Wissenschaftliche Untersuchungen zum Neuen Testament · 2. Reihe

309

Charles A. Anderson

Philo of Alexandria's Views of the Physical World

Mohr Siebeck

Charles A. Anderson, born 1975; MDiv Trinity Evangelical Divinity School (Deerfield, IL, USA); 2009 PhD, University of Cambridge; since 2007 lecturer in New Testament and biblical languages at Oak Hill Theological College (London, England).

ISBN 978-3-16-150640-6
ISSN 0340-9570 (Wissenschaftliche Untersuchungen zum Neuen Testament, 2. Reihe)

Die Deutsche Nationalbibliothek lists this publication in the Deutsche Nationalbibliographie; detailed bibliographic data are available on the Internet at *http://dnb.d-nb.de*.

The book was printed by Laupp & Göbel in Nehren on non-aging paper and bound by Buchbinderei Nädele in Nehren.

Printed in Germany.

Preface

One of the pleasures of finishing such a work resides in the chance to thank the people who have helped along the way. This book began as a PhD thesis for the University of Cambridge. I am grateful to Prof. Markus Bockmuehl, a wise supervisor and friend. The way he incisively holds together the big picture with a careful attention to detail is a model for me. He and Celia have generously opened their home and their lives to us, and to many others. Prof. William Horbury oversaw my work for a year with his characteristically gracious, humble erudition. I thank too my examiners, Dr James Carelton Paget and Dr Sarah Pearce, for their helpful comments and suggestions.

The work was finished at Oak Hill Theological College. The old advice not to take a job before submitting certainly has its merits, yet nonetheless I found a truly supportive environment in which to begin teaching and finish the thesis. Staff and students have looked out for these foreigners in their midst and indulged my propensity to link nearly any topic to Philo. The principal Mike Ovey graciously pastored me through moments of despair about this project, and the librarian Wendy Bell assisted in myriad ways.

While in Cambridge, we were based at Tyndale House, and I am grateful to the warden, the fellows and staff for all their work. I benefited from the fellowship among readers, the resources of the library, and the accommodation. I want especially to acknowledge Jonathan Moo, who was subjected to sharing a carrel with me for three years, and John Yates, who found for me a used Loeb set of Philo, newly-arrived at G. David's that afternoon. I am thankful also for the funding which made the whole enterprise possible, including from the Overseas Research Students Award Scheme, the Cambridge Overseas Trust, the Baker-Bethune and Hort Memorial Funds, and the EAA grant.

I presented aspects of this research in seminars at Cambridge University, the Oxbridge Postgraduate Student Conference, and Kings College London. A special thank you to Eddie Adams whose extensive feedback after my paper at Kings went beyond the norm and helped to re-shape the direction of the overall work. Akiva Cohen, David Rudolph, and Alex Richardson provided much appreciated language help. People who read various portions and improved matters with their comments include Jane Heath, Kate Lewis, Alec Lucas, James Robson, Daniel Roe, Martin Salter, David Shaw, Dan Strange, and Stephen Witmer. Conversations with Brian Hebbelthwaite, Martin Hengel, Hermann Lichtenberger, and David Sedley provided helpful pointers and ideas. Steffen Jenkins helped considerably with the technical matters of formatting and indexing in Nota Bene.

My parents, David and Monette Anderson, first instilled in me a love of learning and a sense that all of life is lived *coram Deo*. Erin's parents, Mike and Julie Abbott, have been a constant source of encouragement in this process to us both.

Finally, I dedicate this work to my wife Erin. During its long gestation, Jack, Theodore, and Adelaide have joined us, and we wondered whether I would ever give birth too (though assuredly not to something nearly so delightful and joyful as they are). She has borne the unexpected turns and developments with great grace and abiding love. I remain amazed and humbled at the chance to share my life with her.

Charles A. Anderson
June 2011

Table of Contents

Abbreviations and Citations

References to secondary literature are given as author-date. Primary sources typically use the abbreviated title and relevant numbering. References to ancient authors in the collection by Long and Sedley feature section number and letter, while references to their commentary give page number. References to Aristobulus, Artapanus, and Pseudo-Eupolemus use the numbering in Eusebius, *Praeparatio evangelica*, unless otherwise noted.

Abbreviations follow the conventions in *The SBL Handbook of Style.*[1] In addition, the following abbreviations are used:

AT	Author's translation
DK	Diels, Hermann, and Walther Kranz, eds. 1951. *Die Fragmente der Vorsokratiker*. 6th ed. 3 vols. Berlin: Weidmann.
DL	Diogenes Laertius. ET 1925. *Lives of Eminent Philosophers*. Translated by R. D. Hicks. 2 vols. Loeb Classical Library. Cambridge: Harvard University Press.
isf	*Incertae sedis fragmenta* (unidentified fragments)
L-S	Long, A. A., and D. N. Sedley, eds. 1987. *The Hellenistic Philosophers*. 2 vols. Cambridge: Cambridge University Press.
PCW	*Philonis Alexandrini opera quae supersunt*. 1896–1915. Edited by Leopold Cohn, Paul Wendland, and Sigfreid Reiter. 6 vols. Berlin: George Reimer.
PLCL	Philo. 1929–1953. *Works*. Translated by F. H. Colson, G. H. Whitaker, and Ralph Marcus. 12 vols. Loeb Classical Library. Cambridge: Harvard University Press.
SPhA	*Studia Philonica Annual*

The Greek text and English translations come from the Loeb edition, with some reference also to the Cohn-Wendland critical edition. Fragments for *QG* and *QE* come from the French edition by Françoise Petit.[2] References to *De Deo* are from the critical edition by Folker Siegert in 1988, as well as his Eng-

[1] Alexander, Patrick H., John F. Kutsko, James D. Ernest, Shirley A. Decker-Lucke, and David L. Petersen, eds. 1999. *The SBL Handbook of Style: For Ancient Near Eastern, Biblical, and Early Christian Studies*. Peabody, Mass.: Hendrickson.

[2] Françoise Petit. 1978. *Quaestiones in Genesim et in Exodum. Fragmenta Graeca*. Les Œuvres de Philon d'Alexandrie 33. Paris: Cerf.

lish translation in 1998.[3] Other fragments come from the edition by J. Rendel Harris.[4] Word searches in Philo utilise either the print or electronic edition of the *Philo Index* by Peder Borgen, Kåre Fuglseth, and Roald Skarsten.[5]

---

[3] Folker Siegert. 1988. *Philon von Alexandrien: Über die Gottesbezeichnung „Wohltätig Verzehrendes Feuer"* (De Deo). *Rückübersetzung des Fragments aus dem Armenischen, deutsche Übersetzung und Kommentar.* WUNT. Tübingen: Mohr Siebeck. Idem. 1998. "The Philonian Fragment *De Deo*: First English Translation." *SPhA* 10:1–33.

[4] J. Rendel Harris, ed. 1886. *Fragments of Philo Judæus.* Cambridge: Cambridge University Press.

[5] Peder Borgen, Kåre Fuglseth, and Roald Skarsten. 2000. *The Philo Index: A Complete Greek Word Index to the Writings of Philo of Alexandria.* Grand Rapids/Leiden: Eerdmans/ Brill. Idem. 2005. *The Works of Philo: Greek Text with Morphology.* Bellingham, Wash.: Logos Research Systems, Inc.

Chapter 1

The Problem of Philo's Ambivalence about the Physical World

> The leper combines as joint causes, God and creation, which are antagonists by nature (θεὸν καὶ γένεσιν, ἀντιπάλους φύσεις). *Leg.* 3.7

> Let therefore even the whole universe, that greatest and most perfect flock of the God who IS (ὁ κόσμος ἅπας, ἡ μεγίστη καὶ τελεωτάτη τοῦ ὄντος θεοῦ ποίμην), say, "The Lord shepherds me, and nothing shall fail me". *Agr.* 52

I. Discovering Philo's Ambivalence

The goal of this work is to examine Philo of Alexandria's ambivalent, seemingly contradictory claims about the ethical status of the sensible world. In some texts, God and creation oppose one another, so that what pleases the one is alien to the other (*Somn.* 2.67). Evil is native to mortality (*Congr.* 84), and sin 'congenital (συμφυές) to every created being (παντὶ γενητῷ), even the best, just because they are created' (παρόσον ἦλθεν εἰς γένεσιν; *Mos.* 2.147). The only answer is to flee this world. People must 'estrange themselves from all that belongs to the world of creation (πάντων ὅσα γένεσιν), and . . . treat all such as bitter and deadly foes' (*Ebr.* 69). Yet in other texts, God's motive for creating the world is his goodness (*Deus* 108). The world is his son (*Ebr.* 30), his gift (*Leg.* 3.78), created in his image (*Opif.* 25), 'the fairest, and greatest and most perfect work of all' (τὸ κάλλιστον καὶ μέγιστον καὶ τελεώτατον ἔργον; *Abr.* 74). By contemplating the order in the world, people can know God (*Leg.* 3.99; *Praem.* 41–42), and by imitating it they can become more like him (*Opif.* 151). The only proper response to the world is praise and thanksgiving to God (*Plant.* 131; *Her.* 200). These divergent ways to evaluate the sensible world run deeply and pervasively through Philo's work.

Understanding this tension, though, is not what I originally set out to write. Many of the most potent ethical issues of our day, like stem cell research or the definition of marriage, turn in no small part on a protological question: Is there something properly basic to being human that depends on how we – and the world as a whole – came about? For those who profess or study Judaism or Christianity, that question has a sharper point, since both affirm that God created all things good, and presumably some kind of order inheres in the creation. To face such questions, therefore, partly entails listening to Scripture and its interpretation. Consequently, I set out to study Paul's ethical appeals to creation in 1 Corinthians, how he argued about sexual immorality (6:16), meat sacrificed to idols (10:26), and head-coverings in the church's public gatherings (11:7–9), by invoking creation traditions.[1] What began, though, as a short exploration of Philo's *De Decalago*, for the sake of comparing him with Paul, grew into one chapter, then to half the original PhD thesis, until finally, it overtook the whole project, as I saw more and more the importance of Philo for this question. Philo stands at the head of a long line of those who join philosophy and biblical revelation. Early Christian theologians like Clement of Alexandria and Origen drew upon Philo for how to interpret Scripture according to philosophical modes of thought.[2] Indeed, Harry Wolfson went so far as to place Philo first in the tradition of a certain 'grand' style of philosophy that would hold sway until Spinoza.[3] Such overreaching aside, Philo makes an ideal test-case for understanding the relative influences of Greco-Roman philosophy and Jewish biblical interpretation, particularly in an area like cosmology, which he treated extensively.[4] For someone with a special interest in the New Testament, Philo also provides an important comparison and contrast.[5] For example, his overwhelmingly positive usage of κόσμος differs from Paul's variable use, and the mostly negative slant taken in the Fourth Gospel.[6] Probing into why these differences exist may enable a better understanding of each. Moreover, Philo is relevant here not least because he holds an important place at the fount of the natural law tradition, despite his neglect

---

[1] The links between creation and ethics in 1 Corinthians remain under-investigated, as far as I can see; I hope to address them in the future. On creation traditions and cosmological language, see, *inter alia*, Badley 2005; Sterling 1995b; E. Adams 2000: 85–150; Schrage 2005; on ethics, Rosner 1994; Wanamaker 2005; Hartog 2006. The literature on particular passages (e.g., 11:3–16) is, of course, voluminous.

[2] On Philo in early Christianity, see Runia 1993a and the many specialist studies.

[3] Wolfson 1947. Wolfson has many strengths, but the sweep of his claims, and a constant impulse to synthesise disparate findings, has led most scholars to reject this reading of Philo.

[4] That is part of the reason Harl 1967 chose cosmology as a test-case for the relations between Judaism and Hellenism for Philo. Sterling 1999a identifies cosmology as one of the three key areas of connection between Philo and Greek-speaking Judaism.

[5] See recently this argument by Siegert 2008 and Sterling 2003a, and as evidence, the volume edited by Deines & Niebuhr 2004.

[6] On Paul, see E. Adams 2000; more widely, Sasse 1965.

at the hands of some contemporary theorists.[7] Thus Philo is well worth studying on the link between ethics and cosmology.

Even a cursory reading of Philo shows how often he appeals to cosmology as ethical justification or motivation. A grasp of the weakness inherent to being a 'created thing' (τὸ γενητόν) should lead to humility (*Spec.* 1.293). The seventh commandment is justified on the grounds that 'nature' makes human beings sociable, and thus murder subverts natural laws and statutes (νόμους φύσεως καὶ θεσμούς; *Decal.* 132). Contemplation of the order of the κόσμος enables perfect obedience to God's commands without any need for intermediaries (*Abr.* 61). Philo repeatedly appeals to the 'created realm', broadly conceived, and how that realm came about, as a basis or justification for ethics.

Such appeals had good precedent in ancient philosophy. According to *Tim.* 90b–d, the way to order the rational soul is to meditate on the harmonious movements of the heavenly bodies.[8] Most famously, the Stoa grounded ethics on cosmology, specifically 'nature'.[9] It was the best starting point for ethics (*SVF* 3.68), and the *telos*, the proper goal of human existence, was life according to 'nature' (τὸ ὁμολογουμένως τῇ φύσει ζῆν; 1.179, 552).[10] One of many names for the active principle in their cosmology, 'nature' was the rational principle which benevolently creates and governs all that exists (Cicero, *Nat. d.* 2.82).[11] Likewise, although the roots are complex and disputed, it seems best to ascribe the origins of 'natural law' to Stoicism.[12] More concretely, Cicero could invoke 'nature' for discrete moral topics like the duty to hold public office on the part of those so gifted (*Off.* 1.72), or the inappropriateness of a father and grown son bathing together (1.129).

Although most attention rightly goes to Greco-Roman backgrounds, one should also note the presence of such ethical appeals to the 'created realm' in Judaism.[13] The discourse remains incipient, yet nonetheless there are biblical

---

[7] For example, John Finnis omits Philo from the classical tradition of natural law in an essay devoted to that topic (2002), as well as in his seminal work, *Natural Law, Natural Rights* (1980). That omission may result from how his conception of natural law differs from Philo's (on specific points of divergence, see below, p.118 n.101; p.138 n.54; p.140 n.70). On Philo and natural law, see p.120.

[8] Betegh 2003: 278–83; Carone 1997.

[9] See especially N. White 1985; idem 1979; Long 1996: 134–55. On parallels here between the *Timaeus* and Chrysippus, see Betegh 2003: 290–93.

[10] *Contra* Annas 1993: 160–66 the nature in view is both human and cosmic (cf. Cooper 1996: 273; Inwood & Donini 1999: 686–87; Betegh 2003: 273–78).

[11] *SVF* 2.937, 945, 1024, 1027; 3.320. *Inter alia*, Inwood & Donini 1999: 682–83; Striker 1996: 229; Long 1996: 141.

[12] See below, p.136 n.42.

[13] On this tradition, see, *inter alia*, F. Horst 1961; J. Barton 1979; Novak 1998: 27–61; Bockmuehl 2003: 87–111.

roots, picked up by Second Temple writers, for the idea that some moral knowledge is accessible from creation.[14] Those roots can be seen, for example, in Amos 1–2. God judges Israel's neighbours for war crimes, some of which clearly have nothing to do with Israel, like Moab burning the bones of the Edomite king (2:1).[15] Amos is not explicit about the standard for judgment, but John Barton calls it international customary law: the universal, unwritten rules of conduct for nations.[16] Amos is similarly silent about how the nations were to have known this standard,[17] but there is a hint – on the analogy of the covenant of kinship (ברית אחים) in 1:9 – they should have known simply by virtue of their common humanity.[18] So in varying degrees, Philo had precedent in Greco-Roman philosophy and Judaism for ethical appeals to the 'created realm'.

There is at least one significant difference between these precedents and Philo that complicates matters and helps explain the more narrow focus of this work. For Greco-Roman philosophy in general, the sensible world was fundamentally good. Theirs overall was an optimistic, positive view of the world.[19] This was derived in large measure from the *Timaeus*, the standard cosmological text of the Hellenistic period.[20] The Demiurge created because of his good-

[14] In Scripture, Gen 4:10–12 (on which, Novak 1998: 31–35); 9:5–6; 18:25; Isa 1:2–3 (the idea of cosmic nonsense from J. Barton 1979: 5–7). There is also the notion of universal practice in the expression 'a thing that ought not to be done' (לא־יעשׂה and variants) at Gen 20:9; 29:26; 34:7; 2 Sam 13:12, which is applied specifically to sexual ethics (F. Horst 1961: 240–41; Rodd 2001: 44–46). In the Second Temple period, see *T. Naph.* 3:2–5; Ps.-Phoc. 70–75, 175–76, 190–92; Josephus, *Ag. Ap.* 2.199. Some of these texts use φύσις – see Niebuhr 1987: 5–72; Sterling 2003b.

[15] John Barton's work, especially his 1980 monograph, is standard here, although he misunderstands Israel's place in the oracles (2:6–8). Juxtaposing their social injustice with war crimes is not a rhetorical trick (*pace* 1990: 60–61) but a contextualisation that shows Israel the true gravity of their sin. Similarly, Israel's surprise at its place in the list is not because they had thought election excused them from judgment (*pace* 1980: 41–42), but because of the realisation that God considered their actions as serious as these war crimes.

[16] J. Barton 1980: 41–45. Elsewhere, he identifies these norms as resting on human consensus (2002: 61–63).

[17] F. Horst 1961: 241–42.

[18] So Paul 1991: 61–63; Bockmuehl 2003: 93; Hubbard 1989: 133–34. Less convincing explanations of this covenant include Andersen & Freedman 1989: 261, who see it between Israel and Tyre (1 Kgs 5:26, 9:31); Wolff 1969: 193–94, who proposes Edom and Israel; and Driver 1897: 137, who suggests Tyre and non-Israelites towns.

[19] Mansfeld 1981: 293–309.

[20] On its influence, see Reydams-Schils 2003; Sharples & Sheppard 2003. There was a second, more negative Platonic tradition, derived from *Phaedrus* and *Republic* (Festugière 1944–54: 2.583–85; cf. Scott 1991: 76), which was picked up by later Platonists, like Numenius and Plutarch (see Dillon 1977: 366–76; and below, p.189).

ness (*Tim.* 29e), and the final product, the κόσμος, was beautiful, blessed, even divine (92c).[21] The Stoics took the view that even the cosmic conflagration was a good thing, since the pure existence of the active principle (i.e. god) was better at that point.[22] Likewise, Jews could look to Gen 1:31 and the divine pronouncement that everything he made was very good.[23] Wisdom of Solomon, from the same intellectual-religious milieu as Philo,[24] adopts a positive perspective on the sensible world.[25] Michael Kolarcik traces how the world for Pseudo-Solomon plays a positive, divinely-directed role in the original creation (1:14), the exodus (16:17, 24–25), and ultimate judgment (5:17, 20).[26] Thus these various writers held an overall positive view of the material world, and on that basis, made their ethical appeals.

Philo held a more complicated view of the sensible world. On the surface, he seems to make contradictory statements about the world and its ethical status, alternately praising and condemning it. This is not to say that only someone who holds a positive view of the sensible realm could appeal to it ethically. For example, Philo supports the prohibition of idolatry by the fact that 'created objects' (γένεσιν) are 'by nature' perishable, precisely because they are 'created' (ὡς γενητὰ καὶ τῇ φύσει φθαρτά; *Spec.* 2.166). So a negative attitude toward the material realm obviously does not prevent it from playing an ethical role. The ambivalence which Philo demonstrates, however, means that it is difficult to determine what kind of role he envisions. What kinds of moral justification or motivation are compatible with how Philo evaluates the sensible world? Does it help all people equally? What are the limits of such appeals? Until we can come to grips with Philo's divided perspective on the world, it will not prove very fruitful to examine how he links ethics to that world. This work, therefore, is aimed at understanding the ambiguity of the

---

[21] On the positive worldview encoded by κόσμος, see E. Adams 2000: 64–69.

[22] Mansfeld 1981: 304.

[23] For a different, pivotal interpretation of Gen 1:31 by Philo, see below, p.174.

[24] Winston 1979: 59–63 argues that Philo influenced Wisdom, but whatever the case, they certainly share a Middle Platonic context within Judaism (cf. Cox 2007: 59–60).

[25] The body-soul dualism of 9:15 does have a moral connotation (*pace* Cox 2007: 78 n.64), since it is the body's burdensome nature that makes humanity weak in reasoning (Hay 1987: 889). In turn, weak human reason is ultimately linked to ignorance of God and idolatry (Wis 13:1; 15:2–3; so Lucas 2009). Nonetheless, the perspective in Wisdom remains a long way from the overwhelmingly negative attitude Philo adopts (on which, see below, p.60).

The other exception is possibly the condemnation of animals that are worshipped (15:18–19; on which, see Kolarcik 1997: 570), but the polemical context means the verses have limited value in constructing the author's views on the physical world. My thanks to Alec Lucas for drawing this verse to my attention.

[26] Kolarcik 1992. See also Collins 1977: 128; Cox 2007: 81–83; below, p.190.

sensible world for Philo, which is the necessary first step toward this larger goal. The ethical status of the material world must precede its ethical function.

II. Attempts to Analyse Philo's Ambivalence

Some ideas for how to analyse Philo's ambivalence toward the physical world do not prove genuinely fruitful due to their intrinsically speculative nature. First, it is not possible to chart a chronological development of Philo's ambivalence, where one side represents an earlier stage which he subsequently changes – either positively or negatively – in later treatises.[27] These views exist alongside each other in the same treatises throughout his corpus. There are relative differences among the treatises, but those are attributable to the intended audiences and aims of the commentary series, not a temporal progression in Philo's thought.[28] Moreover, although some points of connection between chronology and text can be made,[29] no one has yet given a cogent, systematic account of how to organise the treatises chronologically, so we lack even the coherent foundation necessary for such a study.

Second, it is clear that Philo participated in an interpretive community and interacted with other scholars. His treatises are peppered with references to other exegetes, with whom he may agree (e.g., *Abr.* 99) or disagree (e.g., *Mut.* 61).[30] This can be taken a step further by recognising that Philo incorporates exegetical traditions in his work, which may be more or less integrated with his own contribution.[31] This hermeneutical approach, while valid, suffers from a paucity of primary sources, so much of it must remain speculative reconstruction.[32] More to the point, appeal to exegetical traditions does not provide

---

[27] Morris 1987: 841–44 and Royse 2008: 59–62 provide excellent overviews of attempts to locate Philo's writings chronologically.

[28] See p.18 and p.176.

[29] E.g., *Spec.* 3.1–6 likely refers to Philo's involvement in the Alexandrian embassy (Morris 1987: 844). For similar proposals elsewhere in Philo, see e.g., Kraft 1991 and Wong 1992, though the plausibility of such claims varies.

[30] Shroyer 1936; Hay 1979–80. Hay 1991b looks at specific references to other exegetes, from which he concludes Philo saw himself as part of a tradition (1991b: 97). Most likely, this was historical and not invented by Philo (*contra* Dillon 1993: 153–55; 1995: 109 n.5).

[31] In this vein, see Tobin 1983; Goulet 1987; and the Philo Institute's work, e.g. Mack 1984: 241–49; Hamerton-Kelly 1972. See the state of the question at Mach 2005: 128–31.

[32] Sterling 1999b: 151–54 advocates a balanced approach to the evidence for such traditions. For how Philo relates to other Alexandrian Jewish writings, see Borgen 1997: 41–45, and to the world outside Alexandria, Sterling 1999a. On the question of Philo and midrashic interpretation, it is reasonable to suppose some kind of interplay and common exegetical tradition, but proposals that go much further, e.g., Bamberger 1977 or N. Cohen 1995, suffer at

significant help for our study. Philo's divided views of the sensible world are too consistent, pervasive and interwoven to hypothesise that one side is actually a prior tradition which he has adopted alongside his own position. It seems better to approach the problem from the standpoint that this ambivalence belongs to Philo himself.

If neither of those suggestions work, how has previous scholarship accounted for this ambivalence in Philo? If the problem truly is pervasive, then the question has remained surprisingly under-addressed. One explanation could be that the complexity of the task has discouraged investigation, especially if a lexical study is undertaken. The six key terms this work examines appear cumulatively a staggering 2,900 times in Philo.[33] Moreover, cosmology is a central concern – for example, the very purpose of the Exposition commentary series is to demonstrate the harmony between the Mosaic Law and world-order (*Abr.* 1–6; *Praem.* 1–3).[34] Thus studying this ambivalence toward the physical world is a large task.

A second reason for relative neglect of this question may be that it has simply been assumed that on the whole Philo holds a positive orientation on the physical world. There is certainly strong evidence for such a view: the celebration of the κόσμος and its role in knowing and becoming like God, and the ways that God operates through φύσις in creating and guiding the world – these motifs grant a certain presumption to the primacy of the positive viewpoint for Philo. This is reinforced by the manifest importance of the *Timaeus* for Philo's exegetical project, as David Runia magisterially demonstrated.[35] Its positive perspective can then be seen as properly basic for Philo too.

A few scholars, however, have seen the difficulty that arises from Philo's competing statements about the sensible world and tried to account for it. A. J. Festugière devoted some sixty pages to Philo, a thinker whose originality he did not hold in the highest regard, in his four-volume work on Hermeticism.[36] He distinguished between two Platonic traditions in Philo: the contemplation of the world and its renunciation, both of which lead to knowledge of God.

---

the level of details: on Bamberger, see Grabbe 1993; on Cohen, see Birnbaum 1996b; Winston 1996b.

[33] Φύσις appears 1,342*x*, κόσμος 634*x*, γένεσις 438*x*, οὐσία 222*x*, ὕλη 177*x*, and γενητός a mere 97*x*. Relying on Mayer 1974, Runia 1988b: 69 n.2 ranks φύσις as Philo's fourth most common noun, and κόσμος the twelfth.

[34] This framework comes from Mack 1984: 266; similarly, see Bréhier 1925: 11. Reinhartz 1986: 338 and Arnaldez 1984: 40 omit cosmology (at least explicitly) from their construals of the intent of the Exposition. On the importance of transitional threads for such macro-structure, see Borgen 1995.

[35] Runia 1986. My debt to Prof. Runia's work is obvious throughout these pages.

[36] Festugière 1944–54: 2.519–85.

The first corresponds to the *Timaeus* and is a conventional *topos* for Philo without his own passion. The second corresponds to the *Phaedo*, *Symposium*, and *Republic* and holds that contemplation of the self, exemplified by Abraham, is the higher path to knowing God. This is where Philo's sympathies lie, according to Festugière. Philo's singularity is that he put these opposing tendencies together, as Hermeticism did after him, as two stages in one journey.[37]

Richard Baer's seminal study of male and female as categories for Philo looked at this ambiguity of the sensible realm, particularly in an appendix dedicated to 'Philo's attitude towards man's irrational soul and the created world'.[38] He succinctly distinguished between positive and negative orientations in Philo's work. On the positive side are his celebration of the goodness and beauty of the created world in general and the human person in particular, and the usefulness of sense-perception and even passion. On the negative side are the opposition between God and creation, the fact that human sinfulness is attributable to being created, and the severe denunciations of pleasure and the human body. Baer judged that the emphasis falls on the negative side: Philo 'theoretically affirms the goodness of creation, yet throughout most of his writings speaks of the created world as sharply opposed to the transcendent realm of the divine'.[39] Baer further suggested that these orientations tie in with the commentary series and their attention to the biblical text: because it is more directly concerned with the literal content of Scripture, the Exposition is more positive about the created world than the Allegory.

Finally, Alan Mendelson briefly yet perceptively picked up this question in his study on Philo's use of secular education. He agreed with Baer's division between positive and negative orientations, as well as his hypothesis that the more Scripture exerts an influence, the more positive the viewpoint. But he added a distinction between the ideal and the ordinary, the philosopher and the pragmatist. These represent two different perspectives on reality, and in fact, they form the foundation for these alternating evaluations of the sensible world:

> For the philosopher, the created world is necessarily evil – a realm which the sage, in his perfection, transcends. Ordinary men, on the other hand, see the created world as a good, for only through knowledge of that world can they come to know God.[40]

Like Festugière and Baer, then, Mendelson made the higher, more normal point of view for Philo the negative one.

---

[37] Festugière 1944–54: 2.585.

[38] Baer 1970: esp. 89–93.

[39] Baer 1970: 76. Cf. 91: 'far more typical of Philo's writings as a whole are those passages where the created world is portrayed as hostile and antithetic to the good life'.

[40] Mendelson 1982: 34.

There is much to commend in these studies.[41] They perceive not just that there are two equal perspectives, but that there is a hierarchy, and that the negative orientation is accorded the higher status. For Festugière these two ways of relating to the world are tied into how one knows God. In terms of influences on Philo's views, Festugière points to competing Platonic traditions. Baer links Philo's approach to the relative influence of the biblical text and exegetical method. Mendelson's suggestion of a multiperspectival approach is potentially very fruitful, because it suggests categories, proper to Philo, for how to judge the same entity differently, depending on the angle from which it is evaluated.

Even with these strong points, there remains more to do in this area. First, none of these scholars made Philo's ambivalence their focus. Consequently, they lacked the breadth and rigour necessary for an holistic answer. Second, the lack of a lexical approach to the problem is striking. There may well be some correlation between terms used and the evaluation expressed, and so a selective study of key words Philo uses for the sensible world is needed to help shed new light on the problem. That lacuna is part of the problem, for example, with Baer – without lexical study, he overlooks the positive usage of κόσμος and φύσις and so over-estimates the relative prevalence of the negative orientation. Third, the initial insights into the influence of the commentary series and exegetical method need to be put on a sounder footing. Fourth, Mendelson's nascent multiperspectivalism should be taken further. Finally, if these scholars are correct that the negative orientation toward the sensible world is ultimately the higher one, then the entailments for this surprising conclusion should be teased out, particularly how that would situate Philo among other Jewish writers. It appears, therefore, that we have not yet arrived at a sufficient explanation for the co-existence of these seemingly contradictory orientations, and thus further study of this problem is justified.

III. Argument and Plan of the Book

The tension in Philo's positive and negative views on the physical world is a genuine problem, but far less of a contradiction – when properly understood – than it first appears. Philo's ambivalence about the material world is best understood perspectivally. There are higher and lower ways to see the world, and one's vantage point dictates the value judgment made. Ultimately, though, the higher, privileged perspective is negative, because those who advance

[41] There are, of course, many works that deal with individual components of this study (e.g., Philo's use of φύσις), and they are cited at the appropriate points.

toward God and perfection directly must see the sensible world as nothing, or even as an obstacle to overcome. The primary means of establishing this argument is a close textual analysis of the Philonic corpus, particularly through a comprehensive study of key words.

Chapter 2 sets the context in Philo in two ways. First, he wrote his major commentary series, Allegory of the Law and Exposition of the Law, with different audiences and aims. The Allegory was intended for advanced readers, adept in philosophy and familiar with allegorical exegesis of Scripture, to help them progress further, even to the point of perfection. The Exposition, in contrast, was an introduction for beginners, whether Jewish or Gentile, who lacked familiarity with either philosophy or Scripture. This differentiation shapes how Philo evaluates the sensible world, since his distinction between advanced and beginner (or higher and lower) perspectives is embodied in the Allegory and Exposition, respectively. Second, Philo conceptualises Judaism and Hellenism as essentially compatible, with biblical revelation the superior, original source of the good in Greek philosophy and culture. This way of understanding the relation between Judaism and Hellenism helps frame our investigation: to what extent does Philo's attitude toward the sensible realm reflect this conceptualisation? Subsequent chapters will weigh the relative influence of Judaism and Hellenism on Philo's usage of key terms and on his perspectives on the sensible realm.

Chapter 3 begins to lay the foundation and core of the study through a lexical-semantic examination of six key terms which together encompass how Philo refers to the sensible realm. Chapter 3 focuses on terms which express a negative ethical status for the world. That examination begins with οὐσία and ὕλη, which denote the disordered matter from which God made all sensible things. Philo is alternately neutral and negative about this universal matter. His negativity may emphasise either the total passivity of such matter or its chaotic, disordered state. Paradoxically, the worse Philo depicts matter, the greater God looks, because he subdued it and shaped it into its current structure. Nonetheless, from the standpoint of its substance, the sensible world has a negative starting point. Next, the terms γένεσις and γενητός stress mutability and flux, and are primarily – though not exclusively – negative. The transcendent, perfect God is contrasted with a sensible world beset by sin and decline. Γένεσις figuratively may mean vice or anything that impedes communion with God. These four terms predominantly convey a negative evaluation of the ethical status of the material realm. Compared to other philosophical and Jewish usage of these terms, Philo is generally more negative.

Chapter 4 turns to κόσμος, where in contrast, Philo is strongly positive – it is the well-ordered world, the fitting culmination to creation. In celebrating the κόσμος, Philo echoes the philosophical tradition, but he modifies it substantially, because he consistently subordinates the κόσμος to God, its maker and father. Indeed, the κόσμος cannot be rightly understood except in relation to God. The κόσμος represents a way to know God indirectly, since its order testifies to divine design. Even more, imitation of that order can help a person progress toward the religious-ethical *telos*. Abraham's experience in Gen 17, however, establishes the paradigm that ultimately the κόσμος must be displaced in order to reach perfection. The usage of κόσμος encapsulates the wider conclusions in Chapter 2 about the relation of Judaism and Hellenism for Philo: it is impossible to conceive of Philo's understanding of the κόσμος apart from Greek philosophy, but its insights must be corrected and modified in light of Scripture. The result is that Philo's usage of the term overlaps with philosophy and Judaism, but attains something distinctive in its own right.

Chapters 5 and 6 examine φύσις. They form one unified argument stretched across two chapters, due to its length and complexity. Like κόσμος, φύσις for Philo conveys a very positive understanding of the sensible world. Chapter 5 looks at φύσις when it is defined as creative power, essential character and sensible world. Chapter 6 examines φύσις defined as principle of order (which includes 'natural law') and its relation to God. What emerges from this study is the interconnected usage of the term. To speak of φύσις as sensible realm incorporates its work as the power which creates and guides that realm, which in turn, is composed of all the individual natures. Behind and through that stands God, who uses 'nature' as his agent to create and order the world. That divine presence, therefore, gives a normative status to 'nature'. Like κόσμος, Philo's usage of φύσις derives its overall shape and much of its content from Greco-Roman philosophy, yet his Jewish faith decisively modifies this appropriation, so that he uses φύσις (and νόμος φύσεως) in an original way. Thus the Stoic *telos* 'to live in agreement with nature' is redefined so that it becomes equivalent to obeying Mosaic Law and a means by which people may know God. Chapters 5 and 6 conclude the lexical-semantic study.

Before we can build on the findings from the lexical-semantic studies of Chapters 3–6 to discern Philo's views on the physical world, Chapter 7 must address the question of whether every person pursues God in the same way. Philo's answer is no. He distinguishes between a direct, supra-rational, mystical vision of God, and the more normal, indirect, mediated sight of him. The sensible world plays no role in the direct vision – in fact, it must be transcended. But for the indirect vision, it is through God's work in the world that he makes himself known. Hence, the material world has a different ethical status, depending on how one approaches God. Moreover, there are three ideal classes of people, which form a hierarchy in the pursuit of this vision of God. These distinctions in how people pursue God imply that the divergent perspectives on the sensible world may correspond to different classes of people.

Finally, Chapter 8 builds on the preceding investigation to argue that Philo took a multiperspectival view on the ethical status of the sensible world. The ambiguity of 'nature' for Philo is because he holds that there are higher and lower ways to see the material world, of which we enumerate four. First, there is a higher, heavenly part and a lower, sublunary part of the universe. Philo ties this common Hellenistic belief to his ethical evaluation, so that positive statements often pertain to the heavenly part, which is pure and filled with divine beings, while negative statements go with the sublunary realm, which is mutable and full of strife and wickedness. Second, there are higher and lower perspectives on the world depending on whether the vantage point of God or matter is adopted. These perspectives correspond largely to the lexical study of Chapters 3–6. The positive terms (κόσμος, φύσις) stress God's involvement in creating and ruling over this world. The negative terms (οὐσία, ὕλη, γένεσις, γενητός) convey a pessimistic viewpoint, as they focus on the substance of the material world. The two sets of terms denote the same thing but convey different valuations because they take different focal points.

These first two perspectives, however, while important, cannot sufficiently explain Philo's ambivalence. The terminological distinction is by no means absolute: γένεσις may denote the created realm through which a person can learn of God; on the other side, a person ultimately must renounce study of the κόσμος, just as Abraham did, in order to reach perfection. Further probing thus reveals a surprising reversal: the higher perspective now becomes the negative one, while the lower perspective is positive. Accordingly, the third perspective is that the higher method of allegorical interpretation of Scripture leads to a negative evaluation of the sensible world more frequently than does the lower literal method. That is, the more Philo allegorises and departs from the literal content of Scripture, the more likely he is to be negative about the material world. Fourth and finally, the higher path of direct apprehension of God actually necessitates a negative evaluation of the world as an obstacle to overcome, whereas the lower path of indirect vision holds a positive orientation, because the world helps communicate what God is like. The third and fourth perspectives correspond to commentary series: the Allegory expresses and embodies the higher, negative view, while the Exposition belongs to the lower view. Consequently, the Exposition is significantly less likely than the Allegory to express a negative evaluation of the material world. This second set of arguments tips the scales, therefore, to the negative orientation. Philo is divided about how to understand the sensible world, but ultimately the positive orientation belongs to a lesser way of seeing things, and the negative orientation better approximates reality.

The Conclusion analyses how Philo's ultimate negativity about the physical world sets him off from most of his obvious influences and points of comparison. This negative evaluation is not shared by the *Timaeus*, or Wisdom of Solomon, or Paul of Tarsus. It places him closer to cosmological pessimists like the Gnostics or Middle Platonists like Numenius of Apamea and Plutarch. From where does this negativity come? It seems likely that Philo did pick up a second, more negative Platonic tradition, as Festugière suggested. It may be too that a certain Jewish skepticism about the world has shaped him. But it is also likely Philo's own mystical-ascetic impulse influenced this pessimism, so that his negative perspective reflects his own personal outlook. Finally, the Conclusion enunciates the contribution of this study, and makes suggestions for future research, particularly with respect to the ethical function of the sensible world. Given this multiperspectival yet ultimately negative interpretation of the world, the role that the world can play in ethics is limited to the lower level. Those who advance to God indirectly will heed Philo's ethical appeals to the sensible world, but they are superfluous, or perhaps even harmful, for those on the higher path.

Before we can embark on this study, we must address two preliminary matters: the notion that all ethical evaluations of 'nature' are only socially constructed, and the methodology adopted here.

IV. Socially-Conditioned Perspectives on the Physical World

Distinguishing between positive and negative orientations on the sensible world begs the question of how such judgments are made: What determines the ethical status Philo perceives in the physical world? The answer may be that these evaluations are imposed upon the world, a matter of human construct, and conditioned by the social context. What one sees in 'nature' is what one projects.[42] Or, perhaps more precisely, it may be what one chooses from 'nature': Neil Evernden finds that both competition and cooperation are true of the physical environment, but the 'ecology' a person constructs may priori-

[42] So J. Barton 1979: 5 with respect to Abraham's question in Gen 18:25.

tise one over the other.[43] Even a brief historical glance demonstrates the wide array of what has been ascribed to 'nature':

> The fact of the matter is that universally what people have believed in and wanted they have called "natural law," whatever were the real reasons for their preferences. Be it slavery or human freedom, property or selflessness, birth-control or free love, authoritarianism or democracy, they have all at one time or another been identified by their proponents with the very substance of nature and reason.[44]

This kind of empirical survey led Alister McGrath to suggest 'that the concept of 'nature' is a serious candidate for the most socially conditioned of all human concepts'.[45] Moreover, there is an ideological use of such language, often in support of the social status quo.[46]

Some examples in Philo immediately show how the invocation of 'nature' is shaped by social context. He commends gymnasium managers for prohibiting women from attending athletic games, because the will of 'nature' is that men and women not see the other naked (*Spec.* 3.176).[47] Yet to say appeals to 'nature' are *always* guilty of projecting moral values onto the physical world is seriously flawed. It presupposes that reality operates only at a horizontal plane and allows no room for the divine.[48] But if there is a normative, divine presence in and behind the sensible world, then the separation of social, moral norms and 'nature' is not necessarily required – reading 'nature', however difficult it may be, may correspond to how God has structured things. McGrath frames it as the distinction between 'nature' and a Christian theology of creation,[49] but the point is applicable to Philo as well. He saw God at work in and through 'nature', so that it obtains a transcendent foundation.[50] Returning to *Spec.* 3.176, given the divine agency of φύσις, to speak of the 'will of nature' may be a circumlocution for God. Correspondingly, Mosaic Law – which ultimately comes from God (*Mos.* 2.12) – gives commands on sexual purity and modesty. So for Philo the 'will of nature' about nudity among men and

---

43 Evernden 1992: 8–10.

44 Schwarzschild 1962: 55. From another angle, McGrath 2001: 82–88 surveys how differently 'nature' has been personified in Western history.

45 McGrath 2001: 88.

46 E.g., E. Adams 2000: 69–75 looks at κόσμος as a legitimating tool. Naddaf 2005 studies the Presocratics and argues that their περὶ φύσεως tradition explained the universe's origin in conjunction with an examination of the present political order.

47 For other examples, see below, p.115.

48 This is the problem with Evernden 1992 (following Roland Barthes). He allows only for monism (95–96), and consequently clothes 'nature' in religious garb (116–20). Moreover, his search for an unmediated, unenculturated encounter with the physical world is likely to be futile (110–12), since even language is a cultural system.

49 McGrath 2001: 137–38.

50 On God and φύσις, see p.148.

women is not to be disconnected from the divine order. It may still be argued that Philo projects his value judgments onto the sensible world, but it should at least be granted that *he believes* that he is deriving them from how God has structured the world. Correspondingly, this study takes an emic approach to interpreting Philo, while allowing that an etic approach has merit as well.[51]

V. Methodological Approach

In a 1988 essay, Runia identified three main methodological approaches in the history of scholarship on Philo: systematic, doxographical, and contextual.[52] The first takes him essentially as a systematic theologian and synthesises his thoughts into one grand whole. The second probes for the sources behind his ideas and uses him to understand the intellectual context in which he operated. The third takes seriously that he is an exegete, and interpretation of his work starts from the conviction that he utilises philosophy to interpret Scripture. No single approach excludes the others – as Runia's own work proves – rather it is a question of relative balance and overall orientation.

This study broadly adopts a contextual approach, the regnant method today. It gives weight to the fact that the commentary was Philo's chosen genre and that the differentiation between the series with respect to audience and aims is an important influence on how he expresses himself. The focus is on a close textual analysis of what Philo said, a task which occupies the bulk of the work, since such research has not been done before. That analysis is situated within ancient philosophical and Jewish treatment of the same terms and concepts. I also cast an occasional eye toward Philo's social context, both for its influence on his biblical interpretation and for how that interpretation illuminates his social world. This thesis is lightly theorised, although a more hermeneutically suspicious study could helpfully uncover motives and ideologies within Philo's treatment of the physical world. But the primary need is an analysis of Philo's views themselves, and so we concentrate on that first-order task.

Within this contextual approach, there is also a place for systematising. Philo, of course, does not write like a systematician: Monique Alexandre aptly described his repugnance for exhaustive accounts.[53] Yet Philo's own interpre-

---

[51] Emic descriptions use categories native to the actor, whereas etic descriptions work from an outside observer's point of view.

[52] Runia 1988b: 69–72.

[53] Alexandre 1967: 35. E.g., Philo's discussion of natural law (p.135), or how the Logos and φύσις relate (p.143).

tation of Scripture shows evidence of a systematic impulse: faced with Gen 28:13, he feels the need to reconcile why Isaac relates to the deity just as God, but Abraham relates to him as Lord and God (*Somn.* 1.160–63), or why this verse makes Abraham Jacob's father, but at Gen 36:1 Isaac is (1.168–72).[54] His hermeneutical approach takes it that Scripture has a divine author who speaks in a consistent way, and it is the job of the interpreter, when faced with an apparent contradiction, to go beneath the surface to find a deeper consistency.[55] Philo uses philosophical concepts in the service of elucidating the meaning of the biblical text, so it is no surprise the precise concepts may fluctuate, depending on how Scripture presents itself.[56] And Philo certainly does not place his own interpretations on a par with Scripture.[57] Yet for all those caveats, there is a sense in which Philo speaks about the same topics repeatedly, in a way that invites his audience to explore how those statements fit together. One passage (or set of passages), therefore, may serve as an interpretive key through which to read others that initially appear to conflict.[58] As appropriate, we will try cautiously to synthesise Philo's thought.

The bulk and foundation of this book contextually examines Philo's key words for the physical world, most of which are nearly technical terms (Part One).[59] There are other possible approaches: one could focus on specific treatises, like *De Opificio*, or on Philo's interpretation of pivotal biblical texts, like Gen 1. This lexical method, therefore, is certainly not exhaustive, yet nonetheless, it does have some merit. First, Philo's treatment of these themes is diffuse and recurrent, but following key terms, in their context, overcomes that potential obstacle. Similarly, the wealth of material actually proves an asset since it ensures a sufficiently comprehensive base for the ultimate synthesis. Second, this approach has not been taken before, and the lack of it has weakened some previous studies. For example, Baer incorrectly minimised Philo's positive orientation because he focused too heavily on words like γένεσις and not enough on κόσμος or φύσις. Third and importantly, many of these words had become nearly technical terms by Philo's time, and thus they may bear particular insight into Philo's larger views on the sensible world.

---

[54] In both cases, Philo has recourse to the relations among instruction, nature and practice to explain the discrepancies; on this triad, see p.115.

[55] On Philo's understanding of scriptural inspiration, see Burkhardt 1988.

[56] On this relation of exegesis and philosophy, see p.27.

[57] Hay 1991a: 50.

[58] E.g., Winston 1986: 109–10 takes *Spec.* 1.329 as the hermeneutically controlling idea that God's Powers always interpose between him and the sensible world. Thus, although *Opif.* 72–75 seemingly indicates God created many things directly, nonetheless it should be read through the lens of *Spec.* 1.329 to say that he still used intermediaries.

[59] On the pitfalls and promise of word-studies, see Barr 1961; Silva 1994; Walton 1997.

Likewise, because they are semi-technical terms, a diachronic study has some relevance.[60] Fourth, comparing these terms' semantic domains allows for precision by discovering where they overlap and where they are distinct.[61] Thus, although this topic could be approached in more than one way, a lexical-semantic focus is justified.

Finally, something should be said briefly about terminology. The adjectives 'material', 'physical' and 'sensible' are used largely interchangeably, as are the nouns 'world' and 'realm'. The phrase 'sensible world' reflects the Platonic contrast, which is important to Philo, between the intelligible and sensible realms. The difficulty with such language today is that 'sensible' connotes 'prudent' rather than this philosophical sense. Additionally, I try not to make 'creation' language strictly synonymous with the physical world, since for Philo the intelligible world is also created. To speak of positive and negative (or optimistic and pessimistic) perspectives (or evaluations or views) of the material world pertains to whether Philo saw the world favourably, especially with regards to ethics: Does the world advance or hinder the moral life? Finally, for the six main terms examined in Part One, I have opted for Greek script rather than transliteration, not to invest the words with some special meaning, but to maintain the focus on Philo's usage and not an English gloss.[62]

***

Those preliminary matters aside, we are now ready to begin our investigation into Philo's ambivalence about the sensible world. The place to start is with the context for such judgments, both exegetically, in terms of how he wrote his commentaries, and conceptually, in terms of how he understood Judaism and Hellenism.

---

[60] Similarly, E. Adams 2000: 41. On the priority of synchronic study, see Silva 1994: 65–68; Walton 1997: 163–64.

[61] These six terms are not the only possibilities: e.g., τὸ ὄν could be studied too. But these terms do provide a comprehensive yet sufficiently focused and manageable field. Moreover, some reference is made to other relevant terms like various forms of γίγνομαι, ὅλος, and πᾶν.

[62] On the specifics of speaking about φύσις, see below, p.104 n.3.

Chapter 2

The Context for Philo's Ambivalence toward the Physical World

I. Introduction

The goal of understanding Philo's ambivalence toward the sensible world begins with two types of context that affect his interpretation: first, the genre and organisation of his writings, and second, his conceptualisation of Judaism and Hellenism. Both exert a broad, systemic influence on how Philo evaluates the physical world's ethical status. Moreover, the second context provides a foundation from which to assess the relative influences on Philo's views. Does his ultimately negative attitude to the sensible realm mirror or diverge from the larger way he negotiates the relationship between Judaism and Hellenism? Later chapters will face that question, but we must start with a clear idea of the general structure.

Philo composed his major commentary series, Allegory of the Law and Exposition of the Law, with different audiences and aims. The Allegory was intended for advanced readers, adept in philosophy and familiar with allegorical exegesis of Scripture, and designed to help them progress further, even to the point of perfection. The Exposition, in contrast, was for beginners, either Jewish or Gentile, who lacked familiarity with philosophy and Scripture and thus needed an introduction. Second, Philo conceptualises Judaism and Hellenism as essentially compatible, with biblical revelation the superior or original source of all that is good in Greek philosophy and culture. He cannot conceive of either without the other, but it is ultimately Judaism which frames matters and commands his allegiance.

II. Audiences and Aims for the Commentary Series

The treatises are traditionally divided into three commentaries: Questions and Answers, Allegory of the Law, and Exposition of the Law, along with a historical/philosophical category.[1] As its name implies, the Questions series poses questions of the text and offers brief answers, both literal and allegorical, sometimes with a range of exegetical options. It is likely linked both with the synagogue, as commentary on and explanation of the readings from the Torah, and with the other two series, as the skeleton for which they provide the flesh.[2] Indeed, the overall context for Philo's treatises and their audience was homiletic. His repeated references to the Sabbath practice of reading and explaining the Pentateuch point to a similar *Sitz im Leben* for his treatises.[3] Similarly, his idealised depiction of exposition among the Therapeutae likely presents a kindred phenomenon to his practice (*Contempl.* 75–79).[4] Given his frequent favourable references to biblical exposition in these contexts, it makes sense to say Philo saw a positive relationship between these practices and his own writings.

Some have argued that the Allegory and Exposition are actually one series,[5] but their differences are significant enough that they should be seen as separate entities. First, a typical Allegory treatise covers a relatively small portion of the Pentateuch, but in exegeting individual components, Philo ranges far afield, citing and offering capsule interpretations of other passages in support of his exegesis of the primary text, what has been called 'secondary exegesis'.[6] Thus *Quis rerum divinarum heres*, the longest treatise in the series, covers only Gen 15:2–18, but within that, Philo incorporates numerous other texts. For example, he refers to Deut 21:15–17, Gen 29:31 and Gen 3:20, all in service of one sub-point (49–53). Second, the Allegory often presupposes a more advanced knowledge of philosophy. *Quis heres* also features a long

---

[1] Borgen 1987b: 18 labels the last category 'Pentateuchal principles applied to contemporary issues and events'. The treatises *De vita Mosis* I, II are closely linked to the Exposition, likely as an introduction before *De opificio* (Goodenough 1933; Borgen 1987b: 18–19; Morris 1987: 854–55; Runia 2001: 1–4). For heuristic purposes, therefore, references to the Exposition include *Mos.* 1–2.

[2] Royse 1976–77; Nikiprowetzky 1977: 179–80, 231 n.216; Sterling 1991.

[3] *Somn.* 2.127; *Mos.* 2.215; *Spec.* 2.62–63; *Prob.* 81–82; *Contempl.* 30–31; *Hypoth.* 7.12–15. See Borgen 1965: esp. 28–58 for the influence of synagogal sermons on Philo's work.

[4] Leonhardt 2001: 89–95; Bockmuehl 2009: 21–22.

[5] Nikiprowetzky 1977: 192–202 differentiates between the Allegory and Exposition for their purposes of study and argues they form one series (also, along different lines, see Terian 1997: 30–33). Following him, N. Cohen 1987: 168–69 adduces a movement from Greek to Jewish frames of reference. Thorne 1989 goes further and includes the Questions, so that the three series form an integrated whole. His scheme, however, ignores clues that point to a different order, whether internal links between treatises (Runia 2001: 1–4) or probable references to external events (e.g., *Spec.* 3.1).

[6] This phrasing comes from Böhm 2005.

digression about the myriad entities divided by the cutting Logos (τομῆς λόγος), drawing extensively on Platonic and Stoic sources (133–236).[7] Not surprisingly, the allegorical method predominates in this series, while the literal receives little attention, a balance which also presupposes a philosophically-conversant audience.[8]

Exposition treatises, in contrast, cover larger portions of Scripture, hew more closely to its order of events, and do not typically draw as widely on other passages. Whereas five Allegory treatises deal directly with Abraham,[9] the Exposition covers his life in one treatise and carefully chooses which incidents to include.[10] Similarly, in expounding Abraham's life, Philo does not refer to other biblical texts as often as in the Allegory. In terms of methodology, Philo still uses allegory in the Exposition but allows greater room for literal interpretation and takes pains to distinguish between them. The sequence of events narrated in *De Abrahamo* reveals this pattern: Philo starts with a literal exposition of an incident and then explicitly signals his transition to its allegorical meaning.[11] These distinctive patterns between the sets of treatises lend credence to distinguishing them as separate series.

Dividing the treatises into separate series, particularly by virtue of their content, raises the question of who read these works.[12] We should distinguish between empirical readers, those who *actually* read a text, and implied readers, those whom an author *envisions* reading a text.[13] For the latter, can we know from the treatises whom Philo intended as his audience?[14] Unfortunately, he does not provide any explicit markers. It seems reasonable, though, that part of the rationale for the differences in content and methodology between the series is that he conceived of different audiences. The Allegory would be for people familiar with Judaism and particularly the use of philosophy in allegorical exegesis. Based on Philo's references to himself as an exegete in the Allegory, David Hay concludes that 'more than elsewhere, one

---

[7] Dillon 1995: 116–20; Cox 2007: 111–16.

[8] Hay 1979–80: 42–43 finds 39 references to allegorists in the Allegory, 21 in the Questions, 14 in the Exposition. On allegory in Philo, see below, p.28. On distinguishing how the series use it, see Morris 1987: 830–31, 840.

[9] *De migratione, Quis heres, De congressu, De fuga, De mutatione.*

[10] Böhm 2005 argues that Philo treats patriarchal narratives very differently between commentaries (e.g., 115).

[11] E.g., literal migration from Haran (*Abr.* 62–67), its allegorical interpretation (68–88), literal sojourn in Egypt (89–98), its allegorical interpretation (99–106), etc. Cf. Böhm 2005: 142–50 for the alteration of what she labels concrete-historical and universal levels of interpretation in *Abr.* 60–207.

[12] See the review of scholarship by Böhm 2005: 111–14.

[13] Barclay 2002: 140; Böhm 2005: 110.

[14] For a brief, general treatment of this question, see Hay 1991a: 51–52.

gets a sense of an exegete speaking to colleagues'.[15] Perhaps it was connected with a private school setting, where Philo taught advanced exegesis.[16]

In contrast, the Exposition, with its lower demand for prior knowledge,[17] could aim at beginners, which likely included both Gentiles and Jews. Older scholarship sometimes presented these choices antithetically: Philo wrote *either* to Gentiles *or* Jews.[18] We should envision, however, Gentiles as *part* of the Exposition's audience. That is supported by internal clues for the implied audience,[19] and by some evidence about the empirical audience too.[20] Even some of the Jews whom Philo envisioned as his audience might have needed 'missionary' literature, so that the commentary was both external and internal apologetic.[21] Jews with similar interests as Philo could have 'found it easier to cling to Judaism as long as they knew that Judaism stood on an equal level with Hellenism'.[22] For some, perhaps the mounting political and cultural pressures caused them to waver, and the Exposition might bolster their shaky commitment.[23] It seems reasonable, therefore, to conclude that Philo wrote the Exposition in order 'to reclaim the alienated Jews, educate the less knowledgeable ones, assuage non-Jews who may be hostile, and appeal to those who might be interested'.[24]

---

[15] Hay 1991a: 41–42.

[16] Sterling 1999b: 159.

[17] Böhm 2005 draws together evidence from the Allegory (318–20) and Exposition (168–72) that demonstrates what Philo expected of readers' familiarity with the biblical text.

[18] Goodenough 1933 argued the Exposition was outreach to an entirely Gentile audience. Tcherikover 1956: 176–83 argued it must be a Jewish audience since there is no external evidence of Gentiles reading the LXX.

[19] E.g., the Exposition welcomes proselytes (*Virt.* 175–86), while the Allegory is silent on the topic (Goodenough 1933: 117; Birnbaum 1996a: 20). On the Exposition and proselytes more widely, see Rudolph 2006: 130–31; Böhm 2005: 154–55, 197–99, 215–16. Also, Borgen 1997: 143 points to the Jews and Gentiles who celebrated the festival for the Septuagint at Pharos as perhaps a model for Philo's envisioned audience.

[20] Sterling 1999a cites Numenius, Heliodorus, Pseudo-Longinus, and perhaps Plotinus as apparently having read Philo. Cf. Barclay 2002: 141–42. Hilhorst 1992 has questioned whether Heliodorus was actually pagan, but the arguments of Sterling 1999a: 20 n.120 and Runia 1990: 135–36 are plausible in that regard.

[21] Böhm 2005: 174 is too skeptical about a Jewish component to the audience.

[22] Tcherikover 1956: 180. Collins 2000: 14–16 argues that the means by which Diaspora Jews reduced the cultural dissonance between Hellenism and Judaism entailed the intention to address both insiders and outsiders.

[23] Sandmel 1979: 47. Hengel ET 1974: 68 describes a 'temptation to apostasy for political advantage'. Cf. Hilgert 1995: 13–15 on the internal and external tensions.

[24] Birnbaum 1996a: 20. For a summary of the different audiences, see Hay 2001–04: 360; Royse 2008: 33.

Thus it appears Philo differentiated between the Allegory and Exposition in terms of intended audience, method and purpose. Philo often shapes his material differently between the series based on who is reading it. So among other questions, interpretation of Philo should ask to which commentary series a text belongs.[25] In particular, this distinction between the series shapes how he evaluates the physical world. The advanced readers of the Allegory and the beginners of the Exposition do not need to hear the same claims about the sensible realm, and in the end, we will see there is a significant alignment of each commentary series with a particular Philonic perspective on the world.[26]

III. Judaism and Hellenism for Philo

A. Terms and Definitions

Philo is perhaps the quintessential Jewish writer influenced by Hellenism. This certainly affects how he regards the sensible realm, so careful study is needed here. 'Judaism' and 'Hellenism' are complex and much debated terms. Judaism should be seen as ethnic association with the Jewish nation in exclusive worship of the God of Israel and obedience to his Law.[27] This understanding encompasses kinship and cultural practice, both birth and way of life,[28] which were overwhelmingly, though not exclusively, associated with each other.[29] This definition, however, points to an important difference in emphasis from Hellenism, which had become more defined as a way of life, with the kinship portion receding.[30] Dionysius of Halicarnassus defined Hellenicity (τὸ Ἑλληνικόν) as a matter of language, customs, and religion (*Ant. rom.* 1.89.4).[31] The emphasis fell not on ancestry but facility with Greek

---

[25] Birnbaum 1996a and Böhm 2005 utilise these differing audiences methodologically for interpretation. Cf. Runia 2002a: 288.

[26] See p.176.

[27] The definition is from Hengel ET 1974: 3 with modifications by Barclay 1996: 399–444.

[28] So S. Cohen 1990. Barclay 1996: 402–13 includes ancestry and cultural practice within ethnicity. Hall 1997: 19–32, however, distinguishes between ancestry as criterion for ethnicity and cultural practice as indicium.

[29] This allows for both conversion and apostasy.

[30] Hall 2002: 172–228 traces this process back to Herodotus (esp. *Hist.* 8.144.2). Also, Barclay 1996: 410; S. Cohen 1990: 219–21. Isaac 2004, however, points to at least some enduring notions of race as definitionally fundamental among Greeks (and Romans); see esp. 15–39 for his clear delineation of concepts.

[31] Cf. Isocrates, *Paneg.* 50.

language and education.[32] This preference for Hellenism as a way of life constitutes a significant reason someone could be both Jewish and Hellenized without contradiction. The question was not about ancestry but whether these two ways of life could prove compatible.

What did Hellenism as a way of life include? Barclay defines it as 'the common urban culture in the eastern Mediterranean, founded on the Greek language . . . typically expressed in certain political and educational institutions and largely maintained by the social élite'.[33] Hellenism focuses on the Greek cultural side of the encounter.[34] Hellenization represents the process of Greek cultural forms intersecting with native cultures.[35] Local, native cultures remained strong, and their interaction with Hellenism was necessarily variegated and multi-faceted.[36] Johann Droysen famously characterised Hellenism as the 'modernity of antiquity' (*die moderne Zeit des Altertums*) due to its scientific and technological emphases, economic growth of the city, emergence of a cosmopolitan citizen, and movement toward equality of non-Greeks.[37] Hellenization incorporated political, economic, cultural and religious realms, and its extent could vary, as well as its significance in one area as over against another. This engagement occurred at both the societal and individual levels. At the societal level, Jews were certainly Hellenized, as their larger pattern was neither rejection nor adoption of Greek culture but its appropriation and integration into Judaism.[38] Indeed, in a community like Alexandria, allegiance to Judaism and participation in Hellenistic culture constituted the two foci for constructing Jewish identity.[39] The one significant area where Jews Hellenized rather less was religion, for their commitment to exclusive worship of

---

[32] Grabbe 1992: 166.

[33] Barclay 1996: 88.

[34] Walbank 1992: 60–78; Momigliano 1975: 7.

[35] Grabbe 1992: 168; Barclay 1996: 88 defines it as cultural engagement with Hellenism.

[36] E.g., the essays in Kuhrt & Sherwin-White 1987 emphasise the non-Greek elements in the Seleucid kingdom (cf. th examples at Grabbe 1992: 156–64). Some, like Droysen 1836–43 and Smith 1987: 43–61, have stressed the fusion of cultures. Hengel ET 1974: 3 notes the historical development from the penetration of Greek forms to the new forms that emerge from these cultural intersections.

[37] See the defence of this viewpoint in Demandt 1996.

[38] Among others, with varying areas of investigation, Hengel ET 1974; idem ET 1990; Gruen 2002: 11, 231; Goldstein 1981; Modrzejewski 1991. *Contra* Feldman 1993: 3–44, who assumes the incompatibility of Judaism and Hellenism (cf. similar criticism by Grabbe 1992: 151; Barclay 1996: 87–88), and Momigliano 1975: 95–96, who implies it.

[39] Sterling 1995a.

the one God of Israel ran up against a polytheistic, iconic cult.[40] Here, the Jews were unique,[41] but in virtually all other areas, they took on board Greek cultural forms without a particular sense that doing so undermined their identity.[42] For individuals, Hellenization could vary, and particular Jews can be spoken of as more or less Hellenized.[43]

As an individual, Philo is faithfully Jewish and thoroughly Hellenized, without any great tension.[44] More precisely, he is incalculably indebted to Greek culture – one cannot imagine his work otherwise – but not indiscriminately. The criterion by which to evaluate Greek culture was Judaism, particularly Scripture, which was superior and ultimately its original source. This was not just an individual intellectual project – Philo operated in a tradition.[45] Moreover, he worked on behalf of the concrete Jewish community, seen most notably in his leading the Alexandrian Jewish delegation to Rome after the pogrom of AD 38. To substantiate this argument about Philo's identity, we will examine his notion and use of philosophy, his appropriation of and claims to superiority over Greek culture, and his ties to the actual Jewish community.

B. Philo's Understanding of Philosophy

Usually, when Philo is described as Hellenized, what is primarily meant is his relationship to philosophy. The place to start, therefore, is with his use of the

---

[40] This difference does not mean that monotheism was unknown among Greeks (see, e.g., Frede 1999), or that Jewish monotheism may not have some connections to Greek conceptions and practices (see, e.g., Horbury 2004, and an overview of Jewish monotheism in Mach 1999; on the other side, Bauckham 1999).

[41] Momigliano 1975: 7.

[42] Cf. Grabbe 2008 who draws this conclusion particularly for the fragmentary Jewish writings in Greek. Hengel 2001: 10 revised his original argument to reflect more clearly that Judaism could change as a result of outside influences yet maintain its essential identity.

[43] Grabbe 1992: 168; Smith 1987: 59–60. See Barclay's helpful categories of assimilation, acculturation, and accommodation in this regard (1996: 92–101). Sterling 2001 points to the local community as one of the most significant factors in the degree and kind of Hellenization of individual Jews.

[44] Chadwick 1967: 137; Sandmel 1979: 122; Barclay 1996: 91, 161. For Philo with regards to Judaism and Hellenism, see the state of the question in Birnbaum 2006 and Hilgert 1995; and, *inter alia*, the important studies of Heinemann 1932; Mendelson 1988; Niehoff 2001. On some of the tensions in this fusion, see Winston 1990. For the related yet ultimately minor question of whether Philo knew Hebrew, see Sandmel 1978.

[45] Fraser 1972: 1.687–716 provides a helpful survey of the Ptolemaic-era Jewish literature in its historical and social context. For Philo as representative of key elements of Jewish Alexandrian literature, see Borgen 1992a: 123–24; 1997: 41–45. On Philo and his interpretive community and exegetical traditions, see above, p.6.

term φιλοσοφία.[46] Philo sometimes speaks of φιλοσοφία as the preparatory science for wisdom (σοφία). The encyclical subjects contribute to φιλοσοφία, which 'is the practice or study of wisdom, and wisdom is the knowledge of things divine and human and their causes' (*Congr*. 79).[47] This usage of φιλοσοφία also reflects how he is conversant with contemporary philosophical discourse.[48] Second, Philo refers to φιλοσοφία as contemplation of the cosmos.[49] Its proper subject matter is the universe and everything in it (*Congr*. 144). Our sight observes physical and astronomical phenomena, from which the mind reasons there must be a God who created and cares for the universe. On this foundation, φιλοσοφία investigates physics and ethics (*Spec*. 3.185–91).[50] Thus φιλοσοφία is instrumental to knowledge of God ultimately.

The third way Philo uses φιλοσοφία is to describe Judaism. Although not the first to use this language, Philo develops the idea.[51] In *Post*. 100–102, he depicts φιλοσοφία as the royal road that leads to God and equates the speech and word of God (θεοῦ ῥῆμα καὶ λόγον).[52] What God has communicated is philosophy. Thus Philo can refer to the philosophy according to Moses (τοῖς κατὰ Μωυσῆν φιλοσοφοῦσιν; *Mut*. 223),[53] or being a disciple or student of Moses,[54] or the ancestral philosophy (*Mos*. 2.216).[55] Philo has appropriated

---

[46] See Malingrey 1961: 77–91; Nikiprowetzky 1977: 97–116. This schema comes from Malingrey, via the summary by Berchman 2000: 51.

[47] Cf. *QG* 1.6; 3.43. This definition is Stoic (*SVF* 2.36; Cicero, *Off.* 2.5). Similarly, the Stoic three-fold division of philosophy into logic, ethics, and physics (*SVF* 1.45) appears in *Leg*. 1.57; *Ebr*. 202; *Spec*. 1.336; *Virt*. 8; and with an agricultural metaphor in *Agr*. 14–16; *Mut*. 73–75; *Prob*. 80. For philosophy as the means of acquiring wisdom, see *Somn*. 2.170–71; *Contempl*. 28; *QG* 1.57; 3.43.

[48] This category includes typical Greek ways of speaking about philosophy, including references to particular figures and schools, e.g., *Contempl*. 57; *Aet*. 8. On Philo's references to sophists under the term 'philosophers', see Winter 2002: 74.

[49] For the philosophical background of this definition, particularly the influence of Plato's *Tim*. 47a–c, and how Philo shapes this *topos*, see Malingrey 1961: 82–85; Nikiprowetzky 1977: 98–99; Runia 1986: 270–76. For further discussion of contemplation language, see below, pp.86, 121.

[50] Cf. *Opif.* 54; *Abr*. 163–64; *Spec*. 3.1; *Contempl*. 11; *QG* 2.41. For philosophy directed toward virtue, see *Leg*. 1.57; *Congr*. 142; *Somn*. 2.170; *Ios*. 86–87; *Virt*. 8; *QG* 3.43.

[51] In Alexandria, Aristob. 13.12.8; *Let. Aris*. 31. Outside Alexandria, 4 Macc 5:22–25; Josephus, *Ant*. 1.25; *Ag. Ap*. 1.54, 2.47. On Aristobulus and Philo, see Walter 1964: 58–86; Borgen 1987a; Holladay 1995: 65–66. On Judaism as philosophy, see Mason 1996.

[52] See Nikiprowetzky 1977: 115 n.80 for references to the Exodus route as a symbol for philosophy.

[53] Cf. *Her*. 213; *Prob*. 43; *Legat*. 256.

[54] E.g., *Det*. 86; *Deus* 120; *Her*. 81; *Mos*. 2.205; *Spec*. 1.319, 345; 3.1.

[55] Cf. *Somn*. 2.123–32; *Mos*. 2.212; *Spec*. 2.61–63; *Praem*. 66; *Contempl*. 28; *Hypoth*. 7.10–14; *Legat*. 156.

Hellenistic categories to recast philosophy as a communal Jewish enterprise, conducted through study and practice of the Law.

Do these uses of φιλοσοφία cohere in some way? Valentin Nikiprowetzky argued that Philo identifies Mosaic philosophy with contemplation of the truths of nature.[56] Returning to *Mos.* 2.216, where Jews are pictured as gathered for instruction in the ancestral philosophy, Philo further explains this consists of the 'acquiring of knowledge and the study of the truths of nature' (ἐπιστήμῃ καὶ θεωρίᾳ τῶν περὶ φύσιν).[57] Through the study of Scripture the cosmos in its true character is known.[58] The point of both φιλοσοφία and biblical interpretation is ethical, to grow in virtue, especially piety.[59] The Stoic agricultural picture of φιλοσοφία emphasises ethics: the tree (physics) and the garden wall (logic) are only good if they produce fruit (ethics).[60] Likewise, the life of virtue is the sole end of the Law (*Virt.* 15).[61] Elsewhere, Philo connects Stoic definitions of philosophy with study of Scripture (*Prob.* 80) and contemplation of the cosmos (*QG* 1.6). Moses in the Law so precisely captured nature's *logos* that to interpret the former is to understand the latter.[62] So although we must be careful not to over-systematise Philo, he does tie these three senses of φιλοσοφία together, with Jewish philosophy at the centre.[63]

If Mosaic philosophy is the heart of how Philo uses the term, then what can we say about where he stood philosophically? Can Philo be classified according to one of the Hellenistic schools of his day?[64] Thomas Tobin helpfully suggests the question be cast according to an emic-etic distinction.[65] On an emic view, Philo would describe himself as a disciple of Moses (*Her.* 81).[66] But does the same hold true from an etic perspective? Early Christians called him a Pythagorean or a Platonist, the latter cast in the axiom: 'Either Plato

[56] Nikiprowetzky 1977: 102–08.

[57] Cf. *Decal.* 98–100; *Contempl.* 28, 90. On the universal and particular in *Contempl.* 90, see Runia 1997: 16.

[58] On study of Scripture and the world – and the referent for such language – see p.122.

[59] Nikiprowetzky 1965: 151–52; Mach 2005: 131–33.

[60] *Agr.* 14–16; *Mut.* 74–75.

[61] Also, *Spec.* 1.314; *Virt.* 119–20; *Prob.* 80. Cf. N. Cohen 1995: 87–99 on equating Greek virtues and the Law in *Spec.* 4.134–35. This notion goes back at least to Aristobulus (13.12.8); Josephus speaks of Moses subsuming the virtues under religion (*Ag. Ap.* 2.170).

[62] Runia 1986: 536. Cf. Winston 2002: 122 on Moses' direct knowledge of the underlying cosmic structures.

[63] Cf. Nikiprowetzky 1977: 101. Malingrey 1961: 91 speaks of Philo's consecration of φιλοσοφία.

[64] See Sterling 1993: 97–98 for a helpful catalogue of recent scholars' positions.

[65] Tobin 1993: 150. On this distinction, see above, p.15 n.51.

[66] Cf. Runia 1993b: 123; Dillon 1993: 152.

philonizes or Philo platonizes (ἢ Πλάτων φιλωνίζει ἢ Φίλων πλατωνίζει).[67] Today, the consensus is that Philo relates most closely to Middle Platonism.[68] David Runia sets forth a helpful typology of views on Philo and philosophy: the main choices are Philo as a Middle Platonic *de facto*, a biblical exegete with a clear preference for Middle Platonic categories, or an eclectic.[69] To argue the case is beyond this discussion, but the best answer seems to be the second of those options: Philo is a 'Platonizing expositor of Scripture', who aligns most closely with Middle Platonists but still should not be considered one of them.[70] His loyalty is to Moses, his treatises comment on the books of Moses, not of Plato, and he usually invokes and explains philosophical concepts without actually arguing for them.[71] On the whole, Philo finds much in Middle Platonism which is congenial to convictions he holds from Scripture,[72] and thus he often has recourse to it, but it would be misleading to label him a Middle Platonist.

C. Philo's Use of Philosophy

Philo uses philosophy as the indispensable tool for interpretation of the biblical text. The purpose is to explain Scripture according to philosophical categories and unpack its deeper meaning (*Spec.* 3.6).[73] Philosophy is necessary for this exegetical enterprise – one cannot understand the biblical text rightly without it.[74] In so doing, Philo sees himself not as imposing meaning but as revealing the philosophical doctrines '*inherent* in the text'.[75] Philo, though,

[67] As a Pythagorean, Clement, *Strom.* 1.360; 2.482p; as Platonist, Jerome, *Vir. ill.* 11 (references from PCW).

[68] Significant treatments of Philo and Middle Platonism include Theiler 1965; Dillon 1977: 139–81; Tobin 1983: 9–19; Berchman 1984: 23–53. Dillon 1993: 151 asks rhetorically whether there now exists a consensus that Philo is engaged in 'a creative adaptation of the Platonist tradition as it presented itself to him in Alexandria'.

[69] Runia 1993b: 125.

[70] This is the third category in Runia's typology and his own position, as argued in 1986: 505–19 with revisions in 1993b. Note the agreement expressed by Dillon 1993: 152.

[71] For example, Jacobson 2004 points out how Philo at *Somn.* 1.232–33 disagrees with Plato's views (*Resp.* 380d–81d) on the educational value of particular Homeric verses (*Od.* 17.485–87). Such a disagreement by Philo with Moses is almost inconceivable.

[72] E.g., an emphasis on the transcendence of God and the ethical goal of assimilation to him (Tobin 1983: 18–19). Cf. Runia 1986: 507–08.

[73] Cf. Hay 1991a: 46. See Runia 1986: 535–46 on the relationship of exegesis and philosophy. Sterling 2005 finds evidence for Jewish use of Hellenistic philosophy in exegeting ethics, creation, and theology.

[74] Böhm 2005: 292 draws a parallel in Abraham's need for the encyclia to progress to wisdom and virtue through learning. His path to perfection requires Hellenistic education.

[75] Runia 1993b: 129. Cf. Runia 1986: 535; Dillon 1995: 123; Barclay 1996: 165.

nowhere explicitly systematises his approach – perhaps the practice was so established in Alexandria, he saw no need to explain it.[76] He still 'does philosophy' in how he weaves together arguments and draws conclusions through exegesis, but the accent is on Scripture.[77] John Dillon, for example, shows Philo defining happiness according to Stoic, Antiochian, or Peripatetic categories, depending on the biblical text before him.[78] That priority helps explain why his work often lacks arguments to support the philosophical concepts he uses; he is more prone to correlate Scripture with philosophical ideas than to argue for them.[79] That priority also perhaps accounts for his lack of a methodological construct.[80] His concern is to explain the text, to which other considerations are subordinated. Thus there is some truth to the idea of Philo as 'a preacher with a flair for philosophy rather than primarily a philosopher'.[81]

Philosophy is not a neutral tool for exegesis; it affects the *kind* of interpretation derived.[82] As Runia points out, for example, there is an intellectualism to Philo's piety and biblical interpretation that owes a debt to philosophy: it is those who love wisdom and knowledge who will approach God (*Migr.* 57–59); similarly, the relation between humankind and God is at the level of mind (*Opif.* 69–71).[83] The mutual interaction between Hellenism and Judaism emerges from how philosophy and exegesis work for Philo. Philosophy serves exegesis of the Scripture, but that exegesis is certainly shaped by philosophy.

One key tool for philosophical interpretation is allegory,[84] a technique inherited from earlier Alexandrian exegetes.[85] Philo, though, takes allegory

---

[76] Mack 1984: 232–33; Arnaldez 1984: 43.

[77] Cf. Borgen 1995 on this middle way between systematic philosopher and eclectic editor. Berchman 2000: 65–66 sets forward three criteria for Philo's partial approach to philosophy: atomism, fundamentalism, and criticism. His defence, however, of Philo's surpassing subtlety (greater than Plato) probably gives the Alexandrian too much credit (57–58).

[78] Dillon 1977: 146–48.

[79] Runia 1988b: 90; Also, Bréhier 1925: 252, 296, though his view that Philo replaced rational argumentation with an interior, immediate moral awareness is less convincing.

[80] Runia 1986: 512. There are hints, though, to such justification. See below, p.32

[81] Wolfson 1947: 1.97, however, coins this phrase as more characteristic of a position with which he disagrees.

[82] Runia 1986: 540–41; Mansfeld 1988: 75. Cf. Barclay 1996: 164.

[83] Runia 2001: 224 considers this passage 'one of the clearest examples of the strong influence of Greek philosophy on Philo's thought'. Cf. Piccione 2004 on the interplay of biblical text and philosophy at *Mos.* 1.60–62.

[84] On Philo's use of allegory, see Dawson 1992: 83–126; Siegert 1996: 162–89. Mack 1984: 257–62 surveys Philo's other exegetical techniques. Mendelson 1988: 8–15 shows how Philo qualifies his position relative to literalists and allegorists (cf. Hay 1979–80: 51), and Niehoff 1998 demonstrates how his use of allegory can be moderated by other factors.

[85] E.g., Aristob. 8.10.7–9a; *Let. Aris.* 143–61. See Dawson 1992: 74–82; Siegert 1996: 144–62; and Bockmuehl 2009: 22–25 on the Alexandrian tradition.

much further than his predecessors.[86] Allegorical interpretations are treasures for those who can comprehend them (*Cher.* 48; *Plant.* 36) and constitute the Pentateuch's soul, with the laws themselves the body (*Contempl.* 78).[87] The biblical text often demands an allegorical interpretation by including details which, if taken literally, would be horrible (e.g., *Sobr.* 31–33; Gen 9:25). Baudouin Decharneux draws a distinction between a straightforward philosophical approach and the allegorical method.[88] The former relies on systematic coherence, whereas the latter is tied to the particular context of the lemma which it interprets. As a result, an allegorical approach may appear to lack consistency, but that is a consequence of its chosen means of operation.[89]

How does Philo's use of allegory relate to the question of his identity? In one sense it demonstrates his debt to Hellenism because he appropriates a hermeneutical technique from there and applies it to the Pentateuch.[90] David Dawson, however, has argued that allegorical reading is actually a tactic to make Greek culture Jewish.[91] For example, the phrase 'said in his mind' in Gen 17:17 represents swiftness of thought, to which Homer also testifies in the image 'like a bird's wing or a thought' (*Mut.* 178–79; *Od.* 7.36).[92] The Greek poet is enlisted to corroborate the biblical text as it expresses an idea from Greek culture. Philosophical meaning is found in a prior biblical text, and its Greek expression is subordinated to Scripture and made to serve it. So Philo's use of allegory can be part of a strategy of pointing to the superiority of Judaism, even as it manifestly parades his debt to Greek learning.[93]

D. The Superiority of Judaism

Philo continually utilised Greek concepts to serve Judaism. He defined philosophy with Judaism at its centre, considered himself a disciple of Moses, used

---

[86] Unlike Philo, Aristobolus labours to justify allegory (8.10.1–7) and applies it only to anthropomorphisms.

[87] *Abr.* 147. Barclay 1996: 166–67 calls the allegorical method 'the hermeneutical correlate of his Platonic dualism'.

[88] Decharneux 1994: 68.

[89] Dillon 1990: 178 offers two preconditions for writing an allegorical commentary: someone has (1) an authoritative but somehow problematic text, and (2) a coherent intellectual framework in which to interpret that text.

[90] As Dyck 2002 argues. His overall position, however, is flawed by a failure to engage with the range of Philonic texts which assert Jewish superiority.

[91] Dawson 1992: 78–82, 107–10.

[92] Dawson 1992: 109. For other allegorical readings of Homeric texts in Philo, see Lamberton 1986: 49–53.

[93] Birnbaum 2003 has modified Dawson's thesis to point out that the subordination of Hellenism to Judaism, while an important use of allegory, is not the only one.

philosophical concepts in service of biblical exegesis, and employed allegory to elevate Jewish claims. On what grounds did he make such moves? How did he justify this appreciation and yet subordination of Hellenic thought?

The answer in the Egyptian Jewish tradition was relatively clear: Greeks, Egyptians, and everyone else learned from the Jews.[94] Egyptians received astrology from Abraham (Artap. 9.18.1), and boats, armaments and even the animal-cult from Moses (9.27.4).[95] Pythagoras, Socrates, Plato, and Orpheus all learned philosophy from Moses (Aristob. 13.12.4). Nor were such claims isolated to Egyptian Jews. Their fellow religionists in Palestine, and indeed historians and intellectuals of all stripes around the Mediterranean made similar claims for how the best of Greek learning came originally from their own culture.[96] Judaism was superior *because* it was the original source.

Philo too had recourse to this explanation.[97] In explaining Gen 25:28, he says a younger group of philosophers used Moses as a direct source for their opinion that virtue is loved for its own sake (*QG* 4.167). The Greeks took more than just philosophy, though. Their legislators also copied the rule that hearsay is inadmissible evidence (*Spec.* 4.61).[98] This idea could also justify why Philo used philosophical concepts to interpret Scripture, since Moses was their original source.[99] So there is some evidence for Philo asserting Jewish originality.

Nonetheless, such claims do not carry the same weight in Philo as they do for others. First, what appears to be a major argument for Aristobulus is, by comparison, relatively minor for Philo. He claims that the Greeks took something from the Jews about as many times in all his treatises as Aristobulus

---

[94] The best treatment of this motif is Pilhofer 1990: 144–220; also, Droge 1989: 12–48; Roth 1978: 61–67.

[95] See Collins 2000: 39–41 on what he calls competitive historiography in Artapanus. On Abraham as a teacher, see p.89 n.88, and on astrology for Philo, see p.88.

[96] Hengel ET 1974: 1.86, 90 cites non-Jewish and Jewish examples of such claims in Phoenicia and Palestine. Mendels 1988 situates Jewish historiography in the context of the Greek East. Dillon 1977: 119–20 calls this process one-upmanship, which also went on in Greek philosophy. But note *Let. Aris.* 31, 312–16 as an exception.

[97] See Pilhofer 1990: 173–92. I have adopted a modified form of the classification scheme proposed by Runia 1986: 528–35 (528 n.5), having taken into account the valid criticisms by Pilhofer 1990: 190 over Runia's placement of specific passages. Cf. Droge 1989: 47–48. Roth 1978: 64–65 implausibly claims Philo did not choose the Alexandrian option because he was ignorant of it.

[98] *Leg.* 1.108; *Somn.* 2.244; *Prob.* 57; *QG* 3.5, 16; 4.152. *QG* 2.6 is uncertain whether Socrates learned from Scripture or came on his own to the truth about where God placed certain bodily orifices. A few passages (*Her.* 214; *Aet.* 19) state that Moses discovered something first but leave unsaid whether the Greeks were dependent on him.

[99] So Mansfeld 1988: 85–86; Arnaldez 1984: 40.

does in only five fragments.[100] Second, these claims tend not to occur in treatises like *De Abrahamo* or *De vita Mosis*, composed with a partially Gentile audience in mind, but rather in the Allegory and Questions series.[101] Perhaps Philo recognised the relative lack of cogency in these arguments for outsiders and thus confined them mostly to treatises intended only for Jews, where they functioned as internal apologetic.[102] Third, occasionally Philo includes evidence against Jewish originality, most notably in assigning Greek and Egyptian teachers to Moses (*Mos.* 1.21–24).[103] Although Moses quickly surpassed them, this statement could undermine the theoretical basis that Jewish culture is the fount from which everyone else drank.[104] So the 'theft of philosophy' motif does not appear nearly so often nor as widely in Philo.

This relative de-emphasis on Jewish originality is paired with the affirmation that people can reach truth apart from the revelation at Sinai.[105] While the patriarchs are the most obvious example,[106] the more pertinent evidence for us is virtuous non-Jews. Philo rhapsodises about those who 'surpassed their contemporaries in virtue, who took God for their sole guide and lived according to a law of nature's right reason' (*Prob.* 62). This description fits the Essenes (75), but also sages from among the Greeks, Persians, and Indians (73–74). Elsewhere Philo praises all who practice wisdom, whether in Greek or barbarian nations, and live according to nature (*Spec.* 2.44–48).[107] Admittedly these passages can easily be applied to Jews, and the fact that typically the insight gained by non-Jews is attributed to philosophy should remind us how Philo centres philosophy in Judaism. Nonetheless, he grants that some can understand the truth and live virtuously without reference to Moses or the Law.[108]

---

[100] Sterling 1993: 102.

[101] Pilhofer 1990: 188. Roughly half of the examples occur in the Questions, where Philo is more likely to incorporate opinions of earlier exegetes, without endorsing them (see Hay 1991b). Note the harsher tone toward Heracleitus in *QG* 4.152 compared to *Leg.* 1.108.

[102] Sterling 1999a: 6. On his arguments for Jewish superiority, see Mendelson 1988: 128–38; Birnbaum 2001: 45–48; 2004: 147–57; Dillon 1993: 153.

[103] Sterling 1993: 101–02 cites other examples. Cf. Runia 1986: 529.

[104] Pilhofer 1990: 188–89, though he later ascribes it to Philo's confidence in giving Moses such teachers (191–92).

[105] See below, p.141.

[106] *Migr.* 130; *Abr.* 5–6, 275–76; *Mos.* 1.162.

[107] Cf. *Opif.* 143–44; *Abr.* 61; *Spec.* 1.37–40.

[108] Other passages affirm Moses and philosophers hold the same doctrine, without saying anything about the relationship between them: *Post.* 133; *Deus* 22–23; *Conf.* 141; *Migr.* 8, 127–29, *Her.* 83; *Congr.* 89; *QG* 1.99. Runia 1986: 530–31 points to Philo's underlying cosmological and anthropological doctrine as the grounds on which people can come to some awareness of the truth apart from Mosaic revelation. Wolfson 1947: 1.140–43 summarises Philo's multiple explanations for how philosophers and Moses came to the same truth.

What counts for Judaism, therefore, to Philo, is not so much its originality or singularity, but its superior quality.[109] On the surface *Virt.* 65 points to the possibility of coming to the truth apart from Judaism, but indirectly it affirms Jewish superiority:

What the disciples of the most excellent philosophy gain from their teaching, the whole Jewish nation gains from its customs and laws, that is to know the most ancient Cause and reject the worship of created things.

Those without the Law must be disciples of the most excellent philosophy – not just any philosophy – if they want to find the right way. Philo implies their numbers are few, a point he affirms elsewhere (*Spec.* 2.47; *Prob.* 63). But for the Jews, all they have to do is follow the written Law, a privilege granted the entire nation. The Law makes plain to everyone what remains elusive in Greek philosophy.[110] In contrast to how infrequently Philo claims Jewish originality, he often proclaims its superiority, both conceptually and practically. Moses offers better answers to philosophical problems (*Leg.* 2.15),[111] and his surpassing philosophical insight renders anything else second-best: after he has taught that virtue is a thing for joy, what need is there to extol the philosophers who declare virtue a state of happy feeling (*Mut.* 167–68)?[112] Consequently, to use philosophical concepts in biblical exegesis is entirely legitimate, since Moses is the superior, indeed proper philosopher, just as Judaism is philosophy *par excellence.*[113] There is no question of importing 'foreign' methods alien to Scripture, because truth is unified. At a pragmatic level, Jewish superiority encompasses the whole range of life: worship (*Spec.* 2.165), cult (*Abr.* 180), social relationships (*Contempl.* 57–64), marriage and sexuality (*Contempl.* 68; *Spec.* 3.13–19), law (*Mos.* 2.12), and one's approach to death (*Abr.* 260).[114] Why are Jews so superior to everyone else? Because they are the 'race which the Father and King of the Universe and the source of all things has taken for his portion' (*Legat.* 3).

---

[109] Sterling 1999a: 6. On Philo's arguments for Jewish superiority, see Mendelson 1988: 128–38; Birnbaum 2001: 45–48; 2004: 147–57; Dillon 1993: 153.

[110] Cf. the same dynamic in the epistemological priority of natural law (see p.142).

[111] PLCL 1.477 identifies Plato (*Crat.* 401b; cf. 390d) and Pythagoras (*ap.* Cicero, *Tusc.* 1.62) as the philosophers. Cf. *QG* 1.20 for the same passage, but without this contrast.

[112] Also *Opif.* 128 (note the contrast of τιμᾶται and ἐκτετίμται), 131; *Plant.* 14, 18; *Somn.* 1.141; *Abr.* 13; *QG* 1.24; 2.14. For Jewish superiority in philosophy without reference to Moses, see *Somn.* 1.58–60; *Prob.* 88; *Contempl.* 14–16.

[113] See above, p.24

[114] Cf. Mendelson 1988: 133–34 for the social differentiation in such distinctions.

This superiority is ultimately not at the world's expense but for its sake. God has elevated the Jews so they can serve others.[115] Israel is a nation 'destined to be consecrated above all others to offer prayers for ever on behalf of the human race' (*Mos.* 1.149). Jews have a cosmic, priestly role to play on behalf of humanity (*Spec.* 2.163).[116] Part of Philo's strategy for such passages was surely to blunt charges that the Jews hated humanity and set themselves above other nations, while still asserting superiority.[117]

From this vantage point of Jewish superiority, founded in Scripture, inscribed in practice, Philo could appropriate what he found true in Greek culture and criticise what he judged false.[118] His incorporation of philosophy is clear, as is his willingness to point out where philosophers were wrong or had been bettered by Moses (e.g., *Opif.* 170–72).[119] Similarly, Philo benefited from an encyclical education (*Congr.* 74–76),[120] and could enfold such studies into his theological vision of how to approach God,[121] but he also cautioned against its dangers.[122] Likewise, he could appreciate the Greek social world of wrestling or the theatre yet criticise its vices like drunkenness.[123] To be a Hellenised Jew for Philo meant appropriating the best of the former for the ultimate glory of the latter, a typical position for Jewish Alexandria, and the Diaspora.[124] In *Letter of Aristeas*, the translators' answers to the king's ques-

[115] Cf. *Praem.* 114. On particularism and universalism for Philo, see Borgen 1992a: 135; Winston 1984: 398–99.

[116] On this role, see *Abr.* 98; *Spec.* 1.97; 1.168; *QE* 2.42. On κόσμος and cult, see p.84.

[117] The charge of Jewish misanthropy was common: e.g., Hecataeus, 1:26–29; Manetho, 1:78–83; Apollonius Molon, 1:154–55; Diodorus Siculus, 1:181–85; Lysimachus, 1:383–85 (all references in Stern 1974–84). Mendelson 1988: 103–13 discusses this charge and Philo's response. For Philo's use of φιλανθρωπία, see, *inter alia*, *Virt.* 51–174; *Spec.* 4.72, 97; *QG* 3.42; Winston 1984: 391–400; Borgen 1997: 243–60.

[118] Himmelfarb 2005: 95 points to the centrality of Torah as an important reason Jews were able to adapt Hellenism to their purposes and make this critical assessment. See Barclay 1996: 175–76 on Philo's critique of different elements of Hellenistic culture.

[119] Cf. Borgen 1992a: 132.

[120] On this passage's autobiographical character, see Mendelson 1982: 25–26; Feldman 1993: 57–59. This argument follows Mendelson (81–83). On the importance of Greek education to Alexandrian Judaism, see Hengel ET 1974: 1.66, 68–69; Holladay 1992: 144, and for Philo in particular, Borgen 1965: 108–11.

[121] Mendelson 1982: 69–78.

[122] *Ebr.* 49–50; *Congr.* 77–78; *QG* 3.23; *Leg.* 3.167.

[123] Neutral or positive references: *Ebr.* 177, 217–19; *Prob.* 26, 141. Critical references: *Agr.* 35, 113–19; *Ebr.* 20–23; *Contempl.* 40–56; *Flacc.* 4, 136. See Mendelson 1982: 32; Borgen 1992a: 129–30; Feldman 1993: 59–63; Seland 1996.

[124] See Gruen 2002: 221–30; Collins 2000: 24, 157. Holladay 1992: 158 covers the early Ptolemaic era. Modrzejewski 1991: 89–90 and Goudriaan 1992: 90–94 argue the Roman tax system, based on ethnicity, aided the demise of this synthesis.

tions are compatible with Greek philosophy,[125] but even the pagan philosophers acclaim that the Jews surpass them, precisely because all their answers are grounded theistically (*Let. Aris.* 200, 235).[126] Similarly, Aristobulus may appreciate how the Peripatetics recognised the metaphorical connection between light and wisdom, but Solomon's insight was clearer (13.12.10–11).[127] Thus the way Philo appropriates Hellenism and elevates Judaism is part of the tradition.

This intellectual project was not undertaken just for its own sake. Philo carried out his work amid growing ethnic tensions and civil conflict in Alexandria. His identification with and yet subordination of Greek culture should be seen in the context of his work on behalf of the Jewish community,[128] which culminated in leading the delegation to Rome after the events of AD 38.[129] It was a life he sometimes lamented for how it took him from study (*Spec.* 3.1–6), but it obviously corresponded with his sense that the survival of the Jewish community was vital. Philo condemns those who neglect the community and its obligations. God put Onan to death for placing self-interest over family and community (Gen 38:8–11), and Philo affirms such things are worth dying for (*Deus* 17–18).[130] In *Migr.* 89–93, Philo criticises those who allegorise the Law to the point of abandoning its literal observance. Philo agrees with their interpretation but not their application, and he chides them for trying to live as bodiless souls.[131] In contrast, the best path is to obey right reason without neglecting custom (*Ebr.* 30–94), to hold on to the Law's allegorical meaning *and* its literal observance.[132] Philo's philosophical exegesis of Scripture occurs in the context of the concrete Jewish community in Alexandria and throughout the Empire (*Legat.* 190) and is more evidence for how he situates himself with respect to Hellenism and Judaism.

---

[125] Tcherikover 1958: 70.

[126] Barclay 1996: 141–47; Birnbaum 2004: 131–38; Holladay 1992: 147–49. Elsewhere, *Let. Aris.* 139, 143, 161, 177.

[127] Cf. 13.12.6 (on which, see Hengel ET 1974: 1.165; Borgen 1987a: 10). More widely, Holladay 1992: 149–51.

[128] Dawson 1992: 113–26. Cf. Bréhier 1925: 313–14; Arnaldez 1984: 49; Mondésert 1999: 894. Hall 1997: 31–32 argues when a subordinate social group has a negative identity, its members will tend to see themselves as group members first rather than as individuals.

[129] Barclay 1996: 178 argues this role implies Philo's prior political involvement. A few likely allusions include *Somn.* 2.124–29; *Flacc.* 97–100; *Legat.* 178–79.

[130] Mendelson 1988: 24 sees fidelity to ancestral customs as a social concern for Philo.

[131] Cf. Hay 1997; Nikiprowetzky 1977: 120; Himmelfarb 2005: 122–23. Barclay 1996: 177–78 notes the tensions within Philo which this passage exposes.

[132] Nikiprowetzky 1977: 120.

IV. Conclusion

Hellenism and Judaism interact and influence one another in Philo, just as they had done in the Alexandrian tradition of which he was a part. The framework in which this took place was Jewish, and everything else was subordinated to Mosaic Law. Philosophy was most exemplarily study and practice of the Law, and its concepts were harnessed for interpretation of Scripture. Judaism was superior to Hellenism because it was original but even more because of its surpassing quality. All this was in the context of the actual Jewish community of which Philo was a leader. Yet Philo's fusion of Hellenism and Judaism is not perfect. As impressive as his joining of the two is, there are still points of tension where concepts in the two worlds do not mesh exactly.[133] It may be, therefore, that his assessment of the ethical status of the sensible world could either be an example of the fusion or disjunction of Judaism and Hellenism. With the stage set, it is to that initial analysis we now turn.

---

[133] See Winston 2002 for the exploration of some such tensions.

Chapter 3

Philo's Negative Terminology for the Physical World: οὐσία, ὕλη, γένεσις, γενητός

I. Introduction

The previous chapter argued Philo of Alexandria is fundamentally committed to Judaism, but his Judaism cannot be conceptualised apart from Hellenistic philosophy. He is incalculably yet not indiscriminately indebted to Greek culture; it is biblical revelation which is ultimately the superior source for all that is true and good. The question of Judaism and Hellenism is highly pertinent for cosmology. Both Greco-Roman and Jewish writers discussed the subject at length; more to the point, Aristobulus had begun to show how philosophical exegesis of Scripture might interpret topics like God's relation to the created realm (8.9.38–10.17).[1] Indeed, that is why Marguerite Harl chose for the seminal 1966 Lyon *Colloque* to focus on cosmology as the test-case for how Philo navigated the relations between Judaism and Hellenism.[2] In discussing cosmology, Philo draws extensively on both biblical and philosophical sources, and in the course of the following chapters, as we examine Philo's understanding of the sensible realm, we will evaluate how these biblical and philosophical commitments shape his work.

Just as Harl delimited her investigation – by concentrating on the fragmentary treatise *De Deo* – so we will delimit ours, albeit not nearly so tightly. The next four chapters will study how Philo uses terms which denote the concrete, sensible world. That includes surveying every occurrence of six key words: οὐσία, ὕλη, γένεσις, γενητός (Ch. 3), κόσμος (Ch. 4) and φύσις (Chs. 5–6), along with representative instances of other terms (e.g., τὸ πᾶν and participial forms of γίγνομαι). Chapter 3 concentrates on terms which have a negative ethical status, while Chapters 4–6 look at the positive terms. No study of which I am aware has covered all the occurrences of these six terms,[3] but

[1] Aristobulus urges Ptolemy to receive his interpretations φυσικῶς, i.e. in a manner keeping with physics (8.10.2). On this term, see below, p.123 n.120.

[2] Harl 1967; on the place of her study, see Runia 1986: 12–14.

[3] For studies on individual terms, see the corresponding sections or chapters below.

together they give a broad coverage to the material world as a conceptual field. The goal is to map the semantic terrain for Philo's references to the sensible realm.

This terminological study will make two main arguments. First, Philo expresses strongly negative and positive views about the physical world, views which correspond largely to his choice of terms. He tends to use γένεσις and γενητός and derivatives of γίγνομαι which express the idea of 'becoming' in a negative way. In contrast, κόσμος and φύσις are almost exclusively positive terms. Terms for the stuff out of which the physical realm was made – οὐσία and ὕλη – stand somewhat outside this contrast. Philo uses them variously in either a neutral or negative manner. So although the connection is not absolute, there is a substantial link between Philo's choice of terminology for the sensible world and his evaluation of its ethical status. Second, Philo's usage of these terms is fundamentally orientated by Greco-Roman philosophy. His Jewish faith leads him to modify and depart from that tradition, sometimes extensively, yet those philosophical concepts nonetheless lead Philo where other Jewish writers do not venture.[4] This argument appears to stand in a certain tension with the claims of Chapter 2, as it seemingly prioritises the Hellenistic dimension above the Jewish one – that will prove particularly the case here in Chapter 3.

These chapters on the semantic terrain comprise the heart of this study. They will conclusively establish the profound surface contradiction in Philo's attitude toward the sensible world as well as begin to suggest ways forward for understanding it. The final two chapters will build on this foundational lexical semantic study to establish Philo's multiperspectivalism.

This chapter studies the terms which Philo uses in a primarily negative fashion for the sensible world. That starts with οὐσία and ὕλη, which denote the chaotic matter from which God made the universe. Philo uses these terms alternately negatively or neutrally, but virtually never in a positive way, which communicates clearly that whatever the state of the world as finished product, it did not come from glorious beginnings, in so far as the building blocks are concerned. We then consider γένεσις and γενητός, both of which conceptualise the world in terms of 'becoming', the change and flux inherent to anything sensible. There is a range of evaluation for γένεσις – it can sometimes picture the world in a positive or neutral fashion – but the scope for γενητός is more narrow, as it overwhelmingly has a negative hue. Taken together, these four terms overall connote a world which resists God and is far from him, a world

[4] I compare Philo's use of these terms to a set of Jewish writings, which includes the Septuagint, Aristobulus, *Letter of Aristeas*, *Testaments of the 12 Patriarchs*, *Testament of Abraham*, and Josephus.

which a person must flee in order to progress spiritually. Before we begin the terminological study proper, however, we must sketch briefly Philo's overall creation story.

II. The Act and Process of Creation: Bringing Order

Before examining Philo's terms for the material world, it makes sense to begin with an overview of how that world came into existence. Philo weds Greco-Roman views on creation, especially from the *Timaeus*, to the biblical account in Genesis.[5] Among other things, this fusion entails a two-stage creation (*Tim.* 29a). God created the pattern of the intelligible forms, then their sensible copies (*Opif.* 16).[6] On day one, God created the basic forms, and on days two to six, the derived forms and copies; on that sixth day, he also created the noumenal man (Gen 1:26–27) and its copy, the earthly man (Gen 2:7).[7] Of course, Philo informs his readers creation did not literally take six days – Moses employs this device only to demonstrate the order with which it occurred (*Opif.* 13).[8]

That point leads to a second pivotal debt to the *Timaeus*: creation is the move from disorder to order (εἰς τάξιν αὐτὸ ἤγαγεν ἐκ τῆς ἀταξίας; *Tim.* 30a), or correspondingly, from pre-existent matter to the κόσμος.[9] This contrast becomes a primary way for him to conceptualise what occurred at creation: God brought disorder and irregularity into order and sequence (τὴν ἀταξίαν καὶ ἀκοσμίαν εἰς κόσμον καὶ τάξιν ἀγαγών; *Somn.* 1.241; cf. *Gorg.* 504a).[10] Hence, order is characteristic of the created realm (*Praem.* 42).[11] Thus Philo

[5] On this use of *Timaeus*, see the seminal Runia 1986, on the dialogue's wider influence, see p.4 n.20. For the argument that the Aristotelian influence on Philo's cosmology has been under-estimated, see Bos 2009. On the other side, Long 2008 judges that in cosmology, Stoicism does not have a major influence on Philo.

[6] Radice 2008: 132–33 sees a three-phase creation, dividing the creation of the copies into the general and particular.

[7] Wolfson 1947: 1:310; Winston 1985: 24–25. Questions about these two men are, of course, highly controverted; see, *inter alia*, Baer 1970: 20–38; Tobin 1983; Runia 1986: 334–40. The neuter 'its' for the noumenal man reflects how for Philo this intelligible creature transcends sexual differentiation.

[8] Cf. Aristob. 13.12.12.

[9] Runia 1986: 140–48, esp. 140–41; Goodenough 1935: 48. On the biblical roots for seeing creation as the move from chaos to order, see McGrath 2001: 146–48.

[10] Cf. *Opif.* 21–22; *Plant.* 3; *Spec.* 1.48; 4.187; *QG* 1.55, 64.

[11] Τάξις for the sensible realm, often with κόσμος: *Opif.* 13; *Leg.* 2.73; *Her.* 206; *Abr.* 61; *Aet.* 32, 75.

retrospectively sums up *De opificio* as 'the story of the order in which the world was made' (*Abr.* 2).[12]

Philo sees such order as evidence of rationality – that something is ordered implies it has reason, and that something is rational is shown by its order (*QG* 3.3; *Sacr.* 82). But what characterises rational order? Two main traits: sequence and hierarchy.[13] A thing shows order when it exists in the proper arrangement with whatever comes before or after it, and above or below it. So although God created all things simultaneously, yet they are ordered in their design, because 'order is a series of things going on before and following after, in due sequence' (τάξις δ' ἀκολουθία καὶ εἱμός ἐστι προηγουμένων τινῶν καὶ ἑπομένων; *Opif.* 28).[14] Second, the notion of hierarchy recalls the military definitions for τάξις (e.g., *Flacc.* 86) and its use as the post to which God assigns the stars or certain individuals.[15] Philo defines order as the greater lawfully ruling the lesser, whether a king over his subjects (*Fug.* 145), the mind over the senses (*Somn.* 2.152), or the priests over the Levites (*Mos.* 2.277). This hierarchical order encompasses every level of the created realm:

> Now since every well-ordered (εὔνομος) State has a constitution (πολιτείαν), the citizen of the world (κοσμοπολίτῃ) enjoyed of necessity the same constitution as did the whole world (σύμπας ὁ κόσμος): and this constitution is nature's right relation (ὁ τῆς φύσεως ὀρθὸς λόγος), more properly called an 'ordinance', or 'dispensation', seeing it is a divine law . . . (*Opif.* 143)

A descending, inter-linked chain of order stretches from God, divine creator and lawgiver, to the intelligible world, sensible world, human state, and then within the human person (*Opif.* 81).[16] As a result of this rational sequence and hierarchy, order is 'the most beautiful and profitable thing in life' (τό κάλλιστον καὶ λυσιτελέστατον τῶν ἐν τῷ βίῳ; AT; *Spec.* 1.120).[17]

The order in creation comes from God measuring, numbering and shaping what exists into definite form (*Somn.* 1.294). The notion of God measuring

---

[12] Note also the play on words with σύνταξις which means 'treatise' but can also mean the 'order of the world' (LSJ 1724b). On *De opificio* and order, cf. Borgen 1995: 121–22.

[13] Cf. Runia 2001: 160; idem 1986: 101–02. Cambronne 1984 adds the beauty of number. Both traits function within a teleological context: it is sequence and hiearchy that culminate in their proper end which is true order.

[14] Cf. *Prob.* 81; *Aet.* 31, 34. This idea of τάξις as sequence/arrangement is common: e.g., Xenophon, *Cyr* 8.7.22; Plato, *Leg.* 637e; Aristotle, *Eth. eud.* 1218a23; Demosthenes, *Cor.* 2 (from LSJ 1756); *T. Naph.* 2:9; 1 Cor 14:40.

[15] Stars: *Cher.* 23; *Decal.* 104; *Spec.* 2.230. Individuals: *Migr.* 196; *Spec.* 1.114, 345; *Virt.* 127; *Praem.* 152.

[16] Barraclough 1984: 507. Cambronne 1984: 13–14. On reason as a property of φύσις for Philo, see p.130.

[17] *Opif.* 28, 65; *Fug.* 145.

creation is both Platonic and Jewish.[18] Like Plato's Demiurge, God accomplishes this by means of number and the forms.[19] Typically, God does this through the Logos, who measures and divides and wields the forms, and thus brings order to creation, 'for correct division and incorrect division are nothing else than order. And through order equally are made the whole world and its parts' (*QG* 1.64).[20] The Logos is a famously difficult and yet crucial doctrine for Philo. Put broadly, it is 'that aspect of God that is directed towards creation',[21] the intersection between God and all created reality (*Her.* 205–6).[22] The complexities of Philo's Logos-doctrine are better covered elsewhere;[23] for our purposes two points are important: its instrumental role in the act and process of creation, and the variability of how this mediator is identified.[24]

First, the Logos is that through which (δι' ὧν) the κόσμος was made (*Cher.* 127). God used it as his instrument in the act of constructing the universe,[25] and moreover, continues to utilise it in the process of sustaining and guiding the universe (*Deus* 57; *Migr.* 6).[26] Thus creation, as act and process that orders the disordered, does not occur for Philo apart from a mediatorial figure.[27]

Second, however, Philo fluctuates in how he identifies this mediator, as the same instrumental role in creation can be ascribed to the divine potency God (*Mut.* 29) or to Wisdom (*Det.* 54).[28] When Philo schematises the Logos and Powers together, the Logos is higher as that which unites and guides them

---

[18] Platonic: *Tim.* 53ab; Plutarch, *Mor.* 720b; see Runia 1986: 137–38, 291–95. Jewish: Job 28:24–27; 38:5; Isa 40:12; Wis 11:20; *1 En.* 43:1–2; *2 En.* 48:4; *4 Ezra* 4:36–37; *T. Naph.* 2:3 (from Hollander & de Jonge 1985: 303).

[19] *Her.* 156; *Somn.* 2.45; *Spec.* 1.48, 327; *Prov.* 2.50–51; *QE* 2.33, 52.

[20] *Her.* 133–40; *Fug.* 12; *Mut.* 135–36; *QG* 1.4; 4.23. On the Logos-cutter, see Dillon 1995: 116–20.

[21] Runia 2001: 142.

[22] Sandmel 1979: 94; Runia 1986: 449.

[23] These include its complex origins in Platonic and Stoic philosophy, biblical exegesis and Jewish Wisdom speculation; the degree to which the various statements can be systematised; and whether one should speak of levels or stages of the Logos, or even as a hypostasis. See, *inter alia*, Wolfson 1947: 1.226–94, 325–31; Dillon 1977: 158–61; Tobin 1983: 63–77; Winston 1985: 15–25; Runia 1986: 204–08, 446–51; Cox 2007: 87–140.

[24] On the Logos and the act of creation see, in particular, Radice 2008: 136–38.

[25] Cf. *Leg.* 3.96; *Sacr.* 8; *Conf.* 62–63; *Migr.* 103; *Fug.* 95; *Mos.* 2.127; *Spec.* 1.81. In addition to sources previously cited, see Früchtel 1968: 16–17.

[26] Cf. *Fug.* 12; *Mos.* 2.133. That can be expressed as the Logos as charioteer: *Cher.* 36; *Fug.* 101; or as bond of all things: *Plant.* 9; *Her.* 188; *Fug.* 112; *QE.* 2.90, 118.

[27] See Cox 2007 for this figure in Middle Platonism, Judaism, Christianity and Gnosticism.

[28] Cf. for the Powers: e.g., *Plant.* 50; *Her.* 166; *QG* 1.54; for Wisdom: *Ebr.* 31; *Her.* 199; *Fug.* 109.

(*Fug.* 101).[29] There is no clear pattern, however, for the Logos and Wisdom, as either can be primary, or even equated (*Det.* 115–18).[30] The fluidity with which Philo alternates between these entities communicates both the necessity of some kind of intermediary between God and creation, but also that its precise identification can vary, perhaps depending on the exegetical context,[31] or on the interpretive tradition employed.[32] Interestingly, φύσις is never explicitly incorporated into the mix with relation to the Logos. This is despite the fact that Philo sometimes gives 'nature' divine standing and ascribes to it a role in creating and ordering sensible existence. One important difference, of course, is that the biblical text never mandates the use of φύσις as it does for the other terms. We will return to this question later when we consider the relation between the Logos, nature and natural law.[33]

Philo's emphasis on order as foundational for creation seems to reflect an underlying, axiomatic principle.[34] Order is preferred to disorder in every area of life, especially in the realm of human relations. Similarly, the ways he explains that order points to the socially-conditioned nature of the concept. The stress on hierarchy reflects a social conservatism by someone who sat atop the Alexandrian Jewish community. More broadly, it was characteristically Jewish to advocate the benefits of a socially stable, ordered society, even if that was under pagan government.[35] From another angle, Philo lived when the disorder of the civil wars and the *pax Augustana* which replaced them was still recent memory, which his revulsion for disorder may reflect. More pointedly, depending on how much of his output follows the turmoil over the Jewish community's status in Alexandria, this preference for order may have an acutely personal dimension too. This correspondence between order in human society and the universe is, of course, a long-standing feature of ancient cos-

---

[29] *Cher.* 27–28; *QE* 2.68. Berchman 1984: 46 conceptualises Philo's view as the Power being 'an aspect of the Supreme God mediated through the Logos in the universe'. On the Powers in Philo, see Termini 2000 (n.v.); Runia 2004.

[30] Logos: *Fug.* 97; Wisdom: *Leg.* 1.63–65; *Somn.* 2.242–43. *Contra* the systematising of Wolfson 1947: 1.258–61. This may well be because Philo retains prior exegetical traditions (Cox 2007: 90).

[31] Harl 1967: 200. Cf. Runia 2002a: 296.

[32] Cox 2007: 89–90 using the image of Russian *matryoshka* ('nested') dolls. He also notes that Middle Platonism had this same problem of not fixing on a definite identification for the intermediary being (99).

[33] See p.143.

[34] Cf. similar observation by Runia 1986: 141.

[35] Jer 29:7; *m. 'Abot* 3:2; Josephus speaks of the prayer and sacrifices offered for the emperor: *J.W.* 2.197; *Ag. Ap.* 2.77.

mological discourse, and could be used to support the status quo, as evidenced by Middle and Roman Stoicism.[36]

What lessons should one draw from this cosmological order? The story of creation, as Philo tells it, is ultimately ethical. He concludes *De opificio* with five lessons from what God has done (170–72) and promises his readers that learning them will ensure a pious and blessed life. The very purpose of reflecting on these cosmological matters is to enable progress in the ethical-religious life. There is, therefore, something intrinsically ethical to the story of creation. God created and sustains the physical world in an orderly way, and that pattern should shape the order of one's life. Our investigation in Part One will corroborate this point, as each of the terms for the sensible world have a moral torque to their usage.

III. Οὐσία and Ὕλη: The Stuff from which the Physical World is Made

A. Introduction

Since the shift from disorder to order is central for Philo's doctrine of the creation of the sensible realm, we begin logically with the starting point, disordered matter. Philo uses οὐσία and ὕλη to denote the material from which God constructed the visible world.[37] Philo's philosophical usage of οὐσία reflects different emphases than Plato's, who contrasted οὐσία and γένεσις at a metaphysical level as Being and Becoming (*Tim.* 29c) and had Socrates deride the atomists for equating οὐσία with σῶμα (*Soph.* 246a–c). Philo would agree conceptually with such distinctions, but he almost never uses οὐσία to denote true being.[38] He most commonly means the more Aristotelian 'substance'

---

[36] E.g., Cicero, *Resp.* 3.33; *Fin.* 3.68; cf. Simon & Simon 1956: 27–28, 92; J. Adams 1945: 95; E. Adams 2000: 69–75; L-S 1.436. On the sociology of 'nature', see p.13.

[37] His wider usage of these terms holds minimal importance for our study: e.g., οὐσία as property (*Flacc.* 150); ὕλη as wild trees (*Det.* 105), cut wood (*Sobr.* 36), subject-matter (*Congr.* 144) and material resources (*Abr.* 220). Definitions in this section are modified from LSJ 1274b, 1847b–48a. For the full results for οὐσία see Appendix 1; for ὕλη, see Appendix 2. Winston 1981: 7–8 suggests μὴ ὄν as another term for matter (*Mos.* 2.267, *Spec.* 2.225).

[38] The notable exception is his exegesis of Exod 20:21, when Moses enters into the darkness where God resides, the archetypal οὐσίαν of existing things (*Mos.* 1.158; cf. *Mut.* 7), i.e., God as known to himself (so Runia 2002a: 299).

(e.g., *Metaph.* 1017b10; *Cael.* 298a29).'[39] Οὐσία as substance ranges from oil and wine (*Conf.* 186) to all visible and invisible existence (*Congr.* 144). Similarly, ὕλη denotes that from which something is made, from brass and iron for weapons (*Praem.* 132) to the material cause of anything (*Cher.* 125–27; cf. *QG* 1.58).[40] It is these categories under which falls the more specific meaning of the material from which the sensible world is made.[41] When he defines οὐσία and ὕλη this way, they are often interchangeable terms.[42] Such synonymy likely comes from Stoic influence, who defined the primordial matter as an inert quality-less substance (τὴν ἄποιον οὐσίαν τὴν ὕλην; *SVF* 1.85, 87).[43] When οὐσία and ὕλη refer to the stuff from which God made the world, Philo fluctuates between neutral and negative evaluations, but the main point is that for God to make the world as he did, he had to overcome the material he used.

B. Positive and Neutral References to Matter

There are only two passages which refer to universal matter positively using οὐσία or ὕλη.[44] First, God made the original human body from the best, purest matter possible (ἐκ καθαρᾶς ὕλης τὸ καθαρώτατον; *Opif.* 137, 136). This positive statement, though, must be considered in light of Philo's mostly negative treatment of the human body.[45] Second, Philo argues at *Prov.* 2.50 that God used precisely the right amount of material in making the universe, and accordingly, it 'was well made from a perfect substance' (ἐκ τελείας οὐσίας). This is a striking – and singular – endorsement of universal matter. But there are mitigating factors. This treatise records Philo's dispute with his nephew

---

[39] Philo, like Plato and Aristotle, uses οὐσία to denote the essence or definition of a thing, that without which it would cease to exist (def. #3 in Appendix 1; e.g., *Opif.* 54; *Mos.* 1.118; of God, *Post.* 15; *Virt.* 215; of the soul, *Cher.* 65; *Her.* 55). This definition occurs around 55*x*. 'Substance' as used here includes the definitions of 'matter, substance' (#4; around 65*x*) and of the 'elements/individual bodies/things themselves' (#5; around 50*x*).

[40] On the four causes, see p.76.

[41] Runia 1986: 141 blurs this connection when he describes οὐσία in *Opif.* 21–22 as indicating 'neither Platonic 'being' nor Aristotelian 'substance'. This instance is indeed more Stoic, but he overlooks the continuum for Philo between οὐσία as specific substance, universal sensible substance and the raw material for everything.

[42] Interchangeable and positive: *Prov.* 2.50; interchangeable and negative: e.g., *Leg.* 1.31; *Fug.* 8–9; *Spec.* 3.128.

[43] Cf. Runia 1986: 141.

[44] This is excepting the motif with οὐσία that describes heaven (οὐρανός) as 'the purest part of existence/matter' (e.g., τὸ καθαρώτατον τῆς οὐσίας; *Virt.* 85). See also *Opif.* 27, 114; *Mos.* 1.113; *Decal.* 134, 155; *Spec.* 4.235. For similar judgments, see *Decal.* 64; *Spec.* 1.66; *QG.* 4.8. This motif speaks more to Philo's valuation of the supralunary realm than it does how he sees matter. On this high valuation of heaven, see below, p.171.

[45] On Philo's treatment of the body, see below, p.60.

Alexander over divine providence, and thus for rhetorical purposes, Philo may speak positively of how God made the universe – including the material he used – in order to bolster his thesis that God watches over what he has made. Since none of the exegetical commentaries use οὐσία or ὕλη positively in this manner, relatively little weight should be accorded *Prov.* 2.50.

Perhaps somewhat surprisingly, Philo describes matter in a neutral way just as often as in a negative way.[46] Moses fittingly built the tabernacle with 'substances like those (τὰς ὁμοίας οὐσίας) with which the Ruler made the All' (*Mos.* 2.88).[47] Likewise, God could have made Eve in the same way he made Adam, since the material (ὕλη) was unlimited (*Leg.* 2.18). Philo often describes matter as sensible (αἰσθητὴν) or visible (ὁρατή).[48] Both motifs feature οὐσία more frequently than ὕλη. Philo also repeats the traditional claim that all possible material went into creating the cosmos, using either οὐσία or ὕλη.[49] On the whole, though, neutral references about the matter from which God made the sensible realm use οὐσία more frequently than ὕλη.[50]

C. Negative References to Matter

Philo may refer to matter negatively with or without reference to the act of creation. If without, he describes what matter is like now, even after having been given shape. In those cases, the dominant description is to picture matter as lifeless and perishable.[51] The body is like a cross – both are lifeless and perishable matter (ἀψύχον . . . φθαρταῖς ὕλαις; *Post.* 61). Moses ground up the golden calf as a sign that no genuine good can ever come from corruptible matter (ὕλη φθαρτῇ; *Post.* 163). Other negative characteristics – like disorder or formlessness – are true of matter initially but are transformed at creation; lifelessness and perishability, however, remain. In fact, the adjectives ἄψυχος and φθαρτός appear more frequently with οὐσία and ὕλη when Philo is talking about matter as it continues to exist rather than as it is initially.[52] Overall, these negative references to matter's continuing character use ὕλη more than

---

[46] Combining the two terms, there are a little over 40 relevant references on each side.

[47] Other οὐσία neutral references: *Her.* 133; *Migr.* 180; *Decal.* 107; *Spec.* 1.327; 4.237.

[48] Sensible οὐσία: *Opif.* 70; *Ebr.* 61; *Conf.* 81; *Abr.* 77, 88. Visible οὐσία: *Opif.* 111; *Congr.* 144; *Abr.* 69; *Spec.* 3.190.

[49] Οὐσία: *Aet.* 21; ὕλη: *Opif.* 171; *Plant.* 5; *Prov.* 2.50 (2*x*).

[50] Of the relevant occurrences, for ὕλη, 13 are neutral and 26 negative; for οὐσία, 29 are neutral and 15 negative.

[51] ὕλη with ἄψυχος: *Post.* 61; *Deus* 8; *Ebr.* 132; *Decal.* 133; *Contempl.* 4; with φθαρτός: *Leg.* 1.31, 88; *Post.* 115, 165; *Ebr.* 162; *Congr.* 112. Οὐσία does not appear with ἄψυχος; with φθαρτός: *Leg.* 1.31; *Cher.* 48; *Conf.* 108; *Somn.* 2.253; *Mos.* 2.171. Negative texts which include neither adjective: *Leg.* 3.243; *Spec.* 3.180.

[52] The lone exception is *Her.* 160.

οὐσία, which is opposite from the neutral references. This distinction also applies when they are used for the human body.[53] We may speculate this is a matter of the philosophical legacy for these quasi-technical terms. Plato, Aristotle and others used οὐσία more broadly and positively than ὕλη, and perhaps that influenced contemporary practice, or at least Philo's idiolect. This distinction should not be pushed too far, however, since negative passages that do have creation in view employ οὐσία and ὕλη in roughly equal measure.

The second category of negative reference to universal matter is when the act of creation is explicitly in view. David Runia discerns two overlapping tendencies in how Philo depicts the matter used at creation: sometimes it is 'a wholly passive, quality-less substrate', and other times the focus is on 'the negativity of a disorderly material'.[54] Some passages recount just passivity, whereas others describe passivity and negativity.[55] In either case, Philo employs multiple alpha-privative adjectives to stress what matter is not, a kind of cosmological *via negativa.*[56] Οὐσία

> of itself (ἐξ αὑτῆς) was without order (ἄτακτος), without quality (ἄποιος), without soul (ἄψυχος), [without likeness] <ἀνόμοιος>; it was full of inconsistency (ἑτεροιότητος), ill-adjustment (ἀναρμοστίας), disharmony (ἀσυμφωνίας; *Opif.* 22).[57]

Some adjectives show what matter lacks while others predicate negative characteristics. The passive terms depict a raw material which offers nothing: no shape or type (ἀσχημάτιστον, ἀτύπωτον; *Somn.* 2.45), no life or movement (ἄψυχος, ἀκίνητος; *Contempl.* 4), no form or quality (ἄμορφον καὶ ἄποιον; *Her.* 140). Under this set of adjectives, matter simply lies limp and inert. The negative characteristics portray material which had to be subdued and brought into line. The adjective ἄτακτος recurs elsewhere (*Plant.* 3; *Spec.* 4.187), which is not surprising, given Philo's emphasis on creation as the move from

---

[53] Neutral use of οὐσία for the body: *Sacr.* 108; *Her.* 282; *Decal.* 31; *Spec.* 1.263–66; *QG* 2.12. Negative use of ὕλη for the body: *Leg.* 2.51; 3.152; *Post.* 115; *Plant.* 22. The sole negative usage of οὐσία is *Post.* 163. For Philo's views on the body, see below, p.60.

[54] Runia 1986: 144 (emphasis removed). This analysis is superior to his division between negativity and potentiality (452), since those categories actually belong together, as we will see.

[55] Passive only texts include *Her.* 140; *Fug.* 8–9; *Somn.* 2.45; *Contempl.* 4. Passive and negative texts include *Opif.* 21–22; *Plant.* 3; *Her.* 159–60; *Spec.* 3.128–29; 4.187. Although it uses neither οὐσία nor ὕλη, *Opif.* 8–9 fits with the 'passive' texts, for its usage of the Stoic τὸ παθητόν, as well as ἄψυχον and ἀκίνητον, which Philo uses elsewhere for matter (*Ebr.* 132; *Contempl.* 4, respectively).

[56] See Runia 1986: 147 for how such adjectives are typically Middle Platonic.

[57] *Contra* O'Neill 2002: 456 who takes this as intelligible οὐσία rather than pre-existent matter.

disorder to order. That disorder resided in the building blocks with which God had to work. The most negative passage is perhaps *Her.* 160 which damns ὕλη as 'soulless, discordant, and dissoluble . . . in itself perishable, irregular, unequal'.[58] Such matter is a jumbled mess that must be overcome to be used in creation.

Runia analyses the provenance of this mix of passive and negative traits.[59] Philo of course draws extensively on the *Timaeus*, but his terminology differs, and important notions for Plato, like the receptacle, do not appear as such for Philo.[60] What Philo retains is the constructively negative slant on matter and 'the skeletal frame of Plato's text'.[61] Passive traits come more from Aristotle and the Stoics, but the usage of a Stoic adjective like ἄποιος is altered by the fact that Philo can use it alongside terms which actually do predicate certain 'qualities'. That juxtaposition leads Runia to conclude that although Philo sounds Stoic, he must mean something different, since the Stoics stressed the passivity of matter to the exclusion of such predication.[62] Moreover, although Philo resembles Middle Platonists in his adjectival descriptions, the fact that matter itself is ἄψυχος, rather than that describing an evil cosmic soul, differentiates him at least from figures like Plutarch and Numenius.[63] The philosophical strands of Philo's conceptualisation of matter can be teased apart, but the *gestalt* is his own, particularly in the negative emphasis.

Granted the predominantly philosophical background, is there also Jewish influence on Philo's treatment of matter? With respect to this terminology of οὐσία and ὕλη, the answer is very little, if any. The Septuagint uses the words infrequently, and even then, almost exclusively colloquially.[64] A rare exception is Wis 11:17 which credits God with creating the κόσμος from 'formless matter' (ἐξ ἀμόρφου ὕλης). This statement notes a 'passive' characteristic of matter, but nothing 'constructively' negative. Likewise, the terms either do not appear in Second Temple sources, or their usage is overwhelmingly non-

---

58 On *Her.* 160 as a key to interpreting Philo's multiperspectivalism, see p.174.

59 Runia 1986: 142–45.

60 Philo explicitly alludes to the receptacle only at *Ebr.* 61; *QG* 4.160. Cf. Runia 1986: 283–91. Winston 1981: 9–10 does see in Philo, by implication, the idea that the receptacle contains the pre-existent matter.

61 Runia 1986: 144.

62 Runia 1986: 143 (cf. *SVF* 1.85, 87; 2.301, 303). He speculates that in *Opif.* 22 it refers to 'formlessness'.

63 See below, p.189.

64 Οὐσία as property: Tob 14:13; 3 Macc 3:28; ὕλη as woods: Job 38:40; mass: 4 Macc 1:29; subject-matter: Job 19:29; 2 Macc 2:24; fuel: Isa 10:17, Sir 28:10; and earthly matter: Wis 15:13.

philosophical.[65] Josephus never uses οὐσία for matter, but at *Ant.* 1.28, he refers to 'the whole of matter' (τὴν ὅλην ὕλην) at creation.[66] This is his only usage of either term with respect to the act of creation, and there is nothing negative about it. In contrast, he does speak in a few places of the corruptible or perishable matter of the human body or idols (*J.W.* 2.154; 3.372; *Ant.* 8.280). But these examples stand out precisely because of their rarity. There is little Jewish context for Philo's usage of the terms οὐσία and ὕλη to signify the stuff from which the universe was made.

There may be a conceptual Jewish background, however, for God using a disorderly, chaotic material in creation. The תהו ובהו of Gen 1:2, usually translated 'formless and void', may mean a primordial chaos from which creation began.[67] In his *Chaoskampf*, God overcame that poor beginning in order to establish this world. Philo displays no obvious influence from this exegetical tradition,[68] but the idea is similar to his notion about the sorry state of the building blocks for the physical world.

Paradoxically, Philo's negative characterisation of matter dramatises the greatness of what God did in creation. Philo repeatedly inserts the phrase 'of itself' (ἐξ αὑτῆς/ἑαυτῆς) when describing matter.[69] It emphasises the sorry state of matter if left on its own. The strongest contrast comes from the division between God and matter by his nature, which leaves him unable to handle it directly (*Spec.* 1.329). Yet since each of the passages narrate God's creative activity, matter is not left 'of itself'. These descriptions of matter, whether negative or passive, lay great stress on its potential to become something entirely better under God's gracious direction. Such matter is 'capable of turning and undergoing a complete change to the best' (*Opif.* 22), which Philo enumerates as the positive counterparts to the earlier negative adjectives.[70] God perfects this οὐσία into the cosmos (*Somn.* 2.45).[71] Such transformation

[65] Josephus uses οὐσία nearly always for 'possessions'; e.g., *Ant.* 7.114; 17.307; *J.W.* 4.414. He overwhelmingly uses ὕλη for timber (e.g., *Ant.* 4.55; 18.357; *J.W.* 5.107) or materials (*Ant.* 3.103; *J.W.* 7.136). Neither term appears in *Testaments of the 12 Patriarchs*, *Testament of Abraham*, or *Letter of Aristeas*.

[66] He occasionally uses οὐσία for God's being (*Ant.* 20.268; *Ag. Ap.* 2.167), or with ὅλος to denote all of existence (*Ant.* 1.272; 10.278). Aristobulus uses οὐσία to describe 'natural' wisdom (*ap.* Clement, *Strom.* 6.16.138.4b; see the comment at Holladay 1995: 232 n.143).

[67] As the rabbis understood it at *Ber. Rab.* 1:5 (quoted at Levenson 1988: xx). One or both of the terms are applied creationally also at Job 26:7; Isa 34:11; 45:18; Jer 4:23.

[68] The LXX rendering of Gen 1:2 (ἀόρατος καὶ ἀκατασκεύαστος) only appears at *Aet.* 19.

[69] *Opif.* 9, 22; *Plant.* 3; *Her.* 160; *Contempl.* 4.

[70] Runia 1986: 147–48 regards this motif as Philo's own contribution to interpretation of the *Timaeus*.

[71] Cf. *Opif.* 9; *Plant.* 3; *Her.* 140, 160.

is in keeping with the very divine purpose of changing the worse for the better (*Spec.* 4.187). Paradoxically, therefore, the worse the characterisation of matter, the better God appears.[72] Since he lacked a cooperative, perfectly malleable starting point, to produce the cosmos as he has done redounds all the more to his honour. Playing up the resistance of matter further magnifies God.

God activates and directs this potential through the Logos or the forms (*Opif.* 20; *Mos.* 2.127), though properly speaking the former utilises the latter. They are the means by which he imparts structure and order to chaotic matter (*Her.* 140; *Spec.* 1.328).[73] Their work continues in the present, for if the forms were withdrawn, Philo supposes that 'nothing more than shapeless matter' (ἄμορφος ὕλη) would be left (*Spec.* 1.328). Accordingly, matter remains as a substrate of the sensible world. In *Migr.* 180 and *Contempl.* 4, Philo uses ὑποβάλλω with οὐσία and ὕλη, respectively, to indicate that God has laid matter as a foundation for the world.[74] The first passage is entirely neutral about this substrate, and the second describes ὕλη in terms of passivity. Significantly, no passage which pictures matter as a substrate describes it as disorderly, or any other 'constructively' negative trait. It remains lifeless and perishable but not unruly and chaotic.[75] So although the two tendencies of passivity and negativity often overlap, they do not in these passages.[76] This distinction minimises the notion that matter continues to play a negative role in the sensible world. Its confusion and chaos were subdued at the creation. Only by inappropriately systematising Philo can the concept of the material substrate be joined to matter's 'constructively' negative characteristics.[77]

What is the ontological status of matter? Runia detects a studied ambiguity on Philo's part: at *Opif.* 7–8 there is the active cause (δραστήριον αἴτιον), and the passive (τὸ παθητόν), for which αἴτιον is elided. This omission denies

---

[72] *Pace* Reydams-Schils 1995: 90–91 who proposes a multiperspectivalism: matter is passive when seen from the viewpoint of God's power, but negative and disorderly when seen from the viewpoint of evil in the world. Philo actually highlights God's power precisely by the fact that he overcame the disorderly state of matter.

[73] Cf. *Mut.* 135, *Spec.* 1.48 which describe forms and matter but do not use οὐσία or ὕλη.

[74] Cf. Runia 1986: 144 on *Opif.* 8 that ἐν τοῖς οὖσι shows matter 'as an ever-present constituent of reality'.

[75] See above, n.51.

[76] On the difficult case of *QE* 1.23, see Runia 1986: 281–82.

[77] This belies the claim of Dillon 2005: 99, 106 that a figurative interpretation of creation means an irreducibly disorderly element in the cosmos (similarly Bos 2009: 43). Philo distinguishes between matter's disorder pre-creation and its continuing state, which is mutable, but not disorderly. On this question of interpreting the act of creation, see below, p.66.

matter any autonomy.[78] Similarly, Philo is unclear, perhaps intentionally, about its pre-existence. In *Plant.* 3, the temporal clause (ἐπειδή) implies that the disordered, confused οὐσία was already there when God began.[79] The lack of overt reflection on this question by Philo may reflect the constraints imposed by the biblical text as well as the potential pitfalls of raising questions about the ontological relationship between God and matter.[80] Runia points out that the negative attributes of matter would be difficult to square with Philo's repeated claims that God is not responsible for evil (e.g., *Plant.* 53).[81] On the other hand, *Somn.* 1.76 depicts God not just as demiurge but also creator of all things, which could imply his prior creation of the pre-existent matter, but on the whole, the issue lies unaddressed. The assumption is that this matter existed somehow independently of God, without ever threatening his primacy. Thus Philo did not hold to a doctrine of creation *ex nihilo*. This question bears on our topic, because if God unambiguously created the matter from which he made the universe, that would shrink the distance between him and the world; as it is, the gap remains.

D. Conclusion for Οὐσία and Ὕλη

What does Philo's usage of οὐσία and ὕλη contribute to our sense of how he depicted the sensible realm? The starting point for this realm is clearly not positive. It may be passive and quality-less or unruly and chaotic, but it is never good, ordered and pliant. Yet that does not mean Philo regards such matter as intrinsically negative: the balance of neutral to negative occurrences for these terms is fairly even. Nevertheless, there is virtually no notion that what God began with when he created is good. Yet paradoxically, the more the negative is emphasised, the more God's greatness in imposing order in creation is magnified. As for its post-creation status, while this material substrate remains, and it is still perishable, there is no explicit indication that it exerts a continuing negative or evil influence.

The entire discussion of matter is framed philosophically. The terminology comes from there, and Philo's depiction of matter's negativity demonstrates a

---

[78] Runia 2002a: 290–91; Reydams-Schils 1995: 89–91. On matter not being a cause, *Fug.* 8–13; *Spec.* 1.327–29. This diverges from Platonists who establish a three-cause scheme of God, matter and ideas (*Phileb.* 26e; Aëtius, *Plac. Philos.* 1.11.2; Alcinous, *Did.* 1.8–10).

[79] Also, *Prov.* 1.22 at Runia 1986: 156.

[80] Dillon 1977: 157–58 notes Philo's lack of clarity here, but see the astute reflections of Runia 1986: 287–91; cf. Wolters 1994; Winston 1981: 7–13; Berchman 1984: 47–48; *contra* Wolfson 1947: 1.300–05; O'Neill 2002: 456–62.

[81] Runia 1986: 289.

familiarity with prior debate. In contrast, usage of the terms to refer to universal matter is virtually non-existent in Judaism, and even the little there shows nothing of the negativity common to Philo. There is a parallel concept in the *Chaoskampf* myth, but there is no strong evidence of its influence on Philo. Thus for Philo to focus on the matter from which God made the sensible world – and moreover, to evaluate that matter negatively – is evidence of his being shaped more by Hellenistic philosophy than biblical exposition.

As οὐσία and ὕλη refer to the starting point of the sensible world, Philo uses other terms to denote the sensible realm as it continues to exist, and to those we now turn.

IV. Γένεσις: Exemplar of Philo's Varying Views on the Physical World

A. Introduction

How does Philo understand the final product made from οὐσία and ὕλη? When he describes the concrete result with a derivative of γίγνομαι, he tends toward the negative; when he describes it with κόσμος or φύσις, he is almost invariably positive. From the first group, we will focus on γένεσις and γενητός. Philo's use of γένεσις opens a window into his ambivalence toward the sensible world. He uses γένεσις in two general ways: either as generation, the process or event by which something comes into being; or else as its result, the concrete existence of that which has come into being.[82] A summary of the occurrences relevant for this study appear in Figure 3.1.

Figure 3.1 Γένεσις as Generation and Result

	Generation	Concrete result
Positive	57	10
Neutral	151	28
Negative	23	86

What do we notice from Figure 3.1? First, γένεσις as generation appears more often than as concrete creation. Second, the typical valuation differs between

[82] The 441 occurrences of γένεσις for Philo were graphed according to definitions derived from LSJ (see Appendix 3), and then sifted for relevance for Figure 3.1. The general category of 'act' encompasses the definitions of origin, birth, and the process of generation. The general category of 'result' corresponds to the definition of concrete creation. Instances of γένεσις as kind, generation of numbers, or generation/age are rare (e.g., respectively, *Sobr.* 60; *Spec.* 3.36; *Congr.* 91); no instances of *genitalia muliebria* appear in Philo.

these general categories. When γένεσις represents activity, it is predominantly a neutral term; if it is positive or negative, it is due to the subject or object of γένεσις. Thus when God appears in conjunction with γένεσις as generation, the term is nearly always positive. On the other side, when γένεσις represents what has come into being, it is mostly negative, and if God appears, typically he opposes the concrete creation. After an initial overview of γένεσις and comparison with how others use it, this section will briefly examine γένεσις as generation and then more fully as the concrete creation.[83]

The basic contours of γένεσις take their shape from its essential connection to the sensible world, as shown in *Opif.* 12. Finishing his answer to whether the cosmos had an origin, Philo attributes to Moses the awareness that everything sense-perceptible is 'subject to becoming and constant change' (ἐν γενέσει καὶ μεταβολαῖς), which led him, in turn, to call everything which belongs to the sensible realm 'becoming' (γένεσιν).[84] The first instance of γένεσις refers to the process, and the second the result. Although the immediate context does not evaluate such 'becoming', *Opif.* 151 suggests that mutability inevitably entails decline; on those grounds, the first two occurrences of γένεσις in *Opif.* 12 are negative. But then things shift. Because the κόσμος is visible and sensible, it must have originated (γενητός), an origin (γένεσιν) Moses records, 'setting forth in its true grandeur the work of God'.[85] That the biblical cosmogony praises God for the γένεσις of the universe – and adopts that as the name of the first book of the Bible – renders this final occurrence positive. The physical realm came about through a process that entails change, and γένεσις captures both that process and the result.[86] Moreover, because it is God who made it, there is something positive to say. This usage of γένεσις in *Opif.* 12, therefore, shows how the sensible realm is conceptualised according to process and change and how Philo's evaluation of it can shift.[87]

This passage also highlights the philosophical influence on Philo's usage of γένεσις and his differences from other Jewish writings. Runia sees *Opif.* 12 as a 'simplifying but effective paraphrase' of Plato's *Tim.* 28bc.[88] Both γένεσις

---

[83] To avoid repetition, I omit the Greek for γένεσις and γενητός, unless it is significant for the point, and use single quote marks to indicate the corresponding English gloss.

[84] Despite this link to sense-perception, in a few places γένεσις denotes or encompasses the immaterial soul (e.g., *Leg.* 3.73; *Sobr.* 62).

[85] On how Philo interprets the act of creation, see p.66.

[86] Runia 2001: 120 notes the two definitions but not the shift in evaluation.

[87] On the basis of this passage, I sometimes use the 'created realm' for γενητός or γένεσις, without implying that the intelligible realm is not also created.

[88] Runia 1986: 93. He notes that Atticus, frg. 37 and Plutarch, *Mor.* 1016e make similar use of the *Timaeus* (95–96).

as generation and result are amply attested in philosophical texts.[89] If ψύχη can be destroyed, then 'all the heavens and all *genesis*' would be destroyed (πάντα τε οὐρανὸν πάσάν τε γένεσιν; *Phaedr.* 245e) Elsewhere, Plato makes γένεσις and οὐσία metaphysical opposites: 'as Being is to Becoming (ὅ τί περ πρὸς γένεσιν οὐσία), so is Truth to Belief' (*Tim.* 29c). Philo agrees with a contrast between becoming and true reality, though for him, God more accurately defines the latter.[90] Using γένεσις to refer to the concrete result also follows Platonic examples(*Tim.* 29e γένεσις and κόσμος parallel; cf. *Phaedr.* 245e).

The clear precedent in philosophy for how Philo employs γένεσις is not matched in Jewish writings. The Old Greek translations use it exclusively for 'birth' or people related by birth.[91] How Philo differs emerges in his treatment of the *tôlĕdôt* (תולדות) structure in Genesis. The 'generations of Noah' (Gen 6:9) lead him to reflect on kinds of 'generation', from non-existence to existence, as with plants and animals, and from the higher to lower kind, as with Jacob the practiser fathering Joseph the politician – hence the 'generations of Jacob' (Gen 37:2; *Deus* 117–19). Philo is familiar with Septuagintal usage of γένεσις as 'descendants' but turns the word to his own ends and prefers its philosophical meaning, precisely how these parts of the LXX never use it.

The Old Greek books without extant Hebrew originals offer more overlap with typical Philonic usage. In addition to birth-related occurrences, γένεσις refers to the origin of humanity or the origin of all things (2 Macc 7:23; Sus 1:42).[92] Only Wisdom of Solomon, though, comes close to matching Philo's range. The author uses γένεσις with relation to birth (3:12; 14:6, 26; 18:12) and generation (1:14; 7:5; 12:10; 16:26; 19:10), including of the material world (ἀπ' ἀρχῆς γενέσεως; 6:22). But nowhere in the Old Greek does γένεσις denote the concrete creation. It is the same in our set of Second Temple texts: either they do not use γένεσις,[93] or if they do, it is very rarely with reference to creation, whether the act or its result.[94] The virtual absence in Jewish writings

[89] Generation: e.g., *Pol.* 281b; *Resp.* 359a.

[90] On Philo's un-Platonic usage of οὐσία, see above, p.42.

[91] For birth, translating ילד or cognate: e.g., Exod 28:10; Ruth 2:11; Eccl 7:1; Hos 2:5. For generations, translating תולדות: e.g., Gen 2:4; 5:1; 36:1; Num 3:1; Ruth 4:18; 1 Chr 7:2; 9:9. For families/clans, translating מִשְׁפחה: e.g., Exod 6:24, 6:25; 1 Chr 5:7. Ezekiel 4:14 uses it for 'youth', translating נעורים. In contrast, Philo uses γένεσις for birth approximately 100*x* but rarely for birth-relatives (only *Spec.* 3.36, *Deus* 117, 119, *Abr.* 31).

[92] Birth-related: Sir 44:1; 4 Macc 15:25; Jdt 12:18; *Pss. Sol.* 3:9. On allusions to Gen 2:7, 5:1 in 2 Macc 7:23, and its difficult text-critical questions, see Goldstein 1983: 313.

[93] *Testaments of the 12 Patriarchs*; *Testament of Abraham.*

[94] Creation of universe: Aristob. 13.12.3, 9; Josephus, *Ant.* 7.380; of humanity: *Ant.* 20.259; frequently as 'birth', e.g., *Ant.* 2.225; 19.330; *Ag. Ap.* 1.42. 'Kind', *Let. Aris.* 75, 97.

of this definition of concrete creation is striking, as well as the relative absence of its definition as act. Jewish usage of γένεσις, therefore, unlike philosophical texts, offers a contrast to Philo. His handling of γένεσις provides another example where Hellenistic philosophy, rather than Jewish thought, sets the primary orientation.[95]

B. Process of Generation

Philo frequently uses γένεσις to refer to the process of generation, whether of the generation of the seasons (*Virt.* 93), of laughter (*Mut.* 157), or even of a sponge from water (*Conf.* 186). Context determines the term's value, but usually there are not sufficient markers to classify γένεσις other than a default 'neutral'. Positive and negative references to γένεσις as generation take their value based on the subject or object of the act. Thus when God is the subject of γένεσις, the reference is usually positive. God is the primary cause of all things that are sown and come into being (*Her.* 171–72).[96] Indeed, the cause of creation is his goodness and grace (ἀρχὴ γενέσεως . . . ἀγαθότης καὶ χάρις τοῦ θεοῦ; *Leg.* 3.78).[97] The converse holds for negative occurrences of γένεσις: they almost never identify God as subject. Indeed, *Fug.* 70 claims 'God deemed it necessary to assign the creation of evil things (τὴν κακῶν γένεσιν) to other makers' (i.e. the Powers). This passage is paradigmatic for God's non-involvement in the creation of something negative; when it appears that God may be responsible, another agent is introduced as the subject of γένεσις.[98] Likewise, *Fug.* 70 illustrates the role of the object of 'creation'. That it is 'evil things' created leads to classifying this instance as negative. On the positive side for the object of γένεσις as act is the recurring phrase, the

---

[95] See p.64 below, however, for a potential conceptual link.

[96] Also *Fug.* 109; *Spec.* 1.10; *Praem.* 9, 13; *QE* 2.46.

[97] While this instance of ἀρχὴ γενέσεως clearly has an ontological meaning, other occurrences are contested, whether they refer to a literal, temporal beginning of creation, or that the created realm is metaphysically dependent on God. See, respectively, Runia 1986: 96–100; Bos 2009. On that question itself, see below p.66.

The phrase is used in that technical sense (often with λαμβάνω) at *Opif.* 54; *Leg.* 3.78; *Conf.* 114; *Her.* 172; *Abr.* 162; *Aet.* 14, 53, 73, 118; *Prov.* 1.6, 21; in a semi-technical way, see *Mos.* 1.98; 2.80; *Contempl.* 65; *Aet.* 89. Philo often uses it more widely in a non-technical way, to denote the start of life: e.g., *Opif.* 67; *Ebr.* 42; *Conf.* 42; *Decal.* 117.

On this Platonic motif of God creating because of his goodness, see also *Deus* 108 and below, p.77.

[98] On God's involvement in creation and evil, see Winston 1986. Cf. *Fug.* 84. Other negative instances of γένεσις as generation include *Leg.* 2.6; *Congr.* 13, 59; *Mos.* 2.147.

creation of the cosmos (ἡ τοῦ κόσμου γένεσις and variants).[99] This event provides the name to the first book of Scripture (*Abr.* 1) and includes intelligible and sensible bodies (*Leg.* 1.1), and one can deduce from its creation that God wills only the good (*Spec.* 4.187).

One further example highlights how evaluation of γένεσις as generation must be so context-driven. The traditional pairing of γένεσις and φθορά appears often in Philo, but their relationship is not static; as it changes, the valuation of γένεσις correspondingly shifts.[100] In some cases, coming into and passing out of being are indissolubly connected – to become is inevitably to perish. Thus the very creation of the cosmos is the origin of its corruption (γένεσις δὲ φθορᾶς ἀρχή), although God providentially makes it immortal (*Decal.* 58). The inverse is true too: that which has no generation is indestructible (*Aet.* 53). In such cases, γένεσις is negative because destruction is intrinsic.[101] Sometimes, the comparison is simply neutral without any evaluation of γένεσις: becoming and perishing are simply one pair in a long list of opposites, like white and black or right and left (*Her.* 209).[102] And still other times, the terms are contrasted, with γένεσις on the positive side of the ledger. The Law marks the first month of the cultic year in the spring rather than the autumn (Exod 12:2; cf. *Spec.* 1.181), because first things 'should be associated with all the fairest and most desirable things which are the sources of birth and increase (γενέσεις καὶ αὐξήσεις) . . . not with the processes of destruction' (αἱ παλίμφημοι φθοραί; *Spec.* 2.154).[103] The diversity of this motif demonstrates the flexibility in Philo's usage of the term.

C. Concrete Creation in Harmony with God

The valuation of γένεσις when it refers to the concrete creation is not nearly so elastic as it is for 'generation'. Philo frequently uses γένεσις to denote the concrete creation.[104] We will consider positive and neutral occurrences before focussing on the negative ones.

The rarity of positive references to γένεσις as 'concrete creation' is striking: only 10 times amidst 137 instances of this definition. Six of those ten

---

[99] See, *inter alia*, *Opif.* 77; *Migr.* 136; *Spec.* 1.210; with synonyms, *Opif.* 168, 171; *Mos.* 2.51; *Prob.* 80; with constitutents of the cosmos: *Mos.* 1.212; 2.37. More general cosmological examples include *Opif.* 37; *Sacr.* 102; *Spec.* 2.58. On how Philo interpreted this act of creation, see below, p.66.

[100] Runia 1986: 236 does not note this variability.

[101] Cf. comparisons which highlight mutability: *Cher.* 51; *Spec.* 1.27; *QG* 4.8b.

[102] Also *Leg.* 1.7; *Her.* 247; *Aet.* 8, 117, 137.

[103] Also positive, *Virt.* 132.

[104] LSJ 343b explicitly notes this fact for Philo.

occurrences describe God as creator of γένεσις.[105] Philo's usage of κόσμος and φύσις will show that he can speak very positively about the physical world, but he seldom does it with γένεσις. In fact, even the ways he does use it positively tend to be indirect or derivative of patterns that find their true centre of gravity elsewhere. Fo example, one way Philo communicates a high regard for the material realm is by making the divine goodness intrinsic to the creative Power.[106] The Power which established the 'creation' is nothing other than his goodness (ἀγαθότης; *Migr.* 182–83); similarly, it is fitting that the beneficent Power ordered what was 'brought into existence' (*Plant.* 86). The material world owes its existence precisely to the divine Power in which goodness subsists. In a theistic framework, it is hard to imagine a more positive fundamental connection between God and the sensible realm. Yet γένεσις plays only a minor role in this theme: it appears just twice, and even so, other terms like τὰ ὅλα (*Migr.* 182) or κόσμος-cognates (κοσμοποιίᾳ; διεκοσμεῖτο; *Plant.* 86), may account for the positive viewpoint.[107] Similarly, Philo interprets Exod 33:13 as Moses' plea for God to manifest himself directly rather than through 'any created thing at all' (*Leg.* 3.101). This positive evaluation implies elements of the sensible realm can make God known.[108] Yet, rhetorically, it remains secondary to the prioritisation of divine direct self-revelation. In contrast to this implication for γένεσις, Philo explicitly affirms that the κόσμος testifies to God as its Maker (3.99). Finally, just this passage about indirect knowledge of God employs γένεσις – all other instances of this theme assign that role to κόσμος or φύσις.[109] Philo, therefore, is able to use γένεσις positively for the concrete creation, but such cases are rare and hedged by other factors.[110]

Philo refers to γένεσις in a neutral fashion more often than he does positively. Such texts do not deny a disjunction between God and the sensible world, but neither do they make it a cause for judgment on the world. Hence, right reason establishes duty to God, while training and education shape our dealings with 'creation' (*Ebr.* 77).[111] *De posteritate* 172 provides a particularly helpful example of how to conceptualise this gap between God and creation without tracing it to hostility or alienation. According to Gen 4:25, God

---

[105] *Plant.* 86; *Ebr.* 30; *Migr.* 183; implicitly, *Leg.* 3.101; *Post.* 42; *Mut.* 28.

[106] Runia 1986: 134. He cites *Opif.* 21; *Leg.* 3.73; *Cher.* 27; *Migr.* 182–83; *Her.* 166; *Somn.* 1.162–63, 185; *Spec.* 1.209; *QG* 1.57; 2.51, 75.

[107] Cf. *Leg.* 3.78 where γένεσις and κόσμος are parallel.

[108] Note also the synonyms γεγονότων and γενητόν in 3.100.

[109] On which, see below, p.85 and p.121, respectively.

[110] Other implicitly positive passages include *Post.* 42; *Plant.* 130; *Sobr.* 62.

[111] On this neutral contrast, *Post.* 89; *Her.* 206; *Spec.* 1.277. More generally, *Cher.* 62; *Fug.* 173; *Mut.* 18.

raised up Seth, another seed (σπέρμα ἕτερον), after Cain killed Abel. Scripture does not say in what sense he is 'another', but Philo takes it as two-fold: Seth is different from Cain, to whom he is hostile, and different from Abel, to whom he is friendly and related. Seth and Abel differ as, respectively, the beginning from the full-grown, or as that which is friendly toward creation from that which is friendly toward the uncreated (τὸ πρὸς γένεσιν τοῦ πρὸς τὸ ἀγένητον). The comparison to beginning and full-grown implies that γένεσιν and ἀγένητον relate organically and harmoniously. The uncreated is better, but not at the expense of the created. So the contrast of God and γένεσις does not necessarily require opposition.

D. Concrete Creation in Opposition to God

Despite these positive and neutral occurrences, the majority of Philo's references to γένεσις as sensible creation do express something negative. There is an essential contrast between God and the realm of 'becoming' that often pits the one against the other. That is seen, first of all, in how rarely Philo calls God creator of γένεσις in a negative context. The only explicit identification is in the axiom that a 'creature' should come into its maker's presence precisely when it knows its own nothingness (*Her*. 30).[112] The fact that over half of the positive statements – although admittedly a small sample size – name God as Maker, but only a very bare handful of negative texts do so raises two points. First, Philo is hesitant to ascribe a negative sensible world to God explicitly. That distinguishes Philo from Gnosticism, since he does not want to link a negative creation to God. Yet that raises the second point, that it is nonetheless striking how relatively reluctant Philo is to identify God as creator of γένεσις – there are very few explicit indications of such, no matter how they are evaluated. Philo will show no such hesitation with κόσμος.[113] Thus, even though Philo confirms that God made γένεσις, he does not go out of his way to trumpet it.

At the extreme, far from making God creator of γένεσις, Philo depicts them as ontological opponents. In Num 5:2 the LORD commands the Israelites to put outside the camp those unclean from leprosy, a discharge or physical contact with a corpse. Philo interprets these cases as types of souls (*Leg*. 3.7). The leper is expelled for trying to make God and creation joint causes, even though they are actually 'antagonistic natures' (θεὸν καὶ γένεσιν, ἀντιπάλους φύσεις; AT).[114] The idea from *Post*. 172 that the created and uncreated are dif-

---

[112] Also, implicitly: *Mut*. 127; *Virt*. 218.

[113] See p.76.

[114] On Philo's interpretation of Num 5:2–4 and Deut 23:2–4 for those excluded from the assembly, see especially *Spec*. 1.324–45 (Laporte 1972: 168–70).

ferent yet not alien is pushed aside. In its place is a hostility that stems from their intrinsic characters. Hence, the goat sent off into the wilderness on the Day of Atonement stands for the sensible realm (γενέσει), 'a homeless wanderer', banished from wisdom (*Her.* 179). Even Abraham arrives at the consummation of his devotion to find God still 'far away from all creation' (*Somn.* 1.66). These statements reveal a chasm where what pleases God is alien to the created realm (*Somn.* 2.67).[115]

One of the key contrasts between God and γένεσις is with respect to change. God stands steadfast, sharply distinguishing himself from the ever-wavering 'creation' (*Leg.* 2.83). Mutability and movement are characteristic of 'creation', while stability describes God (*Post.* 29–30). Indeed, Abraham comes to perceive 'how changeable and inconstant was creation' precisely through knowing 'the unwavering steadfastness that belongs to the Existent' (*Deus* 4). True knowledge of God leads to true knowledge of the sensible world.[116] Philo goes beyond biblical hints about God not changing, which are not philosophical in substance, to this principle that mutability must not be predicated of God.[117] Given Philo's exposition of sense-perception in *Opif.* 12, mutability is of the essence of γένεσις.

In turn, this mutability helps account for the origin of evil. There is intrinsically a close link between creation and mortality: whatever comes into being will naturally go out (e.g., *Decal.* 58), and Philo often joins γένεσις and θνητός as equivalent.[118] The inevitable mutability of things that are created and mortal, then, leads to sin. Philo explains the Fall by the fact that since nothing in creation is constant (οὐδὲν τῶν ἐν γενέσει βέβαιον), and mortal things are necessarily subject to change (τροπὰς δὲ καὶ μεταβολὰς ἀναγκαίως τὰ θνητὰ δέχεται), 'it could not but be that the first man too should experience some ill fortune' (*Opif.* 151). Because the sensible realm cannot escape change, it is bound to decline – the connection is intrinsic. Runia comments that the generalising tone makes the Fall 'a structural feature of the world of becoming'.[119] This overall pessimism reflects a strand of Greek metaphysical

[115] Also, *Deus* 61; *Plant.* 53; *Her.* 103, 170; *Somn.* 2.28; *Spec.* 1.43; *QE isf* 10.

[116] Also *Opif.* 100; *Cher.* 19; *Post.* 23; *Somn.* 1.244, 249; *Spec.* 3.178. Cf. passages where γένεσις denotes the act of generating, which speak about change: *Opif.* 12; *Cher.* 51; *Decal.* 58; *QG* 4.8b.

[117] Unchanging in being: Ps 102:25–27; Mal 3:6; in purposes: Ps 33:11; Isa 46:9–11. Philo anticipates patristic focus on the question of divine immutability, which for them was connected to Christology and divine impassibility: see Pelikan 1971–89: 1.229–32; Weinandy 1985: xxi-66.

[118] E.g., *Sacr.* 58; *Deus* 77; *Mut.* 13, 48; *Somn.* 2.231. See also the pairing of γένεσις and φθορά above.

[119] Runia 2001: 355–56.

reflection that saw change as inevitably negative: something perfect can only change for the worse. Elsewhere, Philo describes human beings as sinners simply by virtue of being created.[120] Evil is native to mortality (τοῦ θνητοῦ, ᾧ τὸ κακὸν οἰκεῖον; *Congr.* 84). The sacrifice of a calf upon Aaron's installation as high priest shows that sin is 'congenital (συμφυές) to every created being (παντὶ γενητῷ), even the best, just because they are created (παρόσον ἦλθεν εἰς γένεσιν; Lev 8:14–17; *Mos.* 2.147).[121] Questions about a 'Fall' are irrelevant, one's existence as a creature is sufficient to account for evil. Such texts call into question Marcel Simon's distinction that Gnosticism locates the origin of evil within the world, whereas Philo affirms that creation is God's good work and evil comes from without.[122] Simon is right in what he affirms for Philo but suspect in what he denies. Texts like *Opif.* 151 seem to place the origin of evil within creation itself. Because change is inevitable, evil belongs to the essence of γένεσις as concrete creation.

Given this stark contrast between God and the realm of becoming, a person must be careful not to place creation above the deity in any way (*Sacr.* 70–72).[123] Ultimately, the danger from creation is so great that the person who wants to see God must flee it.[124] This is the higher call for those who aspire to see God directly, illustrated by Levi and his descendants. He shows his perfect virtue most clearly when he 'makes God his refuge and forsakes all dealing with the world of created things' (τῶν ἐν γενέσει; *Sacr.* 120). His soul soars 'above created being . . . to hold fast to the Uncreated alone' (*Congr.* 134).[125] Likewise, when the Levites slay their fellow Israelites in the golden calf incident, they do not kill human beings, but rather cut away everything dear to the flesh, because those who minister to God have 'to estrange themselves from all that belongs to the world of creation (πάντων ὅσα γένεσιν), and to treat all such as bitter and deadly foes' (*Ebr.* 69).[126] The hostility between God and the realm of γένεσις forces people to choose sides. To know and be in communion with God, therefore, is to have nothing to do with creation.

---

[120] Baer 1970: 92.

[121] On the relation of γένεσις and γενητός, see p.65.

[122] Simon 1967: 365, followed by Wilson 1993: 90.

[123] Also, *Mut.* 195; *Somn.* 1.77; *Spec.* 2.166.

[124] On the *telos* for Philo, see p.156, and on the two levels for apprehending God, p.158.

[125] On Philo's use of the Platonic heavenly ascent, see p.156.

[126] Similarly, *Sacr.* 58; *Gig.* 53; *Plant.* 64–66; *Her.* 30, 45, 93; *Mut.* 127; *Somn.* 2.68, 273; *Virt.* 218. For the same point with other terms, particularly σῶμα, *Leg.* 3.41–42, 47; *Det.* 158–60; *Ebr.* 99–103, 124; *Migr.* 9; *Her.* 267 (for Philo's views on the body, see p.60). Cf. Winston 1984: 409; Birnbaum 1996a: 79–80. The vast majority of such passages are from the Allegory (cf. below p.176). On Philo and the golden calf, see Feldman 2005.

E. Referent for the Concrete Creation

This discussion about fleeing creation raises the question of what exactly Philo refers to when he uses γένεσις. Does he envision a literal estrangement from the physical world on the part of those who pursue God, or does such creation language function figuratively? Asking this question exposes the range of referents for γένεσις when it denotes what has come into existence.

First, the term sometimes refers to humans as a particular instantiation of γένεσις. The realisation that ashes and water are 'the beginnings of our existence' should humble us (*Somn.* 1.211).[127] Even more specifically, γένεσις can refer to an aspect of a person, namely the body, which Philo calls an 'inferior creation' (τὴν γένεσιν . . . τῶν χειρόνων) compared to the soul (*Leg.* 3.73).

A second category of referent for γένεσις is the whole sensible realm. The infrequent positive occurrences of γένεσις belong here, whether denoting the realm as a whole,[128] or its constituent elements.[129] Some negative instances also refer literally to the sensible world. Those on the higher path to God do not describe him according to 'any of the attributes of created being', which Philo glosses as including humanity, heaven or the cosmos (*Deus* 61–62).[130]

An important third category are negative statements about creation which Philo intends figuratively. When he condemns γένεσις he often means something other than the material world. In *Plant.* 46–72 he interprets Exod 15:17–18 (and Deut 32:7–9) on what is the proper 'portion' (κλῆρος or μερίς) for those who pursue God.[131] Repeated references to γένεσις evoke anything that opposes God and virtue. This realm is the source of evil (53), the scapegoat exalting something other than the First Cause (61), something from which to be purified (64), and property and physical possessions (66). Γένεσις represents a kind of negative inverse of God and stands for whatever philosophical error, moral failure or personal effect that impedes communion with him.

The Levites who kill their fellow Israelites in Exod 32 cut off 'all that is near and dear to the flesh', or put another way, they alienate themselves from everything within creation (*Ebr.* 70–71). This is doubly figurative as the categories of people in the biblical text are allegorised as constituents of creation, which are then taken figuratively. To kill the brother refers to the body, which means the passion-loving element. To kill the neighbour refers to sense-perception, which means not trusting its reliability. To kill the nearest refers to

---

[127] Also, *Det.* 46, 124; *Mut.* 48–50, 156.

[128] *Post.* 42; *Plant.* 86; *Sobr.* 62; *Migr.* 183.

[129] E.g., *Leg.* 3.101; *Sobr.* 62.

[130] Cf. *SVF* 2.1022 for how Stoics did this very thing; PLCL 3.485. Other negative references to the sensible realm as a whole include *Congr.* 134–35; *Spec.* 2.166.

[131] On God as portion and in opposition to γένεσις, cf. *Congr.* 134; *Mut.* 127.

speech, which means forsaking sophistry. The body, sense-perception, and speech are never actually destroyed – such language refers rather to how they are used. Thus γένεσις symbolically evokes the need to cultivate a moderate yet comprehensive asceticism.[132] This interpretation is reinforced in *Ebr.* 73 when Phinehas takes up the spear to search 'the secrets of corruptible creation (τὰ τῆς φθαρτῆς γενέσεως), which finds in food and drink the treasure-house of its happiness' (Num 25:7).[133] Here, γένεσις refers to sensual hedonism, the opposite of asceticism. Moreover, Phinehas attacks not the actual Midianite woman and Israelite man, but rather the belief that anything created is active, whereas really God alone brings things into existence. In *Ebr.* 70–73, γένεσις represents holistically what a person must avoid or control – whether in terms of beliefs or practices – in order to know God.[134]

This category of figurative referent is slightly different than an allegorical usage of γένεσις. The literal content of Scripture often does not call for Philo to speak of the sensible world with γένεσις – that is his allegorical interpretation; within that, sometimes he uses γένεσις for the sensible world and sometimes to symbolise whatever opposes God and pursuit of him. Strikingly, all of the figurative references are negative, and all but one come from the Allegory.[135] This distribution suggests a correlation between commentary series and a negative perspective on the world, a point to explore in Chapter 8.[136]

F. A Gap Between Rhetoric and Meaning in Philo's Anti-Creation Language

As *Ebr.* 70–73 reveals, there is a sizable gap between Philo's anti-creation rhetoric and the more moderate application. The latter, though, sometimes can be hard to detect amidst the negative din, especially Philo's hostility toward the human body.[137] His interpretation of how God kills Er showcases this outlook (Gen 38:7; *Leg.* 3.69–73). God put Er, who symbolises the body, and the serpent, which symbolises pleasure, to death in the same way – summarily, without an open charge (69). Thus the human body is closely linked to plea-

---

[132] Philo describes Jacob as the paradigmatic figure for perfection via practice (ἄσκησις; e.g., *Mut.* 81; *Sacr.* 42). On asceticism, see Bréhier 1925: 261–71; Völker 1938: 198–239; Winston 1984: 405–14. On Philo's Jacob, see Zeller 1990: 95–99; Böhm 2005: 308–18.

[133] Cf. *Conf.* 57.

[134] Other examples include *Sacr.* 58; *Gig.* 53; *Deus* 179–80; *Her.* 45, 179; *Somn.* 2.67–69, 273; *Spec.* 3.178–80. Hay 1987: 901 n.96 also sees *Ebr.* 70 as a potential interpretive key for Philo's harsh language about the body.

[135] The exception is *Spec.* 3.178–80.

[136] See p.176.

[137] On Philo's attitude toward the body, see Pearce 2007: 85–87; Hay 1987: 894–95, 899, though the latter sees more moderation in Philo's attitude than is probably there.

sure, and both are condemned.[138] The body is 'wicked and a plotter against the soul', and in one of Philo's favourite images, 'even a corpse and dead thing' (69).[139] Moreover, Er is slain by God, the creative, beneficent power, in order to show it is 'in the exercise of goodness and kindness' that he destroys the body (73). This last detail seems particularly damning and directly contrasts the idea that God in his goodness made all things.[140] Other negative images include the body as prison,[141] as Egypt,[142] or the soul as alien and stranger in the body.[143] One particularly effective way Philo conveys his hostility is by putting 'pro-body' speeches in the mouths of biblical villains.[144] Thus the Sodomites oppose temperance and claim bodies should be given the materials which belong to them, since souls are not naked (*QG* 4.37).[145] As with γένεσις, Philo finds this negative perspective through allegory. Philo could be positive about the body: the beauty of the first man includes his body, crafted with great skill from the best material possible (*Opif.* 135–36), and thanksgiving to God for the κόσμος and its parts explicitly includes the body (*Spec.* 1.210–11).[146] These positive views have precedent.[147] Despite such state-

---

[138] Baer 1970: 93 notes the connective phrase διὰ τοῦτο.

[139] *Leg.* 1.106–8; *Gig.* 12–15; *Deus* 150; *Agr.* 25; *Migr.* 21. Closely connected is the play on words of σῶμα and σῆμα; on the body as tomb, see *Leg.* 1.106–8; *Spec.* 4.122, 188; *QG* 1.45, 70; 2.69. Plato famously uses this imagery at *Phaedr.* 250c; *Crat.* 400bc; *Gorg.* 493a. Its origins are likely Orphic or Pythagorean: see Philolaus, DK 32b14. Cf. Mansfeld 1981: 292. For later usage, see Epictetus, *Diatr.* 1.9.19; Seneca, *Ep.* 60.4, 82.3, 122.3. See Courcelle 1966: 102–05 on this image specifically in Philo.

[140] See p.77.

[141] Philo can apply this image to all human beings (*Ebr.* 101; *Conf.* 177; *Migr.* 9; *Her.* 85, 273; *Somn.* 1.139, 181), or to the wicked (*Deus* 111–15; *Her.* 109). On the philosophical antecedents and context, see Philolaus, DK 32b14–15; Plato, *Phaed.* 62b, 67cd, 82e–83a; *Phaedr.* 250c; *Crat.* 400bc; Cicero, *Scaur.* 4; *Amic.* 13–14; *Resp.* 6.13–15; *Tusc.* 1.74; Seneca, *Helv.* 11.6–7; *Polyb.* 9.3; *Ben.* 3.20.1; *Ep.* 65.16; 79.12; 102.22–23; Plutarch, *Mor.* 607d (references from Courcelle 1965; see his discussion of Philo on 413). What Powell (Cicero 1990: 154) notes for Cicero also holds true for Philo – he never enunciates 'the logical corollary of the idea, which is that earthly life is a punishment', although others did, e.g., Euxitheus the Pythagorean at Athenaeus, *Deipn.* 4.157c.

[142] E.g., *Leg.* 2.59; *Det.* 38; *Migr.* 77; Pearce 2007: 85–127.

[143] *Conf.* 82; *Her.* 82; *Somn.* 1.181; *QG* 3.45.

[144] Cf. Bréhier 1925: 290.

[145] Also, *Det.* 32–35; *QG* 4.77.

[146] Also *Congr.* 96–97.This Philonic praise works off the macrocosm-microcosm relationship (cf. *Plant.* 28–31); see p.80 n.37. Cf. *Let. Aris.* 153–59 where the body is the occasion for remembering the great works of God.

[147] D. E. Aune 1995: 296–98 argues that philosophers treated the body more positively than is commonly thought, citing *Tim.* 88b; Aristotle, *Protr.* frg. B60; Plotinus, *Enn.* 4.8.1, to which add Xenophon, *Mem.* 1.4.5–7; Epictetus, *Diatr.* 1.16.9–18. But Aune overstates his case and minimises the significance of the countervailing passages. Moreover, *Tim.* 88b

ments, though, in general it may be said that 'the body is for Philo, at best, a necessary evil'.[148]

Upon closer examination, though, it becomes clear that this vituperative denunciation of the sensible realm generally, and of the body more specifically, actually has a far more restrained practical application. The gap between rhetoric and meaning is illustrated by Philo's interpretation of Abraham's calling (Gen 12:1).[149] He allegorises the command for Abraham to leave homeland, family and father's house as the need to depart from body, sense-perception and speech (*Migr.* 2), the same triad as in *Ebr.* 70–71 (though with different biblical referents). In two crucial passages, *Her.* 68–74 and *Migr.* 7–8, Philo explains this interpretation pragmatically and provides a hermeneutical key for understanding his language about leaving the material world.[150] To migrate from body, sense and speech does not mean complete severance from them, since that would be a prescription for death (*Migr.* 7). Instead, it means to 'dedicate and attribute' them to God, who empowers their use (*Her.* 73), and to reject their attempts at mastery by making sure that the mind rules over the self (*Migr.* 8). To leave behind the sensible world, therefore, is not literally a disembodied existence, though the language may sound like that.[151] This explanation from *De migratione*, however, feels like an aside, for as soon as the interlude is complete, Philo again marginalises all things material, particularly the body, that 'foul prison-house', against which a person should use 'every terror' to 'menace the enemy' (9).

Certainly Philo is not the first to use radical language about the body to make a more modest point. With his own execution imminent, Socrates famously described philosophers as those who despise the body and make their chief aim to separate the soul from it; death, therefore, is not to be feared but welcomed as consummation of this goal (*Phaed.* 67b–e). Cicero picks up this motif and makes its moderate application more explicit. The life of the philosopher is preparation for death which means to 'sequester the soul from

---

concerns the operation of body and soul together, not just the body, and in quoting *Enn.* 4.8.1 Aune omits Plotinus' preceding judgment that Plato 'everywhere speaks with contempt of the whole world of sense and disapproves of the soul's fellowship with body and says that soul is fettered and buried in it'. On the Jewish side, Prov 20:12; Sir 16:26–17:14, esp. 17:4–5; *Let. Aris.* 155–56; *T. Naph.* 2:8; *2 En.* 65:2–5.

[148] Winston 1984: 408. Such anthropological pessimism provides some of the closest links between Philo and Gnosticism, so Simon 1967: 366; Pearson 1984: 328–29, 337–38; Wilson 1993: 91.

[149] Bradshaw 1998: 485–87 similarly utilises *Migr.* 7–12 to depict Philo's call for mental detachment.

[150] On this interpretive strategy when reading Philo, see p.15.

[151] On *Migr.* 7–8, cf. Pearce 2007: 101–3.

pleasure . . . from private property . . . from public interests; from any kind of business' (*Tusc.* 1.74–75). He calls on his readers to 'make this preparation and dissociation of ourselves from our bodies, that is, let us habituate ourselves to die'. On the other hand, when *Testament of Abraham* speaks of departing from the cosmos and coming out of the body, it literally means death: the archangel Michael is to tell Abraham the time has come to leave this vain cosmos and come out of the body (rec. A 1:7).[152] Philo, therefore, is more rhetorically extreme than Cicero, but unlike *Testament of Abraham*, figurative in his meaning.

This jarring juxtaposition of moderate explanation and radical imagery provides insight into Philo's perspective on the sensible world. We return to Gen 12:1 but this time to its interpretation in *Det.* 159–60, which offers less realism than *Her.* 68–74 and *Migr.* 7–8. The charged rhetoric sharply separates the material realm and God. Only after Abraham forsakes body, sense and speech does God appear to him (Gen 12:7), which shows 'that He clearly manifests Himself to him that escapes from all things mortal and mounts up into a soul free from the encumbrance of this body of ours' (159). Paradoxically, Philo acknowledges that bodily constraints are unbreakable (ἀρρήκτων σώματος καὶ περὶ σῶμα δεσμῶν), yet he glorifies being freed from them (λυθείς; 158), and the language does sound like some kind of bodiless existence, or even death. This kind of purple prose for the material world is more prevalent in Philo's corpus than nuanced explanations. The overall impact is the radical passages leave the lasting impression, even though they express matters less clearly. As a result, Philo's imagery works at cross-purposes to his intent. The thrust of his response to 'creation' is more radically negative, and only in rare moments does he provide a more restrained interpretation.

G. Conclusion for Γένεσις

Philo's usage of γένεσις ranges across a wide territory. It refers to the process of generation as well as the thing generated and can convey a positive, negative or neutral assessment. The dominant valuation for γένεσις as act is neutral, since it requires clear contextual factors like the subject and object to render it otherwise. Γένεσις as a result can signal how the origin of the sensible world resides in God's goodness and grace, or it can stand for the deep-seated alienation of all things mortal from their Maker. Hence, Philo's usage of γένεσις brings clearly to the fore tensions within his view on the sensible world. How can he conceptualise it both as a means of knowing God and as

---

[152] Also, 8:11, (rec. B) 4:9, 12 .

something alienated from and antagonistic toward him? In Chapter 8, we will wrestle with how to resolve this apparent contradiction.

Although this ambivalence and tension exists in the usage of γένεσις, nonetheless, the two sides are not equally poised – the negative predominates. The connection between γένεσις and mutability may help account for this slant. There seems to be in Philo's writings, as in much of antiquity, an axiomatic aversion to change, a conviction that whatever will pass away is inherently, necessarily inferior. When γένεσις is used, the sensible world is conceptualised primarily according to flux and alteration. The frequency with which Philo employs γένεσις figuratively to stand for philosophical error or moral failings only reinforces this negativity.

This outlook seems to surpass any obvious philosophical or Jewish influence. While ancient philosophers often use γένεσις in opposition to the divine or intelligible realm, it does not tend to connote such hostility between them. On the Jewish side, as with οὐσία and ὕλη, there are few lexical parallels to Philo's negative usage of γένεσις. Perhaps, though, there is a conceptual link. There are some Jewish texts, particularly in wisdom and apocalyptic literature, that view the created realm as bleak and inhospitable.[153] This is especially true in Qoheleth, for whom the cyclical, unending character of the universe leads not to praise of the creator but weariness (Eccl 1:4–7).[154] God is in his heaven, and people are on earth (5:2), which implies a divine distance from, or even an indifference toward, what he has made.[155] The result is that creation becomes beautiful yet incomprehensible to humanity (3:11, 8:17).[156] The Book of Job is more ambiguous about the world. Job calls for a reversal of light and darkness, day and night (Job 3:1–10), but it is unclear whether he refers only to the day of his birth or to all of creation.[157] Similarly, God's coming topples mountains and heralds darkness (9:5–7), but whether this means he directs his wrath against the world is disputed.[158] These texts, however, are

---

[153] On creation and wisdom literature, see Perdue 1994: 41–48; Crenshaw 1995b: 126–27; Dell 2006: 135–46 (esp. for Proverbs).

[154] Perdue 1994: 209–10. See further, Crenshaw 1998: 117–28.

[155] Longman 1998: 151. On the centrality of creation for Ecclesiastes, see Crenshaw 1995b: 121.

[156] On 3:11, Longman 1998: 118–21; Crenshaw 1995a: 552–57. On 8:17, Anderson 1997: 104–05.

[157] Clines 1989: 87 argues for a more limited scope, whereas Perdue 1994: 131–37 and Fyall 2002: 59, 84–85 see it extended to all of creation.

[158] Again, Clines 1989: 229–32 does not see negativity, whereas Perdue 1994: 145 does. Dell 1991: 127 classifies this text as a parody of psalmic hymns about God's creative power.

Other possibly negative texts include Job 30:16–31, where the created realm becomes the means of Job's torment (Fyall 2002: 66–67), and the existence of Behemoth and Leviathan, which points to violence and suffering as part of this realm (Fyall 2002: 173–74).

small strands, rather than the dominant paradigm for the wisdom literature. Moreover, whatever their redaction-critical history, in their canonical form, the narrative frameworks of Ecclesiastes and Job relativise this skepticism about the created world. For apocalyptic literature, a negative view of this world is often thought to be a characteristic feature, and certainly there are texts which seem very negative about the physical world.[159] Yet even here, recent scholarship has questioned whether such pessimism is truly regnant.[160] It seems, therefore, that some strands of Jewish writings do adopt a pessimistic outlook on the created realm. They do not amount to a tradition, nor do they set the overall framework, nor are they negative in the same manner as Philo. With these caveats granted, then there may be some conceptual parallels in the biblical tradition that reflect what Philo is doing with regards to γένεσις.

Perhaps Philo's negativity reflects the perception of someone who distrusts the material world, who resorts to asceticism in order to shut out external temptations and quell internal appetites. This negative usage of γένεσις corresponds to a priority on the mystical experience of the divine. It is perhaps ironic to find such a distrust of the material world in someone who moved in such privileged circumstances. The conviction in *Her*. 93 that the truly great understanding will distrust created being, 'which in itself is wholly unworthy of trust', in order to trust in God alone, may capture a core Philonic belief about how to relate to the sensible world when expressed with γένεσις.

V. Γενητός: The Contrast between God and Creation

A. Introduction

While Philo's treatment of οὐσία and ὕλη as universal matter and of γένεσις as generation carried a long philosophical pedigree, his usage of the adjective γενητός stands out for the opposite reason – it shows up relatively infrequently elsewhere. Philo uses it 97 times, among the most of any extant author. It does not appear in the Septuagint at all and virtually never in Second Temple sources.[161] Aristotle's explanation for its usage describes something that actually or potentially has an origin, possibly through the process of γένεσις (*Cael*. 280b15–20). Alexander of Aphrodisias details three ways

[159] E.g., *2 Bar*. 56:6–10; *4 Ezra* 7:11–14; 9:19–20; also, there is the motif of this age growing old and weak and thus evils increasing: 5:55; 14:10, 17.

[160] J. Moo 2008.

[161] From our set, only Aristob. 13.12.4, where it is neutral.

ἀγένητον and γενητόν contrast, the first of which is particularly relevant: 'ἀγένητον is contrasted with γενητόν, as that whose existence is never the result of γένεσις with that whose existence always and necessarily *is* the result of γένεσις'.[162] Philo does not offer theoretical reflections on the meaning and usage of γενητός.[163] Indeed, most of the passages where he uses γένεσις and γενητός together diverge from such explanations. In a few cases, Philo does depict this relation along the lines of process and result: because there is a creation (γένεσιν) of the irrational part of the soul, it is a created thing (γενητός; *Leg.* 2.6).[164] More typically, though, Philo uses both terms to denote the concrete creation. The nuance varies: γένεσις may refer to the overall realm and γενητός to certain members (*Leg.* 3.101; *Plant.* 66; *Mos.* 2.147), or what is characteristic of that realm (*Spec.* 2.166); or both may refer to created beings in true parallelism (*Cher.* 16).[165] The point is that Philo usually links γένεσις and γενητός in a way slightly different from ancient philosophy.

The first pattern of usage appeared already in our examination of *Opif.* 12. Philo uses γενητός 16 times to affirm that the κόσμος has an origin, which is the teaching of Plato, Hesiod, and, most importantly, Moses (*Aet.* 13, 18–19). It is so important that it is included in the summary of what Moses taught in his account of the creation of the cosmos (*Opif.* 171). The opposite idea, that the cosmos is unoriginate (ἀγένητον), denigrates God, over-values the cosmos and undermines the doctrine of providence (*Opif.* 7–11).[166] While Philo strongly affirms the creation of the cosmos, it is unclear whether that is to be understood literally or figuratively. Does he envision an actual event, or does such language express how the cosmos depends on God for its existence?[167] This question is much debated today, just as it was then. The evidence is closely matched on both sides, but on balance, I narrowly favour the view that

---

[162] This comes from the LCL translator for *de Caelo*, W. K. C. Guthrie, p.104 note b.

[163] Runia 1986: 97.

[164] Also, *Opif.* 12; *Deus* 58; *Aet.* 19.

[165] Cf. *Opif.* 67; *Cher.* 109; *Migr.* 183; *Her.* 206; *Somn.* 2.253; *Aet.* 14, 73.

[166] Runia 1986: 100.

[167] It may do both, if the literal interpretation is adopted, since it can encompass the figurative also (Runia 1986: 429). Among philosophers, it was particularly Platonists who wrestled with Plato's affirmations of createdness (*Tim.* 28bc) and Aristotle's criticism of a literal interpretation (*Cael.* 279b–80a). For a lucid summary of ancient philosophers' positions, see Sterling 1992: 21–32. Modern scholars who find a literal interpretation in Philo include Wolfson 1947: 1.295–324; Runia 1986: 92–103, 148–55, 426–33, 456–57; Berchman 1984: 48; Baltes 1976–78: 1.32–38, 86–93 (not available to me). Those who see in Philo a figurative interpretation of the creation event include Winston 1981: 13–21; Sterling 1992; Dillon 2005; Bos 2009. There are, of course, distinct interpretations within these two broader categories.

Philo affirmed a literal creative event.[168] It is difficult to discern what role a figurative interpretation of disorderly matter would play in Philo's theology. As we saw above, he does *not* describe matter after creation as disorderly,[169] yet on a figurative interpretation, that is precisely what matter represents – the ongoing disorderly element within the universe. Thus the entailments of a figurative understanding of creation clash with what Philo says about matter. So I find a literal reading of Philo's 'creation' language slightly more cogent. Regardless of the specific interpretation, however, Runia points out that it is the sheer createdness of the cosmos that is most important for Philo.[170] This teaching upholds God's care for what he has made and establishes that everything in the cosmos is ontologically different from and dependent on God. It acts as the prerequisite foundation, therefore, for Philo's more common usage of γενητός, to which we turn now.

B. The Divide between God and Creation

Philo's usage of γενητός closely resembles what we saw for γένεσις with one important change: γενητός has a much smaller range than γένεσις. Whereas γένεσις as concrete creation alternated mainly between neutral and negative occurrences, with even some positive instances as well, γενητός is overwhelmingly negative.[171] It nearly always depicts a fundamental contrast with God that leads to alienation. The frequent negative pairing of γενητός with

---

[168] Arguments for a literal-protological interpretation include (1) the frequency of temporal language for the creation event (e.g., *Leg.* 2.2; *Deus* 58; *Decal.* 58), which Philo does not qualify like he does anthropomorphisms (Runia 1986: 432). (2) Though their readings are partly obscured, both *Prov.* 1.6–9 and *Aet.* 13–19 indicate Philo's disagreement with at least some forms of an eternal creation. (3) Philo praises Aristotle for his literal interpretation of Plato (*Aet.* 16). (4) At least some Middle Platonists held a literal interpretation of Plato (Atticus, frg. 37; Plutarch, *Mor.* 1013e–17c). (5) Finally, Runia 1986: 97 points out Philo lacks a theoretical apparatus for a figurative interpretation, unlike Calvenus Taurus' multiple definitions of γενητός (*ap.* John Philoponous, *Aet.* 145.13ff. in Dillon 1977: 242–43).

Arguments for a figurative-ontological, metaphysical interpretation include (1) how the temporal language for creation is consistently interpreted non-literally to refer to order (e.g., *Opif.* 13, 26–28, 65–68; Sterling 1992: 33–34). (2) Most Middle Platonists understood Plato figuratively (see Sterling 1992: 27–32 for references). (3) This is more consistent with God's immutability, because it does not posit some kind of change in him with respect to creation (Winston 1981: 16–17). (4) Finally, since Philo often adopts a hermeneutical approach that allows for higher and lower interpretations of the same datum (e.g., anthropomorphic descriptions of God), it may be that in this case, the literal reading would be the lower one, and the figurative the higher one (Winston 1981: 21).

[169] See p.48.

[170] Runia 1986: 429.

[171] Contrast neutral usage: e.g., Alcinous, *Did.* 10.8.6; 14.3.1; 15.1.2; Numenius, frg. 3.5.

φθαρτός makes that divide clear.[172] The Jewish nation rightly chose to serve the uncreated and eternal God (ἀγενητοῦ καὶ ἀιδίου) rather than anything that has come into existence (εἰς γένεσιν ἦλθε πάντα), because everything 'created' is perishable 'by nature' (ὡς γενητὰ καὶ τῇ φύσει φθαρτά; *Spec*. 2.166). Philo uses γενητός to express a negative viewpoint about the created realm, and because, unlike with γένεσις, there is virtually no offsetting evidence to balance the picture, this valuation comes across all the more starkly.

The prevalent usage of γενητός establishes a contrast to God. At the most basic level, γενητός and ἀγένητος stand on opposite sides. Philo calls on his soul to separate 'all that is created' from how he thinks of God, the uncreated (*Sacr*. 101).[173] The gap separating God from everything created renders it a fundamental mistake to try to understand the former in terms of the latter. For example, mutability is necessary and peculiar to everything 'created', just as immutability is peculiar to God (*Leg*. 2.33). That separation expresses itself functionally in everything God can do that 'created being' cannot, like discern hidden motives (*Cher*. 16), divide things equally (*Her*. 77), or open the womb (*Leg*. 3.180).[174] This contrast is so strong that as with γένεσις, Philo can use γενητός to imply that to be created is necessarily to be sinful. Even a Nazirite makes a sin-offering as he completes his vows to demonstrate that 'the perfect man, in so far as he is 'created being', never escapes from sinning' (*Spec*. 1.252). Again, evil is inherent to existence as a sense-perceptible creature.[175]

This contrast gives rise to an inversely proportional dualism for how humanity relates to God and creation: the closer to the one, the further from the other. So when Leah is unloved, which Philo interprets in terms of her rejection of the passions, her 'estrangement on the human side (πρὸς τὸ γενητόν) brings about fellowship with God' (*Post*. 135). Faith is defined as trust in God and a concomitant distrust in anything created (*Mut*. 201).[176] One particular area in which this division must come to fruition is abandoning idolatry. In the tumult over the golden calf, Moses calls to his side any who hold that God alone, and 'no created thing', rules the universe (*Mos*. 2.168). A

---

[172] *Leg*. 2.99; *Ebr*. 209; *Somn*. 2.253; *Mos*. 2.171; *Spec*. 2.166; *Praem*. 28; *Aet*. 73; *Legat*. 118; and with διαφθείρω, *Post*. 145. The doxographical *Aet*. 7 and 78 are the exception to this negative valuation. Also, like with γένεσις, Philo uses γενητός and θνητός together: *Leg*. 3.31; *Cher*. 31; *Sacr*. 101; *Conf*. 122; *Ios*. 254; *Mos*. 2.6; *Praem*. 39.

[173] Cf., *inter alia, Plant*. 66; *Migr*. 91; *Ios*. 265; *Legat*. 5.

[174] Cf. *Cher*. 77; *Gig*. 26; *Mut*. 22; *Mos*. 1.174.

[175] Note, however, *Sacr*. 139 which may imply that sin, but not weakness, can be purged from 'created being'.

[176] *Congr*. 107; *Praem*. 28. For γένεσις, cf. *Her*. 93; *Virt*. 218.

test of covenant loyalty in the biblical account becomes a problem of blurring the line between creator and created in Philo.[177]

In one instance, however, Philo turns the negative contrast between γενητός and God to positive advantage. Abraham's migration to Haran represents allegorically the command of the Delphic oracle to Socrates: know yourself.[178] For Philo, that self-knowledge comes via an examination of sense-perception which recognises ultimately its intrinsic faultiness. Having thus grasped the nothingness of 'created being' (γενητοῦ), a person makes the dialectical leap to knowledge of God (*Somn.* 1.59–60). This explanation posits discontinuity between the sensible and divine spheres as the basis for knowing God.[179] In fact, self-knowledge recognises 'that God and humans are on different sides of the basic division of reality'.[180] As Baudouin Decharneux aptly puts it, for Philo it is precisely when people are closest and furthest from their own being that they find God.[181] So although the dichotomy between creation and God is typically to the detriment of the former, in this instance, Philo enlists it paradoxically in the quest to know God, precisely because the two are opposed.

Philo occasionally casts the relation between God and creation in a more complementary fashion. The distance between them, established so firmly elsewhere, can shrink. Human beings receive rulership over everything on earth as part of bearing the image of God, 'the visible of the Invisible, the 'created' of the Eternal' (*Mos.* 2.65). Likewise, in showing kindness, people who are 'created' imitate the eternal God (*Spec.* 4.73).[182] Yet that distance can only be bridged at God's gracious initiative: if he stoops 'to visit created being', it is 'in His tender mercy and loving-kindness' in order 'to show His goodness to our race' (*Cher.* 99). Even when viewed favourably, the gap remains one that humans cannot traverse. The contrast between God and creation is fundamental.

---

[177] Similarly, *Opif.* 45; *Ios.* 254; *Mos.* 2.171; *Spec.* 1.13, 20; 2.166; *Virt.* 65, 180; *Legat.* 118.

[178] On this motif in Philo, see Kahn 1973; Courcelle 1974–75: 1.39–43.

[179] Kahn 1973: 304 underplays this opposition and, correspondingly, overestimates Philo's optimism about the ultimate role of the sensible world in the ethical life. All the same, elsewhere Philo explains that self-knowledge leads to divine knowledge through recognising anagogically that just as the human mind rules the body, so the invisible mind rules the κόσμος (*Abr.* 71–72; *Migr.* 184–86). This explanation depends on the microcosm-macrocosm relation (see p.80 n.37), and thus presupposes positive continuity between the sensible and divine spheres. Philo's explanations, therefore, of how self-knowledge leads to knowledge of God are not entirely consistent.

[180] Runia 2002a: 301.

[181] Decharneux 1994: 74.

[182] *Post.* 145; *Ebr.* 84; *QG* 2.16.

C. Referent for the Concrete Creation

As with γένεσις, there is a range of referents for γενητός, though with one important difference – figurative occurrences are rather few. The same three categories of reference apply to γενητός as for γένεσις. First, the term often refers to human beings. A person who obeys mother and father cannot help but win praise, since allegorically, they 'observe the customs that hold among γενητοῖς and . . . also the ordinances of the Uncreated' (*Ebr.* 84).[183] A second category takes γενητός for the entire created realm, whether as an aggregate of individual constituents (e.g., *Leg.* 3.101) or a single collective (e.g., *Cher.* 119).

The third category for γενητός covers those instances where the term is figurative. Here, however, γένεσις and γενητός diverge: γένεσις is often used figuratively, while γενητός rarely is, despite it being the more negative term on the whole. In Leah's 'estrangement on the human side', γενητόν literally refers to her difficult relations with Jacob – a point Philo suppresses – but symbolically to her having nothing to do with the passions or sense-perception, the latter represented by Rachel (*Post.* 135).[184] Similarly, for Abraham to ascend to God requires that his reason, symbolised by the fire and knife in Gen 22:6, cut away everything mortal, leaving 'nothing to the created' (μηδὲν ἀπολείτειν τῷ γενητῷ) and instead making 'God his standard in all things' (*Cher.* 31). This cutting means discerning the divine powers of goodness and sovereignty, along with choosing good and shunning evil (30). So γενητῷ metaphorically means human moral standards, which often turn out to be wicked. These figurative meanings for γενητός resemble what Philo does with γένεσις. But the fact that, on the whole, Philo uses γενητός literally yet negatively, reinforces a sense of cosmological pessimism.

D. Conclusion for Γενητός

The usage of γενητός significantly, yet not wholly, resembles that of γένεσις (when the latter means the concrete creation). It differs by moving further toward the negative end of the spectrum: there is less variation in how Philo employs γενητός – it is more consistently pessimistic and literal in denoting the concrete creation. This relative constancy has implications. For example, the recurring refrain in the motif of γενητός and φθαρτός is that something is

---

[183] See, *inter alia*, *Cher.* 99; *Her.* 143; *Abr.* 206; *Spec.* 4.73. Occasionally the referent may include all living beings: *Opif.* 67; *Ios.* 254. A related category is when γενητός seems to encompass everything universally, but the context applies only to people: e.g., *Leg.* 3.4; *Cher.* 77; *Sacr.* 100; *Migr.* 91; *Legat.* 5.

[184] On Philo's re-reading of Jacob's relations with his wives, see Böhm 2005: 312–15.

'created and perishable'. The repeated pairing of those terms conveys the idea that they are mutually entailing – to be created necessitates perishability, and to perish means something had an origin and now completes that process. So even when only one term appears, a reader may rightly infer the legitimacy of the other. This suggests that references to the sensible world with γενητός may reflect a point of view which emphasises the perishability (and hence mutability) of anything created. That holds true for γενητός in a way that it cannot as easily for γένεσις, given that the latter bears a much wider range of meaning and valuation in Philo's hands. Ultimately, the reasons for using γενητός – particularly given its infrequency in the extant literature – may derive from its contrast to ἀγενητός, which allows Philo to express a central, axiomatic conviction – the ontological contrast between God and everything sensible.

VI. Conclusion

This chapter has examined four terms Philo uses in a predominantly negative fashion for the sensible world. Οὐσία and ὕλη refer to the matter from which the world was made. They are alternately neutral or negative but virtually never positive. That negativity may be expressed in terms of passivity, or in terms of chaos and disorder. It is clear, therefore, that the sensible realm, so far as its substance is concerned, did not come from good stock. Yet two qualifications are important: first, the more negative the portrayal of matter, the more God is glorified, because he overcame it and transformed it into something ordered. Second, that negativity is never predicated of the continuing material substrate. The world has the potential to descend into chaos, if the forms were withdrawn, but that remains hypothetical.

Γένεσις and γενητός refer to the sensible world in terms of its intrinsic flux. Both frequently contrast with, or oppose, the uncreated, immutable God, who is thus their exact opposite. Evil is closely linked to γένεσις/ γενητός: it exists by virtue of them. The two terms are not exactly alike, however, for γένεσις is used with greater variety than γενητός. It has a wider semantic domain, its ethical valuation ranges from positive to negative, and when it means 'concrete creation', it can have a literal or figurative referent.

What apparently unites these four terms is how they connote alteration and change. It is the disorder of matter which God must vanquish in order to create the universe. It is the intrinsic flux of the realm of becoming that leads to the inevitability of sin. It is that constant alteration that makes God and creation mutual antagonists. That mutability culminates in perishability, usually signified by φθαρτός.[185] It is possible to imagine a neutral use of θφαρτός for contingency or dependence – whatever is created is contingent in comparison with an absolute God.[186] But Philo's usage is value-laden. The contrast with God is as much ethical as metaphysical: from God come things good and holy, but 'from the corruptible creation (γένεσις ἡ φθαρτή) come things evil and profane' (*Plant.* 53). Only God is peace; the entire created, perishable existence is warfare (ἡ δὲ γενητὴ καὶ φθαρτὴ οὐσία πᾶσα συνεχὴς πόλεμος; *Somn.* 2.253). On the opposite side of this aversion to disorder and change is Philo's strong preference for order. That inclination is not unusual, but its deep-seated and pervasive character does suggest something of Philo's own personal feelings at play.

Three further points should be raised. First, although γένεσις is predominantly negative, nonetheless, it occasionally can be positive. Usually there are mitigating factors, but the fact remains that even the world of becoming may be seen positively. So even though there is a significant link between lexical choice and ethical status, the tensions within Philo are not entirely explicable on these grounds.

Second, there is at least some connection between how γένεσις is used and the valuation it conveys. The rare positive instances all refer literally to the created realm. Negative occurrences, however, may be literal or figurative. Philo employs γένεσις – and γενητός to a lesser extent – to represent anything that opposes or impedes the pursuit of God. In turn, every figurative occurrence comes from the Allegory, which suggests a link between the commentary series and how the ethical status of the sensible realm is evaluated. It might be argued, however, that this figurative usage renders the terminology irrelevant for our purposes, that it says nothing about his true evaluation of the physical world. On the contrary, the very fact that he so often uses γένεσις to symbolise hostility toward God suggests precisely that he does hold a negative view of the world; otherwise, he would not find the link so congenial. At the same time, Philo's negativity cannot be confined to a figurative level, since he frequently employs γένεσις and γενητός negatively yet literally. This sense that cosmological pessimism marks his basic outlook is reinforced by the gap between his charged rhetoric and moderate application. His infrequent acknowledgment that such anti-creation language means simply to use created things rightly without depending on them, reinforces the impression that his outlook on the sensible world is instinctively pessimistic.

Finally, this negative outlook raises the question of the relative influence of the philosophical and biblical traditions. On the one hand, philosophy exer-

---

[185] For matter, see n.51; for γενητός, n.172; for γένεσις, *Plant.* 53; *Ebr.* 73; *Spec.* 2.166.
[186] Field 2008.

cises a stronger influence. Philo's very terminology, but even more his basic orientation and meaning, all derive from philosophical rather than Jewish sources. That stands in tension with the conclusions of Chapter 2 that Judaism, or more specifically Scripture, provides the controlling framework for Philo. This negative terminology seems at odds with most Jewish thought, although there is at least some precedent for a pessimistic evaluation of the world. At the same time, there is a sense that Philo's pessimism actually exceeds his philosophical counterparts. His usage of γένεσις and γενητός is markedly more negative than Plato and Middle Platonists, and likewise his treatment of the body, while it has precedent, is more one-sided than Plato's, for example. Jaap Mansfeld distinguishes between anthropological and cosmological pessimism with respect to Plato and judges that only the former is true for him.[187] This chapter has begun to show that Philo is clearly at least an anthropological pessimist, but very possibly, also a cosmological one. So while the tension within Philo's views may be attributable in part to an inherent clash in interpreting Scripture Platonically, at least some of the difficulty seems to surpass even that. We will return to this question as the argument proceeds.

These four terms – οὐσία, ὕλη, γένεσις, and γενητός – have depicted an overall negative ethical status for the sensible realm. But they by no means tell the whole story. Other Philonic terms see the world in a strikingly positive light, and so we proceed now to κόσμος.

---

[187] Mansfeld 1981: 294.

Chapter 4

Philo's Positive Terminology for the Physical World: Κόσμος

I. Introduction

Our map of the semantic terrain for the sensible world now ascends figuratively from the valleys to the heights. Γένεσις and γενητός described the sensible world as process and becoming. Κόσμος, in contrast, represents that world as finished product, the worthy result of God's labours. The shift in valuation that accompanies this move in terminology is dramatic: Philo's use of κόσμος is overwhelmingly positive, which opens a wide chasm between it and γένεσις and γενητός. Κόσμος pictures the world as the well-ordered, perfect work of its Creator, and as a result, a way to know him and even become like him. The philosophical tradition fundamentally orientates how Philo employs κόσμος, yet Jewish beliefs substantially modify that, with the result that this distinctive mix reflects tellingly on the larger relationship of Hellenism and Judaism laid out in Chapter 2. This is in contrast to γένεσις and γενητός, where philosophical influence proved much stronger than Jewish.

Κόσμος appears 634 times in Philo, of which 580 denote the world or universe in some way, over 90% of the total occurrences. Alongside that sit the non-philosophical definitions of 'order' or 'ornament, adornment', both of which can helpfully highlight aspects relevant for the cosmological definition too.[1] Moses exhorts those who ascribe causation to heavenly bodies not to worship them and 'all the ordered host of heaven (πάντα τὸν κόσμον τοῦ οὐρανοῦ; Deut 4:19; *Spec.* 1.15). This represents the only cosmological definition of κόσμος in the Hebrew-original portion of the OG.[2] Nowhere else, though, does Philo employ this meaning – and even here it is only by virtue of direct quotation. He typically pairs κόσμος and οὐρανός as a hendiadys for the

[1] There are 17 occurrences of 'order' (e.g., *Her.* 206; *Somn.* 2.51; *Flacc.* 92) and 37 of 'adornment' (e.g., *Sacr.* 26; *Migr.* 97; *Mos.* 1.317).

[2] Gen 2:1; Deut 4:19; 17:3; Isa 13:10; 24:21; 40:26.

universe, a motif which follows the *Timaeus* rather than Scripture.[3] This preference for Greek over biblical modes of expression will recur in Philo's cosmological usage of κόσμος. Next, the inherent approval of something by virtue of describing it with κόσμος is observed in how the Jews learn the Law (*Contempl.* 80; *Spec.* 2.62). The Therapeutae sit in rows (ἐν τάξεσι), but it is really their general demeanour that merits depicting them 'in order' (ἐν κόσμῳ). What represents 'order' is socially-conditioned – using κόσμος conveys approval of that arrangement.[4] Instances of κόσμος as 'adornment' also reflect the dimension of judgment: clothing makes a fitting 'adornment' for a person, but rational speech is 'an adornment of the whole life' (*Somn.* 1.102). Sometimes the order itself is the adornment. On the Sabbath the Essenes sit in rows (ἐν τάξεσιν) from eldest to youngest with the 'adornment' (μετὰ κόσμου) that 'befits the occasion' (*Prob.* 81). Likewise, because crops and trees bear fruit at different times, Moses forbade planting them together,

> so that he introduced order out of disorder (τάξιν ἐξ ἀταξίας εἰσηγούμενος). For order is related to κόσμος, and disorder to ἄκοσμον (τάξει μὲν γὰρ συγγενὲς κόσμος, ἀταξίᾳ δὲ τὸ ἄκοσμον; Lev 19:19; *Spec.* 4.210).

As F. H. Colson admits, an English rendering for κόσμος is difficult, but the sense is that order and arrangement is beautiful and commendable.[5] This connection of order and beauty will appear in Philo's lyrical praise of the κόσμος. So although Philo uses non-cosmological definitions of κόσμος infrequently, such occurrences still can prove illuminating.

II. Definition and Attributes of the Κόσμος

A. Basic Definition

In *Aet.* 4, Philo defines the κόσμος along standard philosophical lines: it refers either to 'the whole system of heaven and the stars including the earth and the

---

[3] E. Adams 2000: 59 n.108. οὐρανὸς καὶ κόσμος preceded by σύμπας (or just πᾶς) appears 17*x*: e.g., *Cher.* 88; *Abr.* 166. Nikiprowetzky 1977: 114 n.73 correctly perceives the influence of *Tim.* 28b, 40b in this formulation but overestimates the simultaneous influence from Gen 2:1 and the Alexandrian synagogue. Elsewhere the hendiadys of οὐρανὸς καὶ κόσμος does not require πᾶς or its compound: *Deus* 30, 62; *Migr.* 138; *Spec.* 1.336; *Contempl.* 90. When οὐρανός is paired with κόσμος, but only the latter is preceded by πᾶς or its compound (e.g., *Ebr.* 75; *Fug.* 103), then the former is only a part of the universe (as elsewhere, e.g., *Somn.* 2.6; *Virt.* 73).

[4] Cf. *Plant.* 162; *Somn.* 2.139; *Praem.* 76. On this topic, see p.13.

[5] PLCL 8.138 note b.

plants and animals thereon', or to heaven alone.[6] Accordingly, though he may use κόσμος for the intelligible world, or more infrequently, as a part of the universe or inhabited world, it usually refers to the sensible universe as an overall system.[7] Some of the central features of the κόσμος can be seen in *Cher.* 127, which uses the four causes-schema: the κόσμος, 'that greatest of houses or cities', has as its formal cause, God, its material cause, the four elements, its instrumental cause, the Logos, and its final cause, the goodness of the demiurge.[8] That God made the κόσμος is perhaps Philo's most fundamental claim for it.[9] In *Opif.* 171–72, he summarises what Moses taught: the κόσμος has come into being and is one like its maker, who exercises providence over it.[10] The createdness of the κόσμος safeguards God's ontological primacy and uniqueness.[11] This clear identification of God as creator of the κόσμος is a standard Jewish claim.[12] How Philo asserts it, however, differs, since demiurgic metaphors, derived from the *Timaeus*, predominate.[13] The contrast is with Philo's treatment of γένεσις, which he seemingly ascribed to God as creator only reluctantly.[14] He shows no such reticence with κόσμος. The major entailment of God as maker of the κόσμος is that he is also its Lord, 'since none could more justly govern what has been made than the Maker' (*Mos.* 2.100). The impact of this overall claim affects nearly every

---

[6] For the first definition, cf. Plato, *Gorg.* 508a; Aristotle, *Eth. eud.* 1216a14; *SVF* 2.527, 945; Aristob. 13.12.13. For the second definition, cf. Isocrates, *Paneg.* 179; Aristotle, *Mete.* 339b17–19; Ps.-Plato, *Epin.* 987b; in Philo, *Somn.* 1.215 and the description of heaven as a cosmos within a cosmos: *Abr.* 159; *Spec.* 3.187; *Praem.* 41; *Flacc.* 169.

[7] For intelligible cosmos, e.g., *Opif.* 36; *Gig.* 61; *Mos.* 2.127; or, for intelligible and sensible together, e.g., *Conf.* 173; *Spec.* 1.302. For part of the universe, *Post.* 144; *Migr.* 105. For inhabited world, *Spec.* 1.331; *Legat.* 309, a usage which E. Adams 2000: 43 notes is rare outside the LXX until later Greek.

[8] On this prepositional metaphysics, also *QG* 1.59; *Prov.* 1.23. Elsewhere, Aristotle, *Metaph.* 983ab; Aëtius, *Plac. Philos.* 1.11.2; Alcinous, *Did.* 8–10; Seneca, *Ep.* 65.7–10. Possible NT texts include John 1:3, 10; Rom 11:36; 1 Cor 8:6a; Col 1:15–20; Heb 1:2; 2:10. On this concept, see Theiler 1930: 17–34; Dillon 1977: 135–39; Runia 1986: 171–74; Sterling 1997; Cox 2007: 43–51.

[9] E.g., *Leg.* 2.3; *Deus* 30; *Mut.* 30; *Abr.* 75; *Spec.* 4.187.

[10] Mendelson 1988: 29–49 proposes *Opif.* 171–72 as the foundation and bounds of orthodoxy for Philo. Cf. *Conf.* 114 where the builders of the Tower of Babel assert essentially the opposite.

[11] E.g., *Opif.* 11–12; *Migr.* 180; *Abr.* 163; *Spec.* 1.13; *Aet.* 19. See p.66 on whether creation is literal or figurative.

[12] 2 Macc 7:23; 13:14; 4 Macc 5:25; Wis 9:9; 11:17; Aristob. 13.12.3, 5; Josephus, *Ant.* 1.26, 31; *T. Ab.* (rec. A) 10:14.

[13] Runia 1986: 107, 420–26. Bos 2003: 314–15, though, detects an Aristotelian influence which moves Philo somewhat away from the Platonic demiurgic construct.

[14] See p.56.

dimension of Philo's understanding about the κόσμος: it shapes which traditional philosophical attributes he keeps and which he discards; it governs how he praises the κόσμος; it enables the κόσμος to have a revelatory function, and it assigns the κόσμος its role in the ethical-religious *telos*.

The other causes in *Cher.* 127 fill out further aspects of Philo's basic definition.[15] For the material cause, that from which the κόσμος was made (ἐξ ἧς), Philo follows the standard claim that it was formed from the four elements, which ensures its completeness (*Her.* 197).[16] He may also speak more generally of the κόσμος being formed from matter.[17] The Logos, as we saw previously, serves as the instrumental cause, that through which the κόσμος was made (δι' ὧν).[18] Philo equates the Logos in the act of creating with the intelligible cosmos (*Opif.* 24), which consists of the ideas and is the model for the sensible cosmos (*Opif.* 16–17; *Conf.* 172).[19] The final cause, the reason for which God creates the κόσμος (δι' ὅ), is his goodness and grace, just as Moses taught (*Deus* 108).[20] This ascription aside, Philo follows Plato (*Tim.* 29e), indicated by his referring to 'one of the men of old' who said the father and maker of the all (πᾶν) created because he is good (*Opif.* 21).[21] But as is typical, Philo also finds a biblical basis for this position in that Noah found grace in God's sight (Gen 6:8). Thus Philo links God's goodness in creation with his grace, joining Platonic and biblical themes.[22] Dieter Zeller describes this creational perspective as ontological grace: the κόσμος itself is gift and divine grace.[23] Placing the motive for creation of the κόσμος in the character of God provides a robust theoretical foundation for Philo's positive evaluation of it.

---

[15] The image which introduces the causes-scheme, the κόσμος as a city-state, appears frequently (e.g., *Opif.* 142; *Somn.* 2.248; *Ios.* 29; cf. use of μεγαλόπολις). There is the concomitant idea of the sage as citizen of this world-city (*Migr.* 59; *Mos.* 1.157; *Spec.* 2.45; but see *Cher.* 120). The imagery is primarily Stoic (*SVF* 2.528; Epictetus, *Diatr.* 2.10.1–12).

[16] *Inter alia*, *Plant.* 6; *Her.* 152; *Decal.* 31; *Aet.* 25. From *Tim.* 32bc; see Runia 1986: 180–83.

[17] From ὕλη: *Opif.* 171; *Plant.* 5; from οὐσία: *Plant.* 3; *Her.* 133; *Somn.* 2.45; *Aet.* 21; from both: *Prov.* 2.50.

[18] See p.40.

[19] Also *Mos.* 2.127. On Philo's cosmological usage of κόσμος νοήτος, see Runia 1999: 154–55.

[20] *Spec.* 4.187; *Leg.* 3.78. With πᾶν: *Opif.* 21; cf. *Deo* 3 God creates from compassion.

[21] On this Platonic motif, see Rist 1962: 30–31; Mansfeld 1981: 295–96. Plato also describes the lack of jealousy among the gods at *Phaedr.* 247a, which Philo quotes at *Spec.* 2.249 and *Prob.* 13; on this, see Zeller 1990: 39.

[22] Runia 1986: 135 judges that 'according to the sources available to us, Philo is the first thinker to associate the goodness of Plato's demiurge with the Judeaeo-Christian conception of God as creator'.

[23] Zeller 1990: 36.

Just as γένεσις for the sensible realm emphasised becoming and change, using κόσμος emphasises order.[24] Straightforwardly, the cosmos is made according to order (τάξις καθ' ἥν ὁ κόσμος; *QG* 1.64). This comes from God's character: because of who he is, it is 'necessary for him to transform order from disorder' (*Aet.* 39). The move from disorder to order which characterised the creative act finds its culmination in the well-ordered universe.[25]

B. Acceptance and Adaptation of the Attributes of the Κόσμος

Philosophers developed a set of attributes for the κόσμος, derived primarily from the *Timaeus*.[26] Throughout his œuvre, Philo demonstrates his familiarity with these attributes but filtered through the lens of Jewish piety.[27] Some he accepts with little, if any, modification. We saw how he held that the κόσμος was made from the fourelements, with nothing left over, ensuring its completeness and perfection (*Spec.* 2.59). Likewise, he thinks the κόσμος will not grow old or sick, though *Spec.* 2.5 adds that this is true 'according to the purpose of Him who made' it, subtly reinforcing how the κόσμος depends on its Maker.[28] The sphericity of the κόσμος appears occasionally in Philo (*Spec.* 3.189; *Prov.* 2.56),[29] although Philo uses it more for heaven, particularly in conjunction with his interpretation of the tabernacle furniture (*Her.* 227–29; *QE* 2.76, 81).[30] Yet Philo also endorses these attributes even when there is little connection to the biblical text. He makes the oneness of the κόσμος a key summary point of Moses' teaching (*Opif.* 171), without adducing biblical support for it, though – this is likely because, as David Runia puts it, there is none.[31] On the whole, Philo takes these attributes mostly as they are from the philosophical tradition, without alteration.

---

[24] Cf. E. Adams 2000: 59 on the importance of order for Philo's usage of κόσμος.

[25] See, *inter alia*, *Opif.* 33; *Somn.* 1.241; *Spec.* 4.237; *Aet.* 75. Also, Plato, *Pol.* 269d–74d.

[26] For an overview of the Greco-Roman philosophical development of κόσμος, see E. Adams 2000: 42–58.

[27] For a thorough treatment of these attributes in Philo, see Runia 1986, esp. 180–98.

[28] Runia 1986: 183. *Tim.* 33a. Also, *Aet.* 25–26 quoting *Tim.* 32c–33b.

[29] Cf. *Tim.* 33bc; also *Cael.* 287b15; Aëtius, *Plac. Philos.* 2.2; Alcinous, *Did.* 12.3.

[30] This is not a case of οὐρανός meaning universe, though, because *Her.* 226 includes it as a part of the κόσμος.

[31] Runia 1986: 176; Mendelson 1988: 44. Elsewhere in Philo, *Conf.* 170; *Migr.* 180. More widely, *Tim.* 31ab; *Cael.* 276ab; Aëtius, *Plac. Philos.* 2.1.2–3; Atticus, frg. 13; Alcinous, *Did.* 12.3; Plutarch, *Mor.* 720b.

The immortality of the κόσμος also belongs in this category. Philo follows Plato rather closely here (*Tim.* 41ab) with little appeal to biblical support.[32] Left to itself, the κόσμος, like γένεσις, is subject to change, weariness and suffering (*Cher.* 88; *Aet.* 59). But this principle of γένεσις and φθορά is rarely enunciated for the κόσμος, because Philo's understanding of it already implies God's involvement and thus a way around that causal nexus. What keeps the κόσμος from the inevitable end befalling all created things is God's providence (*Decal.* 58), his sustaining bond exercised through the Powers (*Conf.* 166) or the Logos (*Fug.* 112).[33] This, of course, is the focus of the treatise *De aeternitate mundi*, where the introduction clearly affirms that Plato, Hesiod and most importantly, Moses, all taught that the κόσμος was γενητός yet ἄφθαρτος. Although the immortality of the κόσμος was mostly a philosophical commonplace at this time, it is worth noting how Philo arrives there. He does not take an Aristotelian route where the κόσμος in itself is eternal, as he judges that denigrates God (*Opif.* 7, 171), but rather he follows Plato that God effects that immortality. That ensures the credit and honour remain with God, and the κόσμος and the deity stand in right relation.

There are a host of typical attributes, however, which Philo rejects or significantly modifies as a result of his Jewish faith. The common denominator seems to be that uncritical acceptance could give the unacceptable impression the κόσμος is autonomous. God as maker of the κόσμος, therefore, is the axis around which the attributes must fit. Moreover, many of the traits, although they were in the *Timaeus*, were picked up especially by the Stoics, which underscores Philo's divergence from them cosmologically.[34] First, Philo avoids calling the κόσμος a living creature (ζῷον).[35] He attributes it to others in *De aeternitate*, and while he mentions it in *QG* 4.188, he never unambiguously claims it in the major commentaries.[36] It is implied in comparing a

---

[32] So Runia 1986: 235; see his discussion at 233–42. Philo quotes *Tim.* 41ab at *Aet.* 13. As PLCL 9.197 notes, Philo's rendering of Gen 8:22 at *Aet.* 19 departs from the actual sense of the text. *De confusione* 166 exegetes Josh 1:5, but the use of δεσμός is not based on Gen 15:2 at *Her.* 23. For the κόσμος as γένητος yet ἄφθαρτος, see Seneca, *Ep.* 58.27–29; DL 3.72; Atticus, frg. 4, 25, 32; Alcinous, *Did.* 15.2; Apuleius, *Dogm. Plat.* 198; Plutarch, *Mor.* 393f, 1002c (references from Runia 1986: 235–36). Other Jewish evidence of this doctrine is scarce, though Schmidt 1974 argues for it in *T. Ab.* (rec. A) 10:2–3.

[33] Powers: *Migr.* 181; *Her.* 23; Logos: *Her.* 188; God's will: *Her.* 246. More generally, *Aet.* 13, 19; *Somn.* 1.158.

[34] *Contra* Bréhier 1925: 161. Reydams-Schils 1995: 92–93 notes how Stoic reception of the *Timaeus* had become so overlaid with the text itself that Philo could not disentangle them; for her larger thesis about Stoic influence on *Timaeus* interpretation, see Reydams-Schils 1999.

[35] *Tim.* 30b; *SVF* 1.110; 2.633–34; Cicero, *Nat. d.* 2.46–47.

[36] *Aet.* 26, 74, 94–95.

human being – the most insignificant animal (τὸ βραχύτατον ζῷον) – to the κόσμος as microcosm to macrocosm, since each possesses a body and rational soul (*Her*. 155).[37] Yet Philo creates some rhetorical distance by attributing the statement to others and assessing it as 'not wide of the mark' (156).[38] Similarly, Philo is ambiguous about whether the κόσμος has a soul (*Tim*. 34b–36b).[39] It is not the functions of Plato's cosmic soul which he questions – those are taken up by the Logos in large measure – but the terminology, probably because it had been adopted by the Stoics and equated with God (*SVF* 1.532; 2.774).[40] Philo's references to the soul of the κόσμος, if made without mention of God, depend on other sources.[41] The exception is *Mut*. 223 where he first identifies 'reasoning' (λογισμός) as 'a piece torn off from the soul of the universe', but quickly amends it to the more reverent and Mosaic description, 'a faithful impress of the divine image'. On God specifically as soul of the κόσμος, Philo is either reserved (*Leg*. 1.91) or outright opposed (*Migr*. 179, 181). It appears, therefore, that Philo does not attribute ψυχή to the κόσμος lest readers become confused and think that, like the Stoics, he is making God immanent in the sensible realm.

A third modified attribute, or at least its terminology, is the self-sufficiency of the κόσμος. Plato used αὐτάρκης not as an ontological claim for cosmic autonomy but to say it had the necessary physical resources (*Tim*. 33cd).[42] Yet although Philo uses the term 46 times, he applies it just twice to the κόσμος and then only in citations (*Aet*. 38, 74). Instead, it is God who is absolutely sufficient, in comparison to whom the κόσμος is not sufficient to serve as a

---

[37] Philo seems to play on βραχύς as small in size and in significance, since a person is a small cosmos (βραχὺν κόσμον); this is better than calling a person the 'smallest' creature (as PLCL 4.361 does with 'tiny'). On macrocosm-microcosm elsewhere in Philo, see *Post*. 58; *Plant*. 28–31; *Mos*. 2.135 (and for microcosm conceptually, *Opif*. 69; *Migr*. 186; *Abr*. 74–75; and *Opif*. 82; *Her*. 88; 233; and again, *Migr*. 220; *Her*. 263). This doctrine underlies and structures much of the *Timaeus* (e.g., 27a; *Phileb*. 29e); elsewhere, Democritus, DK 55a34, Aristotle, *Phys*. 252b26; Cicero, *Resp*. 6.26; Seneca, *Ep*. 65.24; DL 7.138. Borgen 1997: 219 includes a rabbinic parallel from *ʾAbot R. Nat*. 31:3. On this topic in Philo and his predecessors, see Kroll 1914: 233–34.

[38] The case is similar for the κόσμος having a body: *Her*. 155; *Spec*. 1.210; *QE* 2.120; *Aet*. 51; from *Tim*. 34b (cf. *SVF* 2.605). Runia 1986: 198 judges Philo's avoidance of this attribute 'quite deliberate'.

[39] Cf. Runia 1986: 204.

[40] On the Logos as cosmic soul, see *Plant*. 8–9; *Conf*. 136–37; *Her*. 217; *Fug*. 110–12; and Runia 1986: 204–8, 448–49.

[41] *Aet*. 47, 50, 74, 84; *Prov*. 1.33, 40, 45. In the case of *Somn*. 2.2, τῇ τῶν ὅλων . . . ψυχῇ is parallel with νοῦς τῷ τῶν ὅλων (*Somn*. 1.2), and it may be that it is adapted from Stoic sources (PLCL 5.593).

[42] So also Chrysippus (*SVF* 2.604); Alcinous, *Did*. 12.3.

dwelling (*Plant.* 33).[43] At most, Philo will say all the elements together constitute a sufficient material for God to use in creation (*Opif.* 146; *Prov.* 2.50). Likely Philo regarded the possibility of misunderstanding αὐτάρκης serious enough that its omission with respect to the κόσμος is deliberate, so that no allowance is made for even mistakenly understanding the κόσμος as autonomous.[44]

Finally, one of the chief ways philosophers praised the κόσμος was to deify it. Plato called it a blessed, self-sufficient, most perfect, sensible god, and the Stoa were especially fond of labelling the κόσμος god.[45] But Philo draws a clear line between the two: Scripture reveals God is not like the κόσμος or anything created (*Deus* 62), and those who desire genuine piety will not mistake any part of it for God (*Decal.* 58).[46] The significance of the difference should not be underestimated – Abraham migrates from Chaldean astrology and error precisely when he abandons the idea that the κόσμος is God and instead acclaims its true father and maker (*Her.* 97–99; *Congr.* 48–49).[47] Philo opposes here a key tenet of cosmic religion, which was the notion of having reverence for the universe, especially the heavens. This constituted a genuine attraction for the more educated in his day.[48] Yet when people worship the cosmos or its parts rather than God, the fault lies with them, not the κόσμος. If it were not so wonderful and magnificent, the problem would never arise in the first place (*Her.* 97). The closest Philo comes to this deification is to call the intelligible cosmos God's elder son – the Logos's position – and the sensible cosmos his younger son (*Deus* 31–32).[49] Similarly, the κόσμος bears God's image by being created by the Logos, itself the image of God (*Opif.* 25; *Conf.* 147). Both descriptions, however, show the derivative majesty of the κόσμος. Philo is again careful to conceptualise the matter only in such a way that it preserves God's primacy. The way he understands all these attributes, therefore, reflect a consistent pattern of following Greek, particularly Platonic,

---

[43] For God as αὐτάρκης: *Cher.* 46; *Decal.* 81; *Spec.* 1.277; *Virt.* 9.

[44] Runia 1986: 188 underplays this deliberate avoidance of using αὐτάρκης with κόσμος.

[45] *Tim.* 34a, 68e, 92c respectively. The Stoa, *Nat. d.* 1.39; 2.21; Sextus Empiricus, *Math.* 9.81–85; DL 7.137–38, 148. Of course, the Stoic view was a more complicated panentheism, where God is in all things yet not strictly equal to them (with theistic and polytheistic strands too). On Stoic theology, see Algra 2003: esp. 165–70.

[46] Also *QG* 2.54a. 'Visible god' in *Aet.* 10, 20 clearly paraphrases an Aristotelian position and does not reflect Philo's own views.

[47] *Ebr.* 75; *Congr.* 105; *Abr.* 69; *Decal.* 53; *Spec.* 2.255; *Virt.* 212. Cf. Harl 1967: 191. On Chaldean astrology, see p.88.

[48] On cosmic religion, see Pépin 1986: 410–21; Scott 1991: 3–62; Runia 2001: 207–09.

[49] *Ebr.* 30; *Mos.* 2.134; *Spec.* 1.41, 95–96. See Simon 1967: 365–66. Philo more often uses this title for the Logos (e.g., *Agr.* 51; *Conf.* 146–47); it applies by extension to the universe.

philosophy, yet adapting it so as to uphold God's superiority over and separation from the κόσμος.

III. Praise of the Κόσμος to the Praise of God

Since God from his goodness and grace created the κόσμος as the well-ordered world, Philo lauds it, just as philosophers had long done. Here the divergence between γένεσις and κόσμος becomes acute. For the most part, γένεσις opposes God and is to be disdained. But the κόσμος is God's son and to be praised. They connote respectively change versus order, which in one sense accounts for this vast difference, yet nonetheless, the contrast remains surprising, and we will return to this question in Chapter 8.

Although Philo follows the philosophers in praising the κόσμος, in light of his modification of its attributes, it is no surprise that the way in which he praises the κόσμος reflects distinctively his Jewish faith, because he celebrates it chiefly in relation to God its maker and ruler.[50] Thus providing water from the rock (Exod 17) is 'but child's-play to God', and even something more amazing, namely the creation of the κόσμος and all it contains, is 'great and worthy of earnest contemplation' precisely as it leads to knowing God (*Mos.* 1.212–13). Celebration of the κόσμος finds its rightful end in knowledge and praise of God.

That goal may lead Philo to revise how praise accrues to the κόσμος. Attributing divinity and immortality to the κόσμος were primary ways it was extolled in antiquity,[51] and we have just seen that in both areas Philo is keen to make sure such acclamation does not undermine God's greater standing. Yet such constraint does not lead to reticence. Philo often exalts the κόσμος as God's greatest handiwork, simultaneously revealing its magnificence and subordination. He exhorts his readers to a life of thanksgiving and praise to

---

[50] On the magnificence of creation and the consequent praise of God: Neh 9:6; Job 38:4–38; Pss 8:3; 18 (LXX); Isa 40:12, 26; Sir 16:26–17:14; 42:15–43:33; *1 En.* 2–5, esp. 5:2; 36:3–4; 41:5–9; *2 Bar.* 48:2; *Pss. Sol.* 18:10–12; 1QS IX 26–X 7. A key difference between Philo and these examples, however, is that none of them use κόσμος (though Sir 43:27 has πᾶν), while Philo lacks typical LXX cosmological terminology (see below, p.98). He can celebrate the sensible world, however, without using κόσμος: e.g., *Opif.* 114–16; *Post.* 42; *Her.* 31–32; *Mut.* 59; *Spec.* 2.173.

This argument largely agrees with Runia 1986: 459–60, but was reached independently. For a range of positive ways Philo speaks about the κόσμος, cf. Bréhier 1925: 170–72.

[51] E. Adams 2000: 67–68.

the universe-maker and the universe, 'the former', as one has said, 'the best of causes, and the latter, the most perfect of things made' (ὅ τε κοσμοποιὸς καὶ ὁ κόσμος γεραίρηται, 'ὁ μὲν', ὡς ἔφη τις, 'ἄριστος τῶν αἰτίων, ὁ δὲ τελειότατος τῶν γεγονότων'; AT; *Plant.* 131).

Philo quotes *Tim.* 29a but reverses Plato's order by putting God first and the κόσμος second, presumably to reflect the right prioritisation.[52] As Runia points out, τελειότατος is 'Philo's favourite superlative in praise of the cosmos' perfection'.[53] The κόσμος, 'the first and the greatest and the most perfect of God's works' (*Deus* 106), reveals 'the highest art and knowledge' (*Spec.* 1.35), and is 'most venerable . . . in very truth holy' (*Her.* 199), 'the most perfect of all things that have come into existence' (*Opif.* 14).[54] This language of excellence started with the *Timaeus* and grew under the influence of cosmic religion, but many have noted that Philo contains a higher proportion of such praise, which may be attributable to the simultaneous biblical influence.[55]

Yet for all that, the magnificence of the κόσμος must live up to and be worthy of the God who made it (*Cher.* 112). God clearly subordinates the κόσμος to himself. He makes it his footstool to show that its original cause and continued movement are both extrinsic (*Conf.* 98; derived from Exod 24:10). Such subordination sets Philo apart from the philosophical mainstream,[56] but aligns him with other Jewish writers.[57] The κόσμος as footstool pointedly follows directly after praising it as 'the most perfect sense-perceptible work' (*Cher.* 97; AT). Thus Philo robustly affirms side-by-side the greatness of the κόσμος and its lesser status in relation to God. Even the intelligible cosmos is made by God (*Conf.* 172; *Abr.* 88), an odd claim in a Platonic vein, but one that makes good sense in this light.[58] Runia puts it perspicaciously: 'The true philosopher therefore maintains an attitude of *absolute* admiration for God the creator and *relative* admiration for the created cosmos'.[59]

This dynamic of praise and subordination runs throughout Philo's characterisation of God and the κόσμος. There is intimacy and hierarchy in their relation. God's presence pervades the cosmos (*Conf.* 136), filling up his dwelling place (*Congr.* 117), yet he remains so much greater that the vision of

---

[52] A point sorely missed by the PLCL translation.

[53] Runia 1986: 98. Philo uses it 12*x*.

[54] See also *Opif.* 9; *Det.* 154; *Agr.* 52; *Conf.* 97; *Migr.* 220; *Abr.* 74; *Mos.* 2.267; *Aet.* 15.

[55] Nikiprowetzky 1977: 104–05; E. Adams 2000: 59–60. Note, however, the reserve of Runia on this question of relative influence (1986: 459 n.285). From philosophy, see, *inter alia*, *Tim.* 30ab, 68e, 92c; Dio Chrysostom, *Or.* 40.35; Plutarch, *Mor.* 153d; 1014ab.

[56] E. Adams 2000: 64 cites *Conf.* 98 in this regard. Cf. *Leg.* 1.44; *Plant.* 126; *Ebr.* 75; *Migr.* 186; *Spec.* 2.224.

[57] 2 Macc 7:9; 8:18; 12:15; Wis 9:3; 11:22; Aristob. 8.10.9.

[58] Runia 1999: 155.

[59] Runia 1986: 460.

him is more than the κόσμος can contain (*Spec.* 1.44).[60] God rules over the κόσμος as king (*Decal.* 155), yet as a shepherd who provides for it (*Agr.* 52) and providentially cares for it (*Opif.* 171–72; *Spec.* 3.189).[61] The κόσμος belongs to God (*Plant.* 48) and is his gift to give both generally (*Ebr.* 118) and specifically to worthy individuals (*Mos.* 1.155).[62] These patterns – and their pervasiveness – testify to how thoroughly Philo has incorporated Hellenistic praise of the κόσμος with a Jewish piety for God's sovereignty.

The proper response to this greatness of the κόσμος is praise and thanksgiving to God (*Spec.* 1.210).[63] Indeed the κόσμος should give continual thanks to demonstrate its complete dependence on the one who gave it birth (*Her.* 200), and thus render itself an offering to him (*Somn.* 1.243). An important expression of this worship is the cosmological allegory of the Jewish cult. Its underlying basis likely came from the Hellenistic notion of the κόσμος as temple, a motif which Philo adopts.[64] The allegory of the cult reverses that relation, so that the temple/tabernacle and its service signify the universe and its parts. While it appears fleetingly in Wisdom of Solomon and more in Josephus, its fullest development is in Philo.[65] Most parts of the tabernacle are involved: for example, the sacrificial incense symbolises the four elements, that the κόσμος may continually thank God (*Her.* 197–99).[66] Philo especially focuses on the high priest's vestments, down to the pomegranates hanging at his ankles.[67] Linking the high priest and the κόσμος has three purposes: first, the κόσμος and humanity join together in worship; second, the priest should model his life on the κόσμος and be worthy of it, and third, he offers service

---

[60] Filling up: *Post.* 14; *Plant.* 50; *Somn.* 1.185; inability: *Leg.* 1.44; *Deus* 79.

[61] Rulership: *Migr.* 186; *Her.* 99; *Somn.* 1.157; *Abr.* 78; *Virt.* 220.

[62] Possession: *Cher.* 119; *Sacr.* 97; *Spec.* 1.302.

[63] On cosmic thanksgiving, see Laporte 1972: 151–53 (cf. Runia 1986: 460–61). *Contra* Festugière 1944–54: 2.584 this surpasses literary convention and expresses personal conviction for Philo.

[64] Winston 1979: 321. On this motif, see Pépin 1986: 424–29. It originates probably with Cleanthes (*SVF* 1.538) and then extends widely: Dio Chrysostom, *Or.* 12.33–34; Cicero, *Resp.* 3.14, 6.15; Seneca, *Ep.* 90.28; Porphyry, *Abst.* 2.46.1; Plutarch, *Mor.* 477c. In Philo, *Somn.* 1.215 (cf. *Cher.* 100); *Spec.* 1.66; without κόσμος, *Opif.* 55; *QE* 2.85. But cf. *Plant.* 116 that the whole κόσμος is not an adequate temple for God. Cf. Scott 1991: 69; Früchtel 1968: 69–81.

[65] Wis 18:24; *Ant.* 1.144–46; 3.123, 179–87; *J.W.* 5.212–14, 217. See Laporte 1972: 153–59, Pépin 1986: 423. On this characterisation of the temple more generally in early Judaism and Christianity, see Werman 2004; Beale 2004: 45–48.

[66] On the tabernacle and its furniture, see *Her.* 197–99, 221–29; *Mos.* 2.66–108; *QE* 2.56, 73, 76, 79, 85, 91.

[67] *Mos.* 2.109–35; *Spec.* 1.84–97.

not just for the Jews but all peoples.[68] The sum total is that the high priest becomes a microcosm (βραχὺς κόσμος; *Mos*. 2.135).[69] One effect of this linkage, therefore, is social legitimation – the very universe aligns itself with Jewish worship, a powerful stamp of approval. The implication is an endorsement of the dominant social paradigm, represented by κόσμος, but it has been transformed and made Judaeo-centric, the same move we saw in Chapter 2 for Philo's integration of Judaism and Hellenism. There is, of course, a concurrent apologetic aim. If the high priest ministers on behalf of the κόσμος, then the Jews are concerned for the whole world, and the charge of misanthropy loses some of its sting.[70] Finally, to hold the κόσμος as moral model reinforces the inherently evaluative dimension of ancient discourse on this term. The physical order of the sensible realm should have its counterpart in the moral life. Hence, this cosmological allegory fittingly summarises this larger idea of celebration of the κόσμος in Philo. To locate the deeper meaning of the sacrificial cult in this cosmic setting is to praise the κόσμος very highly. This enlists the κόσμος in worship of God which makes clear its subordination. The κόσμος figures grandly but certainly secondarily to God.

IV. The Κόσμος as a Means of Knowing and Becoming Like God

Because the κόσμος is not God and yet constitutes his greatest work which he made, fills up and sustains, it is a means by which to know him. This revelatory function confers a high value on the κόσμος. The overarching principle is that the sensible world serves as the necessary starting point for understanding the intelligible (*Somn*. 1.185–88; *Migr*. 105).[71] The κόσμος provides sense-perception (αἴσθησις) with the phenomena that constitute the subject-matter of the encyclia, the lower school studies,[72] which then 'form the staple of philo-

[68] *Mos*. 2.133–35; *Spec*. 1.96–97; *Somn*. 1.215.

[69] On microcosm, see above n.37.

[70] Cf. *J.W*. 4.324. On these charges, see p.33. This claim fits within the wider Philonic theme of Israel's universal priesthood: see Borgen 1997: 257 and *Abr*. 98; *Mos*. 1.149; *Spec*. 2.163, 167.

[71] *Pace* Van Kooten 1999: 314–15, Philo takes a stronger view on the necessity of the sensible realm for studying the intelligible than Socrates (*Resp*. 529e; on which see Scott 1991: 7). On Philo's epistemological usage of κόσμος νοητός, see Runia 1999: 155–57.

[72] The encyclia (ἐγκύκλια παιδεία) is the seven liberal arts: grammar, rhetoric, dialectic, geometry, arithmetic, music and astronomy, studied in the gymnasium, which prepared a person to undertake public life. On the encyclia in Philo, see Mendelson 1982.

sophy' (*Congr*. 21).[73] It is philosophy, in turn, which grants knowledge of the intelligible world and of God. But in one atypical passage, Philo allows that the encyclia, the lower studies, can lead directly to knowledge of God. Hagar, symbol of encyclical learning, names a well Beer-lahai-roi, 'the one who sees me' (Gen 16:4), which Philo takes to mean that the soul steeped in the encyclia sees God, its Author, reflected as in a mirror (*Fug*. 213). Given that the encyclia is founded on observation of the sensible world, this interpretation of Gen 16:4 ascribes to the κόσμος the capacity to lead people to see God.

More typically, Philo attributes to philosophy, through its connection with the κόσμος, an ability to lead people to know God. *De specialibus legibus* 3.187–91 offers the full narrative. The sense of sight looks upon the heavens, that κόσμος within a κόσμος, and in turn, the mind inquires about the underlying truth of these phenomena. From their order and beauty, the mind reaches the reasonable likelihood (λογισμὸν εἰκότα) that God is their father and maker, and there is but one κόσμος which he watches over providentially.[74] Elsewhere Philo expresses this idea of finding God through the material world in terms of contemplation of the κόσμος: reflection on the things in this world should lead to inquiry about the Father who brought them into existence (*Somn*. 2.26).[75] Philo, therefore, endorses looking to the heavens not ultimately to see them but through them (*QG* 1.6). He depends on Plato's encomium to sight (*Tim*. 47a–c), a motif which had become widespread in antiquity, due to the popularity of cosmic religion.[76] But he alters the tradition by explicitly orientating it to lead to knowledge of God.[77] Of course, in arguing for the existence of God from observation of the κόσμος, Philo follows many before him, who had all pointed to the order, design and beauty of the uni-

---

[73] Cf. *Leg*. 1.25; 2.7–8; 3.49; *Cher*. 58–60; *Her*. 53; *Congr*. 155. On the relation of mind and sense-perception, see Mattila 1996: 114–16. On the senses as bodyguards to the mind, e.g., *Leg*. 3.115; *Somn*. 1.32; *Spec*. 4.92; on this adaptation of *Tim*. 70d, see Runia 1986: 306–08. On the encyclia and sense-perception, see Mendelson 1982: 34–38.

[74] Cf. *Leg*. 3.99–101; *Spec*. 1.33–35; *Praem*. 41; *Contempl*. 5; *QG* 2.34.

[75] For this contemplation (ἡ περὶ τόν κόσμον θεωρία), *Somn*. 2.81, 173; *Abr*. 164, 207; *Spec*. 1.49, 269; 2.52; 3.1. *Legum allegoriae* 3.84 and *Mut*. 76 are positive but speak of a higher way too. On Philo's usage of such contemplation language with respect to the commentary series, see p.176.

[76] For this motif with κόσμος, *Abr*. 156–66; *QG* 2.34; with οὐρανός, *Opif*. 54, 77. See Runia 1986: 270–76. In antiquity, e.g., Cicero, *Leg*. 1.58; *Fam*. 15.4.16; *Tusc*. 1.64 (references from Boyancé 1954: 215 n.1); Plutarch, *Mor*. 550de. Philo sometimes combines this encomium with the notion of contemplation of the κόσμος (e.g., *Abr*. 164).

[77] Runia 1986: 275.

verse as evidence for the existence of the gods.[78] Philo utilises those arguments while grounding them in Scripture. Hence, the city of Zoar, the only one spared in the destruction of Sodom and Gomorrah (Gen 19:22), stands for sight, which leads into this discourse (*Abr.* 156–66). Or, Philo explains that God appearing in the sanctuary made for him means the world (Exod 25:17; *QE* 2.51). The κόσμος, therefore, plays an important role in transmitting knowledge of God.[79] It is not the highest knowledge of God – which is reserved for the mystical, supra-rational direct encounter – but rather, more like a happy guess (*Praem.* 46).[80] Nonetheless, it is commendable to observe the order of the κόσμος and conclude God was its maker (*Leg.* 3.99; *Praem.* 41–42).

In a final set of passages, the κόσμος not only leads to knowledge of God but contributes to seeing and becoming like him, the ultimate religious-ethical *telos*.[81] Philo has a hierarchy for the *telos*, the highest level of which is to see and become like God, but the κόσμος fulfils a secondary role, particularly for those who cannot reach the top rung (*Conf.* 97; *Mos.* 2.135).[82] In *Opif.* 151, Adam grows in likeness to the κόσμος and God (ὡμοιοῦτο . . . κόσμῳ καὶ θεῷ). By making these parallel expressions, growing in likeness to the κόσμος becomes a legitimate stage in assimilation to God.[83] A further dimension of this process emerges in *Spec.* 4.187. God can do both good and evil but wills the good only, which 'his creation and ordering of the cosmos demonstrates' (μηνύει δὲ ἡ τοῦ κόσμου γένεσίς τε καὶ διοίκησις; AT). Rulers must learn from and imitate this divine characteristic. Thus the example by which people see the importance of imitating God expressly involves his work as creator. 'The celebrated Platonic τέλος, ὁμοίωσις θεῷ, is thus brought in relation to God's creational activity'.[84] In these passages from the Exposition Philo

[78] Plato, *Phileb.* 28de; *Leg.* 886a; 966e; Xenophon, *Mem.* 4.3.13; Aristotle, *On Philosophy* frg. 13; Sextus Empiricus, *Math.* 1.20–21; Cicero, *Nat. d.* 2.15; *Tusc.* 1.68–70. In less developed form, Wis 13:12; *1 En.* 36:3–4; *2 Bar.* 54:17–18; *T. Naph.* 3:4. On this background, see still Pease 1941; Festugière 1944–54: 2.229–32; Riedweg 1993: 88–89. For Philo, see Wolfson 1947: 2.75-78; Mendelson 1982: 77–78. Philo's rendition fits well with the Stoic variation on this argument from design, as they tended to emphasise order (Algra 2003: 162 n.24).

[79] Strictly speaking it is knowledge of the Logos (*Leg.* 3.100; *Fug.* 110; *Decal.* 60) or of the Powers (*Post.* 167).

[80] See p.158.

[81] See p.156.

[82] On this hierarchy of persons, see p.162.

[83] Helleman 1990: 59 sees the microcosm notion underlying this text. Runia 1986: 342 proposes that Philo has adapted the 'likeness of the cosmos to its model' motif in *Tim.* 30c–31b to include God and humanity.

[84] Runia 1986: 135.

incorporates the κόσμος into the pursuit of seeing God and becoming like him, and they represent, therefore, perhaps the most optimistic assessment he can make about the sensible realm.

V. Limitations of the Κόσμος

In contrast to γένεσις, we should not speak of a negative usage of κόσμος. No example among the 580 occurrences of the definition of 'universe' merits truly negative classification. Philo never opposes God and the κόσμος as mutual antagonists like he does God and γένεσις (*Leg.* 3.7). We should speak, however, of the limitations of the κόσμος, because despite all its glory, it remains a created thing, liable of itself to destruction. More to the point, though, since the κόσμος is created, ultimately the highest path to God necessitates its abandonment. To reach perfection one must eventually step away from the κόσμος.

Abraham's pilgrimage provides a paradigm for the limits of the κόσμος, which unfold over two stages.[85] First, Abraham migrates from Chaldea, with its astrology, and leaves the κόσμος in the sense that he no longer deifies it but instead worships God as its creator (*Congr.* 48–49).[86] Although he leaves behind astrology, he still engages in φυσιολογία, the study of the sensible realm, which leads to right knowledge of God (*Her.* 98).[87] Abraham does not

[85] Following Philo's own practice, I refer to Abraham as such throughout, except when his prior name factors into the interpretation.

[86] Philo uses the Chaldean-word group (Χαλδαϊ-) 29*x* in connection with study of the heavens, 28 of which are negative (the exception is *Mos.* 1.23). He critiques its methodology (*Praem.* 58; *Somn.* 1.23) and metaphysical conclusions (*Migr.* 177–87; *Her.* 97–99; *Mut.* 16; *Abr.* 69–82; *Virt.* 212), though he can appreciate some aspects (*Migr.* 180; *Congr.* 50). On Philo's understanding of Chaldeanism, see Decharneux 1994: 67–78. Bréhier 1925: 164–70 and Stuckrad 2000: 14 ascribe too positive an attitude to Philo (the latter because of too broad a definition of astrology; cf. Popović 2007: 213 n.10).

Equating Chaldea with astrology was common: e.g., Sextus Empiricus, *Math.* 5; Diodorus Siculus, 2.29–31; 17.112.2–6; Arrian, *Anab.* 7.16.5–6; Cicero, *Div.* 1.2 (references largely from Reed 2004: 125 n.14; Decharneux 1994: 76 n.1). Cumont 1912: 26–28 points out how Philo, Diodorus Siculus, and others retrojected contemporary astrology into this ancient term. On Greco-Roman astrology and astronomy, see Hankinson 2003: 290–94; on its general, underlying principles, T. Barton 1994: 86–113. On the Stoics and astrology, see Jones 2003: 337–42; Long 1982: 167–72. On the Chaldeans as Stoics, compare *Migr.* 181 with *SVF* 1.532, 2.774; cf. Runia 1986: 190; Reed 2004: 155.

[87] Φυσιολογία for Philo encompasses the whole world (*Prov.* 2.40), and can include metaphysics (*Somn.* 1.184), but focuses particularly on astronomy (*Cher.* 4; *Ebr.* 91–92). For his hermeneutical use of φυσιολογία, see p.122. On φυσιολογία in Philo, see Di Mattei 2006: 19–32 and Nikiprowetzky 1965: 151.

set aside the κόσμος all together, only in the restricted sense of how astrology approaches it.[88] This language of 'leaving the cosmos' is like the anti-creation language from Chapter 3: Philo's rhetoric conveys a stronger bias against the sensible realm than does his actual meaning.[89] The first limit on the κόσμος, therefore, is the necessity to recognise it as God's handiwork rather than God himself, and it applies to all people generally.

Second, Abraham receives a new name – and the perfection that signifies – when he turns away from φυσιολογία and contemplation of the κόσμος (ἀπὸ τῆς περὶ τὸν κόσμον θεωρίας) in order to gain ethical philosophy, true knowledge of its Maker and piety (*Mut.* 76; cf. *Cher.* 7). He thus numbers himself among those who belong to God and refuse citizenship in the κόσμος, because it would hinder their pursuit of him (*Gig.* 61). It is noteworthy *Mut.* 76 speaks of 'contemplation of the cosmos', an otherwise positive phrase for Philo.[90] This is not a case of defining κόσμος like the New Testament sometimes does, as 'the world-system in opposition to God';[91] rather, it is that well-ordered world which is elsewhere God's son from which Abraham must turn. So while φυσιολογία in *Her.* 98 was a good thing which Abraham gained from his migration, now it has served its purpose as a way-station and must be set aside in order to reach the highest rung.[92] One cannot hold on to the κόσμος and attain perfection.[93] Accordingly, this second limit seems more final than the first one: there is no corresponding positive view of the κόσμος to replace

---

88 Thus Philo diverges from the Jewish tradition that made Abraham a teacher of astrology to the Egyptians and Phoenicians: Ps.-Eupolemus 9.17.3–4, 8; 18.2; Artap. 9.18.1; Josephus, *Ant.* 1.167–68; Aristob. 13.12.5 (on the latter as Abraham see Riedweg 1993: 86–88; Walter 1983: 224–25). On Abraham as teacher to the Gentiles, see Reed 2004: 129–35; Knox 1935; on Philo and the wider Jewish exegetical traditions about Abraham and astrology, see Calvert 1994: 464–71.

Jewish responses to astrology could be positive (*Treatise of Shem*; 4Q186; 4Q318) or negative (*Sib. Or.* 3.218–47; *Jub.* 12:16–20 [*contra* Bar Ilan 2004: 2032]; *Gen. Rab.* 44:8–12) or mixed (*b. Šabb.* 156ab). The best survey remains Charlesworth 1987 (see as well, Popović 2007: 225–27; Reed 2004: 125–27). Stuckrad 2000 and Bar Ilan 2004 interpret more of the texts along pro-astrology lines than the evidence warrants.

89 Cf. p.60.

90 See p.86.

91 BDAG 562b. E.g., John 14:20; 1 Cor 7:31; Jas 1:27. On the diverse usage of κόσμος in Paul, see E. Adams 2000; for the NT more generally, Sasse 1965: 3.868–95.

92 Both Nikiprowetzky 1977: 104 and Di Mattei 2006: 31 overlook the mediate character of φυσιολογία for Philo. The former takes it too negatively, and the latter too positively. The language of way-station comes from Zeller 1990: 87, who uses it to describe the role of sense-perception for Abraham.

93 Contrast Rom 4:13 where Paul uses κόσμος to denote the new world which Abraham would inherit.

a flawed one.[94] Yet this limit also seems more restricted in scope than the first one: not everyone must treat the κόσμος this way – only those who stand on the cusp of perfection.

Drawing this two-stage distinction in Abraham's departure from the κόσμος differs from much Philonic scholarship. Marguerite Harl, for example, claims that Abraham migrates from astrology to perfection with no intervening positive contemplation of the κόσμος.[95] She bases that on how Philo treats the patriarch's name-change. 'Abram', which means 'uplifted father' (πατὴρ μετέωρος), signifies an 'astrologer and meteorologist' (τὸν ἀστρολογικὸν καὶ μετεωρολοκιόν) who loves Chaldean beliefs, whereas 'Abraham' signifies the sage (*Abr.* 82). Philo conceptualises Gen 12 and 17 as one indivisible event, and the name-change represents the departure from Chaldea.[96] The limits of the κόσμος are the same in this view, but its overall ethical status is much lower, since it plays no positive role ever in Abraham's pilgrimage.

Such an interpretation makes sense for *Abr.* 82, but it does not fit with how the other treatises handle the narrative. Philo gives multiple clues that Abraham continues to study the κόσμος after he departs from Chaldea, and that such study is a good thing.[97] First, the name-change passages are not monolithic. Most of them describe 'Abram' as something good – he is a virtue-seeker (*Cher.* 6), devoid neither of natural gifts nor wisdom (*Mut.* 68), and worthy of esteem (*Leg.* 3.83). Such characteristics do not fit with a Chaldean astrologer who deifies the κόσμος. Second, it is implied that Abram's turning away from the κόσμος in his migration is only temporary – for a short time (ὀλιγὸν χρόνον; *Abr.* 71). Third, and most convincingly, *Her.* 98 explicitly says Abraham migrated from astrology (ἀπὸ ἀστρονομίας) to φυσιολογία, which is what he eventually leaves behind in order to become a sage who loves God (*Cher.* 7). Given his pantheistic background, Abraham must step away from cosmological study for a time, in order to perceive God though self-examination at Haran, but once he has come to know the deity rightly, the proper kind of contemplation of the sensible world is a good thing for the next part of his pilgrimage.

---

[94] Radice 2008: 145 omits these limitations in his portrayal of Philo's positive views about the cosmos.

[95] Harl 1966: 31–32; at 47 n.3 she cites *Cher.* 7; *Abr.* 82; *Gig.* 62–64; *Mut.* 66–76. This interpretation seems particularly French, as Bréhier 1925: 167–70; Festugière 1944–54: 2.575–76; Nikiprowetzky 1965: 150–51; idem 1977: 104; Laporte 1972: 171; and Cazeaux 1965: 209 n.4 all take essentially this view.

[96] Böhm 2005: 299. The name-change is grounded in and already takes place – in a sense – at the migration.

[97] Riedweg 1993: 87 n.262 also limits Philo's rejection of astronomy for Abraham to the Chaldean variety.

Likewise, Harl and others misunderstand *Mut.* 66–76. When Abraham ascends to the ranks of the perfect, he leaves behind this positive φυσιολογία rather than astrology, from good to better rather than from bad to better. Philo makes φυσιολογία parallel to and synonymous with contemplation of the cosmos (τῆς περὶ τὸν κόσμον θεωρίας; 76), and the latter is elsewhere an overwhelmingly positive concept. Most tellingly, none of Philo's key descriptions for astrology appear – he does not mention Chaldea, methodological errors, confusion of the cosmos for God, or astral divination and determinism. None of the clearest, most significant charges against astrology are levied.[98] Combine that with the positive things that are said about Abram (67–68), and it is difficult to claim he is departing from astrology. Clearly, Abraham ascends to something better when he moves from study of the sensible world to piety and knowledge of God, but the limit of the κόσμος here is different from mistakenly deifying it, and properly counts as a separate, second stage.

Only in *Mut.* 76 and *Gig.* 61 does Philo's usage of κόσμος come close to the multitude of passages with γένεσις that speak of alienation from the sensible realm as the prerequisite for relationship with God. That is only two instances out of 580! Nonetheless, this culmination of Abraham's pilgrimage stands in tension with *Opif.* 151 and *Spec.* 4.187 which incorporate κόσμος into the *telos*. Moreover, the claim that study of the heavens contributes nothing to ethics (*Mut.* 72) does not easily harmonise with how key lessons from the biblical cosmogony should shape a person in piety and holiness (*Opif.* 172).[99] Does the κόσμος have an honoured role in the pursuit of seeing and becoming like God, or must it be abandoned in order to reach God? Perhaps the answer is yes to both. This tension shows that further work beyond lexical study alone – foundational though that is – remains for us in thinking about Philo's divided views on the material world.

VI. Comparison to other 'Universe' Terms

A. Ὅλον

Philosophers used terms other than κόσμος, particularly ὅλον and πᾶν,[100] to denote the universe, and Philo is the same. Ὅλον connotes the completeness

---

[98] The closest Philo comes is to say some have called Abram an astrologer (μαθηματικόν; 71). But ascribing the epithet to others creates some distance (cf. *Somn.* 2.114–15; Scott 1991: 85–86), and moreover, Philo's usage of the term elsewhere is uniformly positive: *Opif.* 128; *Cher.* 4; *Mos.* 1.24; *Spec.* 2.40.

[99] On ethics as the proper goal of φιλοσοφία and study of Scripture, see above, p.26.

[100] For these terms, I examined a cross-section of Philo's usage.

of what exists: God used up all matter in the creation of the whole, which helps demonstrate the unicity of the κόσμος (*Opif.* 171).[101] As this example shows, Philo uses ὅλον and κόσμος to refer to the same thing. With one possible exception (*Mos.* 2.191),[102] in no passage are both terms cosmological yet denoting different things. In some cases they seem interchangeable.[103] In other cases, they denote the same thing but with different emphases: each thing that exists needs everything else, so that 'this whole (ὅλον), of which each is a part, might be that perfect work worthy of its architect, this world' (κόσμος; *Cher.* 112).[104] Ὅλον stresses the inclusion of each part, while κόσμος draws its standard praise. Philo's practice was not unusual, for the Stoa explicitly denoted the same thing with ὅλον and κόσμος (*SVF* 2.422–24).[105] This synonymy is reinforced by Philo using ὅλον in the same motifs as κόσμος. God is father and maker of the whole (*Abr.* 9), responsible for its creation (γενέσεως; *Contempl.* 65), and thus its ruler (*Mut.* 13).[106] Most significant for our purposes is that from a cross-section of 95 occurrences, I did not find a single negative example – like κόσμος, Philo values ὅλον positively. It is impossible to praise adequately 'him who brought the universe (τὰ ὅλα) out of non-existence. For it was an exercise towards us of every virtue' (*Leg.* 3.10). On the whole, Philo's use of ὅλον mirrors and reinforces his use of κόσμος.

B. Πᾶν

Πᾶν connotes the totality of what exists, the universe as it embraces everything possible: the eyes look up and reach 'the boundaries of the universe' (τὰ πέρατα τοῦ παντός; *Abr.* 161).[107] The term was used as 'universe' not only in philosophical texts but even occasionally in non-technical writings like Scrip-

---

[101] Similarly, *Plant.* 10; *Aet.* 21, 26, 29, 71; *Prov.* 2.110. Philosophical examples: *Phileb.* 28d; *Tim.* 32c; *Lysis* 214b; Xenophon, *Cyr.* 8.7.22 (from LSJ 1218b).

[102] The sequence is ὑπ' οὐρανοῦ τε καὶ κόσμου καὶ τῆς τῶν ὅλων φύσεως. That could mean heaven, earth, and the nature of the universe; or less likely, heaven, cosmos and the whole (universal) nature.

[103] *Plant.* 8, 69; *Conf.* 98; *Somn.* 1.159; *Praem.* 34; *Aet.* 37.

[104] Also, *Opif.* 171; *Spec.* 1.120; 3.189; *Aet.* 26, 83.

[105] Also, Plato, *Gorg.* 508a.

[106] E.g., father: *Det.* 147; *Legat.* 3; maker: *Her.* 56; *Decal.* 64; ruler: *Opif.* 78; *Plant.* 91; creation: *Her.* 171; *Praem.* 9.

[107] *Opif.* 111; *Det.* 90; *Agr.* 53; *Ebr.* 105, 152; *Mos.* 1.117; 2.120; *Spec.* 1.41. Cf. *Tim.* 41c.

ture.[108] Usually, πᾶν and κόσμος denote the same thing. Sometimes they are seemingly interchangeable.[109] In other cases, they convey distinct connotations: the seventh day is the festival 'not just of any one place' but of the πᾶν and the birthday of the κόσμος (*Opif.* 89). The terms are parallel and clearly denote the same thing, but πᾶν is the appropriate contrast to particular geographic locations.[110] Again, this synonymy is reinforced by the use of πᾶν in κόσμος-motifs, hence the creation of the 'all' (*Plant.* 117) is accomplished by God, its maker (*Praem.* 41), who is also its ruler and father (*Opif.* 135).[111] Not surprisingly, then, πᾶν and ὅλον sometimes both denote the universe, usually without any distinction.[112] Yet, though their semantic domains overlap considerably, sometimes a distinction can be made where πᾶν focuses on totality and ὅλον on unity (even if the difference is admittedly fine-grained).[113] Those who attribute the creation of the πᾶν to multiple causes do not know the one father and maker of the ὅλον (*Conf.* 144). 'Many causes' is paired with πᾶν, connoting totality, whereas ὅλον connotes unity through the stress on the unicity of the creator.[114] Moreover, on occasion, Philo uses κόσμος, πᾶν and ὅλον all to denote the universe without any differentiation. In *Mos.* 1.96, Philo declares the ten plagues unusual because God used the elements of the πᾶν, from which he had produced the κόσμος, to punish the impious, and thereby showed his sovereignty in turning what he had shaped for the creation of the ὅλον to the destruction of the ungodly. All three terms signify the universe without apparent distinction.[115] Judging from the many passages where two or

[108] Philosophical examples: *Leg.* 966e; *Pol.* 270b; *Tim.* 29c. LXX: Sir 42:17; Add Esth C 2/13:2 (o', L texts respectively, on which see Hanhart 1966: 162; Clines 1984: 69–70). There is a less technical usage – though cf. *Cael.* 268a20–23 – of τὰ πάντα for 'all things', i.e. the universe. In Philo, e.g., *Opif.* 135; *Cher.* 66; *Sacr.* 42; *Mut.* 29. In LXX, e.g., Gen 1:31; Jer 10:16; 2 Esd 19:6; 3 Macc 2:3; Wis 9:1; Sir 18:1. In NT, e.g., Rom 11:26; 1 Cor 8:6; Eph 1:23; 3:9; 4:10; Heb 1:3; 2:10; Rev 4:11 (cf. Bertram & Reicke 1967: 5.888–89).

[109] *Leg.* 3.99; *Det.* 75; *Mut.* 27; *Virt.* 73; *QG isf* 10. Philosophical examples: *Pol.* 272e; *Tim.* 30b; 92c; *Mete.* 356b7–9; *Phys.* 196a25–29; Atticus, frg. 4.7.

[110] Cf. *Det.* 8; *Plant.* 4; *Mos.* 2.53; *Flacc.* 123.

[111] Examples are numerous: creation (cf. *Tim.* 29c): *Opif.* 68; *Prob.* 80; maker: *Post.* 175; *Decal.* 51 (cf. *Tim.* 41b); ruler and father together: *Mut.* 127; *Mos.* 2.88 (cf. *Tim.* 28c); and individually, *Sobr.* 62; *Her.* 62; respectively.

[112] I found 17*x* where both terms appear and denote the same thing and none where they denote different things (cosmologically). Of that total, those occurrences which appear interchangeable are *Opif.* 62; *Det.* 147; *Gig.* 40; *Migr.* 193; *Her.* 23, 301; *Abr.* 121; *Mos.* 2.88; *Spec.* 1.294, 307; 3.178; *Virt.* 64–65; *Legat.* 3.

[113] Louw & Nida 1988–89: 63.1–2.

[114] That, in turn, corresponds to the oneness of the universe (*Opif.* 171). Other differentiated texts: *Conf.* 137; *Migr.* 135; *Decal.* 64.

[115] Also, *Deus* 107–8; *Mos.* 2.48, 238; *Spec.* 1.96. Cf. *Conf.* 98; *Aet.* 83 with σύμπας rather than πᾶς.

all three of these terms appear together, therefore, Philo uses each of them to signify the 'universe', though with some nuance between them at times.

In some passages, however, πᾶν and κόσμος seemingly denote different things. If that is the case, on what grounds did Philo make this distinction? The Stoa distinguished between πᾶν, which included the void and was infinite, and the finite κόσμος/ὅλον, a distinction necessary for their doctrine of cosmic conflagration.[116] Philo apparently refers to this distinction at *Ebr.* 199 with questions of whether πᾶν is infinite or finite and the κόσμος created or uncreated.[117] Overall, though, Philo does not hold to an extra-cosmic void, so the Stoic distinction is irrelevant.[118] But theirs was not the only possibility. Aristotle classified πᾶν and ὅλον differently on the basis of order: for πᾶν the position of the contents do not matter, but for ὅλον they do (*Metaph.* 1024a1–4).[119] Given that Philo uses κόσμος and ὅλον synonymously, and order is essential to κόσμος, this holds more promise. That distinction does approximate how Philo occasionally employs the terms together: πᾶν is matter undifferentiated, without order and thus broader than κόσμος. Judah's gift of his seal to Tamar teaches that God gave a seal to the οὐσία of the πᾶν when it was 'without shape and figure', and after he completed it, he sealed the κόσμος with his Logos (Gen 38:18; *Somn.* 2.45). Matter here is in its pre-creation state, and by the Logos, God makes it into the κόσμος. It is possible that πᾶν and κόσμος are synonyms, but it seems more plausible to read them as denoting different things.[120] Similarly, a few texts without κόσμος nonetheless speak of ordering (διακοσμέω) the πᾶν, which may imply bringing order to what precedes the universe.[121] Thus even though such texts are not numerous, Philo at times uses πᾶν and κόσμος to denote different things.

---

[116] *SVF* 5.222–24 and E. Adams 2000: 53–54. On the void, DL 7.140; on the cosmic conflagration (ἐκπύρωσις), DL 7.135–36; Cicero, *Nat. d.* 2.118; and on Stoic cosmology more generally, M. White 2003.

[117] PLCL misses the distinction, translating πᾶν as 'universe' and κόσμον as 'it'.

[118] He is not entirely clear on the topic: *Opif.* 29 locates a creation of the void on day one, but Runia 1986: 182 n.5 points out that §32 interprets that as an intra-cosmic void. Elsewhere, Philo rejects a Stoic void on the grounds that Moses showed that the conflagration is a fable (*Her.* 228; cf. *Plant.* 7–9). Hadas-Lebel 1973: 76–78 judges the concept of a void insignificant for Philo.

[119] Empedocles, DK 21a47 makes πᾶν larger than the κόσμος, but as he posits inactive matter outside the κόσμος, his view is irrelevant for Philo.

[120] Likewise, *Det.* 90; *Plant.* 120; *Mos.* 2.127; *Spec.* 4.127.

[121] *Abr.* 121; *Mos.* 2.99; *Spec.* 1.307. That may hold for ὅλον too at *Mos.* 2.48 (διάταξις), 148 (διοίκησις), but there the substantives may point to the order that currently exists by virtue of the Logos or φύσις. The exact relationship between πᾶν and κόσμος is underdetermined by the available evidence at *Somn.* 2.116; *Abr.* 71; *Spec.* 2.255; *Aet.* 69. Additionally, πᾶν at *Conf.* 56 may refer to God, as at Sir 43:26.

For our purposes, the important summary point in Philo's usage of πᾶν is the same as it was for ὅλον. A cross-section of over 115 instances reveals that Philo employs πᾶν in a consistently positive fashion. God gave birth to the πᾶν through his goodness (*Cher.* 27), and accordingly, the Israelite leaders acknowledge that the πᾶν is his gift (Num 31:49–50; *Ebr.* 117). Regardless of the term used, then, to denote the universe, it appears that Philo overwhelmingly gives it a positive valuation. One difference may be that the positive usage of ὅλον or πᾶν is proportionally smaller than that of κόσμος, which would not be surprising as there were not nearly the developed patterns for those terms as there was for κόσμος. Nevertheless, Philo does not just rate κόσμος favourably because it refers to the universe as well-ordered – he does the same for all these universe-terms.

VII. Comparative Usage of Κόσμος

A. Greco-Roman Philosophy

We have seen throughout this chapter the extensive debt Philo owes to Greek philosophy for his usage of κόσμος. That view came in large part originally from the *Timaeus*, but by Philo's time many of its aspects were commonplace. In general, Philo adopts a more Middle Platonic than Stoic understanding of the κόσμος, with the caveat that these positions had much in common. Still, at least some aspects of the Stoic view, particularly anything distinctively Stoic about the God-κόσμος relation, were avoided by Philo.[122]

Edward Adams's summary of the Greco-Roman philosophical understanding of the κόσμος under five headings provides a helpful grid for evaluating Philo.[123] The κόσμος was characterised by order, unity, was an object of beauty, related to humanity as macrocosm to microcosm, and an object of praise. Each of these five criteria recurs in Philo. He understands order as fundamental to the process of creation (*Opif.* 21–22), reflective of who God is and how he acts (*Spec.* 4.187), and thus constitutive of the universe (*Spec.* 4.237). Second, the κόσμος is one, because it includes all of matter, but even more because it harmonises with the oneness of God (*Opif.* 171). Third, the κόσμος in its order is beautiful to the point that it reflects the image of the Logos (*Opif.* 25). Fourth, Philo repeatedly puts humanity and the κόσμος in a microcosm-macrocosm relationship (*Plant.* 28). Finally, Philo praises the κόσμος repeatedly as the most perfect of God's works.

---

[122] E.g., the body and soul of the κόσμος (p.80) and the stress on its divinity (p.81)

[123] E. Adams 2000: 64–69, which are similar to Sasse 1965: 3.873–74.

But it is on this last point that Philo also departs significantly from the philosophical consensus. We saw that his praise of the κόσμος is rarely for the κόσμος alone but in relation to its maker. According to Adams, one of the main ways to praise the κόσμος was to ascribe divinity to it. Philo diverges from this practice in order to preserve the ontological primacy and uniqueness of God. A passage like *Tim.* 68e offers insight into how Philo charts his own path. Plato identifies the κόσμος as 'most fair and good' (καλλίστου τε καὶ ἄριστου) as well as 'the self-sufficient and most perfect god' (τὸν αὐτάρκη τε καὶ τὸν τελεώτατον θεόν). Philo wholly assents to the first set of adjectives but not so the latter. He may agree with Plato's meaning for αὐτάρκης, but he does not attribute that adjective to the κόσμος, presumably so that its dependence on God remains clear. His overall aversion to deifying the κόσμος is even more apparent and a significant departure from the *Timaeus* and most Hellenistic philosophy.

Philo, therefore, owes an enormous debt to the philosophical tradition, but not an indiscriminate one. He is not some uncritical doxographer, rather he selectively takes up what suits his exegetical purposes and, shaped by Jewish piety, diverges at times from accepted views. Philosophy's understanding of κόσμος, therefore, crucially – perhaps even fundamentally – orientates Philo's usage, but it remains open to significant modification.

B. Other Jewish Writings

Given that his Jewish faith has such an impact on his usage of κόσμος, how does Philo compare with other Jewish writers' usage of the term? Some initial differences impede any comparison: much more of Philo's writings survived than anyone else's, and the style of his commentaries diverges from nearly all others. Both of those mean *prima facie* we should not expect to find κόσμος as frequently in other writers as we do in Philo. Despite that, there are important similarities. Two of Philo's chief assertions about the κόσμος are shared widely in Jewish usage of the term: God made it, and he rules over it.[124] Unsurprisingly, the best single comparison is Wisdom of Solomon, where the word occurs 19 times.[125] The κόσμος is the system of what exists (σύστασιν; 7:17), made from pre-existent matter (11:17). As its maker (9:9), God is so much greater that before him the κόσμος is like a speck of dust or drop of dew

---

[124] See above, n.12. and n.57, respectively.

[125] That includes two textual variants: 7:6, 13:3. Though Aristobulus offers a good comparison substantively, there are too few occurrences in his fragments. On κόσμος in Wisdom, see Collins 1977: 123–28; Cox 2007: 61–62; Kolarcik 1992.

(11:22).[126] At the original creation, the 'generative forces' (γενέσεις) of the κόσμος are salvific (σωτήριοι; 1:14), so that its very structure is 'conducive for salvation'.[127] People should know God through the κόσμος but are prone to worship its parts (13:1–2). Nevertheless, the κόσμος plays a mediatorial role for God, joining him in delivering the righteous at the Exodus (16:17) and in fighting against his foes in the eschatological judgment (5:20).[128] Indeed, salvation is the realisation of God's purposes from the creation of the κόσμος.[129] Michael Kolarcik summarises that the κόσμος plays a positive, divinely-directed role in the original creation (1:14), salvation (16:17), and judgment (5:20).[130] Finally, the κόσμος is connected thematically with the cult (18:24), an intermediary figure like Wisdom (7:17; 9:9; cf. *Det.* 116), the first man (10:1; cf. *Opif.* 143), and the sage (6:24; cf. *Migr.* 59, *Mos.* 1.157). This usage matches well with Philo and further supports the idea of an interpretive community in Alexandria.[131]

But despite these similarities, even with Wisdom of Solomon two key differences remain: there is no comparable praise or displacement of the κόσμος. Neither of the extremes of Philo's perspective on the universe appear. First, the language of excellence which Philo uses for the κόσμος has no parallel here, or in any extant Jewish writings. There is praise of God on the basis of the sensible creation but not this celebration of the κόσμος, particularly in philosophically-derived language. It is not that Philo speaks in the language of Greek philosophy but underneath says the same thing any rabbi would – he has adopted the concepts thoroughly so that it orientates his expression and substance. Second, the notion of surpassing or displacing the κόσμος is also absent from Wisdom. Instead, the κόσμος plays a role in the eschatological deliverance of God's people and judgment on his enemies (5:20).[132] The role of the κόσμος is positive to the end, unlike in Philo.

There are two further areas of difference between Philo and other Jewish writings. First, he uses κόσμος for the universe in much higher proportion than others do. In the Septuagint, the definition of 'adornment' appears far

---

[126] The usage of τὰ πάντα for 'all things' is similarly theocentric, affirming him as creator (1:14; 8:1, 5; 9:1), ruler (12:15) and sustainer (1:7), particularly by means of Wisdom.

[127] Collins 1977: 124 takes σωτήριοι with this more active sense, *contra* e.g., NRSV. Cf. *Let. Aris.* 210.

[128] Collins 1977: 127. This calls to mind the κόσμος enlisted in the plagues (*Mos.* 1.96; cf. *1 En.* 101:1).

[129] Kolarcik 1992: 103.

[130] Kolarcik 1992. See also, Collins 1977: 128; Cox 2007: 81–83.

[131] On that interpretive community, see p.6; on the relation of Philo and Wisdom of Solomon, see p.5 n.24.

[132] Ps.-Solomon also uses κτίσις in this way: 5:17; 16:24–25; 19:6; see Kolarcik 1992.

more.[133] And the one cosmological way the Hebrew-original portions do use κόσμος – host of heaven – appears only once in Philo (*Spec.* 1.15).[134] Similarly, the anthropocentric nuance of 'inhabited' or 'human world' is more frequent in other Jewish texts than in Philo.[135] Even someone like Josephus, who is often similar to Philo, diverges in this case, mostly using the word in a non-cosmological sense, whether for order or adornment.[136] So at a basic level of definition, Philo uses κόσμος to denote the universe much more frequently. Second, his uniformly positive valuation of the term is not universally shared. *Testament of Issachar* praises the genuine man who does not allow his eyes to see 'the evil from the error of the κόσμος' (4:6; AT).[137] *Testament of Abraham* repeatedly connects death and κόσμος and talks of departure from the body and 'this vain world' (ἐκ τοῦ ματαίου κόσμου τούτου).[138] Interestingly, this departure language is not figurative, as we saw with Philo and γένεσις, but means literal death. These differences are even more notable, since *Testaments of the 12 Patriarchs* and *Testament of Abraham* show signs of significant accommodation to Greek culture and thought.[139] Philo is not alone in his Hellenising, yet he is distinct in his usage of κόσμος.

The difference between Philo and Jewish writings cuts the other way too in that some terminology which they use for the sensible world, he does not. First, 'heaven and earth' (οὐρανός καὶ γῆ) is a standard LXX translation for השמים והארץ where it appears approximately 70 times and denotes the entire sensible realm (Gen 1:1; 2:4).[140] Philo, in contrast, uses 'heaven and earth' as a pair but rarely for the universe. He often incorporates it in quotations from Scripture, but that seems not to have made a huge impact on his idiolect.[141] In contrast, he may invoke heaven and earth as just two components among oth-

---

[133] Whether it was originally written in Hebrew or Greek: e.g., Exod 33:5–6; Prov 20:29; Isa 3:19–20; Ezek 23:40; Jdt 1:14; 1 Macc 2:11; Sir 6:30; 21:27. The exception is Wisdom which never uses this meaning.

[134] Cf. p.74.

[135] E.g., Wis 2:24; 9:3; 17:19; *T. Ab.* (rec. A) 10:2, 3; 11:9; 13:4; (rec. B) 10:15.

[136] E. Adams 2000: 77. E.g., order: *Ant.* 1.81; 3.84, 289; 5.132; 14.2; adornment: *Ant.* 1.249; 3.167; 8.135; 18.90.

[137] Most instances of κόσμος in *Testaments of the 12 Patriarchs* appear to be Christian interpolations about the 'saviour of the κόσμος' (e.g., *T. Levi* 10:2; 14:2; *T. Benj.* 3:8).

[138] With death: (rec. A) 16:4, 12; 17:5; 19:7. Vain world: (rec. A) 1:7; (rec. B) 4:9, 12.

[139] On *Testaments of the 12 Patriarchs*, see Kee 1978, though as modified by Slingerland 1986. On *Testament of Abraham*, see Allison 2003: 30.

[140] Also, e.g., Deut 30:19; Ps 120:2; Isa 37:16; 65:17.

[141] 16*x* in quotation: e.g., *Opif.* 26; *Leg.* 1.1; *Det.* 80. Philo uses the terms as a pair to refer to the universe 5*x*: *Opif.* 111; *Somn.* 1.208; *Mos.* 2.105; *Spec.* 2.53; 4.232. Both terms appear in four texts which conceptually refer to the universe but do not use the LXX terminology: *Cher.* 99; *Migr.* 181; *Spec.* 1.92; *Praem.* 44.

ers, which together constitute sensible existence.[142] Or, in even greater contrast, he may allegorically oppose heaven and earth: Cain refuses the things of heaven, if the things of earth are forbidden him, so he turns his back on virtue, because pleasure is denied him (*Det.* 156).[143] So the main LXX terminology for the sensible realm does not play the same role for Philo.

Second, it is a similar case for 'heaven of heaven' (οὐρανὸν τοῦ οὐρανοῦ translating שְׁמֵי הַשָּׁמַיִם).[144] It means something like the area beyond the visible skies which belongs to God.[145] The only time Philo uses it, though, he alludes to Deut 10:14 and interprets it as the distinction between the intelligible and sensible heaven. Thus he takes biblical language and uses it in a different way, as he did with γένεσις at *Deus* 117–19.[146]

Finally, Philo does not use κτίσις to denote the created realm, unlike many Jewish writers.[147] The verb κτίζω in the Septuagint may translate Hebrew verbs for God's creative activity (e.g., ברא Deut 4:32; קנה Gen 14:19), but the noun appears unambiguously only in the Greek-original portions.[148] It can refer to the whole created world, the non-human creation, or created things/creatures.[149] It is used synonymously for κόσμος at Wis 5:17, 16:24, and many of the books in which it appears also use κόσμος.[150] Adams notes an emphasis on using it for the relation of God to the created world.[151] Philo, however, never employs κτίσις in that way. He uses it only at *Mos.* 2.51 with its secular meaning of 'founding' a human city, in contrast to the γένεσις of the 'great-city' (μεγαλοπόλεως), i.e. the world.[152] So again, terminology other Jewish writers use for the sensible realm is eschewed by Philo.

---

[142] *Leg.* 3.101; *Cher.* 62; *Agr.* 51; *Ebr.* 106; *Decal.* 53; *Spec.* 1.210.

[143] *Gig.* 60; *Deus* 181; *Agr.* 65; *Plant.* 145; *Fug.* 180; *Mut.* 258–59; *Abr.* 205; *Mos.* 1.217; 2.194.

[144] Deut 10:14; 3 Kgdms 8:27; 2 Chr 2:5; 6:18; Ps 113:24; 148:4; Sir 16:18; 3 Macc 2:15.

[145] Tigay 1996: 107.

[146] Cf. p.52.

[147] On κτίσις, see E. Adams 2000: 77–80; Foerster 1965: 3.1027–28.

[148] In textual variants at Pss 73:18; 103:24; 104:21; Prov 1:13; 10:15. On the difficulty of text-critical decisions in the OG Psalter, see Boyd-Taylor, Austin & Feuerverger 2001.

[149] Created world: Jdt 9:12 (*contra* E. Adams 2000: 77; Foerster 1965: 1028); Sir 16:17; 49:16; 3 Macc 2:2, 7; 6:2. Non-human creation: Wis 2:6; 5:17; 16:24; 19:6. Creature: Jdt 16:14; Tob 8:5, 15; Sir 43:25.

[150] *Let. Aris.* 136, 139; *T. Naph.* 2:3; *T. Levi* 4:1; *T. Ab.* (rec. A) 13:3, 6; 16:2, (rec. B) 12:12.

[151] E. Adams 2000: 77.

[152] Similarly, at *Pss. Sol.* 8:7 and *T. Reu.* 2:3 it appears with the sense of 'act' with respect to creation. Likewise, Josephus uses κτίσις mostly for founding cities, though see *J.W.* 4.533 for the act of creation.

Overall, Philo's terminology for the sensible realm is fairly different from other Jewish writers. But not matching terminologically is different from not matching conceptually, and that latter question is among those to consider as we conclude.

VIII. Conclusion

The previous section has already summarised Philo's usage of κόσμος through its comparative analysis. Philo takes a high view of the κόσμος with an approach orientated by the philosophical tradition. Evaluating Philo in light of Adams's summary criteria from Greco-Roman philosophy particularly demonstrates this. But we also saw that Philo re-works that tradition. The relation of the κόσμος to God, its maker, father, ruler, sustainer, is central for its identity and function. The dialectic of closeness and subordination, intimacy and hierarchy, runs like a central thread through his usage of the term. What Philo predicates of the κόσμος may be different from most other Jewish writers yet not necessarily in contradiction to them. No one praises the κόσμος like he does, but there is widespread conviction that the world testifies to the greatness of the God who made it and rules it. But at the same time, the philosophical *topoi* and language are not just window-dressing. Philo understands and approaches faith differently because of his philosophical outlook. For example, incorporating the κόσμος as a model for imitation into the goal of human existence is genuinely different than what other Jewish writers say. The interplay of Hellenism and Judaism in Philo's usage of κόσμος is mutual so that he resembles other philosophers and Jewish writers and yet stands unique with respect to both sides.

This list of positive claims for the κόσμος raises three further points of reflection. First, the contrast between γένεσις and κόσμος in Philo is striking. A chasm stretches between these terms for the sensible realm. Γένεσις tends to depict a world alienated from God, their natures mutually hostile, whereas κόσμος is God's son and greatest handiwork. Γένεσις is rarely said explicitly to have been created by God – and when it is, it most likely is a positive statement – but the fact that God created the κόσμος is central. This general contrast, however, is not absolute. Philo also uses γένεσις to denote the material realm as a means of knowing God and attributes its origin to divine beneficence. On the other side, the κόσμος must be left behind when the call for true perfection comes, so its end is the same as γένεσις. But the audiences for these pronouncements do not seem to be the same. What is predicated of γένεσις –

whether bad or good – seems absolute for anyone, but the limitations of the κόσμος seem confined to a small elite (*Mut.* 76; *Gig.* 61). Finally, the philosophical and Jewish influences work differently for the terms: Philo's negative usage of γένεσις is not typical of Jewish sources but also appears to exceed other philosophical writings. In contrast, the positive usage of κόσμος fits with both philosophy and Judaism, even as it is adapted by Philo in a distinctive direction.

The juxtaposition of γένεσις and κόσμος hints that Philo may implicitly adopt a multiperspectival approach to the sensible realm, where the one entity can be described in starkly divergent terms, depending on the viewpoint and audience. Γένεσις is the world seen from the standpoint of matter, the resistant stuff which God subdued in order to create this realm of becoming, which remains inevitably transient and shifting. Κόσμος is that same world seen from the standpoint of God's design which has creatively ordered all things. The κόσμος admittedly remains subject to suffering and weariness and must be preserved by God to remain immortal. But Philo does not focus on these shortcomings, for his interests lie with its well-ordered, beautiful state. Chapter 8 will allow us to test this proposal at greater length, but this suggestion offers at least one way to reconcile partially the wildly divergent claims Philo makes for two terms which both denote the sensible realm.

Second, this dialectic of celebration and subordination of the κόσμος opens up intriguing possibilities for Philo's relation to the dominant culture. Here is the converse of what we saw with universal matter. There, the worse Philo depicted matter, the greater God appeared since he was able to overcome it in creation. Here, the greater that final product, then the more praise accrues to God, because as its maker and ruler, he must be even greater. Instead of praise of the κόσμος threatening the supremacy of God, therefore, by virtue of its inferiority, it only magnifies it. This dialectic could be a way of finding common ground. An educated audience would agree with much of what Philo says about the κόσμος.[153] Its net result of praising the (philosophical) God of Israel might lead an outsider audience to offer a more open hearing for Judaism.

Philo's use of the cosmological allegory of the cult moves things a step further. The foundation consists of these positive statements about κόσμος. But by making the κόσμος a participant in the sacrificial cult, Philo enlists those statements in worship of God. Thus the well-ordered, positive conception of the universe encoded in κόσμος is drafted as part of Jewish service in the temple. On the one hand, this represents a subordination of Jewish worship to Hellenistic philosophy's understanding of the universe. Yet, on the other hand, this is a way of drawing the circle more widely for what constitutes an

---

[153] On questions of audience, both implied and empirical, see p.18.

acceptable understanding of the κόσμος. Indeed, the map is re-drawn so that the Jewish viewpoint is not just one acceptable option among many but at the centre.[154] The κόσμος participates in the particular Jewish cult and implicitly endorses it as the exemplar or deepest understanding of the world. The entailment is that no one can rightly understand the κόσμος apart from Judaism. This is the same dynamic we observed in Chapter 2 in Philo's relation to Hellenism and Judaism. All the treasures of Greek culture and thought find their true home in Judaism – whether by it being the original source or superior expression. So the κόσμος is not rightly understood by mainstream philosophy apart from making this divine dialectic central.

A third, brief point of reflection concerns the relation between the overwhelming majority of positive statements about the κόσμος and the few brief statements that claim the highest relationship with God entails abandonment of the κόσμος. To what extent do these few negative passages undermine or even deconstruct the positive ones? Can a coherent narrative be constructed so that all that is positive about the κόσμος has its appropriate place, along with these few statements that see things otherwise? That, too, is part of the remit of Chapter 8, but we turn now to the important question of Philo's usage of φύσις.

---

[154] On this kind of maneuver with respect to allegory, see above p.29.

Chapter 5

Philo's Positive Terminology for the Physical World: Φύσις Part One

I. Introduction

The final term in our survey of Philo's terminology for the sensible world is φύσις, which resembles in many ways what we saw for κόσμος in Chapter 4. Philo gives a positive ethical status to φύσις so that it belongs with κόσμος rather than γένεσις or γενητός. He appropriates φύσις from Greek philosophy, which profoundly shapes his discourse, yet he adapts the term to Jewish piety to create something distinctive. This is what we witnessed for κόσμος. Moreover, as was the case with κόσμος, God and φύσις are intimately connected. The mode of that relationship differs, however, since broadly speaking, φύσις is an agent through which God operates, whereas κόσμος is an object to which he relates.

While the investigation of previous terms (οὐσία, ὕλη, γένεσις, γενητός, κόσμος) focussed on the times when they referred to the sensible realm, we cast the net more widely with φύσις to all 1,342 occurrences. This broader coverage is necessary for two reasons. First, there is a *prima facie* case for the importance of φύσις in ancient ethics, differently from the other terms. Second, it is often inherently impossible to assign only one definition to a given occurrence. Although I have marked each instance under one primary definition, frequently multiple definitions are in view – approximately 25% of the time. For example, the motif of nature lavishing its wealth, namely air, water, crops, etc., requires φύσις as creative power and concrete creation, the giver and the gift (*Virt.* 6–8).[1] Similar to mediaeval discussion of *fides*, we might say such imagery involves *natura qua creatur* – nature as instrument or act – and *natura quae creatur* – nature as result. Similarly, a thing that happens 'by nature' (φύσει, κατὰ φύσιν) shares in the essential character of that thing as well as in the wider cosmic order.[2] Φύσις, therefore, is a polyvalent term – Nature as creative power forms the individual nature, which shares in the uni-

[1] Also, e.g., *Her.* 76; *Spec.* 2.158; *Praem.* 99.

[2] Cf. Martens 2003: 73.

versal nature, guided by cosmic Nature.[3] This means we cannot stop with just a primary definition of φύσις but must look for other definitions that may be included in a particular instance.[4] There is, thus, an interconnectedness in Philo's usage of φύσις that necessitates examining all of its occurrences.

Philo's usage of φύσις should be understood as one coherent whole, but our argument will encompass two chapters, because of the amount of ground to cover. Chapter 5 covers Philo's usage of φύσις according to its definitions as creative power, the essential character of a thing, and the sensible realm.[5] At the end, we offer preliminary thoughts about the positive ethical status of φύσις. Chapter 6 then examines how φύσις denotes the principle of order in the universe (including natural law) and may be used as a metonymy for God. In reality, φύσις as creative power and cosmic order properly belong together as one principle, but for heuristic purposes, it is clearer to cover them separately. The goal for both chapters is to establish the term's polyvalence and high ethical status. Φύσις for Philo is thoroughly ethical, no matter its definition. It has a positive ethical status, belonging on the side of κόσμος rather than γένεσις when mapping out the semantic terrain for the sensible world. Part of that high status derives from how its definitions are so interconnected. To speak of φύσις as sensible realm includes its work as the power which creates and guides that realm, which in turn, incorporates how God is at work through φύσις. Finally, Philo's usage of φύσις derives its overall shape and much of its content from Greco-Roman philosophy, and accordingly he ventures onto ground no other Jewish writers tread. Yet his faith decisively modifies this appropriation, so that Philo uses φύσις (and νόμος φύσεως) in a distinctive, original way.

---

[3] For clarity's sake, I try to use Nature or *natura creatrix* for the creative principle, nature for essential character, universal nature (or just nature) for the sensible realm, Nature or cosmic Nature for the governing principle, and 'nature' when the term is polyvalent. Additionally, I use φύσις itself for any of the categories. The language of φύσις as 'x' (where x refers to one of these definitions) should be taken as shorthand for 'when φύσις is used to mean or denote x'.

[4] This is not the fallacy of illegitimate totality transfer, since the term itself is polyvalent (cf. Carson 1996: 60–61; Cotterell 1997: 152).

[5] For the categories of Philo's usage, I have drawn initially on Martens 2003: 67–81, who examines φύσις under four main headings: growth and power of life, inherent character of things, order of the cosmos, and the nature of God. It should be clear that I diverge from him significantly at points. The structure in Koester 1974: 267–69 is looser; in Goodenough 1935: 50–51, it is virtually non-existent. Leisegang 1926: 836–45 categorises numerous instances of φύσις but, of course, offers no commentary.

II. Background for Φύσις in Philo

We begin with the background for φύσις, since otherwise we cannot understand Philo's usage – the intellectual context for this term has a profound impact on Philo's own discourse. As was the case with κόσμος, Philo extensively adopts a term little used in Scripture. Φύσις has no clear equivalent in Hebrew, nor did the LXX translators employ it; its only appearances occur in books originally written in Greek.[6] The best single comparison is perhaps 4 Maccabees, even though it uses φύσις only eight times. Of course, 4 Maccabees, like Philo, has been influenced by Greek philosophy, so in many ways they draw their usage of φύσις from the same wells.[7] First, within the context of the martyrdom of the seven brothers and their mother, φύσις is used as creative power, specifically the biological kinship it engenders (13:27; 15:13, 25; 16:3).[8] The powerful pull of parental and brotherly affection, however, cannot overcome the greater call of fidelity to God through his Law, and so the entire family accepts death rather than disobedience. This elevation of piety over 'natural', familial ties appears in Philo too.[9]

Second, 4 Maccabees exploits the interconnectedness of φύσις definitions. Antiochus counts pork among Nature's gifts (τὰς τῆς φύσεως χάριτας), which incorporates φύσις *qua creatur* and *quae creatur*, both act and result (5:9).[10] Pleasure and pain are concerned 'by nature' (φύσεις) with body and soul (1:20), which shows an interplay between the individual human φύσις and the wider cosmic order.

Third, there is reflection on the relation of Mosaic Law and φύσις, but with a different position than Philo.[11] Antiochus rhetorically asks Eleazar why he abominates eating pork, since Nature has granted it to people (5:8).[12] This is φύσις as creative, sovereign power, with an implicit presumption that Nature's actions are inherently right morally. Eleazar responds that as creator and lawgiver, God sympathises with us κατὰ φύσιν in giving the Law (5:25). That presumably means according to human nature, but also likely, according to the

[6] On the challenges of translating Philo into Hebrew viz. φύσις, see Kahn 1986.

[7] But the philosophical influence on 4 Maccabees is more superficial: see Renehan 1972; Barclay 1996: 370–75; Collins 2000: 205–06. D. C. Aune 1994 compares Philo and 4 Maccabees on the *topos* of mastery of the passions.

[8] Cf. below, p.111. On parental affection in 4 Maccabees, see deSilva 2006.

[9] See p.112.

[10] Also, *Let. Aris.* 57.

[11] See p.139.

[12] Chrysippus understood the pig's purpose, in an anthropocentric teleology, as providing delicious food (Cicero, *Nat. d.* 2.160).

cosmic order.[13] Nature and the Law are in harmony, but critically, the priority belongs to the latter. Nature is to be understood only as it conforms to the Law.[14] Thus it follows that Antiochus is wrong, and pork is actually harmful, while meat allowed under the Levitical codes is beneficial (5:26). Philo invokes φύσις as the standard to which the Law conforms, but 4 Maccabees frames things the opposite way, that φύσις must agree with the Law.

This spectrum of usage in just eight occurrences, reveals links between 4 Maccabees and Philo, but significantly, φύσις does not have a clear role as cosmic creative power, nor does it function as divine agent. It is generally the same with other Jewish usage of φύσις where it predominantly denotes essential character.[15] Josephus uses φύσις extensively with a wide range of definitions, but he still lacks the notion that it may stand in for God.[16] I found no instance of another Jewish writer identifying φύσις with God. Thus much of what is noteworthy in Philo's usage of φύσις does not appear in other Jewish writers.

Given the paucity and more limited range of Jewish references, we must look to Greco-Roman philosophy for why Philo found φύσις valuable. But unlike with κόσμος, Plato does not provide pivotal background, since φύσις for him played a rather marginal role. If everything good comes about through either φύσις or τεχνή (*Resp.* 381ab), the latter is preferred (*Leg.* 892b).[17] When φύσις signifies a creative power, Plato understands it as irrational, or non-rational (899bc).[18] Hence he identifies ψύχη as the principle of movement and cause of cosmic order among the sensible phenomena (892ab, 899b).[19] Accordingly, φύσις is a questionable term for reality since it is confined to the

[13] *Contra* Hadas 1953: 174 who limits it to human nature and Koester 1974: 9.266 who takes it as God's nature.

[14] Redditt 1983: 257 rightly sees the referent for φύσις as cosmic order and the harmony between it and Law but does not see the priority given to Law in that relationship.

[15] Essential character: 3 Macc 3:29; Wis 19:20; *Let. Aris.* 250, 257; *T. Reu.* 3:1, 3; *T. Dan* 3:5. Φύσις in *T. Naph.* 3:4–5 is obviously ethically-charged but means 'essential character' of Sodom or the Watchers, who depart from the order proper to them. The sense of 'by' or 'against' φύσις is at Wis 13:1; *Let. Aris.* 44, 288. It is used to mean 'species' of animals at Wis 7:20. Φύσις does not appear in Aristobulus or *Testament of Abraham.*

[16] E.g., *natura creatrix*: *J.W.* 1.465; *Ant.* 6.126; essential character: (human) *J.W.* 7.345; *Ant.* 2.115; (God) *Ant.* 4.269; *Ag. Ap.* 2.168; (universe) *Ant.* 1.24; 3.123; 'by nature': *J.W.* 4.246; *Ant.* 3.190; cosmic order: *Ant.* 17.120; natural law: *J.W.* 4.382. References drawn from Rengstorf 1973–83: 4.337–39. On φύσις in Josephus, see Koester 1974: 9.269–71.

[17] McGrath 2001: 91; Koester 1974: 257.

[18] Kelsey 2003: 85 n.33 notes φύσις is not a principle in *Timaeus*. Contrast *De opificio* where Philo uses φύσις as creative principle 10*x* (44, 67 [2*x*], 68, 79, 85, 113, 124, 133 [2*x*]).

[19] Hahm 1977: 206; McGrath 2001: 92; Kelsey 2003: 85. *Phaedr.* 245c.

material realm (892b). In the later dialogues, Plato more readily invokes φύσις as moral guide, typically denoting essential character, especially of human beings (e.g., 636b; *Tim.* 90d).[20]

We must look, therefore, to Aristotle and especially the Stoa for the formative influence on Philo's usage of φύσις. Instead of Platonic ψύχη, Aristotle returns to φύσις as the source of movement in a thing (i.e. its growth), which provides its form (εἶδος; *Metaph.* 1015a14–19).[21] Aristotle, therefore, pictures φύσις as a creative power, analogous to τέχνη (*Phys.* 192b8–23; *Protr.* frg. 11),[22] even personifying it as an active divine being (*Part. an.* 659b35).[23] Characteristic of the work of φύσις is order (ἡ γὰρ φύσις αἰτία πᾶσιν τάξεως; *Phys.* 252a12),[24] both within an individual thing (*Part. an.* 656b26–27) and across all things, the system of nature (*Metaph.* 1075a12–16).[25] That order is teleological – φύσις is both formal (*Phys.* 198b10–11) and final cause (*Pol.* 1254b22).[26] Although φύσις concerns itself with matter (*Metaph.* 995a17), Aristotle never uses it by itself for the whole sensible realm, though he comes close (e.g., τὴν ὅλην φύσιν; *Metaph.* 1074b3).[27] Nature is not an ethical construct – φύσις engenders neither virtue nor vice, only the capacity for them (*Eth. nic.* 1103a19).[28] Thus some of the main lines of Philo's usage of φύσις appear in Aristotle, especially its creative role and the centrality of order, but its ethical function does not.[29]

Aristotle's understanding of φύσις influenced the Stoa, particularly their definition of it as 'a craftsmanlike fire proceeding methodically to creation' (πῦρ τεχνικὸν ὁδῷ βαδίζον εἰς γένεσιν; *SVF* 2.1133; 1.171).[30] Stoics held that two coterminous principles, passive and active, comprise all reality (2.300). The passive they usually identified as inert, 'quality-less' matter, but the active took several names – god, logos, fate, providence, Zeus, φύσις

[20] Benn 1896. *Pace* Laks 1989: 178. For the context of the *nomos-physis* debate, see McKirahan 1994: 390–413; Long 2005: 414–21.

[21] *Metaph.* 1032a22–25; 1041b27–31; *Phys.* 192b21–22; 193a30–b21.

[22] Hahm 1977: 201. *Gen. an.* 735a2–4.

[23] Koester 1974: 259 n.81. *Part. an.* 654a24–25; 655a17–18; *Eth. eud.* 1247a9–10.

[24] *Gen. an.* 760a31; *Cael.* 301a4–6. McGrath 2001: 94; Kelsey 2003: 86 n.34.

[25] Buchheim 2001: 215–19.

[26] Hahm 1977: 202. *Cael.* 271a33; 291b13; *Part. an.* 641b11; 658a8–9; *Eth. nic.* 1153b32.

[27] Koester 1974: 259. *Metaph.* 984a31; 987b2; 1005a32; also, *Metaph.* 984b9; *De an.* 430a10; *Cael.* 268b11.

[28] Koester 1968: 526.

[29] Cf. Koester 1974: 268 n.168 on the Aristotelian influence on Philo.

[30] The influence is in the craftsman imagery and teleology (Hahm 1977: 200–08); this has been disputed (unconvincingly) by Sandbach 1985: 38–40. On the mundane creative work of Stoic nature, Cicero, *Nat. d.* 2.138.

(2.1027).[31] Φύσις is the active principle understood as a rational, creative force which benevolently governs and sustains all that exists.[32] As 'creator and mother of all good things', nature 'created the structure of the world' (2.1170).[33] Cicero's Stoic speaker, Balbus, defined it as 'the sustaining and governing principle of the world' providing 'order and a certain semblance of design' (*Nat. d.* 2.82).[34] Rationality is a property of cosmic Nature, for the Stoa speak about the 'reason in' or 'of' nature (*Off.* 3.23; *SVF* 2.937).[35] Moreover, all nature is interconnected so that the φύσις of human beings shares in the cosmic φύσις (3.4).[36] Φύσις actually functioned more prominently in Stoic ethics than physics,[37] nowhere more famously than in their formulation of the *telos* as life in agreement with nature (1.179, 552). Φύσις provided the best starting-point for ethics (3.68). Thus, A. A. Long argues 'nature' for Stoicism was 'first and foremost a normative, evaluative' principle.[38]

Given Philo's stress on the orderliness and rationality of the act of creation, it makes sense the Stoic conception of φύσις would prove attractive to him. Its dynamic character, central role in structuring the universe, interconnectedness, and pervasive ethical significance – all these features recur in Philo. The main difference revolves around the immanence of the active principle. Philo clearly separates the transcendent God from the immanent active principle, although the exact relations between God, the Logos and φύσις remain complicated.[39] Nonetheless, as John Martens ably summarises it:

---

[31] *SVF* 1.102, 160; 2.937. From a moral perspective, the principle could be called law or right reason (*SVF* 1.162). This Stoic predilection for stringing together multiple terms to refer to the same thing has been criticised, both then and now (*Nat. d.* 3.26; Striker 1986: 185).

[32] *SVF* 2.937, 945, 1024, 1027; 3.320. *Inter alia*, Inwood & Donini 1999: 682–83; Striker 1996: 229; Long 1996: 141.

[33] Translation L-S 54q. The goodness of nature is presupposed by this function of ordering (Cooper 1996: 273), and by *oikeiōsis*, the notion of human development (Long 1996: 152–53; DL 7.85).

[34] *SVF* 2.912, 945. For that sustaining, see 2.1132 and particularly the notion of *hexis*, 1.528–29; 3.178 (see below, p.110). Fire (1.120, 513) or πνεῦμα (2.441) also held existence together.

[35] Long 1996: 140 n.7. Cf. *SVF* 2.1181; 3.308, 317, 325; Seneca, *Ep.* 124.13–14; Cicero, *Nat. d.* 2.87.

[36] Inwood & Donini 1999: 676. Cf. *SVF* 1.182.

[37] Note the infrequency of φύσις for Stoicism in Sedley's introduction to Hellenistic cosmology (1999), a point he confirmed in private conversation.

[38] Long 1996: 137.

[39] See p.143 and p.148.

Philo finds that the Stoic ideas properly explain God's work in nature, without contradicting Jewish creation accounts, and he believes that the Jewish idea of the transcendent God supplies missing information for the Stoic view of nature.[40]

Philo, therefore, is primarily indebted to philosophical discourse for his usage of φύσις, but he modifies those ideas in light of Jewish theological commitments. We turn now to what that looks like in specific definitions for φύσις.

III. Φύσις as Creative Power

The first category is φύσις as the principle – often personified – which creates and gives growth. Most broadly, Nature is responsible for everything from the stars and heavens above (*Spec.* 1.322) as well as being the 'underlying fact, the fountain or root or foundation' of all things (*Her.* 116).[41] Nature regulates the physical environment: sunlight (*Spec.* 2.210), seasons (*Legat.* 190), rain (*Mos.* 1.117), crops (*Spec.* 2.172). It signifies the development and function of a thing apart from human involvement; it is the contrast between natural and conventional.[42] Unleavened bread is a gift of Nature, but leavened bread a work of art (τέχνης; *Spec.* 2.159). But unlike Plato, who preferred τέχνη (*Leg.* 892b), Philo, driven by the biblical text (Lev 23:6), connects human craft with pleasure and prefers the ascetic workings of φύσις. Philo consistently prioritises the results of *natura creatrix* over those of human effort.[43] Jacob's return to Canaan marks the cessation of all labour and heralds the sudden outburst of all good things by nature and without art (ἄνευ τέχνης; Gen 31:3; *Migr.* 31). Philo then contrasts what the human soul produces with what God gives and recounts how he has experienced this when divine inspiration, and not his own insight, has guided his interpretation (34–35).[44] Thus on one side is human endeavour, and on the other, alternately Nature or God.[45] This passage strongly implies divine activity in Nature, a point to which we will return.[46]

As one would expect, φύσις as creative principle functions particularly in the realm of life. Plants, animals and human beings all owe their existence to

---

[40] Martens 2003: 87. Cf. Mattila 1996: 120–21.

[41] Cf. *Det.* 125; *Spec.* 4.51; *QE* 2.1.

[42] This distinction goes back at least to the Ionian cosmologists of the fifth-century (Long 2005: 415).

[43] See, however, *Mut.* 162 that the *cultivated* vine is Nature's handiwork, an interesting blend of the two.

[44] On Philo's inspiration as exegete, see Hay 1991a.

[45] Other passages contrasting φύσις with the conventional: *Fug.* 169–72; *Mut.* 219, 257–60; *Decal.* 163.

[46] See below, p.148.

Nature. It causes the beginnings of plants (*Her.* 115) and their fullness (*Virt.* 154), as well as holding them together under the Stoic notion of ἕξις, which refers to 'those essential features which make something' what it is.[47] For animals, φύσις works as a consummate artist (*Opif.* 68). Nature is a mother to creatures (*Post.* 162), providing them homes (*Det.* 151), sustenance while young (*Virt.* 143), and even the means of self-defence (*Ebr.* 172; *Mut.* 159).

It is for human beings, however, that Philo most frequently invokes φύσις as creative power. Nature is responsible for every stage of human life and nearly every aspect of a person. Parents play a role in the γένεσις of children, but Nature is 'the original, the earliest and the real cause' (*Her.* 115). It fulfils this duty with aplomb, crafting humankind as the most beautiful creature (τὸ κάλλιστον τεχνιτευούσῃ καὶ δημιουργούσῃ ζῷον; *Spec.* 3.108). Nature forms the marriage-union for procreation (*Abr.* 248),[48] with the womb its workshop (*Aet.* 66).[49] Consequently, nearly every part of the human person is attributed to φύσις: soul (*Deus* 25) and body (*Somn.* 1.210), sense-perception (*Somn.* 1.27), the face (*Post.* 127), lips (*Agr.* 133), teeth (*Spec.* 3.198), a firm chest (*Leg.* 3.115), stomach (*Spec.* 1.217), and the hands for drinking or self-defence (*Somn.* 2.60; *Legat.* 229).[50] The sole exception is rationality, which is attributable to the Logos (*Opif.* 67; *Det.* 82).[51] Interestingly, *Opif.* 146 aligns the mind with the Logos but the physical body with the κόσμος. Since φύσις is responsible for the body, Logos and Nature are on conceptually opposite sides.[52] Nature leads human life along a daily cycle (*Spec.* 2.100–103), and preserves it all the way from breast-milk for infants (*Opif.* 133), through heal-

---

[47] L-S 1.289. On *hexis*, *SVF* 1.528; 3.178. In Philo, *Deus* 35–45; *Somn.* 1.136; *Aet.* 75, and the comments by Long 2008: 134–37. At *Leg.* 2.22–23, each lower form of *hexis* also appears in higher level beings, a twist which Inwood 1985: 25 attributes to Philo.

[48] *Cher.* 43; *Ebr.* 211; *Her.* 164; *Abr.* 137. Nature may stand in for God in these passages, particularly in the interpretation of Gen 1:27 at *Her.* 164.

[49] This is a favourite Philonic phrase: *Mos.* 2.84; *Spec.* 3.33, 109; *Legat.* 56. *De aeternitate* 66 indicates a quote of unknown origin, possibly Peripaetic, since it recalls Aristotle's definition of φύσις as womb (*Metaph.* 1014b17).

[50] Cicero, *Nat. d.* 2.133–53 covers much the same ground.

[51] The specifics on how human rationality is linked to the Logos are scrambled for Philo. He consistently adopts the Platonic view of it being the copy of the image, but is inconsistent with respect to the Stoic notion of it being a particle of aether or of deity (*SVF* 1.1128; 2.633). Occasionally, the two views appear side-by-side (e.g., *Det.* 79–90), and in *Mut.* 223 the copy-image concept is prioritised as more reverent than the part-whole idea. The consistent point is that the immaterial, reasoning part of the person is higher than the body and somehow related to divinity. See Reydams-Schils 1995: 95–102 and Runia 1988a: 66–73, especially his penetrating conclusion on the problems this question poses for delimiting assimilation to God.

[52] On comparing Logos and φύσις in creation, see p.143.

ing sickness (*QG* 2.41), until death, the universal end 'in the due course of Nature' (*Sacr.* 125).[53]

This pervasive role for φύσις in creating humanity engenders a bond among all people. This bond is first a narrow, familial one. Like the Stoics, Philo conceives of parents and children joined together 'by the indissoluble bonds of nature' (φύσεως δεσμοῖς ἀλύτοις; *Spec.* 1.137),[54] expressed through 'the peculiar and intense affection implanted in parents by Nature' (*Virt.* 192). Second, again like the Stoics, Philo conceives of a broader kinship amongst all people, attributable to the common possession of reason, which comes from Nature (*Decal.* 41, 132).[55] There is a tension, however, between the Bible and Philo's exegesis. While Scripture can speak of universal human kinship (e.g., Gen 1:27), it emphasises particularity, especially through boundary-markers like circumcision and dietary laws. Philo's more immediate source for this teaching is Middle Stoicism.[56] Cicero traces the principles of kindness and moral obligation ultimately to the human fellowship established by Nature through the bond of reason and speech (*Off.* 1.50).[57]

The operations of *natura creatrix* are replete with ethical significance for Philo. The presumption is that people should respect and accede to Nature's work. Broadly speaking, that means celebrating the wonder and beauty of Nature's accomplishments (*Sacr.* 75; *Det.* 125), as they should the κόσμος,[58] except that here God is not explicitly incorporated. Perhaps he is already so identified with *natura creatrix* that invocation is unnecessary. More particularly, Philo links a host of ethical *topoi* to φύσις as creative principle. Nature's public generosity in creating the heavens should encourage human generosity (*Spec.* 1.322–23). Slave ownership is contrary to nature, which has borne all men free (*Contempl.* 70).[59] To enshrine child-bearing as Nature's purpose for

---

[53] E.g., *Leg.* 1.107; *Abr.* 257; *Spec.* 4.119.

[54] *Ebr.* 14; *Mos.* 1.32; 2.207; *Decal.* 8, 112; *Spec.* 2.232, 239; 4.178. Stoicism: DL 7.140; Cicero, *Off.* 1.12, 53–54; *Fin.* 3.62.

[55] Cf. *Spec.* 1.294; 2.73; *Virt.* 140; *Praem.* 155; *Prob.* 79; *QG* 2.60; on Nature providing reason, *Cher.* 39; *Aet.* 68; on kinship without reference to Nature, *Mos.* 1.314; *Spec.* 4.14. Striker 1996: 250 regards the step from parental love to wider kinship as crucial for the Stoic theory of *oikeiōsis*.

[56] Bréhier 1925: 253; Winston 1984: 393. Horsley 1978: 49–50 attributes it to Antiochus.

[57] Cicero proves most helpful for this concept. On Nature and such kinship: *Leg.* frg. 2; *Off.* 1.22, 157; *Fin.* 3.63; on the common possession of reason: *Leg.* 1.28–30; *Nat. d.* 2.154; other references: *Off.* 1.149; 3.28; *Fin.* 5.65.

[58] See p.82.

[59] *Spec.* 2.69; 3.137; 4.14, 18; *Prob.* 19. This view goes back at least to the Sophists: Aristotle, *Pol.* 1253b20–23; Alcidamas, Schol. to Arist. *Rhet.* 1373b (cited at J. Adams 1945: 102). On Philo and slavery, see Garnsey 1996: 157–72.

marriage presages a primarily procreationist sexual ethic.[60] Consequently, even marital sex, if it cannot lead to conception – whether because of menstruation (*Spec.* 3.32) or known infertility (3.34, 36) – violates Nature. The broad kinship engendered by φύσις makes all persons equal (*Decal.* 41–43) and, therefore, murder is a violation of natural law (*Decal.* 132).[61] In contrast, the familial bond created by Nature, while important, can be overruled by higher virtues.[62] Hence Abraham does not allow natural affection to prevent him from being ready to sacrifice Isaac (*Abr.* 168), given that it was a divine command, nor does Moses give sway to his 'natural affection for his children' when appointing a successor but instead allows reason to rule and entrusts the decision to God (*Mos.* 1.150; *Virt.* 53). Piety is queen of the virtues (*Praem.* 53),[63] to which natural ties of affinity must be subordinated.[64] Thus the impact of φύσις is not monolithic. Nonetheless as creative principle it has a clear ethical influence and positive ethical status.

IV. Φύσις as Essential Character

A. Basic Sense

Aristotle closely connects the sense of φύσις as creative power, by which he means the principle of movement in a thing (i.e., its growth), to a thing's essential form (εἶδος), or φύσις (*Metaph.* 1015a14–19). According to Thomas Buchheim, the nutritive process of growth preserves the thing's form by giving it an organic unity, hence φύσις appropriately denotes both creative power and essential character.[65] Philo never provides a justification for how the meanings of φύσις relate, but conceptually he too joins them. For example, people 'blessed by the gifts of nature' (εὐμοιρίᾳ χρήσαιντο φύσεως) who do

---

[60] Gaca 1996: 22–27 and Reinhartz 1993: 69 likely overstate the procreationist aim, whereas Winston 2001: 212–13 perhaps underplays it.

[61] Cf. Geiger 1932: 5–6.

[62] Cf. Josephus, *Ant.* 6.127. On the subordination of family ties by Philo, see S. Barton 1994: 23–35.

[63] On εὐσέβεια as greatest virtue, e.g., *Migr.* 44; *Congr.* 130; *Virt.* 216; as queen of virtues, e.g., *Abr.* 270; *Decal.* 119; *Spec.* 4.135. Cf. Winston 1984: 395; Sterling 2006 (my thanks to Prof. Sterling for providing a pre-publication copy of his essay). Völker 1938: 223 notes how Philo occasionally speaks of other virtues as chief (prudence, *Leg.* 1.66–67; justice, *Abr.* 27; temperance, *Spec.* 1.149). Given how consistently he designates piety as preeminent, however, such passages are better taken as rhetorical flourishes than as substantive contradictions.

[64] Also, *Spec.* 1.315–18.

[65] Buchheim 2001: 205–7.

not go astray even when the king does (*Mos.* 1.160), seem to be equipped both by their character and the creative power which so endowed them.[66] To put it more generally, a thing has its φύσις by virtue of the creative work of φύσις. This definition of φύσις as essential character is by far the most common in Philo – around 60% of all occurrences, though most of them do not directly affect our study. Φύσις under this definition does not have an ethical status of its own but always depends on its subject. Philo uses φύσις to denote the essential character of sensible entities like heaven (*Leg.* 1.2), the sea (*Somn.* 2.118), and snakes (*Migr.* 83); intelligible entities like angels (*Abr.* 115), the Powers (*Her.* 172), or the Logos (*Opif.* 146); abstract concepts like self-conceit (*Leg.* 1.52), knowledge (*Somn.* 1.6), and justice (*Ios.* 170); or miscellaneous things like the flight of birds (*Sacr.* 66), stale flesh (*Spec.* 1.220), or the unstable crowd (*Mos.* 1.197). In each of these examples, φύσις expresses what that thing is inherently, its unique constitution.

When Philo uses φύσις as essential character but with a head-noun that pertains to the sensible world, the whole phrase means principally the same as the head-noun alone. When he speaks of the φύσις of 'created things', he is usually negative. Φύσις in *Opif.* 23 can obtain no good thing on its own, because it refers back to the pre-cosmic, disordered οὐσία of *Opif.* 21. Similarly, created things in general (γένεσιν), precisely because they are 'created' (γενητά), are perishable 'by nature' (τῇ φύσει φθαρτά; *Spec.* 2.166).[67] Alternatively, when Philo uses τὸ ὄν or πραγμά with φύσις, the ethical status is neutral or positive.[68] Thus, philosophy takes 'the entire nature of existing things' (πᾶσαν τὴν τῶν ὄντων φύσιν) for its subject-matter (*Congr.* 144), which is virtually equivalent to saying that all of existence falls within its purview.[69] Finally, when Philo refers to the nature of the universe, he basically refers to the universe itself.[70] To describe the φύσις of the κόσμος as 'order of the disordered' (τὴν τάξιν τῶν ἀτάκτων; *Aet.* 75) is conceptually the same as describing the κόσμος itself as 'order of the disordered' (e.g., *Somn.* 1.241).[71] These

[66] Cf. e.g., *Post.* 71; *Agr.* 168; *Migr.* 75; *Praem.* 50.

[67] Cf. *Cher.* 19; *Conf.* 154; *QG* 3.7.

[68] With τὸ ὄν, *Plant.* 79; *Ebr.* 167; *Congr.* 144; *Somn.* 2.115; *Praem.* 11; with πραγμά, *Post.* 93; *Deus* 45; *Agr.* 134, 142. The latter is distinct from the 'things of nature' (nearly always genitive: τῶν τῆς φύσεως πραγμάτων), in which φύσις refers to the sensible world; on this phrase, see p.120.

[69] On Philo's conception of philosophy, see p.24.

[70] κόσμος: *Mos.* 2.135; *Aet.* 37; ὅλος: *Somn.* 2.194; *Mos.* 2.191; *Spec.* 1.96; *Praem.* 23; *Aet.* 59; πᾶν: *Det.* 75; *Ebr.* 141.

[71] Philo himself makes this point further on in *Aet.* 75: if the φύσις of the κόσμος is uncreated and indestructible, then the κόσμος is too. In *Somn.* 1.241 τὸ πᾶν is described in terms of order from disorder. On the κόσμος and order, see p.78.

examples further demonstrate how the term φύσις derives its ethical status from its subject.

Philo's description of the φύσις of God is worth special treatment, because it suffers from the inconsistency typical of his discussion of deity.[72] On the one hand, no positive assertion about the divine nature can be made (*Congr.* 61, *Leg.* 3.207).[73] Yet Philo often attributes incommunicable attributes to God's nature like singularity (*Mut.* 184), immutability (*Somn.* 1.232), simplicity (*Spec.* 1.180),[74] or even more frequently, communicable attributes like graciousness (*Spec.* 2.23), kindness (*Mos.* 2.5), mercy (*Opif.* 169), happiness and blessedness (*Abr.* 87), and goodness (*Fug.* 66).[75] This bifurcation generally correlates to the commentary series.[76] The Allegory tends to claim nothing positive can be said about God's nature, but if it does say something, it pertains to incommunicable attributes. The Exposition is more likely to speak about the moral attributes of God's nature. We may hypothesise that the difference corresponds to the commentaries' respective audiences. Advanced readers of the Allegory knew better than to ascribe anthropomorphic qualities to the deity, who, properly speaking, transcends all such categories. But the beginners reading the Exposition needed the concession that pictured God in moral terms.

B. *Φύσις and Essential Human Character*

As he did with the *natura creatrix* definition, Philo focuses particularly on humankind for φύσις as essential character. There is an universal human nature (*Post.* 160; *Ios.* 25), which can be further analysed along various axes: mortal-immortal (*Opif.* 134),[77] body-soul (*Mos.* 2.288), irrational-rational

---

[72] Philo likely would claim his inconsistency is inherent to human efforts to speak about God. Martens 2003: 77–80 makes this its own category, mainly as an argument against the claim that φύσις equals God. On the inherent slipperiness of language when predicated of the deity, see Runia 1988b.

[73] Passages that describe God as unknowable without reference to φύσις include *Post.* 168–69; *Mut.* 9–10; *Somn.* 1.184; *Praem.* 40; *QE* 2.68. On this negative theology in Philo, which mixes confidence in knowing God's existence with the inability to know his essence, see Sterling 2007: 151–53; Runia 1988b; Runia 2002a: 303.

[74] Cf. *Leg.* 2.2; *Cher.* 86–87; *Mut.* 140; *Spec.* 1.300; *Praem.* 46; *Legat.* 310; *QE isf* 3.

[75] Cf. gracious: *Conf.* 181; *Fug.* 141; *Mos.* 2.61; *Spec.* 1.310; 2.196; merciful and kind: *Mos.* 1.72, 101; *Spec.* 1.97; 2.253; happy and blessed: *Opif.* 135; *Deus* 108; *Somn.* 1.94; *Spec.* 3.129; 4.48, 123; good: *Conf.* 180; *Decal.* 177. The multitude of such references belies the claim by Martens 2003: 78 n.23 that Philo only 'slips up a few other times'.

[76] On the commentaries' different audiences and aims, see p.18.

[77] Cf. *Det.* 87; *Decal.* 99, 101; *Virt.* 203; *Legat.* 91.

(*Fug.* 72),[78] vice-virtue (*Praem.* 62).[79] Φύσις points to human limitations in seeing God (*Spec.* 1.44), comprehending much from physics (*Prob.* 80), or finding the goal of knowledge (*QG* 4.9).[80] The idea that things are either appropriate or inappropriate for human nature conveys an essentialist understanding of human identity at physical and moral levels. For example, physically, Egypt is fruitful for what human nature needs (*Mos.* 1.5); and morally, homosexuality both debases and adds to nature (*Spec.* 1.325). In the case of the latter, φύσις likely refers to human nature and cosmic order together. Texts that thus describe human nature reveal how usage of φύσις is socially-conditioned.[81] Some examples demonstrate this particularly clearly. 'Nature' conceals human genitalia in order to promote decency (*Mut.* 246).[82] Φύσις here likely means *natura creatrix*, human nature and cosmic Nature, which aptly illustrates the interconnectedness of definitions. Similarly, it is obvious that Philo's statements about φύσις and women, like Nature exempting them from combat (*Mos.* 2.236), or their having little sense by nature (φύσει; *Prob.* 117), strongly reflect his social context.[83] Thus the ethical status of φύσις as essential character can only be grasped in relation to its subject and these wider social-intellectual contexts.

C. Divinely-Endowed Individual Φύσις

Philo treats not only general human nature under the term φύσις but also individual natures.[84] For our purpose of assessing what ethical status he assigns to φύσις, the case of Isaac, the one who attains perfection through φύσις, bears special interest. It was generally accepted in antiquity that education or moral progress required instruction, nature or practice.[85] Philo allegorises this triad so that Abraham, Isaac and Jacob represent the three means respectively; each

---

[78] Cf. *Leg.* 3.24; *Det.* 83; *Migr.* 210, 212; *Spec.* 3.99, 103; *Virt.* 168; *Aet.* 68.

[79] Cf. *Opif.* 73; *Mut.* 197.

[80] Cf. *Ebr.* 166; *Mut.* 186; *Spec.* 2.51; 4.175; *Virt.* 172; *QE isf* 3. Koester 1974: 255 notes the wider frequency of this motif (e.g., *Theaet.* 149c; Aristotle, *Pol.* 1286b27).

[81] Cf. p.13.

[82] Cf. *Somn.* 1.97, 102. Similarly, see Cicero, *Off.* 1.126–29.

[83] Cf. *Somn.* 1.123; *Mos.* 1.8; *Spec.* 4.225; *Contempl.* 33. On Philo's views on women and gender, see, *inter alia*, Baer 1970; Sly 1990; Mattila 1996; Runia 2001: 359–61; Winston 2001.

[84] Positive examples of specific human φύσις include Phinehas (*Mut.* 108), Moses (*Mos.* 1.83; *Virt.* 80), Flaccus (*Flacc.* 4). Negative examples tend to identify nameless groups, e.g., *Deus* 63; *Ebr.* 25; *Decal.* 110; *Praem.* 83. See Martens 2003: 71–73 for how Philo relates universal human nature with specific human natures.

[85] For examples, see below in correlation to Philonic passages. On the triad in philosophy and how Philo relates to those traditions, see Zeller 1990: 83–86; Völker 1938: 154–55; Wolfson 1947: 2.196–98.

achieves perfection especially through 'their' component.[86] Sometimes the three means are interdependent (*Abr.* 53; *Praem.* 64–65).[87] Φύσις, defined as intrinsic character, provides the base on which instruction and practice build.[88] It implicitly holds the lowest rank, since it must be improved upon in order to progress.[89] At other times, φύσις is set over against instruction and practice and represents the consummation of virtue, the highest way to perfection. Such texts entail the independence of the triad members, with each potentially self-sufficient.[90] Usually, in those cases, φύσις holds the highest rank and represents the best way to perfection.[91]

How does Philo define φύσις in those passages where it represents the best way to perfection? It still denotes the essential character of Isaac (or the Isaac soul-type). Yet in contrast to *Mut.* 211, where the φύσις of an individual is like smooth, impressionable wax,[92] in *Somn.* 1.162 it describes the soul 'good and perfect from the outset'. How does φύσις acquire this higher ability? Philo exploits the term's semantic range and polyvalence and makes φύσις more than just human nature – it has a divine element as well, which enables it to surpass instruction and practice. In this vein, Philo sets out three potential sources from which a person acquires perfect virtue: from one's self, from

---

[86] The precise allegory changes. The patriarchs may represent the virtue gained by these three means (*Abr.* 54), the types of souls that rely on these means (52), or the means themselves (*Ios.* 1). On Philo's treatment of the patriarchs, see Böhm 2005, as well as Völker 1938: 154–239; Zeller 1990: 83–99; Satlow 2008: 508–11.

[87] So Xenophon, *Mem.* 3.9.1–3; Aristotle, *Eth. nic.* 1099b, 1103a; Ps.-Plutarch, *Mor.* 2ab; Alcinous, *Did.* 28.4.

[88] *Mut.* 210–13; *Mos.* 2.66; *Decal.* 59; *Spec.* 2.21; *Legat.* 320. Note, however, these passages mostly refer to the triad in an axiomatic fashion, without the allegory of the patriarchs.

[89] As is clearly the case for Aristotle, who also speaks of universal human nature, rather than specific natures (*Pol.* 1332ab; Zeller 1990: 85). In *Somn.* 1.169, however, φύσις is simultaneously foundational and highest in value. Völker 1938: 156 overlooks this text and, therefore, too rigidly separates passages where φύσις is the foundation and those where it is the consummation of virtue. Cf. *Leg.* 3.113 where the inverse relationship is true for pleasure, which is both the foundational vice and the worst of them all.

[90] Völker 1938: 158. On such independence, *Somn.* 1.167–68; *Praem.* 27; elsewhere, Plato, *Meno* 70a; *SVF* 1.567; 3.223. Bréhier 1925: 309 lays too much stress on the contradiction between independence or interdependence. Zeller 1990: 85 is right that Philo takes over different school traditions and is not entirely concerned to reconcile them. See the similar point by Daubercies 1995: 187–88 with respect to Philo's varying definitions of virtue.

[91] E.g., see where Philo uses the preeminence of φύσις to solve exegetical conundrums in the Pentateuch: *Congr.* 34–38; *Mut.* 88; *Somn.* 1.160–72. Witmer 2008: 45 recognises this exegetical function but not that such solutions come precisely through the elevation of φύσις. Elsewhere, φύσις ranks above just instruction (*Leg.* 3.135; *Sacr.* 78; *Mut.* 101–102) or just practice (*Migr.* 26–27, 33; *Fug.* 43).

[92] Cf. the image's Platonic roots (*Theaet.* 191cd) and Philo's usage of the imagery elsewhere (*Deus* 43; *Her.* 181).

'nature' or from God. *Fuga* 166–72 puts the three sources side-by-side: among those who 'do not seek yet find' is included every self-learned and self-taught sage (πᾶς αὐτομαθὴς καὶ αὐτοδίδακτος σοφός; 166).[93] Philo explains, though, that 'self-learned' actually means God and φύσις do the teaching.[94] As evidence, he refers to how plants in the jubilee year grow of their own accord, 'by nature' (φύσεως; Lev 25:11), which means that they do not require human attention, but in reality God grows them (*Fug*. 170). Likewise, the culmination of learning takes place by the φύσις of the student and by 'God alone, the best nature' (ὁ θεὸς μόνος, ἡ ἀρίστη φύσις; AT 172).[95] Hence to be self-learned or self-taught is to ascribe that learning simultaneously to φύσις and to God.[96]

In *Fug*. 166–72 Philo exploits the semantic range of φύσις so that the definition of essential character includes a direct divine endowment. Multiple passages show this overlap between the self, φύσις and God in the pursuit of virtue, as Figure 5.1 shows.

Figure 5.1 Self, Nature and God as Means to Virtue and Knowledge

Text	Self	Nature	God	Example
Sacr. 6–7	Self-learnt knowledge		Pupil of God	Isaac
Sacr. 79	Self-taught wisdom		God causes shoots to grow	
Deus 92–93		Richly blessed by nature	Delivers wisdom without toil	Jacob
Congr. 36	Self-learnt kind		Rains down good	Isaac
Fug. 166–72	Self-learnt and self-taught	Beautiful by nature; comes by nature at its best	Wisdom from heaven; God delivers; he alone produces completion of learning	Isaac
Mut. 88	Self-taught, self-learnt kind	Made by nature not diligence		Isaac
Mut. 255–56	Self-learnt kind		Brings this kind into being	Isaac
Somn. 1.160	Self-heard, self-taught, self-learnt	Knowledge gained by nature		Isaac

[93] On this passage, see Witmer 2008: 47–49.

[94] Plutarch, *Mor*. 973c–e; 991e–92a makes the same equation of self-taught and φύσις.

[95] PLCL mistakenly translates φύσις to refer to God, rather than his essential character.

[96] Cf. the comments of Borgen 1965: 119 on *Mut*. 253–63: Philo 'understands by nature God and his activity, so that the "selftaught" by "nature" means the one who is the object of divine grace'.

Text	Self	Nature	God	Example
Abr. 6	Self-heard, self-learnt	Eager to follow nature		Patriarchs
Abr. 16	Received self-learnt hope	Hope from law written by nature		
Praem. 27	Self-heard, self-learnt virtue	Gifted by nature		Isaac

This table highlights two important points. First, every passage except *Fug.* 166–72 includes only two of the categories, not all three. Second, we should note in what combinations those categories appear. The self is virtually always the middle term, linked either to φύσις or God, so that to learn from one's self is to learn by 'nature' or from God. The latter two, however, are rarely connected directly. Hence, conceptually φύσις and God are equivalent means for attaining virtue, but Philo is reticent to make that link explicit in the text.[97]

This set of passages confirms this special kind of φύσις bears a two-sided definition: it stands for the intrinsic character of the Isaac-soul and the operations of God in that soul. Thus Philo places natural endowment and divine inspiration under φύσις.[98] God imparts virtue, even if phenomenologically it appears to come entirely naturally from within a person. The semantic range of φύσις allows Philo to hold the two sides together, a fact not always duly recognised. Émile Bréhier spoke of the sage by nature receiving wisdom from outside, with Philo putting that which cannot be acquired by the self at the centre of the moral life.[99] These claims are true to a point, but they overplay the divine dimension by failing to allow for how Philo defines φύσις as the intrinsic character of the human agent. The ethical status for φύσις as intrinsic character is, therefore, very positive in such cases, since it effortlessly leads a person to perfection, because God works through it.

D. Ethical Status of 'Essential Character' Definition

The key ethical implications from φύσις as essential character relate to its usage for human beings. Just as for φύσις as creative power, 'nature' is the norm worthy of adherence.[100] There is often an underlying movement from 'is' to 'ought' in Philo's identification of the φύσις of a thing.[101] Accordingly, φύσις has a teleological sense. The presumption is that because something has

---

[97] See p.148.

[98] Montefiore 1895: 517. My thanks to Stephen Witmer for this reference.

[99] Bréhier 1925: 277.

[100] With the caveat that the subject of φύσις must be considered.

[101] In contrast, John Finnis's contemporary natural law theory disavows moving from 'is' to 'ought' (Finnis 2002: 4); see the exchange between Veatch 1981 and Finnis 1981.

a particular φύσις, then that arrangement is right and should be followed.[102] Thus moral qualities that belong or conform to human nature, like kindness (*Praem.* 92) or goodness (*Mut.* 197), are held up as imperatives, for to do otherwise is to depart from what human nature should be. The use of the dative φύσει or κατὰ φύσιν matches this ethical thrust. For something to be 'by nature' means it agrees with the specific φύσις in view as well as the wider, cosmic order of which it is a part.[103] In summary, φύσις as essential character reveals not only what is so but thereby what should be so.

V. Φύσις as Universal Nature

A. Polyvalence of Φύσις when Denoting Universal Nature

Under φύσις as essential character, we briefly examined Philo's references to the nature of the universe, which equate semantically to the universe. Such texts also provide a transition to φύσις itself denoting the sensible realm. For example, the phrase τὴν τῶν ὅλων φύσιν in *Somn.* 2.194 is ambiguous. It could mean 'the nature of the Whole' or 'the whole nature'.[104] Both possibilities denote the sensible world, but φύσις refers in the former to the essential character of the world, while in the latter to the world itself.[105] From there, it is only a small step to use φύσις alone for the world.[106] Perhaps the jump was based on the idea that the aggregate of natures which comprise the physical world have a unity by virtue of Nature, the creative power.[107] It is then logical to conceive of all those individual natures as one collective nature. Such a rationale would again show the interconnectedness of the definitions of φύσις.

[102] Moreover, if God operates through 'nature', that would reinforce why φύσις is granted this default position. See below, p.148.

[103] And conversely, παρὰ φύσιν indicates that an action violates both human and cosmic nature. Things may be opposite 'by nature' (*Sobr.* 67; *Abr.* 256), or good (*Migr.* 156; *Decal.* 6), or free (*Spec.* 4.14), or have authority (*Mos.* 2.211). On the other side, something can be 'by nature' for the individual but not in line with the cosmic order: e.g., savagery's craving for slaughter 'by nature' (*Sobr.* 46). Cf., e.g., *Leg.* 2.47; *Agr.* 37; *Virt.* 36; *Flacc.* 59.

[104] The latter, adopted by PLCL, presumably requires reading τῶν ὅλων as a reverse genitive of quality (or attributed genitive). See BDF §165; Wallace 1996: 89–91.

[105] Cf. Aristotle, *Metaph.* 1074b3 (τὴν ὅλην φύσιν); *Cael.* 268b11 (τῆς τοῦ παντὸς φύσεως).

[106] It is not a necessary step: Aristotle spoke of τὴν ὅλην φύσιν (*Metaph.* 1074b3), but never of φύσις alone for the sensible realm. Such usage, though, becomes well-attested later on: e.g., Cicero, *Nat. d.* 2.29, 77, 81–82.

[107] On this idea, cf. Collingwood 1945: 43–45.

Philo uses φύσις to denote universal nature around 90 times.[108] Typically, it emphasises the constituent elements which make up the sensible world. What is in bloom now is always better than what bloomed in the past, whether animals, plants, fruits, or anything else in nature (ἄλλο' τι τῶν ἐν τῇ φύσει; *Opif.* 140).[109] Similarly, the high priest, in his cosmologically representative role, prays for the whole human race and 'the parts of nature (ὑπὲρ τῶν τῆς φύσεως μερῶν), earth, water, air, fire' (*Spec.* 1.97).[110] This general feature is reinforced by frequent references to the 'things of nature' (τῶν φύσεως πραγμάτων), or how it is always contemplation of the 'things' of nature (τῶν τῆς φύσεως; *Spec.* 1.176), never of φύσις as a singular entity.[111] This predilection for the parts of nature indicates that φύσις as sensible realm includes φύσις as creative power. *Natura quae creatur* incorporates *natura qua creatur*. This is confirmed by *Prob.* 74, where Philo describes the Magi's research into the 'works of nature' (τὰ φύσεως ἔργα). In the first instance they study universal nature, but in doing so they examine what Nature has wrought.

Nature as 'sensible realm' may also include the definition of the principle of order which directs that realm.[112] *De Abrahamo* 58–61 illustrates this interconnectedness. Philo assures his readers that anyone who knows not only the things in nature (τἄλλα ὅσα ἐν τῇ φύσει) but also sees their Father and Maker advances to the heights of *eudaimonia* (58).[113] The plural substantive and prepositional phrase suggest φύσις as concrete creation. Philo then turns to Abraham who sought to obey God's verbal commands and those made known by 'nature' through clearer signs (τὰς διὰ τῆς φύσεως τρανοτέροις σημείοις δηλουμένας), which are apprehended by sight (60). The genitival φύσεως, object of διά and subject of the participle δηλουμένας, implies a definition of 'the principle of order and creation in the universe', yet the fact that these commands are 'made known' to sight also involves the sensible realm. Finally, the need for verbal commands is relativised for those who can learn

---

[108] This is a high enough frequency that it is curious that Martens 2003 refers to it, at best, obliquely (e.g., 73) and moves straight from 'essential character' to 'order of the cosmos'.

[109] Things in nature: e.g., *Opif.* 53; *Migr.* 46; *Her.* 235; *Congr.* 52; *Mut.* 231; *Mos.* 2.180; *Virt.* 117; *Contempl.* 54.

[110] On the parts/elements of nature, e.g., *Somn.* 2.122; *Mos.* 2.37; *Prob.* 43. On the κόσμος in worship, see p.84.

[111] Πραγμάτων of nature: *Leg.* 3.12; *Her.* 213, 246, 279; *Fug.* 122; *Somn.* 1.53, 172; 2.44, 186; *Prob.* 50 (elided), *Contempl.* 64. Simple neuter plural substantive: *Her.* 152; *Mut.* 86; *Decal.* 100; *Aet.* 130; *QE isf* 4. On contemplation of φύσις, see n.115.

[112] This makes sense, given that φύσις as creative power is already present in the 'sensible realm' definition, and properly speaking, creating and ordering are two aspects of the same definition.

[113] On the *telos* according to Philo, see p.156.

from 'the order in nature and the constitution enjoyed by the world-city' (τὴν ἐν τῇ φύσει τάξιν καὶ τὴν . . . πολιτείαν, ᾗ χρῆται ὁ κόσμος; 61). The primary definition for φύσις is ambiguous: the prepositional phrase suggests sensible realm, but according to *Opif.* 143, the constitution of the κόσμος is 'the right reason of nature' (ὁ τῆς φύσεως ὀρθὸς λόγος), that is, cosmic order. Thus in this last instance both definitions vie equally. Using Stoic categories adapted to a Jewish sensibility, Philo idealises the sage who can obey God on the basis of his commands revealed in and by φύσις. Definitions of 'sensible realm' and 'cosmic order' may be inherently inseparable. The same holds true for the 'contemplation of nature'. People ponder the things of φύσις in order to perceive their beauty and order, and through that, ultimately, God and his handiwork (through *natura creatrix*). Thus φύσις as sensible realm looks beyond that realm to incorporate the power which creates and orders that realm on behalf of God.

B. God's Relation to Universal Nature

Although prior definitions have hinted at the close connection between God and φύσις, when φύσις denotes the sensible realm, Philo distinguishes it from God. Like Aristotle (*Metaph.* 995a17), he confines φύσις to the three dimensions of sensible reality (*Decal.* 24–25). Consequently, God abides outside of material nature (*Migr.* 192) and sovereignly rules over its parts (*Prob.* 43), which are at his disposal to command (*Mos.* 2.63).[114] All the same, it is striking how few times Philo clearly distinguishes between φύσις and God, especially in comparison to his usage of κόσμος or γένεσις. Particularly infrequent are texts which describe God as creating φύσις (i.e., sensible realm). He is called its sovereign but rarely its maker. Perhaps we should attribute this to the polyvalence of φύσις. Because the idea of the creative, governing principle is so often present when Philo employs φύσις for universal nature, he is reluctant to name God as creator, especially given the ways that φύσις serves as divine agent. So while on the one hand, Philo clearly portrays God as transcendent and distinct from universal nature, nevertheless he obscures matters more than one might expect.

Nonetheless, the entailment of distinguishing between God and universal nature is the latter now can reveal the former. It is the same dynamic we saw in Chapter 4 – neither κόσμος nor φύσις are exactly the same as God, yet they are closely connected to him, so they can disclose his existence. Reason examines 'the whole nature' (ἡ ὅλη φύσις) and concludes it did not come into exis-

[114] Cf. *Abr.* 58, and God as distinguished from the essential character (φύσις) of the All (*Somn.* 1.241) or the Whole (*Somn.* 2.194; *Mut.* 23).

tence on its own (*QG* 2.34a).[115] To see the concrete physical realm, but even more, the creative, organising principle behind it, is to become wise to how God works in the world through φύσις, and thus ultimately to know him.

C. Finding Φύσις (Universal Nature) in Scripture

1. Introduction

Philo forges a close connection between φύσις, defined as the sensible realm (with the creative, ordering power behind it), and Scripture, so that to study the biblical text rightly is to discover Nature. Scripture discloses the true picture of the world and how it operates. This connection bestows a positive status on φύσις, since biblical study is such a high calling for Philo. This connection comes from three areas: the hidden φυσιολογία uncovered through allegory, the polyvalence of φύσις where it simultaneously denotes Scripture's essential character and the sensible realm, and the motif that Sabbath synagogue attendance consists of contemplation of φύσις (or the κόσμος). With the last area, we will also address the arguments of Valentin Nikiprowetzky that such language is not literal but figurative.

2. Scripture's Hidden Φυσιολογία

Chapter 4 briefly touched on the φύσις-cognate, φυσιολογία, which means study of the sensible world.[116] Such study rightly leads to knowledge of God (*Her.* 98), but the person who reaches the cusp of perfection, like Abraham, must eventually transcend it (*Mut.* 76). Philo sometimes uses φυσιολογία to refer to teaching about the sensible world, hidden by Moses in Scripture, which a careful, knowledgeable interpreter can discover by means of allegory. Φυσιολογία is Scripture's hidden content, and allegory the means of finding it.[117] For example, Jacob puts a stone under his head in order to sleep at Bethel (Gen 28:11). That elicits admiration for its literal interpretation, which commends toil and endurance, and for how it reveals the lawgiver's 'hidden treatment and *physiologia*' (τὴν ἐν ὑπονοίαις πραγματείαν καὶ φυσιολογίαν

---

[115] Contemplation of 'things' of nature (overlapping with the categories in n.111): *Her.* 246, 279; *Mos.* 2.216; *Decal.* 98; *Spec.* 1.176; 2.45; *Prob.* 63; *Contempl.* 64, 90. Although Philo never relativises contemplation of φύσις language as he did with κόσμος, the difference is probably not significant, not least because he does relativise the cognate φυσιολογία at *Cher.* 7 and *Mut.* 76; see p.89.

[116] See p.88 n.87.

[117] When Di Mattei 2006: 29 identifies scholars who have taken φυσιολογία as a technical term for allegory, on some he is clearly right (e.g. Harl 1966: 13 n.1), but his criticism misreads Nikiprowetzky (see 1965: 152; 1977: 113 n.63) and Goulet 1987: 34.

αὐτοῦ; AT; *Somn* 1.120). The hidden treatment and φυσιολογία are parallel and both belong to Moses. The specific φυσιολογία concerns the ladder in Jacob's vision, which allegorically is the air, the home of incorporeal souls (1.133–45). Thus Moses encoded teaching about the universe within the biblical narrative of Jacob's flight from Esau.

Often, it might appear that φυσιολογία and allegory are synonymous, like when Philo speaks of Moses omitting something so that those uninitiated in φυσιολογία will not go astray (e.g., *Leg.* 1.60). But with φυσιολογία referring to study of the world elsewhere in Philo and other authors,[118] it is better to distinguish between the terms.[119] These texts indicate that Philo regards the study of the sensible world as something Moses wrote cryptically in the biblical text; the interpreter's task is to uncover it through allegory. Properly understood, Scripture is a source of knowledge about the sensible world.[120]

3. The Φύσις (Essential Character) of Scripture and Φύσις (Universal Nature)

Philo sometimes claims not just that Scripture contains teaching about the sensible world but that its very subject-matter is φύσις. He plays on the word's polyvalence, where φύσις in the first instance is Scripture's essential character, but also includes the sensible world (and its organising principle). This double meaning has sometimes eluded scholars.[121] At *Somn.* 1.160–72 Philo resolves allegorically two exegetical difficulties that arise from how God addresses Jacob at Gen 28:13. What is important for our purposes are the side comments Philo makes to emphasise the deeper, allegorical level. Upon resolving the first problem, Philo lauds the Law for enabling us 'to judge of the real nature of things, and not merely rely on the literal sense' (ὡς φυσιο-

[118] See the references at Di Mattei 2006: 19–21.

[119] Other 'hermeneutical' usage of φυσιολογία: *Cher.* 87; *Mut.* 62; *Prov.* 2.40 (with reference to Homer and Hesiod rather than Moses).

[120] The same distinction holds for Philo's use of the adverb φυσικῶς: it does not signify allegory but rather the 'physical' rationale behind the biblical depiction (so again, Di Mattei 2006: 14–19; cf. Sedley 1997: 337; *contra* e.g., Pépin 1967: 132 n.1; Koester 1974: 269 n.188). Philo writes that 'we must examine the more philosophical aspect (τὴν φυσικωτέραν θεωρίαν) through allegory' (*QG* 4.241; cf. 4.89). Moreover, φυσικῶς relates to physics rather than φύσις – it encompasses the latter but in Philo's time also incorporates topics like God's existence and operations of the soul (cf. *Prob.* 80; *Somn.* 1.184; DL 7.132–33; *contra* Goulet 1987: 36, 544–45; Pépin 1976: 240–41). Typical occurrences of φυσικῶς include *Leg.* 1.25, 100; *Fug.* 194; *QG* 4.8; in Aristobulus, see 8.10.2.

[121] Both Di Mattei 2006: 8 and Nikiprowetzky 1977: 102–03 miss this polyvalence. Di Mattei sees only the intrinsic character of Scripture, the 'reality' of the thing, as he puts it, while Nikiprowetzky does not acknowledge this definition as the first and baseline meaning in these instances. Similarly, Koester 1974: 269 n.185 misses 'essential character' for *Contempl.* 28 and moves straight to 'sensible world'.

γνωμονεῖν καὶ μὴ μόνον τοῖς ῥητοῖς ἐφορμεῖν; 1.164). This φύσις-cognate speaks to the essential character of the sacred text but does not say anything about universal nature. After solving the second difficulty, Philo again addresses his readers and asks, 'Do you by this time perceive that the discourse before us is not about mortal men, but, as already stated, about the facts of nature?' (ὡς ἐλέχθη, περὶ φύσεως πραγμάτων; 1.172). Steven Di Mattei argues that 'Philo's use of the term φύσις [here] hardly merits that we equate it with Physis or Nature, the object of physiological study'.[122] But Philo's use of πρᾶγμα as head-noun and φύσις in the genitive says otherwise. This construction always denotes the sensible world, never just the essential character of a thing.[123] For example, Philo acclaims Moses as the interpreter of the things of nature (ὁ τῶν τῆς φύσεως ἑρμηνεὺς πραγμάτων) for writing in Gen 15:10 that things which exist in division must be set opposite each other (*Her.* 213).[124] There is no compelling reason to interpret περὶ φύσεως πραγμάτων in *Somn.* 1.172 in any way other than 'sensible world'. Philo, therefore, says the biblical narrative is not really about human beings but universal nature.

This interpretation of §172, however, leads us to re-visit our prior assessment of §164, because Philo claims he already made this point (ἐλέχθη). The logical place to find that prior claim is at §164. If φύσις in §172 refers to the sensible world, and Philo claims to have made this point already, then there must be a second layer of meaning for φυσιογνωμονεῖν at §164. The primary referent remains the essential character of Scripture, but universal nature is also in view. So just as Scripture has two levels of meaning, literal and allegorical, its true character has two levels, its own 'nature' and 'nature' as the sensible world. Scripture contains hidden truths about *natura quae creatur*, which reflect the essential character of Scripture itself.

4. Contemplation of Φύσις Literally and Figuratively in the Synagogue

The most well-known evidence that biblical interpretation uncovers universal nature are those apologetic passages where Philo describes religious instruction in terms of the contemplation of φύσις (or κόσμος).[125] The Sabbath is for philosophy with time for contemplating the things of nature (φιλοσοφοῦντας

---

[122] Di Mattei 2006: 8.

[123] See the references at n.111.

[124] The fact that the πρᾶγμα-φύσις construction is tied to the sensible creation and the subject-matter of Scripture contradicts the claim by Goulet 1987: 36 that references to φύσις and Scripture signify a concept of φύσις far removed from the sensible creation.

[125] On this motif with κόσμος, see p.86; on φύσις, see p.121. See p.24 for Philo's understanding of philosophy.

καὶ θεωρίαις μὲν τῶν τῆς φυσέως σχολάζοντας) and meditating on its lessons (ἐπιθεωρῇς τὰ φυσέως; *Decal.* 98, 100).[126] Valentin Nikiprowetzky, however, has objected to taking such language literally. Observation of natural realities, he argues, is meant either figuratively or historically, and in neither case does Philo call for readers to study the physical world.[127] Philo gives an impressive sheen to the study of Mosaic Law with this cosmological contemplation language. No one, however, could expect the entire community to engage in real scientific investigation – such meditation is actually a midrashic or homiletic activity tied particularly to the interpretation of the first chapters of Genesis.[128] Elsewhere such language describes historically the origins of philosophy or the patriarchs and Israel as a nation (e.g., *Opif.* 54–61; *Abr.* 161–64).[129] In so far as these texts elicit a response from Philo's readers, it is for them to devote themselves to Scripture, the truest meaning of φιλοσοφία.[130] Given the figurative or historical intent of this contemplation language, Nikiprowetzky concludes, therefore, that this terminology should not be interpreted as a call for Philo's readers to engage in study of the sensible realm.

Nikiprowetzky is certainly right that Philo's cosmological language is often figurative and that his main focus is for readers to study Scripture rather than the starry skies above. Nevertheless, two lines of response demonstrate that Philo at points does endorse real study of the physical realm by his audience to discover truth.[131] First, Nikiprowetzky has likely constructed a false antithesis between scientific investigation and textual study. Di Mattei has pointed out that such activities need not be so different, when understood properly in their ancient context:

> Just as a student in another philosophical school might study *physiologia*, not necessarily by sitting outside for long hours contemplating the heavens, but by studying a text which purports to be a contemplation of the cosmos, such as the *Timaeus*, likewise the Jews, through their

[126] Also, *Mos.* 2.216; *Contempl.* 28–30, 64, 90.

[127] He does not consider, however, the negative figurative usage of Philo's cosmological language; see p.59.

[128] Nikiprowetzky 1965: 150.

[129] Nikiprowetzky 1977: 106–08. Cf. *Leg.* 3.99; *Congr.* 21; *Abr.* 57; *Spec.* 3.190–91; *Praem.* 41–42; *QG* 2.34.

[130] Nikiprowetzky 1977: 103, 108; idem 1965: 152; see above, p.24.

[131] There is, however, a wrong way to study the world, that is often linked to Chaldeanism, which tries to answer questions beyond human competence (*Migr.* 184; *Somn.* 1.53–54; *Praem.* 58) and is actually 'opinion' (δοξά) rather than knowledge (e.g., *Gig.* 62; *Her.* 289; *Abr.* 70). On Chaldeanism for Philo, see p.88 n.86; on Philo's Platonic epistemological skepticism about the sensible world, cf. Runia 1986: 122–30; Nikiprowetzky 1977: 183–91, 208–14. The right methodology does not bore down to the same level of detail but focuses instead on the philosophical entailments, especially in ethics.

reading and studying of Moses' Scripture are also studying *physiologia*, the goal of which is the recognition and worship of the cosmos' Creator, the one and only God to which all philosophical schools adhere.[132]

Scientific investigation and exegesis of an ancient 'mythical' text written by the founder of the philosophical school are not mutually exclusive. A disciple of Moses, as Philo considered himself, could legitimately practice φυσιολογία through textual study, in a manner recognisable to Hellenistic philosophy. The difference would be the scope: while relatively few would sit down with the *Timaeus*, thousands of Jews gathered in synagogues to hear the Pentateuch expounded. Obviously, Philo frames things this way for apologetic purposes, but that does not mean such language is solely metaphorical. To peer into Scripture at the allegorical level is truly, in his estimation, to discover the sensible world. The first problem with Nikiprowetzky's argument, therefore, is that he distinguishes between two activities that actually are the same thing.

Paradoxically, the second problem is that Nikiprowetzky inappropriately combines two things that are actually separate. Philo sometimes does distinguish between study of the sensible realm and of Scripture so that both are valid. Nikiprowetzky relies on the Essene approach to philosophy (*Prob.* 80).[133] They reject logic altogether, from physics they cull only the existence of God and the creation of the universe (τοῦ παντός),[134] and in ethics they take guidance from the Law. Nikiprowetzky notes that their physics is precisely what Scripture covers and concludes, therefore, that it consists of allegorical interpretation of these revealed doctrines.[135] But the text does not justify this leap, for Nikiprowetzky has overlooked an implicit epistemic distinction between physics and ethics. Although the existence of God and creation of the universe are taught in Scripture, Philo does not mention that when he describes physics for the Essenes. Only for ethics does he invoke the ancestral laws (πατρίοις νόμοις); for physics he remains silent on the source of knowledge. It almost assuredly includes Scripture, but the omission leaves open other possibilities. That is reinforced by *Her.* 246–48 where Philo identifies as friends those philosophers who contemplate 'nature', even though they clearly do not study Mosaic Law. But if they conduct their investigations rightly, they should be in harmony with biblical interpretation. Philo's readers, therefore,

---

[132] Di Mattei 2006: 32.

[133] Nikiprowetzky 1965: 150–51; idem 1977: 104.

[134] Romans 1:20 appeals to these same areas, though without mentioning physics.

[135] Nikiprowetzky 1977: 104.

legitimately can reach knowledge of God and the world independently of Scripture, even if such study is generally less reliable.[136]

5. Conclusion on Scripture and Φύσις

Philo's clear testimony is that Scripture teaches about φύσις, by which he means the material world and the creative, organising power behind it. That teaching is often hidden and must be uncovered through allegory. Yet it is there and available not just to the elite, but all who gather in the synagogue every Sabbath for instruction. At times Philo joins the sensible world to the very φύσις (essential character) of Scripture. Φύσις as universal nature, therefore, holds a positive ethical status, since Moses (and God) communicated so much about it through the Bible.[137]

This union of φύσις and Scripture, though, does raise a pointed question about Philo's true estimation of both. Scripture contains a hidden φυσιολογία, and likewise to reach perfection a person must transcend and leave behind φυσιολογία. In both cases this refers to study of the sensible world. If there is this close identification, therefore, between the sensible world and Scripture, does that mean Scripture also must be transcended? Will the sage leave behind the Bible and specifically Mosaic Law?[138] Philo never addresses such a question, but even the fact that it can be asked shows how tensions within his views on the physical world can spill over to implicate other areas as well.

D. Preliminary Conclusion: Ethical Status for Φύσις as Physical World

The question of what ethical status Philo assigns φύσις when it denotes the physical world is best approached by comparing it with our other main terms, namely κόσμος and γένεσις. Examining passages where φύσις is paired with either term yields minimal fruit. When φύσις and κόσμος are in tandem, typi-

---

[136] Some texts Nikiprowetzky classifies as historical (e.g., *Leg.* 3.97–104; *Praem.* 40–46) invite readers to locate themselves in their categories and imply that the indirect knowledge of God through cosmological study is available to them too. Nikiprowetzky presumably would not say that contemplation of the sensible world in these texts means study of Mosaic Law, since that would place the Law on the lower level, and one would have to surpass the Law in order to know God directly – a point he strongly opposes: e.g., 1977: 122–23. Other texts which push beyond his historical boundary include *Abr.* 61; *Spec.* 1.32–35 (note the first-person plural); 2.44–48.

[137] Philo, of course, privileged the Pentateuch within Scripture. At *Cher.* 49 Jeremiah is depicted as a similar, though lesser, keeper of the divine mysteries, like Moses, and someone whose disciple Philo became. On Philo's 'canon', see Burkhardt 1988: 132–43; Siegert 1996: 175–76; Neudorfer 1990: 90–91.

[138] This touches on the relation of natural and Mosaic Law; see below, p.139.

cally the former is the principle of order which guides the latter.[139] On occasion, however, they both denote the sensible realm, either interchangeably,[140] or from different angles, where φύσις emphasises its plurality of parts and κόσμος the overall system (*Spec.* 2.45). For φύσις and γένεσις, the results are even smaller, since only *Opif.* 139 features them as both referring to the sensible realm,[141] and they are parallel, both connoting an entire realm or class.

Textual comparison of φύσις with κόσμος and γένεσις affords little insight, therefore, other than to confirm that Philo can use either pair in parallel. Thus a more general approach is needed. While φύσις and κόσμος can connote the same thing, typically φύσις focuses on the individual components, by consequence of *natura creatrix* in the background, and κόσμος on the overall system.[142] Order and a positive ethical status are characteristic of both.

Pairing φύσις and γένεσις, however, is a story of contrast rather than comparison. Yet interestingly, the terms have more in common than one might expect. Both include the idea of change. But the change in γένεσις is negative, usually a decline, whereas the change in φύσις is due to growth, something commendable. Moreover, both terms can be defined as the act and result of 'creation'. For γένεσις that produces a split: its definition of 'generation' was typically neutral, though with God as subject, it was positive. But that did not carry over to the definition of 'concrete creation', since it was strongly negative. But there is overlap with φύσις: its meaning of 'sensible realm' incorporates its meaning of 'creative power'. The physical world as denoted by φύσις includes the power which made it, and both are positive. Thus even the similarities between the two terms ultimately serve to highlight their differences.

Philo uses the terms differently in relation to God. Γένεσις typically is used to express creation separated from God, but the relation between God and φύσις, while complicated, clearly and positively identifies them together. Philo's usage of φύσις for the sensible realm, therefore, stands much closer to κόσμος than γένεσις. Moreover, its positive ethical status reflects its polyvalence: the sensible realm when referred to by φύσις is the result of a creative power, with possible divine overtones, that has made the world a well-ordered place. So it is to φύσις as the principle of order within the world which we now turn.

---

[139] See p.129.

[140] *Somn.* 1.157; *Abr.* 58, 61; *Mos.* 2.263. With τὸ πᾶν at *Mos.* 2.127–28.

[141] Elsewhere together, φύσις is essential character (*Leg.* 3.78; *Deus* 77; *Spec.* 2.166) or creative power (*Post.* 5).

[142] Of course, exceptions occur: *Sacr.* 97 has the constituent elements in view but sums them up as κόσμος.

Chapter 6

Philo's Positive Terminology for the Physical World: Φύσις Part Two

I. Φύσις as Cosmic Order

A. Φύσις Rules and Guides the Sensible World

Chapter 5 closed with reflections on the ethical status of φύσις when it refers to the sensible realm. Our investigation in that section and throughout the chapter glimpsed repeatedly how Philo uses φύσις to refer to the principle of order which governs the sensible world. We have distinguished for heuristic purposes between φύσις as creative power and as cosmic order, but Philo held them together as one principle. For example, Moses prohibited the breeding of an animal like the mule because its birth is contrary to 'nature' (παρὰ φύσιν; *Spec*. 3.47). 'Nature' is the creative power which normally brings animals into existence, but it is also the cosmic order which regulates life. To create is necessarily also to order a thing. Similarly, the phrase 'by nature' (φύσει; κατὰ φύσιν) encompasses both the individual essence of a thing and the cosmic order. Moreover, to contemplate 'nature' is to look at the sensible world in order to understand its order and providential design. The Stoics justified such interconnectedness on the grounds that the active principle 'is present in all things which exist and happen, and in this way uses the proper nature (τῇ οἰκείᾳ φύσει) of all existing things for the government of the all' (*SVF* 2.945; L-S 55n). Put another way, φύσις (creative power) gives each thing its φύσις (individual essence), and in turn, φύσις (cosmic order) uses those individual φύσει as the means by which it governs the universe. Philo never offers such a rationale, but it seems consistent with his practice. Thus he often builds on other definitions of φύσις to include the principle which governs and guides the sensible world.

Cosmic Nature has mastery over all (*Ios*. 28) and governs justly human and divine things (*Spec*. 2.231). Philo does not elaborate on those 'divine' (θεῖα) things, but even if it is a rhetorical flourish, it gives a sense of the heights on which cosmic Nature stands. Often, it is specifically the κόσμος – with all it encompasses – which φύσις rules. Hence, the universe and the first man lived under the same constitution (πολιτείαν), 'the right reason of nature' (ὁ τῆς φύσεως ὀρθὸς λόγος; *Opif.* 143).[1] The Stoics commonly described reason as a property of φύσις and right reason as the standard of human life, but Philo puts them together.[2] David Runia judges that was 'to emphasize that [right reason] is not confined to humans, but pervades the whole of the reality, so that a correspondence can exist between human action and universal law'.[3] Accordingly, cosmic Nature is characterised by order: the chain around Tamar's neck symbolises the orderly sequence (εἱρμόν) which marks the 'things of Nature' (τῶν τῆς φύσεως πραγμάτων; Gen 38:18; *Somn.* 2.44). Here φύσις means the creative and ruling principle and its instantiation in the sensible world.[4] Philo also communicates the rulership of φύσις by the metaphors of it as judge or king-maker.[5] Through all these expressions, in a manner consistent with Stoicism, Philo clearly attributes the order and structure of the universe to φύσις with the difference that he places God above cosmic φύσις.

B. Cosmic Order as Ethical Standard: Following Φύσις

This order of the universe is inherently ethical: the actions of φύσις in the κόσμος are always free from evil, and people should acquiesce to them (*Praem.* 34). That means φύσις as cosmic order explicitly incorporates human behaviour within its sphere.[6] There is harmony between human nature at its best and how φύσις governs the whole universe. Counting Abraham's faith as δικαιοσύνης (Gen 15:6) was an act in conformity with nature (*Her.* 95).[7] Faith, defined as trust in God to the exclusion of any trust in created being

---

[1] Also, *Opif.* 3; *Ios.* 29; *Mos.* 2.48, 209; *Spec.* 2.52, 150; 4.131; *Praem.* 34.

[2] On reason as a property of nature, see *SVF* 2.937; 3.308, 317; Cicero, *Leg.* 2.10; *Off.* 3.23; *Nat. d.* 2.87 and the insightful comments by Long 1996: 140 n.7. On right reason and ethics for the Stoics and for Philo, see p.134.

[3] Runia 2001: 341. Also *Ios.* 31; *Mos.* 1.48; *Spec.* 1.191; 2.29; *Virt.* 127; *Prob.* 62; *QE* 2.3. Although, Runia notes this phrase is only found in Philo, it probably comes from Stoic sources no longer extant. On reason more generally as a property of nature, see *Migr.* 104, *Ios.* 29, *Mos.* 2.52. Based on *Ios.* 29–31, it appears that reason and right reason were sometimes interchangeable for Philo.

[4] Also, *Aet.* 112; *Abr.* 61. Cf. p.38 on order and the act of creation.

[5] Judge: *Deus* 112; *Abr.* 38; *Decal.* 111; *Spec.* 3.136. King-maker: *Opif.* 85; *Mut.* 151; *Somn.* 2.243–44; *Ios.* 38; *Legat.* 50.

[6] Cf. *SVF* 3.4.

[7] Thus Philo obliquely touches on the debate on whether Old Testament righteousness language is primarily creational or covenantal (see, *inter alia*, respectively, Seifrid 2001–04; Ziesler 1972: 38–43, 52–69).

(γενέσει; 93), corresponds to the structure of the sensible world.[8] Elsewhere, Philo glosses the biblical promise that those who are pleasing 'to nature' (φύσει) are sons of God (Deut 13:19–14:1; *Spec.* 1.318).[9] Hence conformity to φύσις plays a role in relating to God. Likewise, the ultimate aim of φύσις as ethical standard is to facilitate relationship with God: the road according to 'nature' should culminate in the Father (τῆς κατὰ φύσιν ὁδοῦ . . . ἐπὶ τὸν πατέρα τῶν ὅλων τελευτῶσα; *QE* 2.26).[10] Such a progression shows how Philo alters this Stoic expression – φύσις is not God but rather leads to him.[11]

Amidst his multiple formulations of the ethical-religious *telos*, Philo often utilises the Stoic expression, 'the life according to nature' (τὸ ἀκολούθως τῇ φύσει ζῆν).[12] By his time, this had become a common formulation.[13] Built on a theory of development that emphasised reason as constitutive of human existence,[14] it was also understood as the virtuous life, since nature guided people to virtue (DL 7.86–87; Cicero, *Off.* 3.13). Stoics from Posidonius on frequently understood the Platonic 'assimilation to God' (*Theaet.* 176ab) and the life according to nature as equivalent expressions (Cicero, *Nat. d.* 2.153; Seneca, *Ep.* 50.47, 50).[15] This equation makes sense, for if 'nature' and God are the same thing, differing only in function (*SVF* 2.1024), it is logical for Stoics that the life according to nature is also imitation of or assimilation to God. So, 'if we live according to nature (as understood by the Stoics) we are obtaining likeness to nature or God'.[16]

In some places Philo employs the 'nature' *telos* like a normal Stoic. In *Mos.* 2.174–86 Philo depicts the Levites' complaint about Aaron being selected high priest as an attack ultimately on Moses' integrity and status as a prophet (Num 16:1–3). The Lord vindicates Moses and Aaron by causing Aaron's staff alone to bloom overnight (17:16–24 LXX). The staff bears

---

[8] On the occasional opposition of φύσις to other terms for the physical world, see p.147.

[9] Colson notes that Philo creatively combines the ending of one paragraph and the beginning of the next to construct this promise (PLCL 7.284 a).

[10] Similarly, φύσις leads Philo to the proper interpretation of Scripture (*Spec.* 1.267–73; 3.180). On φύσις as general ethical standard, cf. *Plant.* 159; *Abr.* 6; *Decal.* 150; *Spec.* 4.131.

[11] On Stoicism and God, see p.150.

[12] On the *telos* for Philo, see p.156.

[13] DL 7.87; Stobaeus, 2.75.11–16, 77.16–21; Cicero, *Fin.* 3.16–21. For a good overview, see Striker 1996: 224–31.

[14] On the theory of οἰκείωσις, see Inwood & Donini 1999: 677–82; Pembroke 1971.

[15] Theiler 1930: 106–07 ascribes the connection to Posidonius misreading *Theaet.* 176c.

[16] Rist 1962: 162.

almonds,[17] which signify perfect virtue, for just as the beginning and end, that is, the seed and fruit, are identical in a nut, so too with virtue.[18] Each virtue is both self-generated and a *telos*, since virtue itself is the aspiration of the life according to nature (2.181).[19] Philo does not tie his exegesis, however, back to the text, thus leaving readers to wonder about the actual significance of this symbolism for God's vindication of Moses and Aaron. Philo here uses the Stoic *telos* in an entirely standard way.[20]

In other places, Philo invokes 'life according to nature' but shifts its meaning into a new key, as he adapts it to his theology. Philo quotes Gen 12:4 that 'Abraham journeyed even as the Lord spoke to him' and explains:

> This is the aim (τέλος) extolled by the best philosophers, to live agreeably to nature (τὸ ἀκολούθως τῇ φύσει ζῆν); and it is attained whenever the mind, having entered on virtue's path, walks in the track of right reason and follows God, mindful of His injunctions, and always and in all places recognizing them all as valid both in action and in speech (γίνεται δέ, ὅταν ὁ νοῦς εἰς τὴν ἀρετῆς ἀτραπὸν ἐλθὼν κατ' ἴχνος ὀρθοῦ λόγου βαίνῃ καὶ ἕπηται θεῷ, τῶν προστάξεων αὐτοῦ διαμεμνημένος καὶ πάσας ἀεὶ καὶ πανταχοῦ ἔργοις τε καὶ λόγοις βεβαιούμενος; *Migr.* 128).

The logical structure sets out 'to live agreeably to nature' (τὸ ἀκολούθως τῇ φύσει ζῆν) as the main explanation for the verse and then elucidates it through multiple formulations of the *telos*: 'virtue's path', 'walking by right reason', and 'following God'. The path of virtue is the attainment of the *telos*, and there is a bond between reason and φύσις standard to Stoicism.[21] To follow God is a Pythagorean expression of the *telos*, which Philo often utilises.[22]

[17] A more precise translation of κάρυον for Num 17:8 (LSJ 881a), though for symbolic purposes, it makes no difference (more generally, Forstner 1967: 174).

[18] In *Opif.* 43–44 fruit, as both end and beginning, represents the divine course of Nature; other plant symbolism, *Leg.* 1.56–57; *QG* 4.1; *QE* 2.76. Plants and flowers were often associated with character traits or divine figures in antiquity. For the symbolic interpretation of the nut, see Forstner 1967: 173–76; more generally, de Vries 1974: 345, particularly its meaning of 'hidden wisdom'; for mythological associations of plants, Gordon 1977: 9–16; on the social and cultural meaning of flowers in the ancient Mediterranean, Goody 1993: 28–72.

[19] Note the standard Stoic connection of virtue and the life κατὰ φύσιν.

[20] *Contra* Völker 1938: 327 n.3 who sees this in relation to keeping God's commandments. Nikiprowetzky 1977: 127–28 rightly cautions that Völker over-interprets how often Philo infuses 'life according to nature' with a distinctively Jewish meaning. Other Stoic-like instances of the *telos* include *Ebr.* 34; 55; *Spec.* 4.46.

[21] See p.108.

[22] In Philo, *inter alia*, *Mut.* 45; *Abr.* 60; *Spec.* 4.187. Plato hints at a link with assimilation (*Phaedr.* 248a; *Leg.* 716bc), but later philosophers like Eudorus of Alexandria make it explicit (Stobaeus, *Ecl.* 2.49.8–18); also Plutarch, *Mor.* 550de; Iamblichus, *De vita Pythagorica liber* 137. See Dillon 1977: 122–23; Runia 2001: 343.

Viewed from this angle, the emphasis in *Migr.* 128 falls on 'life in agreement with nature', which the other expressions serve to explain.

The thematic centre of the extended passage, however, focuses on following God, chiefly understood as keeping the Mosaic Law.[23] Right after this citation, Philo hones in on the phrase 'as the Lord spoke', which he takes to indicate that the deeds of the wise do not differ from the divine words (τὰ ἔργα τοῦ σοφοῦ λόγων ἀδιαφορεῖν θείων; 129). To explain the equivalence of divine law and speech, he quotes Gen 26:5 that Abraham did all God's law. He summarises by declaring that the *telos* is to follow God (τέλος οὖν ἐστι . . . τὸ ἕπεσθαι θεῷ). He adds to that Deut 13:4 that a person should go in the steps of the Lord, which signifies not physical movement but compliance with divine ordinances (131). Finally, Philo advises his readers to cleave (κολλᾶσθαι) to God (132).[24] The primary concern, therefore, in explaining Gen 12:4 is not agreement with nature but following God through obedience to his commands. The parallelism between *Migr.* 128 and 131 is instructive. In the first, Philo expresses the *telos* as 'life according to nature', but he builds up in the second, to explaining that as following God. Rhetorically, the passage utilises the Stoic *telos* to explain obedience to divine law, rather than the other way around. Based on this movement of thought, 'life in agreement with nature' becomes an explanation or even a means by which to follow God.[25]

Other passages bear this judgment out. God made no provision in the Mosaic Law for worship of other gods, because he wished to lead people to himself, 'so that following nature (ἑπόμενον τῇ φύσει) they might win the best of goals, knowledge of Him that truly IS' (*Decal.* 81). The end goal is knowledge of God; the path to reach that destination is to follow φύσις. Nature, therefore, functions as the means by which to attain such knowledge, and as with *Migr.* 128–31, the notion of obedience to divine law is invoked as well.[26]

The conclusion of *Quod omnis probus liber sit* at first looks like a standard repetition of the Stoic formula, even featuring a rare reference by name to the school's founder Zeno. Souls that receive first the encyclia and then philosophy will reach the *telos* 'which Zeno, or rather an oracle higher than Zeno, bids us seek, a life led agreeably to nature' (τὸ ἀκολούθως τῇ φύσει ζῆν; *Prob.*

---

[23] On 'follow God' as obedience to his commands, see *Migr.* 143; *Decal.* 100; *Praem.* 98; Nikiprowetzky 1977: 128.

[24] Böhm 2005: 275.

[25] Cf. Völker 1938: 327; Nikiprowetzky 1977: 128; *pace* Helleman 1990: 60 who sees the flow of thought in what we have called the logical structure. From a synthetic point of view, though, she regards the Stoic *telos* as a different stage in assimilation (59).

[26] Nikiprowetzky 1977: 128 implies that the signification of following nature as following God applies only in cases of the 'unwritten Law'. Here, however, clearly the written Mosaic code is in view.

160). Two larger contextual factors, however, point to this passage as a reinterpretation of the Stoic *telos*. First, Philo's rhetorical correction of himself, that an oracle higher than Zeno – presumably Moses – gave this maxim, puts the concept on different footing. The ultimate authority invoked is not that of Stoicism's founder but the Jewish Lawgiver. Moreover, this invocation comes on the heels of praise for philosophy, which recalls how Philo places the study of Mosaic Law at the centre of philosophy.[27] Second, this passage concludes a treatise which has found the highest exemplar of the freedom of the good man in the Essenes, who are trained for virtue by the ancestral laws (*Prob.* 80). They who study and observe the Mosaic Law best fit this *telos*. Considered in this light, the reference to life in agreement with nature means something different than what Zeno taught, for it involves giving heed to the transcendent God who revealed himself and his law at Sinai.

What is the significance of passages like *Migr.* 128–31, *Decal.* 81 and *Prob.* 160? Because Philo distinguishes the transcendent God from immanent Nature, even as he exploits their overlap, to follow nature becomes a means of following or becoming like God. Philo sets these two expressions of the *telos* in close relation without signifying exactly the same thing. John Dillon notes that what it means to live according to nature changes when God is transcendent and the soul can escape this material world.[28] Unlike in Stoicism, φύσις does not stand for the highest principle in the universe, nor does it simply provide another name for God. Philo subordinates Nature to the Existent and his Logos, so it logically holds a lesser position in a hierarchy of the ways to formulate the *telos*.[29] Strictly speaking, it is the divine agent in the sensible realm. God intends people to know him by following Nature. Thus, the life according to nature can be parallel to following God and yet the means to that end as well.[30] Philo's usage of this formulation clearly implies a high ethical status for φύσις, and it also demonstrates how he adapts what he receives philosophically to fit Jewish piety.

Rendering the cosmic order as ethical standard means operations that characterised the universe as a whole do the same for the human realm. That per-

---

[27] Cf. p.24.

[28] Dillon 1977: 148. His prior statement, that "'living in conformity with Nature" is simply "following God"' (146) inadvisably lacks nuance.

[29] *Contra* Völker 1938: 57 who says Philo indifferently interchanges assimilation and following nature. On the relation of φύσις to the Logos, see below, p.143; to God, p.148.

[30] Helleman 1990: 59 calls assimilating to nature a different stage in the process of assimilation to God. Cf. Geiger 1932: 12. *Contra* Lilla 1971: 106–07 who classifies this *telos* at the lower level of ethics by contrasting *Opif.* 143 with *Gig.* 61. He fails to read *Opif.* 143 with §144 to see that life according to nature and assimilation to God go together. He does, however, perceptively grasp the tension over how to relate to the physical world.

tains specifically to the role of reason. Stoics identified the active principle, when applied to human actions, as right reason (ὀρθὸς λόγος). It carries the force of law and offers a more exact means of explaining how to live according to 'nature' (*SVF* 3.4). We saw previously Philo's application of right reason to the cosmic order, but it predominantly serves for him as a specification of the ethical standard.[31] Right reason is 'the sole source and fountain of virtues' (*Mos.* 1.48) and commands what should be done and prohibits what should not (*Ios.* 29).[32] The moral authority of φύσις is mediated to a person through right reason which interiorises that standard.[33] The question then becomes whether the substance of right reason is the same for the Stoics and Philo. In Stoicism, only the sage had right reason (*SVF* 3.614), and it was more a matter of correct dispositions than content.[34] For Philo, right reason ultimately is linked to Mosaic Law (*Migr.* 128–31), so the rational course of life becomes equivalent to obedience to the Sinaitic legal code.[35] Yet this ethical standard – however conceived – can be defied, whether in breeding a mule which is against 'nature' (παρὰ φύσιν; *Spec.* 3.47), or in the admiration of festival-goers for debauchery, contrary to what 'nature' prompts (*Cher.* 92).[36] To invoke φύσις as ethical standard at the level of cosmic order, rather than at the level of basic, and therefore unalterable, human nature, inherently allows for its transgression. Nonetheless, in structuring and ruling the sensible world, φύσις also establishes a moral norm.

C. Place of Natural Law

Philo often specifies φύσις as cosmic order and ethical standard through the idea of 'natural law' (νόμος φύσεως).[37] Natural law is an extension of creative and cosmic Nature and calls special attention to two characteristics we have already observed: first, its rationality and order, and second, its (ethical) regulation of the cosmos and human life. This relationship is best seen in passages that refer to the concept of natural law by just φύσις. The single constitution

---

[31] Myre 1972: 223 n.61.

[32] On right reason and virtue, *Plant.* 121; *Spec.* 2.29; *Virt.* 127. 'Commanding and forbidding' is Stoic (*SVF* 3.314, 614; Cicero, *Leg.* 2.10). See Horsley 1978: 37 on connections between *Ios.* 29 and Cicero, *Resp.* 3.33.

[33] Myre 1972: 240.

[34] This is the case even without Vander Waerdt's thesis about the paradoxically non-law like origins of natural law (see n.42). On virtue as dispositional, see *SVF* 3 Diogenes 45; Annas 1993: 162; Striker 1996: 239–48.

[35] Cf. Wolfson 1947: 2.194. See above, p.132 and p.139.

[36] E.g., *Sacr.* 21; *Conf.* 68; *Mos.* 2.139; *Spec.* 2.23. Martens 2003: 77; Myre 1972: 239.

[37] This is the main, but not only, way of expressing the idea. Martens 2003: 143–44 also surveys, for example, θεσμὸς φύσεως.

and law for the κόσμος is Nature's reason (λόγος . . . φύσεως), which commands and prohibits, and if necessary, opposes positive law (*Ios.* 29–31).[38] Both the rational and regulatory character of φύσις are in view, and conceptually it is clear that φύσις is law-like. Similarly, Philo commends the patriarchs for following cosmic Nature (ἀκολουθίαν φύσεως), since they saw it as the oldest statute (πρεσβύτατον θεσμόν) – 'thus their whole life was one of happy obedience to law (ηὐνομήθησαν; *Abr.* 6).[39] Natural law, therefore, makes explicit what is already present in Philo's understanding of φύσις. But if that is the case, what is the difference between φύσις and νόμος φύσεως? Naturally, Philo never makes it explicit, but we can suggest two differences. First, most of the references to natural law are in relation to 'moral' rather than cosmic concerns.[40] Attaching νόμος to φύσις allows the notion of ethical standard to be clearer. Second, and more tentatively, natural law, as a phrase, allows Philo to describe this standard with greater specificity. So particular moral *topoi* are legitimated more frequently in terms of natural law than of 'nature'.

From where did Philo draw his notion of νόμος φύσεως? The origins of the concept and terminology are famously murky, leading to no small amount of scholarly hypotheses.[41] It seems best to conclude that although the general concept had multiple roots, its actual formulation and terminology came from Stoicism, particularly its Middle and Roman stages.[42] This development was

[38] Also, *Agr.* 43; with νόμος φύσεως, *Ebr.* 37; *Migr.* 94. Goulet 1987: 38–42 sees such texts – as over against those that depict the harmony of natural law and Mosaic Law – as evidence of Philo's uneasy, ambivalent adoption of a prior, radically allegorical exegetical tradition. On his general thesis, see Runia 1989; on this point, the problem is overstated, since Philo is contrasting *human* law with natural law, and Mosaic Law, although it has a human author (*Mos.* 2.3), is attributable to a greater, divine author (e.g., *Decal.* 15; *Mos.* 2.12–13). Cf. Winston 1988: 453; Wolfson 1947: 2.306. In contrast, Cicero opposes natural and positive law (*Leg.* 1.44; 2.11), and even though Roman law is vastly superior to all other codes (*Leg.* 3.12), it still does not match natural law (*Off.* 3.69).

[39] See *Prob.* 62 where the right reason of nature is a law. Cf. Najman 2003a: 83 on Philo's equation of natural law and right reason. Jackson-McCabe 2001: 89–95, however, focuses too much on right reason for natural law in Philo, and not enough on the more important component, φύσις.

[40] On not making this distinction for Philo, however, see p.137.

[41] Martens 2003: 13–16 surveys these options well.

[42] On these roots (e.g., Plato, *Leg.* 890d; Aristotle, *Rhet.* 1373b), see Koester 1968: 522–23; Long 2005; J. Adams 1945. On Stoic origins, see *inter alia*, Striker 1996: 209–20; Mitsis 1994: 4824–50. There is the related question whether the content of natural law for early Stoicism comprised actual rules or the inner disposition of the sage. See respectively Mitsis 2003 and Vander Waerdt 2003 for recent entries in this debate. On the change in Middle and Roman Stoicism, possibly under the influence of Antiochus of Ascalon, see Watson 1966: 69–74; Horsley 1978: 43–50; Vander Waerdt 1994: 4854–55. More specifically, on Cicero, see Watson 1971: 224–36; Van Zyl 1986.

due partly to changing social contexts for νόμος: classical thinkers thought of the separate, sometimes contradictory νόμοι of individual city-states; Hellenistic schools worked under the influence of Alexander the Great and a burgeoning sense of universality; and finally, Romans prized law as a basic thought-structure and means of running the empire.[43] This social development allowed greater ease in reconciling what were once considered antithetical notions and thereby making φύσις a universal νόμος. So it is perhaps not coincidental that the first true attestation of the terminology comes via Cicero and Philo.[44] The latter, however, worked not with Roman law, but Mosaic Law, which ultimately he extends beyond Judaism.[45]

That difference between Cicero and Philo raises the question whether the philosophical tradition is sufficient for explaining Philo's use of natural law. As we saw in Chapter 1, although most attention rightly goes to such backgrounds, one should nonetheless also note the existence of an incipient Jewish natural law tradition.[46] Philo may draw on these inchoate roots, as well as the more dominant philosophical tradition, for his view of natural law. Indeed, although Helmut Koester erroneously attributed the origins of natural law to Philo, he rightly perceived the Alexandrian's creativity in fusing cosmic φύσις with Mosaic Law.[47] Moreover, unlike Stoicism, for Philo, God gives the natural law yet remains separate from it.[48] Philo's natural law, therefore, melds philosophical and biblical traditions into something original and distinctive.

The function of natural law for Philo is to order all things rationally and thus morally, both at the cosmic and human levels. Although we may distinguish heuristically between these levels,[49] Philo likely would have rejected such bifurcation – especially if 'human' actually means 'moral'.[50] There is

---

[43] This is implicit in the analysis of Long 2005 but never brought out clearly.

[44] By comparing Philo to Cicero, Horsley 1978 demonstrated Koester's error in claiming Philo to be the originator of natural law.

[45] E.g., in Gentiles eschatologically turning to Mosaic Law (*Mos*. 2.44). Niehoff 2001: 251–52 speaks of 'an assimilation of others' to Mosaic Law rather than 'a universalization of its principles'. Cf. Borgen 1997: 141. For opposing views on eschatology in Philo, see Borgen 1992b and Mack 1991.

[46] See p.3.

[47] Koester 1968: 536, 540. For this judgment, see Runia 1986: 466 n.333 and the related point on Horsley not giving sufficient weight to this development (only 1978: 56 n.62). On φύσις and Mosaic Law, see below, p.139.

[48] Martens 2003: 86; Grant 1952: 23; Wolfson 1947: 2.180. Horsley 1978: 53 attributes too much of this distinction to Middle Platonism and not enough to Scripture.

[49] Long 2005: 413 differentiates laws of nature ('physical regularities') from natural law ('moral code'). Philo, however, like Seneca (see Long 2005: 426 n.14), conflates them.

[50] Martens 2003: 76, 85. Myre 1972: 220–21 posits one law for Philo applied in two ways, either to the natural course of things (*d'agir naturel*) or the κόσμος as city.

nothing outside the moral sphere – cosmic φύσις is inherently ethical, even when it operates 'scientifically'. Usage of νόμος φύσεως sometimes is at the general level of cosmic order (*Plant.* 132) or of ethical standard (e.g., *Post.* 185).[51] More typically, Philo invokes natural law for specific actions or commands. At the cosmic level, natural law makes sensory perception mind's handmaiden (*Mos.* 2.81) and requires God to exercise providence for what he has made (*Praem.* 42).[52] References to natural law and numbers also belong to this level (*Opif.* 13; *Spec.* 2.58).[53] Agricultural matters bridge the cosmic and human levels: Philo draws out moral implications for humankind from the work of natural law in regulating plant and animal life.[54] Cross-breeding violates natural law (*Spec.* 4.203–4; Lev 19:19), but Philo extends the principle behind this prohibition – to join only homogeneous things – to a prohibition of adultery.[55] At a specifically human level, many natural law references concern sexuality and the family, which is not surprising, given Philo's frequent usage of φύσις as creative power in human reproduction and kinship.[56] Procreation is a natural law (*Praem.* 108), but illicit sex, such as homosexuality (*Abr.* 135), or even marital sex without the possibility of reproduction (*Spec.* 3.32), violates it.[57] Because φύσις has made us, natural law also establishes standards for interpersonal conduct. Again, that begins with the family. By natural law, parents care for their offspring, just as God cares for what he has made (*Opif.* 171–72), but they do not inherit from them (*Mos.* 2.245).[58] Infanticide (*Virt.* 132; *Spec.* 3.112) and murder more generally are forbidden (*Decal.* 132). Slavery violates natural law (*Prob.* 37, 79).[59] Finally, natural law extends not just to human relations but also to human-divine relations for celebration of the Sabbath (*Mos.* 2.211) or the tithing laws (*Spec.* 1.155).

Looking more closely at the citation of these examples reveals a correspondence between frequency of usage and commentary series – the Exposi-

---

[51] Also, *Somn.* 2.174; *Spec.* 1.306; 2.170; *Aet.* 59; *QE* 2.3b.

[52] On the cosmic operation of νόμος φύσεως in Philo, see Koester 1968: 537–38. Some take 'natural law' more broadly to refer to all law-like operation in the physical world: e.g. Wolfson 1947: 1.332–43; Myre 1972: 217–29. On providence, cf. *Opif.* 171–72; *Spec.* 3.189 (following Myre 1972: 218 n.10); with φύσις alone, *Ebr.* 13.

[53] In this regard, Goodenough 1935: 52–53 overstates how a natural law of matter conditions God's creating.

[54] Contrary to contemporary natural law theorists who see moral principles as derivable only from human nature (e.g., Finnis 2002: 4).

[55] Cf. *Spec.* 3.46–48; 4.212–15; *Agr.* 31, using a variety of φύσις expressions.

[56] See p.110.

[57] On procreation, cf. *Abr.* 249; *Spec.* 2.233; *Contempl.* 59; *QE* 2.19; on homosexuality, cf. *Spec.* 3.37–38. On this procreationist sexual ethic, see above, p.111.

[58] On inheritance-law, cf. *Sobr.* 25, and with φύσις alone, *Spec.* 2.130.

[59] See p.111.

tion refers to natural law more than all the other series combined.[60] This is likely because a significant portion of the Exposition focuses on particular laws, in line with our earlier claim that natural law lends itself to greater specificity than φύσις does. It may also reflect the implied audience of the Exposition: perhaps Philo uses νόμος φύσεως to legitimate Mosaic Law to those with less familiarity with it.[61] In turn, that suggestion links with the fact that invocation of natural law seems more *ad hoc* than systematic.[62] The range of topics for which Philo utilises it appears wide but, at least on the surface, sporadic, especially in contrast to his orderly interpretation of the special laws in the Pentateuch. These reflections thus raise the question of how Philo relates natural law (or 'nature') and Mosaic Law.

D. Relation of Nature/Natural Law and Mosaic Law

1. Harmony of these Laws

The ethical standard established by φύσις finds concrete expression in Mosaic Law. Philo depicts a deep harmony between the two. By opening the Pentateuch with the story of the creation of the κόσμος, Moses implies

> that the world is in harmony with the Law, and the Law with the world (ὡς καὶ τοῦ κόσμου τῷ νόμῳ καὶ τοῦ νόμου τῷ κόσμῳ συνᾴδοντος), and that the man who observes the law is constituted thereby a loyal citizen of the world, regulating his doings by the purpose and will of Nature (πρὸς τὸ βούλημα τῆς φύσεως), in accordance with which the entire world itself also is administered (καθ' ἣν καὶ ὁ σύμπας κόσμος διοικεῖται; *Opif.* 3).

There is agreement between the κόσμος and Mosaic Law, and because φύσις directs the κόσμος, it shares in that harmony.[63] The underlying notion is likely the macrocosm-microcosm link: the law that governs the world is the same in substance as that which should govern human society.[64] Philo is sure that whoever observes the Law will also follow φύσις so that the harmony between the two is matched by a harmony between one's words and deeds (*Mos.* 2.48).[65] Following 'nature' is not another step beyond obedience to the Law – they are one and the same thing.[66] This harmony extends down even to spe-

---

[60] Exposition: 29*x*; Allegory: 12*x*; Questions: 2*x*; Non-exegetical: 10*x*.

[61] On this suggestion, which comes most recently from Hindy Najman, see p.141.

[62] This is the analysis of Sterling 2003b: 79 for selections from Philo, Pseudo-Phocylides, and Josephus.

[63] Borgen 1997: 146 points to words like συνᾴδω and ἁμονία reinforcing this concord. Also, Runia 2001: 99. Long 2008: 138 points to this passage's close similarity to Chrysippus' work *On Ends* (*SVF* 3.4).

[64] E.g., *Opif.* 3; *Mos.* 2.51–52; *QE* 2.46. See above, p.80 n.37.

[65] Also, *Abr.* 5, 275; *Spec.* 2.150; *Contempl.* 2.

[66] On Philo's use of the Stoic *telos*, see p.132.

cific commands: obedience to tithe-laws is described as following the laws of nature (τοῖς τῆς φύσεως νόμοις; *Spec.* 1.155).[67] The harmony between φύσις and Mosaic Law is thus broad and deep.

Such harmony, however, is not absolute, despite the claims of some scholars.[68] In an apparently unique passage, Philo opposes Mosaic Law to the will of Nature. Numbers 35:25 requires a person who commits manslaughter to remain in a Levitical city of refuge until the death of the high priest. Philo explains that the high priest must keep himself free even from involuntary sin, and hence be separate from anyone who kills involuntarily. Such people are still somewhat excluded by the Law, even though they have faithfully served the will of cosmic Nature (τὰ μάλιστα τοῖς τῆς φύσεως ὑπερετῆσαι βουλήμασιν; *Spec.* 3.136). Someone may follow the cosmic order yet not have acted perfectly under Mosaic Law. This surprisingly overlooked passage is, I think, the only time Philo finds disagreement between φύσις and the Law. It does not outweigh the mass of evidence on the other side, yet nonetheless it undermines too grandiose a claim of absolute harmony between the two laws.

Nonetheless, the source of this harmony is God, author of Nature and Mosaic Law. All things owe their existence to him, including φύσις and its law: the right reason of 'nature' is a divine ordinance (*Opif.* 143). Moreover, all laws take God as archetype (*Spec.* 1.279). Mosaic Law in particular consists of divine oracles (*Decal.* 15), and its statutes 'are most excellent and truly come from God' (*Mos.* 2.12). Maren Niehoff suggests that cosmic Nature and Mosaic Law for Philo are 'like two sides of the same coin deriving from the same source'.[69] Indeed, prefacing the Law with the cosmogony shows 'the Father and Maker of the world was in the truest sense also its Lawgiver' (*Mos.* 2.48). The harmony between natural and Mosaic Law ultimately derives from its common divine source.[70]

2. Distinguishing between Ontological and Epistemological Priority

There has long been debate on the precise relationship for Philo between φύσις and Mosaic Law. Some scholars, many from a previous generation, see natural law as superior.[71] Philo labels Mosaic Law a copy either of the patri-

---

[67] Biblical passages referred to include Lev 6:38 (LXX); 7:21–24 (LXX); Deut 18:3.

[68] Nikiprowetzky 1977: 122, 'The Law of Moses never finds itself in conflict with the Law of Nature'.

[69] Niehoff 2001: 252.

[70] This marks another difference between Philo and contemporary theory. Philo considers Mosaic Law a copy of natural law, a position Finnis 2002: 21 disavows for natural law theory.

[71] E.g., Goodenough 1935: 88–94; Sandmel 1955: 191–98; Myre 1976.

archs' lives – who embody natural law (*Abr.* 3, 275–76) – or of the patterns in the virtuous human soul (*Mos.* 2.11).[72] Such Platonic imagery necessarily implies the intrinsic inferiority of the copy (cf. *Praem.* 29). Thus, no matter how praiseworthy the Law is, it remains 'at best a copy, and thereby inescapably secondary'.[73] More recently, however, many scholars argue for the complete equality of natural law and Mosaic Law in value and rank.[74] For divine authorship makes a perfect copy possible.[75] Hindy Najman has furthered this argument by explaining the texts which seem to elevate natural law over Mosaic Law as an apologetic that validates the authority of the latter in terms intelligible to a Hellenistic audience.[76] Thus, texts which seem to elevate natural law over Mosaic Law are substantially rhetorical and do not genuinely speak to their relation.

Both positions have their weaknesses. The superiority view drives so large a wedge between the two laws it threatens the harmony which Philo clearly depicts. Furthermore, its stress on natural law's superiority ignores Philo's emphasis on biblical exegesis. It requires that he spent the majority of his time and intellectual effort on a Law he considered inferior. On the other hand, the equality position takes seriously the harmony Philo envisions between the laws, and Najman's argument makes sense of his use of natural law in light of his implied audiences. But this view is in danger of not taking seriously numerous texts that do seem to accord some kind of priority to natural law.

Given the weaknesses of each position, perhaps another brief attempt at formulating matters is in order. Thinking in terms of either superiority or equality does not allow for sufficient precision. The relationship between natural law and Mosaic Law may be conceived along two axes, one ontological and the other epistemological.

On the first axis, natural law holds an ontological priority for Philo. First, natural law chronologically precedes Mosaic Law, and the Jewish patriarchs and pagan sages could obey God perfectly by obeying φύσις alone.[77] Obeying

---

[72] On these links, cf. Najman 2003a: 88.

[73] Sandmel 1955: 197.

[74] E.g., Nikiprowetzky 1977: 117–55; Borgen 1997: 144–48; Runia 2001: 106–08 (and idem 1986: 467 n.335).

[75] Martens 2003: 118–21 contrasts Philo with Cicero, who devalues positive Roman law over against natural law.

[76] Most fully, Najman 2003a: 70–107, but also 1999; 2003b. She points out that this apologetic motive does not exhaust Philo's intentions in appealing to natural law (1999: 57). Similarly, Kleinknecht & Gutbrod 1967: 4.1053 call attention to how this question would also have been supremely personal for Philo.

[77] Patriarchs: *Abr.* 5–6, 275–76; the first man: *Opif.* 143; pagan sages: *Prob.* 62–63. The rabbis interpreted Gen 26:5 as Abraham obeying the pre-existent Torah (*m. Qidd.* 14:6).

unwritten law is worthier than obeying written law (*Spec.* 4.150), which implies a priority – if not higher valuation – for unwritten law.[78] Second, Philo uses mimetic imagery which makes Mosaic Law a copy, albeit a perfect one (*Abr.* 3, *Mos.* 2.11), and φύσις a seal that authenticates the Law (*Mos.* 2.14). In a Platonic framework, with its consistent presupposition that the pattern is better than the copy, Philo would need to send very clear signals that labelling Mosaic Law a 'copy' did not imply the ontological priority of the original – but such signals never come. Third, Philo validates Mosaic Law in terms of Nature and never vice-versa. The Law wants to follow φύσις (*Spec.* 2.129), and in fact it always does so (*Virt.* 18–19).[79] Cosmic Nature is the prior given to which Mosaic Law must be calibrated. Clearly, an apologetic is at work here, but that explanation does not exhaust the evidence – this consistent pattern of setting φύσις as the standard to which the Law must conform inevitably prioritises Nature. These three arguments establish, not the superiority, but the ontological priority of natural law in the pursuit of God.

On the second axis the Mosaic Law has epistemological priority. The crippling problem for natural law remains its inaccessibility to all but the rare few. Because it is unwritten, it must be discerned by reason, which is beyond most peoples' abilities (*Prob.* 63), and Philo is concerned not just with the few but the many. Mosaic Law, on the other hand, presents the contents of natural law perfectly and clearly to anyone. Hence, Philo sets himself to interpreting the Pentateuch, as over against his *ad hoc* appeals to natural law. His systematic interpretation of the Law offers an epistemological leap forward. Moreover, even the patriarchs, of whose lives the Law is a copy, can only be known through Scripture (*Abr.* 61) – only special revelation can impart knowledge of those who obeyed apart from special revelation. Thus Mosaic Law transposes natural law into the human realm and renders its requirements intelligible.[80] Finally, Philo holds an eschatological vision of Gentiles turning to the Mosaic Law, which shows that natural law may be chronologically prior but not chronologically ultimate – the blueprint for this time of restoration comes from Mosaic Law, indicating a final triumph for its epistemological priority.

---

[78] *Contra* Najman 1999: 66–68; but similar to Martens 2003: 106–09. There is also the question of whether the referent of ἄγραφος νόμος is sometimes Jewish oral law or always Greek conceptions. For the former, see Wolfson 1947: 1.188–94; N. Cohen 1995: 256–77. For the latter, Heinemann 1927: 152–59; Goodenough 1935: 78–79; Sandmel 1955: 17–19; Martens 2003: 86–90, 123–24.

[79] This latter passage is echoed by Aquinas who says positive law must be directly derived from or consistent with natural law (*Summa Theologica* Ia IIae q95 a2; cf. Bix 2002: 71).

[80] Nikiprowetzky 1977: 122; Runia 2001: 107.

This proposal for how to relate φύσις and Mosaic Law should by no means obscure their harmony. The content of natural law and Mosaic Law are the same,[81] so that the ethical standard that is cosmic φύσις or natural law is known fully in Mosaic Law. The ethical status, therefore, for φύσις as cosmic order is very high, as it implicitly shares in all the praise Philo lavishes upon the Law, and it itself actually holds an ontological priority.

E. Relation of Logos and Φύσις as Creative, Cosmic Principle

Our investigation of φύσις to this point paints a picture strikingly similar in many ways to the Logos.[82] Both are close to God, act as creative principle by which all things are made, hold the sensible world together, and govern and order it. Are then the Logos and φύσις different names for the same thing?[83] Does Philo have the same referent in mind, though he uses different words, depending on the exegetical context or tradition?[84] There is no straightforward answer, and we are reminded of the axiom of Philo's repugnance for exhaustive accounts.[85] We must try to piece together an answer from indirect clues.

From the outset, we confront two difficulties. First, the Stoic background does not provide a clear account of the active principle. The Stoa sometimes speak of the Logos/reason as the active principle, equated with God, without reference to φύσις (*SVF* 2.300).[86] At other times, they set the Logos and φύσις alongside each other as ways to refer to the active principle: 'the very fate, nature and Logos in accordance with which the All is ordered is God' (*SVF* 2.945).[87] Still elsewhere reason is a property of φύσις and subordinate to it: Chrysippus believes that 'common Nature and the common reason of Nature (ἡ κοινὴ φύσις καὶ ὁ κοινὸς τῆς φύσεως λόγος) are fate and providence and Zeus' (*SVF* 2.937).[88] The Stoic legacy, therefore, already jumbles attempts to sort out how Logos and φύσις relate.

The second difficulty precedes directly from the first and concerns Philo's own somewhat muddled usage of the terms and concepts. On the one hand, as

---

[81] With the possible exception of *Spec.* 3.136; see above, p.140.

[82] Cf. p.40.

[83] Goodenough 1935: 58 and Nikiprowetzky 1977: 150 n.84 answer yes. Martens 2003: 80 n.27 is not entirely clear. There is an unfortunate tendency among scholars to focus more on 'natural law' than 'Nature' with respect to the Logos – of course, given their overlap in meaning, this is not wrong, but there is a certain logical primacy for φύσις, as well as much greater frequency, so I prefer it here to natural law.

[84] Respectively, Harl 1967: 198 and Cox 2007: 89–90.

[85] Alexandre 1967: 35.

[86] Also, *SVF* 1.102; 2.634; Calcidius 293 (L-S 44e).

[87] Translation modified from L-S 55n. Also, *SVF* 2.599, 937; Cicero, *Off.* 1.14.

[88] Also Cicero, *Nat. d.* 2.86–87; *SVF* 1.161, and see above, p.108.

we saw earlier, Philo makes right reason a property of φύσις and a divine statute (*Opif.* 143).[89] Linking right reason and φύσις in this way makes it explicit that right reason is subordinate to, or at least the manifestation of, φύσις. On the other hand, at *Agr.* 51, Philo identifies right reason as the Logos, set over the universe as God's viceroy (Exod 23:20). There is no mention of φύσις as cosmic, creative principle.[90] Based on *Opif.* 143 and *Agr.* 51, therefore, one might hypothesise that either φύσις and Logos refer to the same thing, or even that φύσις is greater.

That may be the case, but it demands further precision, namely distinguishing between the mundane and antemundane Logos (*Mos.* 2.127; *QG* 3.3), or as Roberto Radice puts it, a 'Logos in the world' and a 'Logos in itself'.[91] The mundane Logos operates in the sensible realm, akin to φύσις, while the antemundane Logos operates at the intelligible level, clearly transcending the sensible, unlike the Stoic Logos. Φύσις, however, remains tethered to that sensible realm;[92] there is virtually never a connection between Nature and the intelligible realm.[93] So any link between φύσις and the Logos must keep that distinction in mind. If φύσις can stand in for Logos in *Agr.* 51, it will be because Philo has in view the Logos in its mundane role, not in its entirety.

Moreover, it is striking that Philo never directly juxtaposes Logos and *natura creatrix*. A few times he speaks of the Logos at work in φύσις, meaning the sensible realm,[94] but he never uses them side by side to refer to a creative principle. This is in contrast to the Powers or Wisdom, which he does schematise on occasion (e.g., *Fug.* 101).[95] So the murkiness in how to relate φύσις and Logos is due in part to Philo's own imprecise terminology, the need for clear conceptual distinctions, and his reticence to relate them to one another explicitly.

---

[89] See p.130.

[90] Goodenough 1935: 57. In *Agr.* 51 φύσις means 'heavenly realm' (οὐρανοῦ φύσιν).

[91] Radice 2008: 138. This distinction with the Logos does not split it into separate entities, nor does it imply a position on its ontological status; see p.40 n.23.

[92] Di Mattei 2006: 7 n.16 makes too strong a claim for how Philo ties φύσις to the sensible world, while Goulet 1987: 36 pulls them too far apart.

[93] It can signify an intelligible φύσις as essential character (*Opif.* 35; *Sacr.* 69; *Post.* 99; *Deus* 55; *Conf.* 173; *Her.* 66; *QG isf* 2) or the intelligible realm (*Abr.* 77, 88). In this regard, Mattila 1996: 128 helpfully contrasts Wisdom, which is 'supracosmological', with Nature, whose sphere of activity remains confined to the κόσμος.

[94] *Opif.* 139; *Plant.* 9; *Her.* 235; *Mos.* 2.128.

[95] See p.40. Cox 2007: 102 identifies θεός, κύριος, Sophia, and the Forms as all belonging to the intermediary nexus that is represented overall by the Logos, but he omits φύσις from consideration. Similarly, in his discussion of the role of the powers and the Logos in creation, Radice 2008: 135–42 never mentions φύσις.

Since no single text explicitly relates φύσις as cosmic principle with Logos, we must compare them more generally. We discover that while they broadly fill the same roles, almost always we need to make distinctions. First, they both stand in close relation to God, but not in the same way. Philo clearly speaks of intimacy between God and his Logos, which is his image (*Her.* 230), his first-born (*Conf.* 63), 'with no intervening distance' (*Fug.* 101), and is even sometimes identified as God, or a second God (*QG* 2.62), although not properly so (*Somn.* 2.238–39).[96] In contrast, for Nature, the relationship is always by implication; Philo never makes the connection between God and φύσις explicit, though he does juxtapose them enough that we can speak, in a manner, of φύσις as divine.[97] Second, both participate in the act of creation, but at different levels. The Logos has a general, holistic role of giving form and shape to the κόσμος (*Leg.* 3.96) or to all the different kinds (*Conf.* 62–63). Nature tends to work at a more specific level, creating particular things, like produce (*Spec.* 2.205), or fish (*Ebr.* 182), or even lips (*Somn.* 2.262) and human kidneys (*Spec.* 1.216).[98] Comparable specifics for the Logos are lacking. Third, they both hold together and unify what exists, but at different levels. The Logos permeates all that exists and serves as the bond that holds it together (*Her.* 188).[99] But Nature is used more specifically to unify particular entities, whether as *hexis* in organisms, or simply as the φύσις of something, which gives it form and definition.[100] Finally, even in their common role of giving order and structure to what exists, φύσις has in the background the idea of the individual essence of each thing as the means by which φύσις orders the world (cf. *SVF* 2.945). The analysis, therefore, is that the Logos and φύσις have the same roles, but the Logos operates at a broader, generic level, while φύσις tends to work with particular things.

We conclude that φύσις and the Logos are closely related, but simply to equate them, as E. R. Goodenough or Valentin Nikiprowetzky do, smoothes over too many distinctions.[101] Sometimes the Logos itself acts to create and

---

[96] For these descriptions and others, *Leg.* 3.96, 207; *Conf.* 41, 62, 146–47; *Her.* 205–6; *Somn.* 1.215, 228–30; *QG* 3.34. On God and the Logos, see Cox 2007: 94–102.

[97] See p.148.

[98] This distinction, of course, is not absolute. E.g., Nature in *Opif.* 130 creates everything according to an intelligible pattern, just like the Logos does.

[99] On this function of the Logos, see above p.80.

[100] On φύσις and *hexis*, see p.110.

[101] Goodenough 1935: 58 equates Logos and natural law too glibly, proposing that whenever Philo uses Logos, one may substitute the Law of Nature. Nikiprowetzky 1977: 150 n.84 is more circumspect, yet to say, 'Nature is then exactly the Logos of God immanent in the universe', still misses the mark, because it glosses over the distinctions we have just observed. Myre 1972: 225 rightly distinguishes between 'le-tout-près-de-Dieu' and natural

give order to the sensible world (which may be denoted by φύσις), and sometimes it operates at the level of or in the guise of φύσις.[102] The Logos, unlike Nature, stretches across the intelligible and sensible worlds, and when it projects into the latter, it may do so via φύσις, which gives its activity a greater specificity. This connection is analogous to how the Logos relates to the Powers. Philo often ascribes the same function to them, but in those passages where he joins them, the Logos is the source of the Powers (*QE* 2.68) and unites them (*Cher.* 27–28; *Fug.* 101). In the same way, Logos serves as the source of φύσις. This might also be the implication of *Somn.* 1.62 that God has filled the Logos completely with the incorporeal powers, if φύσις is considered a power. Though no passage actually brings the Logos and φύσις together, this seems a reasonable hypothesis. Intriguingly, because φύσις creates and governs, theoretically it encompasses both the creative and sovereign Powers, God and Lord.[103] The overlap between all these entities, and yet their lack of connection in Philo's corpus, demonstrates both his relative lack of concern for systematisation, and perhaps the lack of integration of concepts.

F. Conclusion: Ethical Status of Φύσις as Cosmic Order

Our coverage of φύσις as cosmic order has been lengthy, due to the need to treat both the 'following nature' *telos* and natural law. What should be clear throughout, though, is the positive ethical status of φύσις. As Nature orders and guides the world, it is free from evil in all its actions, characterised by the highest measure of rationality, and actually the means by which the Logos may operate. Because right reason is shared by human beings and the κόσμος, the entire structure of the universe from top to bottom is inherently moral. Whether as φύσις or νόμος φύσεως, this cosmic order leads ultimately to virtue and knowledge of God. To the extent that this order is instantiated in those texts where φύσις refers to both cosmic order and the sensible realm (e.g., *Abr.* 58–61), the physical world, as denoted by φύσις, receives an even higher ethical status.

---

law, but does not spell out sufficiently why. Runia 2001: 341 hedges his bets and allows that Philo 'might be prepared' to identify natural law and the Logos.

[102] This language of 'at the level of' or 'in the guise of' is from Runia 1986: 450 relating God and the Logos.

[103] In this connection, it is intriguing that in *Deo* 6, on the basis of the seraphim in Isa 6:1, Philo defines the Powers in terms of 'artistic fire' (πῦρ τεχνικὸν in the Greek retroversion of Siegert 1998), the very definition the Stoics also give to φύσις (*SVF* 2.1133; 1.171) and sometimes to God (2.1027). This is the only explicit place in the Philonic corpus where the deity (here through his Powers) is defined in terms that also properly describe φύσις. See the comments at Siegert 1998: 19–20, who approaches the passage from a different angle.

In his development of φύσις as cosmic order, Philo has crafted something indebted to Stoicism and yet original. Philo would agree with the Stoic definition of φύσις as the 'rational, creative force which benevolently governs and sustains all that exists'.[104] Thus Philo speaks of φύσις from a basic Stoic orientation. But his re-definition of 'following nature' to mean obedience to Mosaic Law, with the transcendent God behind and ahead, means that Philo has established something decisively different. Just as we saw with κόσμος in Chapter 4, Philo's usage of φύσις is orientated by philosophy but re-shaped by Jewish piety. The relationship between natural law and Mosaic Law, therefore, takes on further significance as a possible measuring stick for which influence is stronger. Trumpeting the superiority of natural law over Mosaic Law could reflect greater philosophical influence, whereas holding them as exactly equal may align with the Jewish side. A nuanced interpretation that assigns different kinds of priority to the respective laws acknowledges the distinct and original product of this fusion of philosophical and biblical influences.

Finally, we consider the rare instances that seem to pit φύσις as cosmic order against other terms which denote the sensible realm. *Quis heres* 93–95 presents a test-case.[105] Philo defines faith like a two-sided coin: trust in God alone and distrust in 'created being (γενέσει), which in itself is wholly unworthy of trust' (*Her*. 93).[106] Γένεσις seems to refer to anything sensible, though perhaps with special reference to the human realm. That faith which puts no trust in anything created is then commended as 'an act of justice and conformity with nature' (ἀκόλουθον τοῦτο τῇ φύσει; 95). To distrust in created being is to conform rightly to the order of the sensible world. This text, then, means that the world, as a result of φύσις, should lead a person to trust only in God rather than anything created. This claim is unremarkable in itself for a staunch monotheist, but hints at a certain instability in Philo's usage of φύσις. On the one side is γένεσις, referring to the sensible realm, and on the other side, is φύσις. In this case φύσις does not denote the sensible realm, but the interconnectedness we observed in the term's usage, particularly between the definitions of sensible realm and cosmic order, creates some tension. Thus the ambivalence which characterises Philo's views toward the sensible world finds an interesting counterpart in the semantic range of φύσις.

---

[104] See p.108.

[105] The same arguments apply to *QG* 2.3b.

[106] Also, *Leg*. 2.89; *Mut*. 201; *Virt*. 218. On this understanding of faith, particularly for Abraham, see Böhm 2005: 162, 282–83.

II. Φύσις as Divine Metonymy

Intimations of God's involvement in the operations of φύσις have repeatedly emerged so far. What comes suddenly and freely to a person Philo ascribes alternately to Nature and to God (*Migr.* 31–35). The specially-gifted individual φύσις attains perfection, because God works through it (*Fug.* 166–72). Celebration of Nature does not tend to invoke God (*Sacr.* 75; *Det.* 125) – unlike similar passages about κόσμος – perhaps because it would be redundant: to ascribe something to φύσις is already to include God. Lastly, φύσις as the principle which creates and guides the sensible world is a more specific manifestation of the Logos. Apart from any systematic consideration, therefore, it is already clear that some kind of close connection does exist between God and φύσις.

These links between God and φύσις have led many scholars to identify Nature with God. Goodenough famously claimed,

> It is quite to be expected that Philo should speak of the Law of Nature as the regimentation of the material cosmos, a Law within the material cosmos, as well as the Law of God since Nature is God.[107]

Hans Leisegang simply says that Philo equates φύσις with the God of the Old Testament.[108] Their influence has carried on, as later writers frequently cite them en route to the slightly more circumspect conclusion that Philo sometimes identifies φύσις with God.[109]

Recently, Martens and Sharon Lea Mattila have challenged this interpretation, chiefly because it fails to account for God's transcendence. Martens approaches the debate conceptually rather than via the passages usually cited – the φύσις of God is transcendent and unknowable, and his separation from the sensible world precludes the possibility of equating him with φύσις.[110] Identifying φύσις as God is a category-mistake: it uses an immanent concept for the transcendent deity. Mattila characterises Nature in Philo as a semi-immanent organism with divine characteristics, but which is not God.[111] They overlap in function, but 'nowhere in Philo are Nature and God identified'.[112]

---

[107] Goodenough 1935: 51.

[108] Leisegang 1894–1972: 20.1 col. 1160.

[109] E.g., Koester 1968: 531–32; Nikiprowetzky 1977: 150 n.84; Runia 1986: 185 n.9; Reinhartz 1986: 341–42; Bockmuehl 2003: 108.

[110] Martens 2003: 77–80. On the untenability of saying that Philo consistently claims God's nature is unknowable, see above, p.114.

[111] Mattila 1996: 120–29.

[112] Mattila 1996: 124.

These recent challenges compel us to re-examine the text and received interpretations. Philo does employ φύσις as metonymy for God so that, in certain circumstances, it is appropriate to identify them with each other. Nature is not God, but is so associated with him as his agent in creating and ruling the universe that Philo can elide the difference between them, so that what φύσις does, God does. In one text, the comparison extends beyond functions to encompass qualities, where the same incommunicable attributes are ascribed to φύσις and God. But although they are identified, they are not equated. Φύσις may refer to God but cannot be wholly interchanged with him. This functional and qualitative identification between God and φύσις occurs in relation to creation and judgment. In turn, these patterns correspond with *natura qua creatur* and *quae regit.*

Before considering the evidence, two caveats are in order. First, the answer a person reaches is significantly shaped by their methodology. Martens and Mattila seem to approach it systematically with an implicit, underlying stress on God as He Who Is, the Existent (ὁ ὤν). When that is primary, it follows almost necessarily that God must be separate from φύσις. There is support for this view in *Spec.* 1.329, which separates God from chaotic matter by interposing the forms.[113] The counter-question is whether such methodological rigour best reflects Philo's own approach. Clearly, φύσις is not identified with God as Existent but rather at the level of his mundane Logos, as our study has already shown. But Philo does speak repeatedly of God at work in the world, and by that he means the singular deity, even if from a systematic perspective he would caution that it is the Logos or the Powers to which Scripture is referring (*Mut.* 27–31).[114] This looseness of language is in large part, no doubt, because he follows the biblical text and yet interprets it according to philosophical categories.[115] In *Opif.* 72–75, in resolving the plural of Gen 1:26 (ποιήσωμεν), Philo has God utilise intermediaries for creation, but only for humanity – just as the biblical text indicates.[116] He admits his explanation is tentative but surmises the plural is because a human being is a mixture of virtue and vice, and thus God calls in 'assistants' (cf. *Tim.* 41c). Those beings in

---

[113] Cited by Mattila 1996: 122. See, however, Wolfson 1947: 1.274–81 who classifies those forms as immanent, which if true, would eliminate the implication that God is separate in the creative act.

[114] Runia 1986: 246 n.7 This text makes 'quite clear . . . that God, in creating via his powers, still himself creates'.

[115] On the inherent difficulties for Philo in naming God, see Runia 1988b; Sterling 2007: 151–53.

[116] On this question of intermediaries, and particularly Philo's use of them for theodicy, see Runia 1986: 242–49 and Winston 1986. On God's direct creation, see e.g., *Mos.* 1.97 and Wolfson 1947: 1.281–82.

which there is only virtue, like the heavenly bodies, or those in which there is neither virtue nor vice, like the animals and plants, God himself creates. This practice means that texts which juxtapose God and φύσις should not be marginalised. For even if it is God the creative Power in view, still it is the one 'God' at work. In fact, Nikiprowetzky suspects that there is a calculated lack of rigour on Philo's part when identifying God and φύσις.[117] So our analysis will work from these categories as Philo himself presents them.

The second caveat is we must distinguish how Philo identifies God and φύσις from Stoic practice. According to Stoicism the two basic principles in the universe are God and matter, active and passive, coterminous and encompassing everything (*SVF* 2.300).[118] God animates matter, particularising each body. Thus, Stoicism is panentheistic, since God is in all things, yet strictly speaking, not equal to all things. As we saw earlier, this active principle went by many other names – Logos, fate, providence, Zeus, and φύσις – which may be set alongside each other and interchanged.[119] Sometimes this interchange is explicit, as Seneca asks, 'For what else is Nature but God and the Divine Reason that pervades the whole universe and all its parts?'[120] Elsewhere, Stoicism predicates the same thing of God and Nature: both are defined as a craftsman fire that creates methodically (*SVF* 1.171; 2.1027), and both act as *hexis* to hold the world together (DL 7.139, 148–49). At the same time, Stoics can describe God rather theistically. He is 'a living being, immortal, rational, perfect or intelligent in happiness, admitting nothing evil, taking providential care of the world and all that therein is' (*SVF* 2.1021), a description Philo could easily endorse. In the midst of such fluidity,[121] though, what remains constant is divine immanence. The active principle, whether God or φύσις, subsists in matter, without a transcendent dimension.

In contrast, under biblical and Platonic influence, Philo sharply distinguishes between God and the world, whether denoted by γένεσις, κόσμος, or even φύσις (*Migr.* 192). Even in using the language of active cause and passive object (*Opif.* 8), Philo makes clear contextually the cause's transcendence (16–25).[122] Unlike Seneca, Philo never explicitly says that Nature is God, despite Goodenough's confident claim.[123] Moreover, Philo can describe the

[117] Nikiprowetzky 1977: 151 n.84. Runia 1986: 185 n.9 in this regard remarks that 'Philo's lack of terminological rigour should always keep his reader on their toes'.

[118] On Stoic theology, see Algra 2003: esp. 165–70.

[119] See p.143.

[120] Also, Seneca, *Nat.* 2.45; Cicero, *Nat. d.* 2.33–36.

[121] The description by Algra 2003: 169 for the multiple strands of Stoic theology.

[122] See p.45 n.55. Runia 1986: 115–16 ably covers the various philosophical influences at play.

[123] Goodenough 1935: 51.

Logos under a litany of names and thereby sound Stoic, but in reality, the names all derive from Scripture, and φύσις is not included (*Conf.* 146–47). Thus while there is undoubtedly Stoic influence on Philo's identification of φύσις and God, he is clearly not Stoic, because he refrains from explicitly equating them, and God is transcendent in a way φύσις cannot be.

Philo identifies φύσις with God in relation to the act of creation rather frequently.[124] We begin with texts where the same activity is attributed to God and Nature, but the degree to which they are joined is left open.[125] God provided in advance everything living creatures need, and it was there by the 'foresight of nature' (*Praem.* 9).[126] The sheaf offering recognises God as 'the true cause of the good harvest', and in that harvest, 'what we owe to nature is all indispensable and useful' (*Spec.* 2.171–72). Nature bestows the gift of quick learning, therefore, a person should 'be a retentive steward of God's gracious gifts' (*Agr.* 168). It is clear φύσις works on behalf of God, who thus can be said to accomplish what φύσις does.

The two passages which most clearly reveal the overlap of God and Nature in creation are *Her.* 114–17 and *Sacr.* 98–101. In the former, Philo comments on the command to receive Israelite first-offerings (ἀπαρχάς) and asserts that Moses taught that 'the beginnings of things both material and immaterial are found to be by God only'. He then presents evidence for this claim by looking closely at the sensible world and arts and sciences. In each area, he emphasises not God as the beginning but Nature.

What of the first beginning of plants? Do they consist in the droppings of the seed by the farmer, or are they the invisible works of invisible *nature*? What of the generation of men and the other animals? Are not the parents as it were the accessories, while *nature* is the original, the earliest and the real cause? So again with the arts and sciences. Is not *nature* the underlying fact, the fountain or root or foundation, or whatever name you give to the beginning which precedes all else, and is not the lore of each science a superstructure built on *nature* . . . (*Her.* 115–16; emphasis added)

What does Philo conclude from the fact that all these things were begun by Nature? That 'not without reason then did the oracle dedicate "beginnings" to the great Leader, God' (117). In order to demonstrate that *God alone* is the beginning of all things, Philo constructs an impressive list of how all things owe their origin to *Nature*. The functional equivalence between God and φύσις is so close that it fosters identification between them.

---

[124] Goodenough 1935: 50–51 and Koester 1968: 531–32 explicitly note this pattern.

[125] This does not include, therefore, instances where the same activity is attributed to God and φύσις, but not in the same passage. E.g., rational speech is a gift of God (*Somn.* 1.103; *Mos.* 1.84) and of Nature (*Post.* 103; *Congr.* 17; *Her.* 302; *Somn.* 2.262; *Spec.* 2.6); cf. Cicero, *Nat. d.* 2.149; *Fin.* 2.51 on speech as Nature's gift.

[126] Cf. Koester 1974: 268 n.169.

In *Sacr.* 98–101 the identification between God and φύσις extends beyond mutual creative functions to encompass attributes too. While enumerating the gifts Nature provides to humanity, Philo characterises it as unborn, unchanging, and uncreated (ἀγένητον). Just a few lines later, he instructs his soul to separate 'all that is created, mortal, mutable, profane' from its conception of God 'the uncreated (ἀγενήτου), the unchangeable, the immortal, the holy and solely blessed'.[127] Nature is unchanging and uncreated. God is unchanging and uncreated. This juxtaposition becomes all the more significant, when we remember that for Philo, the contrast between God as uncreated and all of created reality is fundamental.[128] Mattila claims that *Sacr.* 98–100 sets up Nature as somewhat independent of the transcendent God,[129] but actually it seeks to minimise, or even undo any independence. Not only does Philo attribute the same work in creation to God and Nature, he can even describe Nature in terms of incommunicable divine attributes.

God and Nature are also sometimes identified with respect to judgment, though this pattern is not as strong as the first one.[130] For example, uncertain cases of adultery come 'before the tribunal of nature (εἰς τὸ τῆς φύσεως ἤγαγε δικαστήριον). For men can arbitrate on open matters, but God on the hidden also, since He alone can see clearly into the soul' (*Spec.* 3.52).[131] There is overlapping agency since God operates through the court of Nature in such a way that they are parallel. Furthermore, men who marry women whom they know to be barren become 'adversaries of God' and 'enemies of Nature' (*Spec.* 3.36). When Noah is declared 'well-pleasing to God', Nature bestows the epithet (*Abr.* 35). Similarly, both Nature and God appoint kings (*Mut.* 151; *Somn.* 2.243–44). The evidence from the pattern of judgment is not as strong as from the pattern of creation: the functional equivalence between Nature and God is less extensive, and there is no comparison in terms of shared qualities.

---

[127] Note too the tension between 'created' (γενητόν) on one side and implicitly φύσις on the other.

[128] For the contrast of the uncreated God and the created realm, see p.67.

[129] Mattila 1996: 122.

[130] The only reference I found was Nikiprowetzky 1977: 150 n.84, who cites *Spec.* 3.52 but does not allude to a larger pattern. Neither Martens nor Mattila acknowledge this category. For God as judge, see *Opif.* 155; *Leg.* 3.205; *Cher.* 72; *Her.* 271; *Mos.* 2.228, 238. For Nature as judge, see above, n.130.

[131] The Greek phrase is ambiguous, since δικαστήριον can mean court or judge (LSJ: 429b). If Philo makes φύσις the judge for adultery, then the parallelism to God is all the more striking, and the interchangeability between them strengthened. The context, however, seems to indicate that φύσις as δικαστήριον should be understood as court. There is overlapping agency – God renders a verdict through Nature, but the distinction between them remains.

Nonetheless, the evidence from this pattern supports identifying Nature with God.

In summary, the two main functions of φύσις as principle – to create and to govern – overlap with what God does. He uses φύσις for his purposes of creating and governing to the extent that divine activity can be attributed to what Nature does, and what Nature does is evidence that God has done it. The arguments of Martens and Mattila ultimately fail to overturn this interpretation.[132] This use of φύσις as a metonymy for God is significant, because it showcases the divine import of Nature. Nikiprowetzky finds that it endows φύσις with theological value which it never loses, even in texts that can be explained wholly by Greek philosophy and without reference to Scripture.[133] When φύσις operates as the creative and governing principle in the sensible realm, it does so on God's behalf as his agent. Because of the polyvalence of φύσις, this divine value likely extends indirectly to the results of that creative, governing work: φύσις as individual essence and as sensible realm. Both of them may carry a secondary theological weight, since God identifies with φύσις. The ethical status of φύσις reaches its heights because of this identification. A contrast with Philo's use of κόσμος may prove helpful in showing where φύσις stands. The κόσμος is the most perfect of God's works and his younger son. But φύσις functions as God's agent in the κόσμος and is drawn into the divine orbit. To utilise φύσις, therefore, is to invoke divine sanction and approval, a powerful legitimating tool.

III. Conclusion

These past two chapters have been complex. We have tried to sketch how Philo uses φύσις, by classifying it according to five main headings, and covering a fair sample of its 1,342 occurrences. It may be helpful, therefore, to recap briefly the argument, though in a different order than it was laid out originally. The one God is at work in the sensible realm through his Logos, or more specifically, through φύσις. Nature, therefore, operates as divine agent: God creates and governs specific things by means of, or in the guise of, φύσις. That overlap is so close that at times Nature may be identified with God. The result of this creating and ordering is universal nature, which still includes, in

[132] Martens simply does not engage sufficiently with the actual texts adduced here. Mattila does, and acknowledges the shared functions of Nature and God. But her preference for speaking of φύσις as organism is barely supported by the evidence – only *QG* 3.48; 4.188.

[133] Nikiprowetzky 1977: 150 n.84.

the background, the Power that brought it about and sustains it. This interconnectedness means that when φύσις denotes the sensible world (*natura quae creatur*), it has a divine stamp, the direct result of *natura qua creatur*. Universal nature is composed of individual φύσεις which share in the wider order. The standard to which individual natures and universal nature conform is expressed in the unwritten νόμος φύσεως and then in Mosaic Law, which represents Nature perfectly. The ethical status for φύσις, as Philo uses it, is therefore consistently and pervasively positive. The sensible world bears the imprint of God who made it and sustains it through φύσις, and by contemplating the things in universal nature, he may be known.

Philo has crafted something distinctive in his usage of φύσις. Throughout Chapters 5–6, we have seen how Philo is incalculably dependent on the philosophical tradition, particularly Stoicism, for his handling of φύσις. The interconnectedness of its definitions, its status as normative ethical standard, the dual role of creating and ordering the sensible world – all these facets have their direct antecedent in the Stoic understanding of φύσις. But for all that, two key differences alter the *gestalt* so that Philo charts a new path. First, God is other than φύσις. He works through it so intimately that he can be identified with it, yet he transcends it and directs its as he will. Second, the ethical standard expressed by φύσις in its regulation of the κόσμος and human life corresponds to Mosaic Law. That evinces a deep harmony between God's law for his people and the law by which he directs the universe. Philo makes the audacious claim that there is actually a written version of the νόμος φύσεως that rules all things. These modifications – motivated by Jewish faith – render Philo's usage of φύσις different from Stoicism in important ways.

The last three chapters have shown clearly the very positive ethical status bestowed upon κόσμος and φύσις. In particular, both are intimately connected with God. The κόσμος is his son and greatest handiwork, while φύσις is his agent in that κόσμος. Moreover, both of them reveal to the careful observer an order and design, which point back to the Father and Maker of all. This intimate connection to God presumably should accord a certain privilege to these terms when it comes to resolving the ambivalence in Philo's views toward the sensible realm. The fact that κόσμος and φύσις are friendly to God, in contrast to his opposition to γένεσις and γενητός, would seem to align them with a more direct or fruitful path to God. On this reading, expressions of hostility between God and either γένεσις or γενητός, are less important. We will test that assumption in Chapter 8 when we seek ways to understand Philo's ambivalence.

Chapter 7

Higher and Lower Approaches to God

I. Introduction

The lexical-semantic study of Chapters 3–6 revealed a deep divide within Philo's views on the physical world. When he denotes that world by γένεσις or γενητός, he typically sees it as alienated from and hostile to God. When he denotes it by κόσμος or φύσις, he sees it as intimately connected to God, a fitting display of his power and grace. How could one person refer to the same entity in such divergent, even contradictory, ways?

Before we can face that question, we must address a preliminary matter, which will significantly shape our ultimate answer. The lexical study has discovered hints that Philo envisioned more than one way to approach God and understand the sensible world. The very fact that his negative and positive perspectives on the world correspond largely – though not entirely – to his choice of terminology already implies multiple, perhaps equally valid, ways to understand the world. Moreover, that Philo praises the κόσμος as God's greatest masterpiece, and yet counsels that its study must be abandoned in order to reach perfection, suggests that a person's viewpoint can change, depending on where one stands with respect to God. If these pieces of evidence belong to a bigger picture, then a satisfactory resolution to the tension within Philo's views on the physical world will require taking account of the multiple levels or ways he believes that a person can approach God.

For Philo the highest *telos* of human existence is to see God and become like him. That vision may come directly from God himself or indirectly through what he has made. Philo divides humanity into idealised, hierarchical classes that characterise where one is in that pursuit and what progress is possible. This distinction between higher and lower ways to approach God will provide a crucial framework for our argument in Chapter 8 on how Philo understands the physical world.

II. *Telos* of Human Life: To See and Become Like God

At the centre of the ethical life, and indeed all of existence, is God, who has 'ontological priority' for Philo.[1] Philo's summary of the ethical life, as a paraphrase of Deut 10:12–13, relates everything to God: loving him, doing everything in order to please him, serving him whole-heartedly (*Spec.* 1.299–300). Moral activity is always oriented to the goal of knowing God.[2] To express that goal, Philo draws from philosophy and Scripture multiple, overlapping formulations of the *telos*. Like the philosophical tradition, to attain the *telos* is to reach εὐδαιμονία, or happiness, understood as human flourishing both objectively and subjectively.[3] Not surprisingly for Philo, εὐδαιμονία supremely focuses on God, knowledge of whom is 'the consummation of happiness' (τέλος εὐδαιμονίας), the very *telos* of the *telos* (*Spec.* 1.345).[4] The knowledge that chiefly constitutes εὐδαιμονία consists of the vision of God.[5] To see him represents 'the beginning and end of happiness' (*QE* 2.51) and the summit of εὐδαιμονία (*Abr.* 58). Drawing on the Platonic motif of the heavenly ascent (*Phaedr.* 246d–49e), Philo depicts the mind soaring past the heavens into the intelligible realm to gaze upon the ideas and then, urged on in a sober intoxication, up further to see God himself, until it is overwhelmed by the streams of light pouring forth from him (*Opif.* 69–71).[6] This quest to approach and see God represents the central and ultimate *telos* for Philo.[7]

The main entailment of the vision of God is assimilation to him (ὁμοίωσις θεῷ).[8] They are like two sides of the same coin: to behold God is inevitably to become like him.[9] That is partly because a person does not just see God but is

[1] Sterling 2007: 148–57.

[2] Bréhier 1925: 251; Winston 1984: 372.

[3] Long 1989: 79–80. On εὐδαιμονία broadly, see Annas 1993; for Philo, Runia 2002b.

[4] *Opif.* 172; *Post.* 185; *Spec.* 2.38; *Contempl.* 90; *QG* 4.4. Long 2003 argues that a theological focus was standard for philosophers' conception of εὐδαιμονία.

[5] For a helpful overview on this theme, see Hagner 1971.

[6] Other heavenly ascent passages include *Her.* 126–28; *Spec.* 1.37–40, 207; 2.44–46, 164–66; 3.1–6; *Praem.* 30; *Legat.* 5–6. On this motif generally, see Runia 2001: 229–33; Borgen 1993; on its Jewish character, Borgen 1997: 235–42.

[7] It can be represented as 'mystical attachment to God' (Winston 1984: 376) or migration (Nikiprowetzky 1977: 239; cf. Runia 1986: 524–26).

[8] For assimilation, see *Opif.* 144, 151–52; *Deus* 48; *Abr.* 87; *Decal.* 73, 101, 107; *Spec.* 4.186–88; *Virt.* 8, 168; *QG* 4.188. Bradshaw 1998: 489 also notes this link.

[9] On that general, conceptual link, *Legat.* 5; *Mos.* 1.158–59; *Virt.* 51; *Praem.* 114. The dynamic is derived from Plato. Betegh 2003: 280 describes the 'affinity argument' where 'the knower becomes like the known' (*Phaed.* 78b–80b; also, *Resp.* 500c). In turn, this link involves Plato's theory of vision, which unites the observer and the thing observed (*Tim.* 45b–d); cf. Scott 1991: 69; Mackie 2009: 27 n.7.

also seen *by* God, which is similarly transformative (*Somn.* 2.227).[10] These formulations quickly overlap: for example, the *telos* of εὐδαιμονία is assimilation to God (*Decal.* 73).[11] Philo at *Fug.* 63 acknowledges the Platonic origins (*Theaet.* 176ab), though anonymously, transferring the cosmological dualism into a moral one.[12] A person must flee from the earthly realm, the residence of evil things, to heaven; and such flight is to become like God, just and holy with wisdom. Thus assimilation to God entails turning away from the sensible world. Like Plato and others,[13] Philo finds virtue essential to becoming like God, both as its means and ultimate outcome.[14] Foundational to assimilation is the underlying kinship between human beings and God's Logos via the mind (*Det.* 83–84).[15] This kinship enables assimilation and makes God the archetype for human behaviour, particularly his love for the world and humanity.[16] Assimilation is certainly not the only way Philo expresses the *telos*, but it is the main way, and linked to the vision of God, it represents the aim of human life.

---

[10] Bradshaw 1998: 490.

[11] Cf. *QG* 4.147. Philo links assimilation to 'following God' (*Opif.* 144; see above, p.132); 'pleasing God' (*Opif.* 144) and 'imitation of God' (*Abr.* 143–44; *Spec.* 4.186–88; *Virt.* 165–70). *Contra* Wolfson 1947: 2.195–96, imitation and assimilation are not synonyms, but rather imitation is the means toward (Bradshaw 1998: 489) or a 'preparatory form of "assimilation"' (Helleman 1990: 58). See the Platonic hints at this relation at *Resp.* 500c.

[12] Plato, *Resp.* 613b; *Leg.* 716bc; *Tim.* 90c. On the background, see Merki 1952: 1–35. The cosmological context is properly Platonic (Betegh 2003: 281 n.19), but Merki 1952: 37 takes this moral interpretation as Philo's awkward exploitation of Plato. It should rather be seen as Philo's skillful appropriation of this motif for his own ends. There are biblical hints at assimilation in the command 'Be holy as I am holy' (Lev 11:44–45; 19:2, etc.), and in the critique that idolators become like the gods they worship (Ps 115:4–8), but except for *Spec.* 2.256, Philo does not allude to them.

[13] *Theaet.* 176ab; *Resp.* 613ab; Eudorus (Stobaeus, *Ecl.* 2.48.8–18); Plutarch, *Mor.* 550de; Alcinous, *Did.* 28.

[14] *Opif.* 144; *Ebr.* 82–83; *Mut.* 81–82; *Virt.* 8; *Legat.* 5; *QE* 2.51. Cf. Helleman 1990: 62–63. On virtue for Philo, see Daubercies 1995; Lévy 2008: 150–54.

[15] Runia 1986: 341 (also Winston 1984: 372–73; Helleman 1990: 56–57). To the Logos: *Plant.* 18–19; *Decal.* 134; to God: *Spec.* 4.123; *QG* 2.45; *QE* 2.29. This surpasses Plato's heavenly bodies (*Tim.* 47bc, 90cd) and is more like the Stoics (Cicero, *Leg.* 1.23–24, 56; *Nat. d.* 2.133, 154; Epictetus, *Diatr.* 1.3.1–3; 9.4–5; 2.8.14). On it being by virtue of reason, see *Opif.* 77; *Spec.* 4.14; and above, p.110 n.51. Whether human beings assimilate to the Logos or God is not because Philo failed to integrate this material theologically (per Merki 1952: 44) but because of the fluidity of language about God (cf. *QG* 2.62, overlooked by Merki according to Runia 1986: 343); on the problem of language about God, see above, p.114 n.72.

[16] Geiger 1932: 12–13. Lévy 2008: 148–49 recognises the significance of assimilation as an overall ethical framework for Philo.

III. Indirect versus Direct Vision of God

If the highest *telos* for human existence is to see God, how does that happen? Philo distinguishes between indirect and direct apprehension.[17] The contrast is between, on the one hand, an indirect, reasoned approach that inductively works up from the sensible world to God's existence and attributes, and on the other, a direct, supra-rational mystical vision that sees God through himself. Figure 7.1 schematises important points of comparison and contrast between the indirect and direct vision of God.

Figure 7.1 Indirect versus Direct Vision of God

	Indirect Vision	Direct Vision
How God is seen	Through God's work in world (*Leg.* 3.97–99; *Praem.* 41) Through divine creative and ruling acts (*Abr.* 122)	Through God himself: as light by light (*Praem.* 45–46) Directly from First Cause himself (*Leg.* 3.102)
Role of reason	Reasoning from order and beauty of sensible world (*Leg.* 3.97–99; *Praem.* 41–42)	Without any reasoning process (*Praem.* 43) Higher than thinking (*Abr.* 123)
What is seen	Creative and sovereign powers (*Abr.* 121) Artificer (*Leg.* 3.99, 102)	One who IS (*Abr.* 122) Logos, Uncreated One, First Cause (*Leg.* 3.100–101)
Certainty of vision	Shadows (*Leg.* 3.102) Amounts to a happy guess (*Praem.* 46)	Clear vision (*Leg.* 3.102)
Type of person	Not yet initiated into highest mysteries (*Abr.* 122)	Perfect, cleansed, initiated into great mysteries (*Leg.* 3.100)
Representatives	Bezalel (*Leg.* 3.102)	Moses (*Leg.* 3.101) Abraham (*Abr.* 122) Jacob (*Praem.* 44)
Evaluation	2nd-best with an element in it which God approves (*Abr.* 123) 'Truly admirable' (*Praem.* 43)	Divinely-approved way and the truth (*Abr.* 123) True friend of God (*Praem.* 43)

What do those who come to God indirectly see? In one place Philo says the Dyad, the two chief powers, God and Lord (*Abr.* 121); elsewhere he identifies the Artificer (τεχνίτην) or the Logos (*Leg.* 3.99–100). Perhaps from a synthetic point of view, we can go a step further and claim that the indirect vision

[17] Esp. *Leg.* 3.97–102; *Abr.* 119–25; *Praem.* 40–46; also, *Fug.* 97–98; *Abr.* 69–71; *Spec.* 1.37–50. Cf. Sandmel 1951: 138–39; Winston 1984: 374–75; Sterling 2006: 117–18. Birnbaum 1996a: 79–80 finds three paths to the vision of God: contemplation of creation, practice of virtue, or God himself. But virtue is intertwined with the other two – whenever Philo discusses multiple paths, it is the comparison of creation and God himself.

of God also sees Nature. The indirect way reasons from the evidence of God's work in the sensible world, particularly its order and design, the very things for which Nature is responsible. Nature may be the guise taken by the Logos, or it can substitute for God while remaining distinct, so that a person who saw it could be said to have seen God indirectly. Philo does not explicitly incorporate Nature into this indirect vision, but it could be consistent with his other ideas to make this connection. Whatever is seen, though, because this method works through the sensible realm, it requires the use of reason and offers no guarantees. Its tools are 'conjecture and theorizing and all that can be brought into the category of reasonable probability' (*Spec.* 1.38). At the end, this method amounts to a grasping of shadows or a happy guess.

The direct apprehension of God transcends the world. Indeed, direct vision of the One lies beyond the power of anything in the created realm (*QG* 4.8). Figures such as Moses and Jacob perceive the First Cause from or through himself, beyond his work in the physical world. Philo compares this way of seeing God to how we can only see the sun by means of the sun, or as 'light by light' (τὸ φῶς . . . φωτί; *Praem.* 45).[18] This well-known image perhaps points to 'the ascent of the soul above the multiplicity of the sense-perceptible and discursive world to the unity of the Logos where God could be perceived intuitively'.[19] This vision occurs apart from or above reasoning, for reason cannot ascend to God (*Legat.* 6).[20] Due to its supra-rational character, therefore, direct vision is a mystical experience.[21] The ascending soul is 'seized by a sober intoxication' (*Opif.* 71), 'possessed like bacchanals or corybants until they see the object of their yearning' (*Contempl.* 12). As a result, nothing from the material realm obscures this clear and certain vision of God.

What exactly do people see directly? Scott Mackie has recently argued that a significant range of texts from across the commentaries identify the Existent One (τὸ/ὁ ὄν) as the object of the direct vision.[22] In the Exposition, in an allegorical interpretation of the theophany to Abraham at Mamre (Gen 19), Philo claims that the purified mind sees the middle visitor, ὁ ὤν, whereas the lower mind sees only the other two visitors, the senior Powers, θεός and κύριος (*Abr.* 119–23).[23] The Existent One also appears as the object of sight in the

[18] Plotinus famously uses the same imagery at *Enn.* 5.3.17.34–38. Cf. Winston 1984: 374–75 on the Middle Platonist tradition here.

[19] Sterling 2006: 118; cf. Runia 1986: 437.

[20] Cf. Bréhier 1925: 314–15.

[21] Hagner 1971: 88 describes this vision more as an experience than an apprehension with the mind. On Philo's mystical theology, see Winston 1985: 43–59; idem 1996a.

[22] Mackie 2009.

[23] Likely too are *Abr.* 79–80; *Mos.* 1.158 (Mackie 2009: 44).

Questions and Answers (*QG* 4.2, 4–5, 8) and the Allegory (*Leg.* 3.100).[24] Mackie discounts much of the evidence often deployed against naming τὸ ὄν as the object of vision, or relativises it in its larger literary context (e.g., *Conf.* 95–97; *Ebr.* 152).[25] Thus a broad, consistent strand in Philo's works grants to those who achieve the direct vision the highest honour possible, the opportunity to see the Existent One.

In another set of texts, though, as Mackie himself acknowledges, Philo judges it impossible for a person to see the Existent One. God tells Moses that neither he nor his Powers can be seen in their essence (*Spec.* 1.41–50). His invitation in Deut 32:39 to 'see that I am' (ἴδετε, ὅτι ἐγώ εἰμι) is to recognise that he exists – anything more is impossible, because created beings simply cannot perceive the Existent One (ἀμήχανον γὰρ τὸν κατὰ τὸ εἶναι θεὸν ὑπὸ γενέσεως τὸ παράπαν κατανοηθῆναι; *Post.* 167–68). Rather, it is the Logos whom one sees, the greatest of the cities of refuge (Num 35:6; *Fug.* 94–99), the only source of knowledge of God (*Leg.* 3.207), the mediator between Creator and creation (*Her.* 205–6).[26]

Given the two sets of texts, an undeniable contradiction ensues, especially since *Abr.* 119–23 is so clear that Abraham does see the Existent One.[27] Mackie, though, goes too far in redressing the previous imbalance. There is more evidence for the Logos and less for the Existent One than he renders it. A better reading of *Leg.* 3.100 sees the Logos as the object of direct vision.[28] While he is technically correct that *Somn.* 1.63–67 'nowhere states that the

---

[24] See, respectively, Mackie 2009: 38–42, 35. Also in the Allegory, see *Ebr.* 82–83; *Mut.* 81–82 (Mackie 2009: 38). Elsewhere, add *Legat.* 4–6; *QE* 2.51.

[25] Mackie 2009: 32–33, 34. He interacts primarily with David Winston (e.g., 1985) and Ellen Birnbaum (1995 and 1996a).

[26] See above, p.40 on the Logos.

[27] We cannot resort to the sometimes useful explanation that Philo's loose usage of θεός really means the Logos, since he has already identified one of the other visitors as θεός and declared specifically that Abraham saw ὁ ὤν.

[28] The phrase in question is ὡς ἀπ' αὐτοῦ αὐτὸν καταλαμβάνειν καὶ τὴν σκιὰν αὐτοῦ, ὅπερ ἦν τόν τε λόγον καὶ τόνδε τὸν κόσμον. Does the relative pronoun ὅπερ refer just to σκιάν, so that God's shadow encompasses the Logos and cosmos (so Mackie 2009: 35), or to the entire clause, making Logos parallel to αὐτόν and κόσμον to σκιάν (so Bradshaw 1998: 494 n.30)? If the former, then the direct vision is of the Cause/Uncreated one (τὸ αἴτιον/τὸ ἀγένητος), and not the Logos. If the latter, then the direct vision is of the Logos.

In context, σκιά can refer to the Logos (3*x* in 3.96) or to the world (3.99; indirectly, 3.100), which would incline toward Mackie's view (Bradshaw overlooks 3.96). But Bradshaw points out that σκιά is feminine, while ὅπερ is neuter, which strikes against Mackie (who does not consider the gender). Thus ὅπερ refers to the whole clause, which means that *Leg.* 3.100 inter-changes Logos with Cause or Uncreated One as the object of the direct vision, *contra* Mackie.

Logos is seen instead of God',[29] the tenor of the passage belies that claim, for even from the Logos, 'apprehension of Him is removed to a very great distance from all human power of thought' (1.66). Moreover, one key passsage overlooked in the discussion is *Somn.* 1.232. Incorporeal souls may see God as he is (οἷος ἐστιν), but embodied souls only see an angelic likeness, which in context presumably means the Logos (1.229–30). That divine appearance is such that people 'take the image to be not a copy, but that original form itself' (1.232). People actually see the Logos yet think that it is God. Such a statement might even act as a hermeneutical key for organising other material.[30]

The tension between the Logos or the Existent One as the object of vision, although not resolvable, may be mitigated somewhat. First, Philo's exegetical orientation explains some passages. He denies human ability to see τὸ ὄν at *Mut.* 15–23, because Gen 17:1 says Abraham sees God and the Lord, the two chief powers. Yet he affirms the opposite at *QG* 4.2, 4–5, because of the shifting singular and plural pronouns in Gen 18. The biblical text directs where Philo goes, even sometimes in opposite directions. Second, the context of the commentaries provides help.[31] In *Abr.* 122, that Abraham sees ὁ ὤν magnifies his greatness, which aligns with the Exposition's aim of extolling Jewish heroes for beginners and outsiders. Moreover, with such an audience, *de Abrahamo* makes the simpler claim, while *Legum allegoriae*, for advanced readers, differentiates and invokes the Logos.[32] Ellen Birnbaum notes how the Exposition discusses divine intermediaries infrequently compared to the other two series.[33] While true, of course the applicability here is weakened by the fact that *Abr.* 122 does mention the creative and sovereign Powers! Third, Mackie wonders whether the inconsistency is Philo's 'deliberate effort to appropriately represent both the complexity and uncertainty of a mystical experience that is ultimately inscrutable'.[34] In sum, Philo vacillates whether the direct vision truly sees the Existent One or an intermediary, yet clearly it still constitutes something greater than indirect vision.

How does Philo evaluate these two ways of seeing God? Obviously, he greatly prizes direct vision. It is the divinely-approved way, the truth (*Abr.* 123), the path on which the true friend of God treads (*Praem.* 43). Even though direct apprehension carries greater worth, Philo still confers value on the indirect path. Seeing God through the sensible realm, while only a happy

---

[29] Mackie 2009: 33.

[30] On this practice, see above, p.15.

[31] As argued for by Birnbaum 1996a: 89–90 and Mackie 2009: 45–46. See above, p.18.

[32] Mackie 2009: 45, though, notes that *Spec.* 1.41–50 makes the opposite move, in a rather complex fashion, and it belongs to the Exposition.

[33] Birnbaum 1996a: 89. She notes *Abr.* 121–22 as an exception.

[34] Mackie 2009: 46–47.

guess, counts as something 'truly admirable' (*Praem.* 43) and contains an element of which God approves (*Abr.* 123).[35] Philo does not disparage the second path, at least partly because there is no guarantee someone will ascend to the first.[36] To see God directly in a supra-rational, mystical experience surpasses what someone can accomplish on their own, so a person may work hard to advance and yet only see God indirectly. Philo does not denigrate that possibility. The sensible realm has relative value, therefore, since one can see God through it. The *telos* of human existence is to see God, and the best way to do that is to apprehend him 'as light by light', but those who cannot attain those heights may still approach him through what he has made.

IV. Idealised Categories of People in Pursuit of God

The distinction on how to see God leads logically to distinguishing between types of people in their pursuit of the *telos*. If only a few can ascend to see God directly, while most see him indirectly, then it makes sense to search for some underlying categorisation of people and how they seek the ethical life.[37]

The most basic classification distinguishes between higher and lower ways. The higher, advanced way is preferred, yet the lower way holds some merit. This scheme underlies numerous topics for Philo. There are higher and lower ways to interpret Scripture. Philo admits that those who interpret the Tower of Babel literally for the origin of languages may have some truth, but he urges them to press on allegorically to recognise 'the letter is to the oracle but as the shadow to the substance' (*Conf.* 190). Philo greatly prefers allegorisation – the text's real, true meaning – but that does not entail rejecting a literal approach.[38] Those on the higher path grasp that anthropomorphisms are not true statements about God, but those at the lower level require them and may benefit from the untruth (*Deus* 61–64).[39] Thus the proper interpretation of Scripture manifests this higher-lower division: there is an advanced way to exegete the text, but the lower way is not thereby dismissed. This categorisation also fits the relationship of philosophy and the encyclia. The best course is to follow them both, but if not, the encyclia bears at least a lesser value

---

[35] Cf. *Mut.* 59, God extends his benefactions (εὐεργεσίας) to some through the created realm and to others through himself alone (τοῖς δὲ δι' ἑαυτοῦ).

[36] Mendelson 1982: 62.

[37] On such classification in general in Philo, see Runia 1986: 125–26.

[38] *Cher.* 48; *Plant.* 36; *Abr.* 147; *Contempl.* 78. Shroyer 1936: 282–84 notes that Philo opposes literalists who themselves oppose allegorisation.

[39] Cf. Mendelson 1988: 3–5. *De confusione* 98 appears to include all humanity within the orbit of needing anthropomorphic expressions in order to understand God.

(*Ebr.* 33–35). This also describes how to handle the passions: it is better like Moses to eradicate them (ἀπάθεια), but failing that, like Aaron, it is good to moderate and control them (μετριοπάθεια; *Leg.* 3.128–30).[40] Eradication belongs to the perfect, while moderation is for those making progress (131–32). Likewise, the question of obedience to natural or Mosaic law divides along the higher-lower paths.[41] This distinction is fundamental for how to pursue God via the *telos* and recurs as an architectonic principle in his work.[42]

This higher-lower division is Philo's most general classification. In numerous places, though, he gives a more specific, three-fold categorisation of people in their relationship to God and virtue (see Figure 7.2).[43] He attaches various labels to these groups: the God-born, heaven-born and earth-born (*Gig.* 60–61); the perfect, neutral and bad (*Leg.* 1.92–94); those focused on God, the in-between and those focused on creation (γένεσιν; *Her.* 40–62).

Figure 7.2 Categories of People in Relation to the *Telos*

	God-born	Heaven-born	Earth-born
Place of existence	Intelligible realm (*Gig.* 60–61) Heights (*Somn.* 1.151)	Midway between heights and depths (*Somn.* 1.151)	Hades as home (*Her.* 45; *Somn.* 1.151)
Type of existence	Never constrained by a body (*Her.* 45) Above genus and species (*Sacr.* 8)	Impress of divine image (*Her.* 57) Between dead and living (*Somn.* 2.234)	Moulded clod of earth (*Her.* 57) Lives by (irrational) blood-soul (*Her.* 61)
Relation to God	Calls him God and Lord (*Mut.* 19) Borderline between God and humanity (*Somn.* 2.229)	Calls him God (*Mut.* 19) Possessed by God (*Her.* 46)	Calls him Lord and Master (*Mut.* 19) Greatly need God's help (*Her.* 58)

[40] Sorabji 2000: 385–86 calls Philo the originator of distinguishing between ἀπάθεια and μετριοπάθεια for different classes of people. D. C. Aune 1994: 128 emphasises Philo's adaptability to people at any stage of development (contrast Seneca, *Ep.* 85.3–6, 116.1). Winston 1984: 400 n.97 and Lévy 2008: 160–61 argue for Philo's independence in this area from Middle Platonism and Stoicism, respectively.

[41] See p.141.

[42] Winston 1985: 14 argues that Philo, as a result of his higher-lower distinction, may adopt an intentional ambiguity when his philosophical approach would clash with Judaism.

[43] See the discussion at Mendelson 1982: 48–59, and the similar table at Hay 1987: 903 [with discussion 902–7]. Cf. Winston 1984: 404; Lévy 2008: 165–66. Simon 1967: 365 notes the Gnostic parallels in such classification.

	God-born	Heaven-born	Earth-born
Relation to Law	No need for injunction, prohibition or exhortation (*Leg.* 1.94)	Need for instruction and exhortation (*Leg.* 1.92–93)	Need for prohibition and injunction (*Leg.* 1.93–94)
Role of reason	Reasoning has God as its owner and companion (*Gig.* 64)	Loves learning and encyclia (*Gig.* 60) Lives by reason (*Her.* 57)	Turned from reason to flesh (*Gig.* 65)
Representative figures	Moses (*Sacr.* 8) Abraham (*Gig.* 64) Generic man created after His image (*Leg.* 1.92)	Adam (*Leg.* 1.92) Abram (*Gig.* 62)	Nimrod (*Gig.* 65–66) Eve as mother (*Her.* 52–53) Esau (*Leg.* 3.2)

Philo takes a Peripatetic position by stressing the possibility of moral progress.[44] The well Beer-lahai-roi (Gen 16:4), named by Hagar to reflect her imperfect vision of God, is rightly located between Kadesh and Bered, for they represent the poles of holiness and evil, and the person 'in gradual progress is on the borderland between the holy and the profane' (*Fug.* 213).[45] Most people reside in this land of progress, and Philo directs his attention to helping them improve. He likely envisions his audience as those capable of making progress, so such exhortations are meant to urge them on down the path.

In this scheme, the God-born clearly take first place (*Her.* 47). They inhabit the intelligible realm and live at the heights (*Somn.* 1.151). Like the Logos, they have a mediatorial role, belonging to neither the divine nor human genus (*Somn.* 2.229–30). Two types of figures inhabit this class.[46] Some like Isaac or Moses reach perfection with little or no toil (*Sacr.* 8–9), but they are rare. More common is someone like Abraham, who worked hard to ascend from the heaven-born, where he perceived God's powers, to the God-born, where he reached the Logos (*Gig.* 62–64).

Regardless of whether the perfect have toiled, though, it is God who bestows wisdom and virtue on them.[47] That is particularly clear for Isaac or Moses,[48] but it also holds true for Abraham. Even if he attained his perfection through much effort, still it came from God. Philo emphasises that everyone who comes to know and see God does so because he enables and draws them;

---

[44] Contrast the Stoic idea of no middle ground – everyone is either a sage or a fool (DL 7.127; Seneca, *Ep.* 75.8, 18).

[45] *Mut.* 226–29; *Somn.* 1.151–52; *QG* 4.243.

[46] Winston 1984: 404.

[47] Mendelson 1982: 52; Bréhier 1925: 275. Mendelson contrasts this to Seneca who affirms that mortals may reach ἀπάθεια, if they will only apply themselves (*Ep.* 116.8).

[48] See further, p.115.

every path to perfection is by God's grace (*Abr.* 54).[49] Even the desire to work hard and a strong love of effort comes from God (*Post.* 154–57). This necessity of grace is the correlate of Philo's theocentric ethics.[50]

Although it is nowhere explicit, the God-born category corresponds to the higher path and those who see God directly. Moses belongs to both camps, and the thrust of the descriptions for both groups coincides.[51] One difference, however, is the place of reason. The direct vision of God occurs apart from reason (*Praem.* 43), yet Abraham finds his reasoning owned by God (*Gig.* 64). Perhaps since the supra-rational, mystical element of directly seeing God does not factor into the latter passage, the formulation about Abraham represents a different expression for something higher than thinking (cf. *Abr.* 123).

The heaven-born are fundamentally the people in the middle.[52] The mixed life is inspired by God yet sometimes reverses course (*Her.* 46). Midway between the wise and the wicked, the heaven-born move up and down the stairway to perfection (*Somn.* 1.151–52; cf. 2.234–36). An important characteristic is that progress is possible, either into the God-born, like Abram becoming Abraham (*Gig.* 62–64), or through the heaven-born, as the category can further divide into beginners, those making progress, and the perfect (*Agr.* 157–58).[53] Each of these sub-types is still advancing – even the perfect person is like a house-builder putting the finishing touches on a building not yet firmly settled. Philo hopes for progress in virtue even when things appear bleak and exhorts readers to fan even the barest ember in the hope of causing it to grow and spread (*Sacr.* 123).[54]

The heaven-born category corresponds to the lower way, and to it belong those who see God indirectly.[55] The heaven-born live by reason (*Her.* 57), which recalls the importance of reason in the indirect vision (*Leg.* 3.97–99). They love learning and pursue the encyclia (*Gig.* 60–61), an integral part of working upwards from the world to God, which is the key characteristic for the indirect vision of God.

The earth-born are opposite from the God-born. They have turned from reason to the flesh (*Gig.* 65–67) and live by bodily pleasure (*Her.* 57; *Gig.* 60–

---

[49] Barclay 2006: 142; Zeller 1990: 85, 105–06; Hay 1987: 906. *Leg.* 1.38; 3.136; *Det.* 95; *Post.* 16; *Ebr.* 11; *Sobr.* 18; *Congr.* 130; *Abr.* 80; *Virt.* 164; *QG* 1.96; *QE* 2.51.

[50] Cf. Völker 1938: 221, 328–30.

[51] Sandmel 1951: 138–39 implicitly connects these two groups in Abraham.

[52] Mendelson 1982: 55.

[53] Cf. D. C. Aune 1994: 131. The perfection is relative: it still requires constant practice (*Agr.* 160) and can be lost (169–71). Cf. Seneca, *Ep.* 75.8–18 for a similar classification. Bréhier 1925: 267 also cites *Plant.* 157–75.

[54] Cf. D. C. Aune 1994: 131–32.

[55] So Mendelson 1982: 76–79.

61). Far from the intelligible realm, they make their home in Hades (*Somn.* 1.151; *Her.* 45). The only possible progress is to accept rebuke and slavery to a better person, as Esau should accept from Jacob (*Leg.* 3.192–94; *Prob.* 57), but that is only an improvement within their class, not out of it.[56] Philo's description of the earth-born is unremittingly negative.[57] It is doubtful he envisioned any of them as among his audience – the very interest in reading such a treatise would indicate that a person belonged rather to the heaven-born. The earth-born category in that sense serves as a warning and foil, against which Philo's readers may measure themselves.

If the God-born see him directly and pursue the higher way, and the heaven-born see him indirectly on the lower way, where do the earth-born fit? The initial answer is easy – nowhere, for they pursue neither God nor the *telos*. But juxtaposing the two-fold distinction of how to see God with the categories of *Her.* 40–62 complicates matters, because the sensible realm fits in very different places. This is true not with different terms being used but just γένεσις alone.[58] In the indirect vision of God, γένεσις has a positive function as a means through which God reveals himself (*Leg.* 3.101). *Quis heres* 40–62, on the other hand, betrays a relentlessly negative perspective on the sensible realm denoted by γένεσις. The life that looks to 'created things' (τὸ δὲ πρὸς γένεσιν; 45) makes its home in Hades, is dead to the life of the soul, lives by blood and the pleasures of the flesh and is only a moulded clod of earth. Understood from the vantage point of the types of lives that pursue God, therefore, the physical world holds a negative place.[59] This juxtaposition raises anew the question of how to solve this tension, the task to which we turn in Chapter 8.

V. Conclusion

This chapter has shown how Philo establishes higher and lower ways to come to God with corresponding ideal classes of people. The higher, preferred way

[56] Cf. Böhm 2005: 310.

[57] Compare the Apostle Paul: the flesh (σάρξ) is hostile to God; the mind set on it is death (Rom 8:5–8); those who sow to it reap corruption (Gal 6:8). Cf. Gal 5:16–21. Paul's understanding of σάρξ has long been argued; see Dunn 1998: 62–70 for the spectrum of Pauline usage and the view that it represents the integrated continuum of human mortality; on the other side, see Bultmann ET 1952–55: 1:232–46 for σάρξ as hostile cosmic power.

[58] On γένεσις denoting the sensible world, see p.54.

[59] Mendelson 1982: 56–57 fails to consider this passage, so he is only partially correct when he says that those on the higher way of seeing God do not have an expressly negative orientation toward the created realm.

is to see God directly in a mystical experience, illuminated by the deity himself. To this higher way belongs allegorical interpretation of Scripture, philosophy, complete eradication of the passions, and natural law. The higher way is the privilege of the few, those who are either perfect from the outset like Isaac and Moses, or who have arrived there, like Abraham. The lower way to approach God sees him indirectly from evidence of his work in the sensible realm. It does not refuse the help offered by anthropomorphisms in Scripture, or moderation of the passions, or the Mosaic Law. This lower path is home to all those who desire to make progress toward the human *telos*. It is not easy work to see God and become like him on this way, but progress is possible. In contrast to both higher and lower ways, there are those who do not see God at all, who remain mired in evil.

This architectonic principle of higher and lower ways begins to shed light on Philo's attitudes toward the material realm. Clearly, it does not belong to the higher way. The direct vision of God must be unimpaired by anything sensible, thus it rises above the world. Key passages like *Leg.* 3.97–102, *Abr.* 119–25 and *Praem.* 40–46 do not speak negatively about the material world so much as they imply its superfluity for those few people able to see God directly. For those on the lower way, the sensible world has genuine value – it is the means by which they come to know God. Yet there is a tension, since too great a focus on that world (as designated by γένεσις) is what characterises the earth-born, who are enslaved to their flesh and passions. The same entity, therefore, is viewed differently depending on which path a person takes, or whether they take a particular path at all. This multiperspectivalism is a vital concept for analysing Philo's overall assessment of the sensible world, the question to which we now finally come.

Chapter 8

The Ambiguity of the Physical World: A Multiperspectival Approach

I. Introduction

The pieces are now in place to construct an answer to our guiding question: How did Philo hold together seemingly contradictory views on the ethical status of the sensible world? Previous chapters mapped the semantic terrain for Philo's views and begun to give clues on how to read the map, and it now remains to provide the legend by which to make sense of it all. We have witnessed up close the mountains and valleys of Philo's assessment of the material world but not yet grasped the overall geography. Chapter 8 provides that orientation.

The apparent contradictions within Philo's views about the sensible world are because he took a multiperspectival approach to its ethical status. There are simultaneous higher and lower ways from which to evaluate the material world, which we consider in two sets. First, and most basic, there is a cosmological and ethical distinction between the higher, purer heavenly realm and the lower, wicked sublunary realm. Second, adopting either the vantage point of God or the material world shifts the perspective. God's viewpoint emphasises his power and skill in creating the world, which corresponds largely to usage of κόσμος and φύσις. The world's viewpoint emphasises its mutable character, which corresponds largely to usage of οὐσία, ὕλη, γένεσις and γενητός. The two sets of terms denote the same thing but convey vastly different valuations because of their focal points.

To this point, the higher perspective is positive and the lower perspective negative. But further probing reveals a surprising reversal with the second set of arguments. Now the higher way to God entails a negative perspective, and the lower way is positive. These higher and lower perspectives are embodied particularly in the Allegory and Exposition commentary series, respectively. First, the higher method of biblical interpretation, allegory, leads more frequently to negative evaluation of the sensible world than does the lower literal method. Second, the higher, mystical approach to seeing God regards the world negatively as an obstacle to be overcome, whereas the lower approach sees it positively, because the world is a medium through which God communicates. This second set of arguments tips the overall scales for Philo to a pessimistic outlook on the sensible world. Ultimately, the positive perspective belongs to a lesser way of approaching God, and the negative orientation better approximates reality.

II. Panoramic Review of Philo's Positive and Negative Perspectives

Before laying out the argument, it will help to review the map for a panoramic vision of Philo's positive and negative perspectives on the sensible world. The positive perspective is conveyed primarily through the use of κόσμος and φύσις, though occasionally with γένεσις too. The world is intimately connected to God. He operates in the guise of φύσις to create and guide the world (*Her.* 114–17; *Sacr.* 98–100), so that the world referred to as φύσις bears a divine stamp, the imprint of him who made it. The well-ordered κόσμος reflects God's own character (*Aet.* 39; *Spec.* 4.187), and in fact, his goodness was the reason he created (*Cher.* 127). Thus it is the image of the Logos (*Opif.* 25), God's son (*Ebr.* 30), his greatest masterpiece (*Deus* 106), his treasured possession (*Spec.* 1.302), and the temple in which he dwells (*Somn.* 1.215).

Accordingly, there is a harmony that encompasses all things. The intelligible κόσμος is nothing other than the Logos engaged in creating (*Opif.* 24), and the sensible κόσμος takes the intelligible for its pattern (*Conf.* 172). The universe is ruled by φύσις which is one divine law for the world and humanity (*Opif.* 143), which means that everything should obey either natural law or its perfect representation in the human sphere, Mosaic Law (*Opif.* 3).

That harmony means the sensible world can help lead people to God. Through contemplation of either the κόσμος or φύσις people can know God's existence and identity as father and maker (*Spec.* 1.41). Moreover, the material realm can help a person move toward the *telos*. Conforming one's life to the pattern of rational order in the κόσμος enables a person to become like God (*Opif.* 151). Following Nature is a means of following God and equivalent to obeying Mosaic Law (*Migr.* 128–31). In Philo's natural theology, the sensible world communicates sufficiently to allow a person to know God and obey his will.[1]

[1] Contrast Rom 1:19–20 where God has revealed himself in the sensible world sufficiently that people are without excuse in judgment, but not that they may be saved through such knowledge.

The only proper response to this good news is praise and thanksgiving. The mind should give thanks for God's creation of the κόσμος both as a whole and its parts, even down to the human body (*Spec.* 1.210–11). The world itself gives thanks, as the κόσμος participates in the sacrificial cult and worships God (*Somn.* 1.215; *Her.* 199). Philo's positive view on the sensible world, therefore, closely joins it to God and bestows on it an honoured place in helping humanity pursue him.

Philo's negative perspective sees the sensible world very differently. On this side belong the terms οὐσία, ὕλη, γένεσις (usually), and γενητός. The starting point for the world was poor, because it came from disorderly, chaotic matter (*Opif.* 21–22). God overcame that negativity at creation, but what nonetheless remains is lifeless, perishable matter, from which nothing good can come (*Post.* 163), and which is destined for destruction (*Somn.* 2.253). To be created is intrinsically to be perishable, as a result of the sheer mutability – the characteristic instability and flux – that belongs to the sensible realm (*Spec.* 2.166; *Aet.* 73). Change belongs to the created 'by nature' (γενόμενον φύσει; *Cher.* 19); it is an attribute of the world, just as unchanging stability is of God (*Leg.* 2.33–34; *Post.* 29–30). Indeed, this difference forms the crux of a sharp distinction between the created realm and God (*Leg.* 2.83).

Change ultimately and inevitably means decline and sin for the sensible realm, particularly human beings. Sin appears to have entered the world not because of a Fall but by the fact that everything created is subject to change (*Opif.* 151). Even the best person, like the high priest or the Nazirite, cannot escape from sinning by virtue of their belonging to the material realm (*Mos.* 2.147; *Spec.* 1.252). This inescapable reality leads to a profound division between God and the world. From God come things good and holy, but 'from the corruptible creation come things evil and profane' (*Plant.* 53). This moral chasm even becomes an ontological opposition. God and the realm of becoming are 'antagonistic natures' (*Leg.* 3.7). Even though God created γένεσις, Philo rarely makes that claim when giving it a negative value. He does not deny it, but it seems like a truth he wants to suppress. God, the uncreated, is far away from the things of the creation (τὰ τῆς γενέσεως; *QE isf* 10).

Because of the evil intrinsic to the sensible realm, and the antagonism between God and creation, the person who wants to see God finally must flee the world. The body, as an instantiation of the created realm, is especially noxious, and those who long to see God try to make their home as far from it as possible (*Ebr.* 124; *Det.* 158–60). Leah experiences fellowship with God as a result of her estrangement from creation (*Post.* 135). Those who minister to God, like the Levites, must 'estrange themselves from all that belongs to the world of creation, and to treat all such as bitter and deadly foes' (*Ebr.* 69). Figuratively, this language refers to cultivating a moderate asceticism and not trusting in created things. The body and γένεσις are totems for all that is evil and opposed to God. But the very fact that this figurative association comes so easily conveys the negative status of the sensible world. Moreover, even a positive term like κόσμος shares in this ultimate separation. To attain perfection requires transcending the well-ordered world (*Cher.* 7; *Mut.* 76). In the final analysis, to know and be in communion with God, is to have nothing to do with the sensible world.

These dual perspectives are not easily disentangled. How is the body a cause of praise and thanksgiving when it is a prison and a corpse? How can one know God through 'creation' (γένεσις; *Leg.* 3.101), when it is hostile and opposed to him? How is the κόσμος God's son and yet ultimately an impediment to perfection and true knowledge of him? Such questions are joined by those texts where these contrasting perspectives closely co-exist. The κόσμος has been made by God through his Powers and is his sanctuary, the radiance of his sanctity (ἁγίων ἀπαύγασμα; *Plant.* 50). Yet 'from the corruptible creation (γένεσις ἡ φθαρτή) come things evil and profane' (53). At the installation of Aaron and his sons as priests, Moses offered a calf and two rams. The calf signified 'that sin is congenital (συμφυές) to every created being (παντὶ γενητῷ), even the best, just because they are created' (παρόσον ἦλθεν εἰς γένεσιν; *Mos.* 2.147), whereas the first ram was a thanksgiving for how God has ordered the universe and for all the benefits humanity receives from it (2.148). Philo's ambivalence about the ethical status of the sensible world runs very deep.

III. Distinction between Higher and Lower Aspects of the Physical World

A first way to understand this tension over the sensible world comes from Philo's differentiation between its higher, heavenly and lower, sublunary parts. This motif is widely recognised, but it has not explicitly been applied before to help explain this ambivalence.[2] As was common in Hellenistic cosmology, Philo differentiates between heaven, composed of a higher, purer

[2] E.g., both Baer 1970: 89–95 and Mendelson 1982: 34 omit it.

substance, and everything sublunary, which is mixed from the four elements.[3] More significantly for our purposes, he often attaches an ethical dimension, where heavenly bodies are harmonious and well-regulated, but 'earthly things are brimful of disorder and confusion and in the fullest sense of the words discordant and inharmonious' (*Ios.* 145).[4]

One way to distinguish, therefore, between Philo's higher and lower perspectives is which part of the sensible world he has in view. Heaven is the 'best and greatest of created things' (κράτιστον ὄντα τῶν γεγονότων; *Congr.* 50).[5] He singles the stars out for praise, those 'images divine and exceeding fair' (*Opif.* 55).[6] Philosophy arises from observation not just of any part of the κόσμος but particularly of the heavenly bodies and their orderly movement (*Opif.* 54; *Spec.* 3.187–88). In contrast, every sublunary thing is full of battles and strife (*QG* 3.7). The undying impiety of Cain means that good things come from heaven and hasten back there, but evil makes the mortal realms its haunt and can never be shaken (Gen 4:15; *Fug.* 62).

The basis for this heavenly-sublunary distinction comes from a familiar axiom. Heaven is better because it 'alone is unchangeable and self-consistent', whereas sublunary things are 'mutable and changeable' (*QE* 2.83).[7] The preference for immutability over mutability, previously applied to God over against the sensible world, now distinguishes between parts of the world.

Appreciation for the stars, of course, comes from the widespread philosophical idea that the stars were higher beings, even divine.[8] Philo understands this tradition and follows it in part, but not wholly. He repeatedly refers to the stars as divine, on occasion even calling them 'sensible gods'.[9] Like-

---

[3] *Her.* 227–29; *Mos.* 2.194; *QG* 1.64; 3.6; 4.8; *QE* 2.33, 56, 73, 81, 85. This notion derives originally from Aristotle (*Cael.* 268b11–69b17). See the concise treatment by Harl 1966: 90–92. At *Somn.* 1.21, however, Philo places questions about the nature of heaven beyond human comprehension.

[4] Cf. *Opif.* 73, 168; *Fug.* 62; *QG* 4.87, 157; *QE* 2.33.

[5] Cf. *Abr.* 272; *Spec.* 3.202; *QG* 4.87. Philo uses οὐσία 12*x* to call heaven/stars the purest part of existence: e.g., *Opif.* 27; *Decal.* 64; *Virt.* 85.

[6] *Opif.* 114–16; *Mos.* 1.212–13; *Spec.* 1.210; *Contempl.* 5.

[7] *Congr.* 103–5; *Somn.* 1.134; *Mos.* 2.121; *QG* 4.8, 87; *QE* 2.91. Cf. Aristotle, *Cael.* 270b. See Scott 1991: 65; Bousset 1915: 29 n.3.

[8] *Tim.* 40b, 41a; *Leg.* 899b; 931a; *Epin.* 977a; 983e–84d. Scott 1991: 7, 17–18, however, points out Plato's relative reserve on the topic. From the Stoics, *SVF* 1.165, 510, 530; 2.1049; Posidonius, frg. 127–28; Seneca, *Ben.* 4.23.4. On Scripture's treatment of the stars, see Fyall 2002: 58–59.

[9] Stars as divine: *Opif.* 84, 144; *Gig.* 8; *Migr.* 184; *Abr.* 162; *Decal.* 64, 104; *QG* 4.188. Sensible gods: *Opif.* 27; *Spec.* 1.19; *QG* 1.42; 4.157. This evidence renders implausible Wolfson's claim that Philo's language is like referring to days by names derived from pagan deities without thereby endorsing such religious views (1947: 1.173).

wise, he refrains from criticism, and while aware of the suggestion that the stars exhibit rivalry like human beings, distances himself from it (*Somn.* 2.114–15).[10] Yet for all Philo's appreciation, the stars remain explicitly under God's authority and control. He condemns Chaldean astrology which glorifies the heavenly bodies and considers them and the universe divine (*Virt.* 212–13; *Migr.* 178–83).[11] Everything in the sublunary realm is subject to the heavenly bodies, but they remain only lieutenants of the Father and must copy him in order to rule rightly. Thus, the cause behind all events should be ascribed to God the charioteer rather than the stars (*Spec.* 1.13–14).[12] As Alan Scott puts it, 'Philo takes away with his right hand what he gives us with his left'.[13] This treatment of the stars reveals Philo's characteristic use of philosophy adapted to Jewish piety.

This bifurcation within the sensible realm is not unique to Philo.[14] In the Dream of Scipio (Cicero, *Resp.* 6.9–29), the great Roman hero tells how his grandfather appeared to him in a vision on the eve of the Third Punic War. He promised that those who serve their country well receive a special reward in the heavens. That afterlife is true life, whereas life now in the body is like death (14). The divine temple is composed of the stars and everything visible in the heavens, but the only way to ascend there is for God to free a person from the prison of the body (15).[15] Here in Cicero is the same mix of reverence for the stars and disdain for the body, one part of the material realm valued, and the other part denigrated.

A first way, therefore, to understand the tension between positive and negative views of the sensible realm is that the two often refer to different parts. When Philo focuses on the celestial sphere, he tends to be positive, but when his attention turns to the sublunary side, he is much more likely to be negative. Jaap Mansfeld describes the phenomenon for Plato as being anthropologically

---

[10] Cf. Scott 1991: 85–86. Contrast how Philo speaks about the body: occasional positive claims dwarfed by frequent negative denunciation; see above, p.60.

[11] On Chaldean astrology, see p.88 n.86.

[12] *Opif.* 46, 60–61; *Cher.* 24, 88; *QG* 4.51; *QE* 2.51. Philo regards astral worship as wrong but not as egregious as idol worship (*Decal.* 66; *Conf.* 173).

[13] Scott 1991: 74; on Philo as a whole, 63–75. Runia 2001: 207–09 also describes Philo's attitude as ambivalent.

[14] Scott 1991: 65; Festugière 1944–54: 2.525; see Aristotle, *Cael.* 270b; *Mete.* 340b; Stoics, *SVF* 2.668 (cf. Plutarch, *Mor.* 933d, 935b), 671, 674. In contrast, Scripture typically does not distinguish between heaven and earth ethically, though *T. Levi* 14:3 does make this cosmological-ethical split.

[15] Similarly, Seneca *Ben.* 3.20.1. On Cicero's influences here, see Kroll 1914: 234; Harder 1929: 118–23; Boyancé 1954: 215–16; on the Dream as a whole, see Powell's commentary at Cicero 1990: 119–33, 149–66.

but not cosmologically pessimistic.[16] At first, this seems to fit Philo too, but we will argue that ultimately he is pessimistic on both counts.

IV. Perspective of God Versus the Perspective of Substance

Distinguishing between the higher and lower parts of the sensible world is a necessary but not a sufficient explanation for Philo's ambivalence. Even though he is usually negative about the human body, he praises it at some points (e.g., *Opif.* 136–41; *Spec.* 1.210–11). Moreover, many of the negative statements appear all-encompassing for the sensible world. Indeed, Philo firmly places the stars within the created realm and calls them our brothers (*Decal.* 64; *Congr.* 50). Thus even the heavens cannot entirely escape his pessimistic assessment. Our analysis must go further.

Philo's positive and negative orientations on the physical world are a case of multiperspectivalism. They are simultaneously true, because they look at the material world from different vantage points. The positive perspective sees God's active involvement to create and sustain what he has made and is typically expressed by usage of κόσμος and φύσις. The negative perspective sees the lifeless and perishable substance from which the world is made and is typically expressed by usage of γένεσις and γενητός. This argument significantly helps decipher the map we drew of Philo's lexical-semantic treatment of the world because it proposes how these views could exist side-by-side and remain coherent.

Quis heres 159–60 provides a hermeneutical key for this dual reading. In context, it talks about the proportional equality in God's work, the underlying principle being that God applies the same art (τέχνη) to everything he does, regardless of its size or the materials used (156–57). In contrast to human artisans, 'with God no kind of material is held in honour' (τίμιον δ' οὐδὲν τῶν ἐν ὕλαις παρὰ θεῷ; 159). It quickly becomes clear that Philo is not restating God's impartiality (as in 157), but rather has in mind the negative, unruly matter from which God made the universe. Philo quotes Gen 1:31 that God saw all the things he had made were very good, and explains:

> Now God praised not the material which He had used for His work (τὴν δημιουργηθεῖσαν ὕλην), material soul-less, discordant and dissoluble (τὴν ἄψυχον καὶ πλημμελῆ καὶ διαλυτήν), and indeed in itself perishable, irregular, unequal (ἔτι δὲ φθαρτὴν ἐξ ἑαυτῆς ἀνώμαλόν τε καὶ ἄνισον), but He praised the works of His own art (ἀλλὰ τὰ ἑαυτοῦ τεχνικὰ ἔργα), which were consummated through a single exercise of power equal and uniform, and through knowledge ever one and the same (*Her.* 160).

[16] Mansfeld 1981: 294.

Philo distinguishes between two aspects of sensible existence: there is the matter used, worthless and condemnable in itself, and there is the craft God applied in using it, particularly his power and knowledge. When God pronounces everything very good, Philo explains that is not all-inclusive but has specific reference to his own craftsmanship. It is possible to praise the sensible realm and not intend for it to encompass the realm *qua* realm but just one dimension. It is striking that Philo takes a biblical verse that could argue against his negative orientation and neutralises it by specifying that God's praise is self-referential.

This distinction between God's art and the matter used applies more broadly as an overarching principle for the terminology from Chapters 3–6. Philo uses κόσμος and φύσις to stress God's active involvement in the sensible world. That God made the κόσμος is perhaps Philo's central claim for it and thus the axis on which all other statements turn.[17] God operates through φύσις to create and govern the world such that φύσις may be equated with him.[18] Denoting the sensible realm by φύσις incorporates the creative, organising power behind it, and so impresses a divine stamp upon the world. Both terms emphasise how God has crafted and sustains the sensible world. They are consistent, therefore, with Philo's interpretation of Gen 1:31, since they see the world from the vantage point of God's art. When they praise the world they do so on the basis of God's involvement.

The negative terminology of γένεσις and γενητός fits the other vantage point in *Her*. 160. Earlier we posited a connection between these terms and Philo's words for matter, οὐσία and ὕλη, on the basis that they all connote change, culminating in perishability.[19] Philo is fond of listing multiple negative traits for matter considered in itself, but nearly all of them are ameliorated by God at creation – except for lifelessness and perishability, which remain constant.[20] That perishability is what condemns γένεσις and γενητός – they are the sensible realm in the process of becoming and passing away. To use these terms, therefore, to refer to the material world, or the stuff from which it was made, emphasises the substance itself, as it shifts and never remains stable. Thus the negative perspective excludes God from active consideration and evaluates the world from the standpoint of its substance. On those grounds, there is nothing to praise, and the world merits a pessimistic judgment.

This interpretation of *Her*. 160, combined with the lexical study in previous chapters, establishes that Philo's divided views about the physical world

---

[17] See p.76.
[18] See p.148.
[19] See p.71.
[20] See p.44.

should be understood multiperspectivally. Both viewpoints describe things as they really are, but it depends on the angle from which the world is evaluated. When Philo uses κόσμος and φύσις, he looks from the angle of God's creative involvement, and when he uses γένεσις and γενητός, it is the angle of the substance itself from which the world is made. There is far less contradiction in Philo's views than might first appear, because he implicitly holds that both views are true, but neither exclusively nor exhaustively so.

V. Higher and Lower Approaches to God and the Physical World

A. Commentaries and the Physical World

This multiperspectival argument offers significant explanatory power for resolving the tensions within Philo's views about the ethical status of the sensible realm. Yet it does not account for all his ambivalence, because it cannot explain the limits of the κόσμος. When Abraham reaches the cusp of perfection, he must leave behind contemplation of the κόσμος and study of the world (φυσιολογία) in order to join the ranks of those who know God truly (*Mut*. 76; *Cher*. 7).[21] To reach the highest level, he must disregard or transcend the κόσμος. But κόσμος is the world seen from the higher perspective of God's creative art. So to attain perfection requires that Abraham displace the positive view of the sensible realm. That implies there may be a still higher, negative view of the sensible world, and that the previous argument for multiperspectivalism is not sufficient for explaining this conundrum.

An initial way into the problem comes from the observation that *Mut*. 76 and *Cher*. 7, with their call to set aside study of the κόσμος, both belong to the Allegory. Is there perhaps a correlation between commentary series and outlook on the sensible world? Three pieces of evidence suggest so.

First, the Allegory and Exposition do not handle this contemplation of the world language in exactly the same way. Overall, they do both use it positively.[22] But the Allegory at multiple points counsels that such contemplation must be superseded in order to attain perfection, whereas the Exposition

---

[21] Cf. p.89.

[22] This survey is based partly on lexical criteria (e.g., ἡ περὶ τὸν κόσμον/τὴν φύσιν θεωρία; φυσιολογία) but also takes conceptual factors into account: e.g., not all instances of φυσιολογία are relevant (e.g., *Somn*. 1.184), and some passages are relevant where contemplation language does not appear (e.g., *Leg*. 3.101). Allegory: *Ebr*. 91–92; *Her*. 98, 246, 279; *Mut*. 220; *Somn*. 2.26, 81, 173. Exposition: *Opif*. 54, 77; *Abr*. 164, 207; *Mos*. 2.216; *Decal*. 98; *Spec*. 1.33–35, 176, 269; 2.45, 52; 3.1, 191, 202. On the specifics for κόσμος, see p.86; for φύσις, see p.121.

makes that claim only once.[23] Thus the Allegory seems more ready to call its audience to move past the sensible world when it comes to knowing God.

A second piece of evidence comes from how Philo treats the body of the first man in the two series. In the Exposition, the body of the first man was 'noble and good' (καλὸς καὶ ἀγαθός), because God made it with consummate skill out of the best, pure material possible (ἐξ ἁπάσης τὸ βέλτιστον, ἐκ καθαρᾶς ὕλης; *Opif.* 135–37). In the Allegory, Philo interprets the exact same verse – Gen 2:7 – but omits physical beauty and instead emphasises the contrast between the heavenly man with no share 'in corruptible and terrestrial substance (φθαρτῆς καὶ συνόλως γεώδους οὐσίας), and the earthly man, 'compacted out of the matter scattered here and there' (ἐκ σποράδος ὕλης; *Leg.* 1.31).[24] The point of view in the Exposition is positive about this particular instantiation of material existence, but the Allegory is negative.

A third, more systematic line of evidence for the commentary series comes from the usage of γένεσις to denote the sensible world. Chapter 3 showed that this definition is predominantly negative, but we did not investigate whether it appeared uniformly across the commentaries.[25] Philo defines γένεσις as sensible world in the Allegory and Exposition 125 times. The results appear in Figure 8.1.

Figure 8.1 Γένεσις as Physical World in the Allegory and Exposition

	Allegory	Exposition
Positive	10	0
Neutral	22	6
Negative	78	7

What stands out in comparing these totals is the sheer difference in usage. Philo rarely uses γένεσις to denote the sensible world in the Exposition. It is not as if he ceases to use the word altogether, because he still defines it as 'generation' in roughly comparable numbers across the two commentaries.[26] Moreover, he uses κόσμος and φύσις (when it denotes the world) in roughly

[23] Allegory: *Leg.* 3.84, 101; *Cher.* 7; *Mut.* 76. Exposition: *Praem.* 43. The treatises use contemplation language positively (*Prob.* 63; *Contempl.* 64, 90; *Aet.* 138; *Prov.* 2.40) without ever relativising it, which makes sense given that their audience is likely very similar to the Exposition's.

[24] Pearson 1984: 328 highlights this contrast without noting how the interpretations occur in different series or drawing out the implications. On Philo and the body, see above, p.60.

[25] The Questions and the historical/philosophical treatises provide only four instances of this definition, an insufficient amount for analysis.

[26] Generation (broadly defined): Allegory: 136*x*; Exposition: 104*x*.

equal measure across these commentaries.[27] Compared to the Allegory, we should expect to see γένεσις defined as the sensible world much more frequently in the Exposition than we do. The fact that we do not is a statistically significant variation at a 99% level of confidence.[28] We may hypothesise that the variation is based on the fact that Philo typically uses γένεσις negatively when denoting the physical world. This analysis is supported by his usage of γενητός, which is also predominantly negative, and which is also much more weighted to the Allegory than the Exposition.[29] This difference offers a significant confirmation that the Allegory inclines toward a more negative perspective on the world.

All this evidence suggests that Philo takes a more negative perspective on the sensible world in the Allegory than in the Exposition.[30] Why, then, is there this difference? It comes from how Philo writes and for whom he writes in the respective series. Philo is more prone to be negative about the sensible world when he uses the allegorical method of biblical interpretation and when he addresses those readers who may be able to approach God on the higher path and see him directly. This provides the second set of arguments for resolving the ambiguity within Philo's views, but it is a multiperspectivalism of a different sort than before. It is not a contrast between positive and negative perspectives, but rather a contrast between a more explicit, ultimately negative view and a mixed positive and negative view.

B. Interpretation of Scripture and the Physical World

Philo tends to handle Scripture differently between the Allegory and Exposition.[31] Allegory treatises typically begin with a biblical quotation and then range far afield, particularly through secondary exegesis of other passages, all of which are usually allegorical. The cumulative effect is that interpretation is less tied to the plain sense of Scripture. In contrast, Exposition treatises follow

---

[27] Κόσμος (definition #5a in Appendix 4): Allegory: 216*x*; Exposition: 161*x*. Φύσις (definition #4 in Appendix 5): Allegory: 40*x*; Exposition: 55*x*.

[28] This conclusion was reached through a chi-square analysis, for which I thank Barry Danylak, James Robson, and Tom Watts.

[29] Of its 63 negative occurrences (out of 97 total), 42 are in the Allegory and 16 in the Exposition. He uses it positively or neutrally much less frequently, but there is no variation between the commentaries in those categories.

[30] Baer 1970: 95 briefly proposed this with respect to the predominance of the allegorical method in the Allegory, and Mendelson 1982: 34 implicitly included it in his distinction between ideal and ordinary views of the world. For both scholars, however, it was more a hypothesis than developed argument.

[31] See p.18. It is important to remember that these differences are general patterns rather than rules.

the Pentateuchal narrative more closely, assume less prior knowledge, and are more likely to concentrate on one passage at a time. They also feature a higher proportion of literal interpretation. The series differ, therefore, in their typical treatment of Scripture and how they balance interpretive methodologies.

These differences are significant because the more directly Philo focuses on a single biblical text in literal interpretation, the less likely he is to express a negative view on the sensible realm.[32] This contrast and its implications are illustrated by Philo's handling of Deut 25:11–12 in *Spec.* 3.175–80 and *Somn.* 2.68–69. In Deut 25:11–12 the Israelites are commanded to cut off the hand of a wife who grabs the genitals of her husband's opponent. In *Spec.* 3.175–80 Philo focuses on this passage alone. He first literally explains and approves of the law (175–77). In fact, he commends the managers of gymnastic competitions who go further and bar women from even watching naked male competitors. He then turns to the allegorical sense (178–80). The male soul clings to God, the maker of all things, whereas the female soul clasps hands in friendship with the world of created things (γένεσιν) and its constant changing. Understood allegorically, therefore, the command to cut off the wife's hand in Deut 25:11–12 symbolises excising 'the godless thoughts which take for their basis all that comes into being through birth' (179).[33] Γένεσις figuratively represents the theological error of not making God the ground of all thought. When the biblical text is read literally, the sensible realm is nowhere to be found; when it is read allegorically, that realm is condemned.

In *Somn.* 2.68–69 Philo gives the same allegorical interpretation as in *Spec.* 3.178–80 but without any corresponding literal explanation. He speaks only of cutting off the hand if it begins to lay hold of the sensible world but says nothing about a literal application of the law. Thus the sole interpretation for Deut 25 is pessimistic about the material creation. Moreover, Philo only refers to Deut 25 briefly in secondary exegesis as support for what it means in Gen 37:33 that the wild beasts devoured Joseph (65). Before and after this interpretation of Deut 25, Philo allegorises other biblical passages to produce similarly negative statements about the world. He refers to Lev 10:1–7 when Moses forbade Aaron from mourning for Nadab and Abihu after the Lord killed them with fire (67). A surface reading of Lev 10 makes clear that God struck Nadab and Abihu down for their sin. But Philo interprets their death positively, as a consummation of their zeal for piety, which is alien to creation but akin to God (γενέσεως μέν ἐστιν ἀλλοτρία, θεοῦ δὲ οἰκεία). Likewise, immediately after invoking Deut 25, Philo explains Adam's condemnation in

---

[32] Baer 1970: 95; Völker 1938: 87–89.

[33] Ironically, Philo's negativity toward γένεσις comes from his following 'nature' (ἀκολουθίᾳ φύσεως; 180).

Genesis on the grounds that he touched the tree and revered 'the created (τὸ γενόμενον) rather than the maker' (70). Thus, Philo takes Lev 10 and Gen 3 in the same negative way he does Deut 25:11. The reader is inundated with a rapid succession of biblical passages that are all interpreted as hostile to the material realm.

This comparison of *Spec.* 3.175–80 and *Somn.* 2.68–69 illustrates the connection between exegetical method and the outlook on the sensible world. The literal interpretation of Deut 25 in *Spec.* 3.175–77 does not mention the world, while the allegorical interpretations in both passages carry an unfavourable judgment. Moreover, in *Somn.* 2.68–69, Philo refers quickly to multiple biblical passages, all of which are interpreted as negative toward the sensible world. In broader perspective, therefore, because the Allegory utilises allegory more extensively, often without an adjoining literal interpretation, it takes a more negative view of the world.[34] The Exposition employs literal and allegorical exegesis and is accordingly less negative about the world. Put another way, the more directly Philo focuses on a single biblical text in literal interpretation, the less likely he is to express a negative view on the created realm. Thus there is a general correlation between the interpretive methodology in each series and their views on the ethical status of the world.

C. Implied Audiences and the Higher-Lower Paths to Perfection

Even more fundamental than this distinction of allegorical versus literal interpretation is the question of implied audience. Whom is Philo addressing? Based on its wide use of Scripture, philosophy and the allegorical method, the Allegory implies an advanced audience eager to progress in its pursuit of God. Conversely, with its fewer assumptions and balance of literal and allegorical interpretation, the Exposition envisions beginners who need initial instruction in this pursuit. In turn, we map that advanced-beginner split onto the architectonic distinction from Chapter 7 between higher and lower approaches to God.[35] The Allegory's readers are presumably mostly on the lower path, but they are aware of and should aspire to the higher path, which only a few will ever travel. The beginners of the Exposition are just learning how to pursue God and thus are only on the lower path – the higher way must come later. So the Allegory has in mind both approaches to God, while the Exposition confines itself primarily to the lower one.

---

[34] The rabbis neither adopted allegory to this degree, nor viewed the world so negatively; cf. Urbach 1987: 249.

[35] See p.162.

Putting the implied audiences and the higher-lower principle together is crucial, because the higher and lower approaches to God do not use the sensible world in the same way. Seeing God directly is a supra-rational, mystical experience which transcends the world. Seeing him indirectly, however, discerns his existence from the order in the world. Thus for the higher approach, the sensible world is, at best, superfluous, and quite possibly an impediment. For the lower approach, the world is a necessary good apart from which God is not known. That produces a second multiperspectival analysis of the world, which this time depends on the audience for whom Philo writes. Put simply, the Allegory, as it calls people to see God directly, unimpeded by the physical world, adopts a more negative perspective, while the Exposition, concerned to encourage people at least on the lower path, is less so.[36] Put more precisely, when Philo addresses advanced readers who might ascend to the direct vision of God, he is alternately positive and negative. He is positive because most – probably all – of his readers are on the lower path, and thus need help knowing God through the sensible realm. But he is more manifestly negative at other times, because his readers also may aspire to the higher path and thus need to know that cosmological study has its limits and cannot take them to the highest level. In contrast, when Philo addresses beginners who, at best, see God indirectly through the sensible world, he is less negative.[37]

The Allegory features multiple texts which connect a negative view of the sensible world with the higher path to God. The crucial link is that it is only by travelling along the higher path that one is able to adopt this negative perspective. This link emerges especially in light of the body and its negative status.[38] After condemning the body as a corpse and avowing that it was because of God's goodness that he killed Er, the symbol of the body, Philo admits that not everyone can see things this way. It is only apparent to God and anyone dear to God that the body is a corpse.

---

[36] Mendelson 1982: 34 briefly mentioned this advanced-beginner split as an explanation for Philo's dual perspectives but neither correlated it with the commentary series nor incorporated exegetical support from them. Cf. Chadwick 1966: 292–93, 'According to Philo, it is the insight of the religious man that the world is transient'.

[37] The more prevalent Jew-Gentile distinction is an intriguing parallel for this knowledge of creation. Pseudo-Solomon condemns Gentiles for not knowing God via the world, hypothesising they become distracted by its beauty (Wis 13:1–9). Paul judges Gentiles for the same failing but ascribes it to their suppression of the truth by their wickedness (Rom 1:19–20). While this basic distinction and the reasons Gentiles fail to understand the world correctly have some parallels in Philo, his advanced-beginner division cuts across Jew-Gentile lines (i.e. a Jew could easily be still a beginner, and a Gentile could theoretically be advanced).

[38] Cf. p.60.

For when the mind soars aloft and is being initiated in the mysteries of the Lord, it judges the body to be wicked and hostile; but when it has abandoned the investigation of things divine, it deems it friendly to itself, its kinsman and brother. . . . When, then, O soul, will you in fullest measure realise yourself to be a corpse-bearer? Will it not be when you are perfected, and accounted worthy of prizes and crowns? For then you shall not be a lover of the body, but a lover of God. (*Leg*. 3.71, 74).

How someone sees the body depends on the degree of intimacy with God. Mystery-language and the heavenly ascent of the mind identify this person as someone on the higher path to the direct vision of God. They, and only they, who have progressed to more advanced study of divine things recognise the body's corruption. Those who have not reached perfection see the body positively. The real state of the sensible realm, instantiated here in the human body, becomes apparent only when someone is on the higher path.[39] This distinction exemplifies what Tzvi Novick has called 'perspectival exegesis': correct interpretation of the textual proposition must take into account the point of view of the speaker.[40] Only the soaring mind can adopt a negative point of view about the physical world. This viewpoint cannot be universalised across Philo's corpus for all readers, because not all belong to that category.

In two further passages, Philo explicitly designates the negative view of the world as an entailment of the higher path. In a fragment of the lost treatise *Leg*. 4, Philo interprets Deut 30:15, 19 and the covenantal offer of life and death.[41] In the process, he lays out general hermeneutical principles for reading those scriptural passages which address the dialectic of divine and human agency: 'There are two main points from the Lawgiver: the one, that God does not direct all things in a human way; the other, that he does train and chasten in a human way'.[42] Philo then crucially connects these principles with his architectonic higher-lower distinction. Passages which follow the first main point describe God as the cause of all things. Passages, however, which ascribe to human beings the power to choose good and shun evil belong to the lower principle that God addresses us in a human way. So, Philo asks rhetorically, why even have scriptural passages that seem to allow independent choice to human beings? God would respond,

---

[39] Cf. *Deus* 4 awareness of the mutability of creation comes through knowledge of God's immutability, and *Leg*. 3.100 the person who sees God directly can apprehend not just God, but also his shadow, which in context includes at least the cosmos (Bradshaw 1998: 494).

[40] Novick 2009: 49.

[41] The fragment appears in Harris 1886: 8. The translation is mine, though I have been helped substantially by Barclay 2006: 145–46.

[42] Cf. *QG* 2.54, Philo says the former statement is the truth, and the latter is for the sake of teaching and learning.

Of such things hear a more elementary explanation: For these things are said to those not yet initiated into the great mysteries about the sovereignty and authority of the Uncreated and about the surpassing nothingness of the created (ἄγαν οὐδενείας τοῦ γενητοῦ).

In the first instance γενητοῦ refers to human beings, but the phrasing suggests the entire sensible realm is in view too. As in *Leg.* 3.71, Philo employs mystery language to describe the difference between the higher and lower paths.[43] At *Somn.* 1.60, Philo speaks of 'the nothingness in all respects of created being' (τὴν ἐν πᾶσι τοῦ γενητοῦ σαφῶς προλαβὼν οὐδένειαν).[44] There the dialectic is knowledge of self versus knowledge of God. Only through distrusting oneself does a person begin to know God. Philo thus seems to appeal to the nothingness of creation in order to safeguard and uphold the centrality of God. Though the sensible realm comes from God's grace, it does not convey any grace from itself, except insofar as God works through it. Only those on the higher path grasp what this nothingness means and the true place of the material world. Those on the lower path operate under a necessary, biblically-sanctioned illusion that accords them a measure of responsibility and ability.

Finally, in *Deus* 179–80, a pessimistic view about the world again goes hand in hand with the higher path:

The two sayings, 'the matter of creation is all of it nothing' (τὸ γενέσεως πρᾶγμα ὅλον οὐδέν ἐστι) and 'we will journey along the mountain country', come from the mouths of the same speakers. For it cannot be that he who does not walk in the upland paths of definition should renounce mortal things and turn aside therefrom and make his new home with things indestructible.

Unless someone is on the higher path, they are unable to see the sensible world negatively. They cannot agree that 'the matter of creation is all of it nothing', because they need the material world – it is the means by which they know God. To take it a step further, it would be inappropriate for those on the lower path to adopt this negative perspective, because it would be inconsistent for them to denigrate the material realm so long as it helps them on their way to God. Thus the negative view of the sensible realm is properly – and perhaps exclusively – for those on the higher path to perfection. Philo engages in perspectival exegesis by necessarily linking the judgment about creation to the viewpoint of the mountain traveller. The first statement is only true if uttered by someone who also adopts the second.

This final argument represents a surprising reversal in evaluating the world. Under the first case of multiperspectivalism, the positive perspective was positive, precisely because it focused on God's involvement with the world, and the negative perspective was negative, precisely because it disregarded that

[43] On this passage in connection with Philo's mysticism, see Winston 1996a: 77.

[44] Cf. p.69.

divine involvement and focused on the substance of the world. For a profoundly theocentric thinker like Philo, one would presume that the viewpoint which privileges God's involvement would be 'higher' – yet this ultimately proves not to be the case. Paradoxically, the terms that highlight God's opposition to the sensible world, like γένεσις and γενητός, belong to the higher approach. Those who would see God directly must set themselves against the physical world, and thus minimise God's role in that world.

Someone might object that this interpretation has reversed the weight of evidence. How can just a few texts that link the higher path with a negative cosmological perspective overrule hundreds of texts that use κόσμος and φύσις to speak glowingly of God as creator and Lord of the sensible world? The key is that these few texts tap into Philo's architectonic principle of higher and lower, better and lesser, ways to live. This distinction is part of the spine of his entire output, cropping up repeatedly: it shapes how to interpret Scripture, speak about God, deal with the passions, and relate natural and Mosaic Laws. These few texts, therefore, fit well in the macro-structure of Philo's thought, and the many texts that convey a positive perspective on the sensible world cannot overturn them.

VI. Conclusion

This chapter set out to analyse the deep ambivalence Philo expresses about the sensible realm. How can the negative and positive perspectives which we saw in Part One fit together in any coherent way? Four arguments were offered for how to resolve this tension.

First, there is a distinction within the sensible realm. Philo differentiates between its higher celestial and lower earthly aspects. He lauds the stars but denigrates the body. Second, a person may look at the world from more than one perspective: from the vantage point of God there is evidence of his creative art, but from the vantage point of matter itself there is evidence of its worthlessness. The positive and negative perspectives see different aspects of the same entity and thus exist side-by-side. Both are true yet neither are exhaustively true.

More importantly, there are multiple perspectives, depending on where one stands in relation to God. For those on the lower path, the sensible realm is good. The order and design of the κόσμος testify to God. Those in progress need it in order to see God, just like they need the literal interpretation of Scripture to know how to pursue him, anthropomorphisms to understand him, moderation of the passions to be fit to approach him, and the Mosaic Law to obey him. But its value is contingent and relative – it is there for those who cannot scale the heights. For those on the higher path to God, the sensible realm is irrelevant or even an obstacle. They can approach him directly, their way illuminated by the deity himself. Anything mortal or sensible only obscures the vision or slows down the journey. Where one stands in relation to God determines how the sensible world is evaluated.

The lower perspective that regards the sensible world positively is legitimate. Philo affirms that the indirect vision of God is commendable. Moreover, it is inappropriate for someone on that lower path to take a negative view of the world – they *should* see it positively. Yet if the person on the higher path is supposed to adopt the negative perspective, it raises the spectre of an instability within Philo's thought. There is a certain conceptual incoherency to how Philo evaluates the world that no multiperspectivalism can alleviate. If the truer approximation of reality is that God's involvement in the sensible world is second-best, it calls into question the repeated claims that God created the κόσμος from his goodness and that people can know and become more like him by looking to his world. Are such statements the noble lie to placate the vast majority who will never attain the mystical vision of God? To ask it this way admittedly may push things too far, but it is the logical trajectory of the path that Philo himself marks out in the Allegory. The scales finally seem tipped toward the negative, and the ambivalence in Philo's views of the physical world is ultimately resolved by prioritising the pessimistic outlook.

Chapter 9

Conclusions

I. Summary

This book set out to account for Philo of Alexandria's ambivalence about the physical world. On the surface, his strongly positive and negative evaluations of the material world seem contradictory, so this study sought to analyse how such divergent views could cohere. The method consisted primarily of a close textual analysis of Philo focusing on six key terms (οὐσία, ὕλη, γένεσις, γενητός, κόσμος, φύσις) that together provided comprehensive coverage for his views of the sensible world (Chs. 3–6). The beginning of Chapter 8 summarised those findings, so there is no need to repeat them in full here.[1] Put briefly, the first set of terms, οὐσία, ὕλη, γένεσις, and γενητός, typically convey a negative evaluation of the sensible world and connote a state of flux which culminates logically in destruction. The second set of terms, κόσμος and φύσις, virtually always convey a positive evaluation and connote the world as the place of God's active involvement and a means by which to know him. That lexical study laid the necessary foundation for evaluating the tensions.

Chapters 7–8 took up the task of synthesising these apparently contradictory sets of terms. The answer is that Philo's ambivalence to the sensible realm should be understood multiperspectivally. First, his perspective may be positive because he focuses on the unchanging, morally superior heavenly realm, and at other times it may be negative because he focuses on the mutable, wicked sublunary realm. Second, he sees the world positively when he looks at it from God's vantage point and stresses its divine craftsmanship and presence. Alternatively, he sees it negatively when he looks at it from matter's vantage point and stresses its intrinsic perishability and worthlessness. This multiperspectivalism corresponds largely to the six key words, and it shows how the same entity can be evaluated very differently depending on which dimension is highlighted. The third and fourth arguments are based on Philo's architectonic higher-lower distinction in how people may approach God.

[1] See p.169.

Third, allegory is the 'higher' method for interpreting Scripture, and it is more likely to take a negative perspective on the world. Fourth and finally, the higher way sees God directly without any sensible intermediary, and accordingly it evaluates the world in pessimistic terms. The lower way sees God indirectly through the universe and thus adopts a positive perspective on the world, since without it God remains unknown. The fact that the 'higher' avenue to Scripture and God both evaluate the world negatively means that ultimately Philo is a cosmological pessimist, and the ambivalence is resolved toward the negative orientation.

II. Whence this Negative Perspective? Comparative Analysis

A. Judaism and Hellenism

We have steadily assessed the influences on Philo's evaluation of the sensible world. Having concluded his outlook is ultimately negative, it is appropriate to weigh how that judgment compares with Philo's predecessors and contemporaries.

Chapter 2 argued that Judaism and Hellenism cannot be conceptualised for Philo without the other, but that Scripture is the superior and original source of everything good in Greek culture and thought. As a disciple of Moses, Philo utilises philosophy in service of biblical exegesis. But this overall formulation does not play out precisely that way in Philo's views on the sensible realm.

Chapters 3–6 showed how philosophy orientates Philo's terminology for the sensible world, providing its general framework and much of its content. Yet his negativity with terms for matter and γένεσις and γενητός even appears to exceed philosophical influence in some ways. Jewish influence is barely discernible on the negative terminology. Making the mutable γένεσις God's ontological opponent lacks precedent. It was suggested, however, that there were conceptual ties between Philo and wider Jewish reflection on creation, which could sometimes be skeptical or even pessimistic.[2] The major obstacles to such a comparison, however, are the paucity of texts that are actually negative about the physical world, and even more importantly, how those texts fit in their wider contexts. The negative views about the world in Ecclesiastes and Job are a minor strand in what is overall a relatively more positive interpretation, due in part to their narrative frames. It is the same dynamic for the wisdom literature genre more widely: the mixed reports of Ecclesiastes and

[2] See p.64.

Job must be set alongside the strongly positive outlooks on the material world of Proverbs or Ben Sirach.[3] Even an apocalypse like *4 Ezra*, long thought to be profoundly negative in its cosmological outlook, has recently been shown to boast actually 'a surprisingly traditional, essentially positive view of the material creation'.[4] In contrast to all this, while Philo is certainly mixed in his assessment of the physical world, his overall evaluation is negative. So the controlling frameworks are different between Philo and these other authors. Hence, if there is any Jewish background from these negative texts, it is relatively slight. Philo charts his own course with this first, negative set of terms.

The biblical influence is much stronger for the positive terminology, the second set of terms. The κόσμος is subordinated to the God who made it and now rules it, both of which are common Jewish claims. Placing the κόσμος in the sacrificial cult sets the Jewish viewpoint as the truest view of the world. Philo makes φύσις a means by which God creates and rules the world, and aligns it with Mosaic Law so that people can follow Nature through this written translation. The biblical influence decisively modifies the philosophical framework for Philo's positive terminology, and it exemplifies the conclusions in Chapter 2 about the overall framework of Judaism and Hellenism.

In contrast, Chapter 8 saw the relative eclipse of Jewish influence on how Philo ultimately resolves the ambiguity in his views about the sensible world. There is little biblical precedent for an ethical distinction between the higher and lower parts of the universe. Philo interprets Gen 1:31 so that it praises God's creative skill in what he has made but not the stuff from which it is made. That allows him to hold simultaneously positive and negative perspectives, but a critical reader may suspect that a more holistically positive exegesis of Gen 1:31 is just as – if not more – legitimate. The correspondence between allegory and a negative perspective on the sensible world reinforces the sense that Philo must depart from the literal content of Scripture in order to support his cosmological pessimism. Finally, if the negative viewpoint about the world is ultimately the higher one, then it seems clear that contrary to the overall findings in Chapter 2, Scripture does not have the upper hand for how Philo evaluates the physical world.

B. Two Strands of Platonism

Does the relative lack of Jewish influence on Philo's ultimately negative views mean the philosophical influence is decisive? Not necessarily. A. J. Festugière diagnosed Philo's ambivalence as reflective of two Platonic tradi-

[3] On Proverbs, see Dell 2006: 139–46; on Ben Sirach, see Perdue 1994: 290.

[4] J. Moo 2008: 201.

tions: the pessimism coming from the *Phaedo, Symposium* and *Republic*, and the optimism from the *Timaeus*.[5] There is a chronological progression: the *Republic* advocates bypassing the material world in order to reach the intelligible forms, but by the *Timaeus*, Plato is positive about reaching the ideas through the κόσμος. Thus Philo's prioritising of the negative perspective means he prefers the earlier stage in Plato's thinking. More importantly, it runs contrary to the profound influence that the *Timaeus*, his 'exegetical blueprint',[6] had on him. Philo departs from the *Timaeus* and adopts ultimately a pessimistic outlook. That pessimism, however, exceeds the other Platonic tradition too, since Plato focused more on the body than the universe. Jaap Mansfeld categorised him as an anthropological rather than cosmological pessimist.[7] Philo is certainly an anthropological pessimist, but Chapter 8 showed that his views are finally cosmologically pessimistic too. Philo, therefore, goes beyond Plato when he holds this negative perspective on the sensible world. This pessimistic Platonic tradition is catalytic for Philo's views, but the Alexandrian takes them much further.

Perhaps, then, Philo should be classified with those second-century Middle Platonists who enshrine evil as a cosmological principle, like Plutarch (*Mor.* 369cd), or who hold that matter itself and any incarnation of the soul are necessarily evil, like Numenius or Harpocration.[8] Alan Scott describes this position as a fusion of Plato's negative statements about the body with his suggestion in *Leg.* 896d of an evil world soul to create a pessimistic, but legitimately Platonic cosmology.[9] Philo certainly agrees with this view of the body, but the Logos is no evil soul. Moreover, despite his negative perspective, his endorsement that the *one* God created (*Mut.* 27–31),[10] and that what he created is good (*Leg.* 3.78; *Spec.* 4.187) sets him apart from this particular cosmological pessimism. Yet Festugière pointed out that Philo, and Hermeticism after him, joined those traditions, and so in that sense is a pre-'cosmologically negative' Platonist. Thus there are latent connections between Philo and these Middle Platonists, but his clear positive statements prevent that from proceeding further.

---

[5] Festugière 1944–54: 2.583–85.

[6] Runia 1986: 409.

[7] Mansfeld 1981: 294.

[8] Plutarch, *Mor.* 371a–72a; 428f; 1014b; 1026e–27a; see Dillon 1977: 199–208. Numenius and Harpocration: frg. 52; Iamblichus, *de Anima* 23 (Stobaeus 1.375.12–15); 29 (1.380.13–17); see Dillon 1977: 373–74, 260–61.

[9] Scott 1991: 83–84.

[10] Runia 1986: 246 n.7. This disagrees with Numenius, frg. 12; cf. Cox 2007: 37.

C. Wisdom of Solomon

Wisdom of Solomon presents the most likely Jewish point of comparison for Philo, since they come from the same intellectual-religious milieu,[11] and used κόσμος similarly.[12] But Pseudo-Solomon holds a consistently positive perspective on the sensible world without an accompanying negative pole – it is essentially the positive half of Philo's presentation. There is a profound continuity in how God deals with the sensible world: from its very foundation the κόσμος has a role in salvation (1:14),[13] which it carries out (in parallel with κτίσις) in the Exodus (16:17, 24–25) and in eschatological judgment (5:17, 20).[14] In Wisdom, God delivers his people by the κόσμος,[15] whereas in Philo, ultimately God must deliver his people from the κόσμος. So there is nothing determinative about a Jewish environment influenced by Middle Platonism that must lead to a negative perspective on the sensible world. That may indicate that the impetus for Philo's views comes from somewhere else.

D. Paul of Tarsus

The title for Chapter 8 echoes Rudolf Bultmann's characterisation of Paul's perspective on creation.[16] Like Philo, Paul certainly holds both positive and negative perspectives. Positively, God is creator of all things (1 Cor 8:6), and this world testifies to him (Rom 1:19–20). The mediator for salvation and creation is Christ (Col 1:15–17),[17] a role which brings the two orders together and implicitly confers a high value on the sensible world. Since, therefore, the earth and everything in it belongs to the Lord (Ps 24:1 in 1 Cor 10:26), nothing should be considered unclean (Rom 14:14, 20), and all things should be received with thanksgiving (1 Cor 10:30). Paul's positive perspective on divine activity in the sensible world can be summed up in 1 Cor 8:6: all things

---

[11] See above, p.5 n.24.

[12] Cf. p.96.

[13] Collins 1977: 124 n.16.

[14] Kolarcik 1992.

[15] Cf. Cox 2007: 81 There is 'no antipathy between the cosmos and of human salvation' in Wisdom.

[16] Bultmann ET 1952–55: 1.230. I thank Jonathan Moo for drawing my attention to this allusion. On Philo and Paul, see Chadwick 1966; Runia 1993a: 66–74; topic-specific studies like Zeller 1990; Barclay 2006; and the relevant essays in Deines & Niebuhr 2004.

[17] Pauline authorship of Colossians is, of course, disputed; in its defence, see D. Moo 2008: 28–41; Johnson 1999: 393–95.

are from the one God, the Father, and we are for him, and all things are through the one Lord, Jesus Christ, and we are through him.[18]

At the same time, although God created this world, it lies under the sway of hostile, evil forces. There is a god of this age at work to blind people to the gospel (2 Cor 4:4), and those outside of Christ are in bondage ὑπὸ τὰ στοιχεῖα τοῦ κόσμου (Gal 4:3). Likewise, creation as a whole is in bondage to decay and corruption (Rom 8:19–20). Paul can describe the κόσμος as a system of values and priorities opposed to God, whose rulers crucified the Lord of glory (1 Cor 2:8) and whose wisdom God makes foolish (1 Cor 1:20). Its present form, along with its rulers, is passing away (1 Cor 7:31; 2:6). As a result, Paul urges believers not to be conformed to this evil age (Rom 12:2), and believers are saved out of it (Gal 1:4).[19]

For Paul, however, unlike Philo, the positive perspective is ultimate, based on both protology and eschatology. First, Philo seems to hold that sin is intrinsic to the sensible world by virtue of the change endemic to this realm of becoming.[20] But for Paul, sin entered as alien force into the universe (Rom 5:12). The fact that creation was subjected to the bondage of corruption against its will implies that its original state was otherwise (Rom 8:20). As pervasive and deep-rooted as the problem is in this age, for Paul it is not intrinsic to the creation per se. Second, this difference between Paul and Philo on how the problem began leads logically to a difference also over its solution. For Philo, the ultimate goal is to escape and cast off the material: that takes the form of a moderate asceticism in this life, and an immortality of the soul after death. For Paul, the ultimate resolution comes through resurrection and new creation, the transformation of the world, not its abandonment.[21] Believers will receive glorified bodies like Christ's, who is the pattern and firstfruits in his resurrection (1 Cor 15:20–23). While it is undoubtedly difficult to say what kind of body that will be, the analogies of 1 Cor 15:36–41 point to an irreducible materiality. Likewise, all of creation will be set free from its bondage and participate in redemption (Rom 8:21). Thus, a comparison of Philo and Paul illuminates how they both experienced this tension over the sensible realm, and yet differed fundamentally over its diagnosis and solution and thus its ultimate ethical status.

---

[18] *Contra* Murphy-O'Connor 1978, this verse has both cosmology and soteriology in view. See Thiselton 2000: 635–38. On the possible background in Jewish Wisdom traditions and their influence in Corinth, see Sterling 1997: 235–36; Cox 2007: 141–61.

[19] E. Adams 2000 has argued that Paul alters his κόσμος-language between Romans and 1 Corinthians based on the needs of his audience, which would correlate with Philo's differentiation between commentary series.

[20] Cf p.57.

[21] For the connection of eschatology and creation for Paul, see the seminal Dahl 1956.

E. Gnosticism

Given that Philo's ultimately negative perspective sets him apart from either the Wisdom of Solomon or the Apostle Paul, and even the Platonic influence is not what one might expect, perhaps he is closer to Gnosticism. They took a negative view of the world and saw it as something to be delivered from for salvation. There are certainly areas of overlap between Philo and the Gnostics, particularly within anthropology, but significant differences remain. Philo is clear that the Existent, through his Logos or creative power, is the Father and Maker of the universe.[22] There is no other god to which creation of the world can be attributed. All the same, the omission of this claim when γένεσις is used negatively raises questions.[23] Does Philo inadvertently open up space for another creator of the world when it is seen negatively? Likely not. Rather, this reticence is precisely so that he does not have to attribute the 'evil' sensible world to God and thereby call God's character into question. Instead, Philo robustly affirms that the supreme God created the universe out of his goodness. That deals a fatal blow to considering him as a Gnostic proper. Philo is not Gnostic in the technical sense, nor is he its forerunner, in the sense of one link in a chain that culminates logically in Gnosticism.[24] Rather, in the terminology of the Messina Colloquium, Philo is pre-Gnostic, for he holds to themes and motifs that will also appear in full-blown Gnosticism.[25]

F. Mystical-Ascetic Impulse

This section began by asking from where does Philo's ultimately negative perspective on the sensible world come? On the whole it does not come from Scripture – despite the wisdom texts which are skeptical towards creation – which is corroborated by how Wisdom of Solomon and the Apostle Paul both see the world positively (though Paul is ambivalent as well). It is not from the *Timaeus*, despite its great influence on Philo, and even what Platonic negative roots there are, Philo seems to surpass. Yet he is not a Middle Platonist who holds to evil as a cosmological principle, nor is he a Gnostic who attributes the creation of this world to some lesser, perhaps evil, god. Philo resolutely and repeatedly affirms that the one and only God created the world out of goodness. Such claims may suffer theoretically from a conceptual instability,

---

22 This distinguishes him from later Gnostics; cf. Baer 1970: 76. On the names ascribed to God as creator, see Wolfson 1947: 1.211.

23 See p.56.

24 On this view of Philo and Gnosticism, see Chadwick 1966: 302–06; Simon 1967; Pearson 1984; Wilson 1993.

25 Bianchi 1967: xxvii.

but nonetheless they clearly remain true for Philo and distinguish him from these other camps.

If Philo's negative perspective does not find an explanation, therefore, in any of these places, we may speculate that a general mystical-ascetic impulse helped shape this pessimism. We have already seen how the ultimate *telos* for human existence is a mystical, direct vision of God. Practice also holds a foundational place for Philo.[26] Its associated virtue is self-control (ἐγκράτεια), the most profitable of the virtues (*Spec.* 1.173), and the foundation for the Therapeutae to attain the others (*Contempl.* 34).[27] Practice requires hard work, concerned as it is to supplant the passions, but if successful, it may lead to the vision of God (*Mut.* 81–82). The mystical-ascetic impulse encompasses these points, and it refers to a general temperament too, or what Carlos Lévy has described as Philo's 'absolute adherence . . . to the ethics of ascetic and mystic detachment'.[28] Its focal point is the body, which Philo actively disdains in frequently colourful, expressive language. The gap between this language and its moderate application only emphasises how deeply ingrained the ascetic impulse is for Philo. Rarely does he explain what his anti-creation language actually means. Thus what lingers for readers is its harsh rhetorical impact rather than its restrained application. There is a sense with Philo of someone who laments and even detests physical existence. That is corroborated from another direction by the correspondence between allegory and the negative perspective. Once Philo is (relatively) unmoored by the constraints of the literal biblical text, his allegorical interpretation could theoretically go any direction. It is instructive, therefore, that it so often moves toward a negative interpretation of the material world – even when the literal text had nothing to say about it. It is as if Philo is driven to this perspective. Perhaps, therefore, this mystical-ascetic impulse helps shape, at an underlying level, his preference ultimately for a negative evaluation of the world.

III. Contribution of this Book and Further Research

This book has advanced scholarship in three ways. First, it has established decisively Philo's ambivalence about the physical world. Often in the past this has either been overlooked or treated cursorily. This study, however, has shown how pervasively these positive and negative perspectives run throughout his œuvre. The method adopted here of a close, lexical-semantic reading

[26] See p.60 n.132.

[27] Runia 1997: 11–12.

[28] Lévy 2008: 151.

of a wide range of Philonic texts in his own terms has been both necessary and profitable in establishing these dual perspectives. In the process, it has advanced our understanding of some of Philo's key terms, particularly φύσις, for which this book now represents the most thorough treatment. Second, it has explained how these seemingly contradictory perspectives fit together through a multiperspectival interpretation. There had been hints of this approach in the past, but this study sets the argument on a sure footing, especially with reference to Philo's own distinctions between commentary series and ways by which to approach God. Third, the book has teased out the implications for Philo's ultimately negative view and shown how it sets him off from most other philosophical or Jewish influences and contemporaries.

In terms of further research, two important areas should be highlighted. First, a significant *desideratum* is more extensive comparison of Philo's views with other ancient writers. The burden of this study has been to investigate Philo himself. This was necessary because of the need to do justice to the volume and complexity of Philo's own views. Now these results should be brought into much deeper conversation with other ancient philosophical and Jewish-Christian sources. For example, Qumran could prove fruitful, since there is an ascetic tendency but not the same philosophical influence there, and that might yield sharper insight into the influences on this negative perspective. Similarly, the New Testament is famously ambivalent – if not hostile – about the cosmos, which on the surface diverges from Philo. Perhaps, however, there is an underlying similarity in meaning just in a different key. Finally, it would be good to study patristic writers influenced by Philo, namely Clement of Alexandria and Origen, to see whether they followed Philo's cosmological pessimism, and to what extent Christian commitments lead to its reinforcement or modification or neglect.

Second, further study should return to the question that helped launch this work: What ethical role does the sensible world play for Philo? Now that its ethical status has been established, it is possible to study its ethical function. We may hypothesise it will play a part only within the lower approach to God, as a 'way-station' for moral progress. Numerous questions require investigation. For what kinds of moral *topoi* is the sensible realm invoked? Does it ground those commands, or does it corroborate commands established on other grounds (namely Mosaic Law)? May ethical appeals to the physical world be overruled by other 'higher' kinds of warrant? Finally, given the hints we saw of a gap between cosmic Nature and the sensible realm when signified by γένεσις, is there an underlying instability, or even incoherence, to how Philo links ethics and cosmology?

Appendix 1

Philo's Usage of Οὐσία

The appendixes list the definitions for every occurrence in Philo of οὐσία, ὕλη, γένεσις, κόσμος, and φύσις and thus provide the basis of the analysis in Chapters 3–6. The term γενήτος is omitted, since Philo's usage of it is rather straightforward and monochromatic. Hopefully, these appendixes will render my work more transparent and so allow for better engagement with it.

How these findings are presented requires a brief explanation. A forward slash (/) between definitions means it was not possible to decide for that occurrence (for statistical purposes, though, only the first definition listed is counted). An ampersand (&) between definitions indicates the word has more than one referent. An en dash (–) indicates the word has just one referent, but that it bears more than one meaning. That occurs especially with φύσις.

For οὐσία in particular, all occurrences were categorised on the basis of definitions modified from LSJ 1274b–75a. Definitions #3–#5 are on a continuum, so distinctions were sometimes fine, or not possible. Each occurrence of 'matter' (#4) was assigned a positive (pos), neutral (neu), or negative (neg) value.

1. That which is one's own, substance, property

Philosophical meanings

2. Being, reality, opposite of becoming
3. Essence, definition of a thing
4. Substance, matter; existence generally
5. Elements/individual bodies/things themselves
6. Opposite of κατὰ δύναμιν ἢ ἐνέργιαν

Opif. 18	5	*Opif.* 49	2
Opif. 21	4-neg	*Opif.* 54	3
Opif. 27	4-pos	*Opif.* 55	4-neu
Opif. 29	3	*Opif.* 66	3
Opif. 43	3	*Opif.* 67	5

Opif. 69	3/4-neu
Opif. 70	4-neu
Opif. 78	3
Opif. 92	4-neu
Opif. 97	4-neu
Opif. 97	4-neu
Opif. 98	3
Opif. 111	4-neu
Opif. 114	4-pos
Opif. 132	5
Opif. 132	5
Opif. 132	5
Opif. 135	4-neu
Leg. 1.31	4-neg
Leg. 1.61	6
Leg. 1.61	6
Leg. 1.62	6
Leg. 1.62	6
Leg. 1.62	6
Leg. 1.66	5
Leg. 1.91	3
Leg. 1.91	3
Leg. 1.100	6
Leg. 2.81	4-neu
Leg. 3.206	3
Cher. 48	5
Cher. 65	3
Cher. 89	4-neg
Cher. 114	3
Sacr. 108	5–4-neu
Det. 76	5
Det. 76	5
Det. 80	3
Det. 80	3
Det. 81	3
Det. 83	3
Det. 91	3
Post. 15	3
Post. 163	4-neg
Post. 168	3
Post. 169	3
Deus 46	4
Agr. 156	1
Agr. 156	1
Plant. 3	4-neg
Ebr. 22	1
Ebr. 73	5
Ebr. 88	3
Ebr. 191	5
Conf. 81	4-neu
Conf. 85	4-neg
Conf. 89	5/4-neu
Conf. 108	4-neg
Conf. 184	5/4-neu
Conf. 186	5
Migr. 7	5
Migr. 180	5–4-neu
Her. 55	3/4-neu
Her. 56	3/4-neu
Her. 133	4-neu
Her. 140	4-neu
Her. 145	1
Her. 158	5–4-neu
Her. 188	3/5
Her. 247	3
Her. 282	4
Her. 283	5
Congr. 144	4-neu
Fug. 8	4-neg
Fug. 26	5
Fug. 148	4-neg
Fug. 165	3
Fug. 165	3
Mut. 7	2
Mut. 10	3
Mut. 91	1
Mut. 200	3
Somn. 1.30	3
Somn. 1.145	4-neu
Somn. 2.28	3
Somn. 2.45	4-neg
Somn. 2.253	4-neg
Somn. 2.253	4-neg
Abr. 13	5
Abr. 69	4-neu
Abr. 77	4-neu
Abr. 88	4-neu
Abr. 113	5/2
Abr. 162	3/4-pos
Abr. 163	3
Abr. 252	1
Ios. 257	1
Mos. 1.65	5
Mos. 1.70	5

Mos. 1.99	5
Mos. 1.113	4-pos
Mos. 1.118	3
Mos. 1.141	1
Mos. 1.158	2
Mos. 2.76	5
Mos. 2.84	3
Mos. 2.88	5–4-neu
Mos. 2.119	5
Mos. 2.155	5
Mos. 2.158	5
Mos. 2.171	4-neg
Mos. 2.245	1
Mos. 2.254	4-neu
Decal. 30	4-neu
Decal. 31	4-neu
Decal. 64	4-pos
Decal. 107	4-neu
Decal. 122	1
Decal. 134	4-pos
Decal. 155	4-pos
Spec. 1.20	4-neu
Spec. 1.32	3
Spec. 1.36	3
Spec. 1.39	3
Spec. 1.41	3
Spec. 1.47	3
Spec. 1.49	3
Spec. 1.66	4-pos
Spec. 1.179	5
Spec. 1.263	4-neu
Spec. 1.264	4-neu
Spec. 1.266	4-neu
Spec. 1.300	5
Spec. 1.327	3
Spec. 1.327	4-neu
Spec. 1.328	4-neg
Spec. 1.333	5
Spec. 2.32	1
Spec. 2.56	3
Spec. 2.87	1
Spec. 2.94	1
Spec. 2.124	1
Spec. 2.127	1
Spec. 2.129	1
Spec. 2.131	1
Spec. 2.177	5/4-neu
Spec. 2.212	5
Spec. 3.163	1
Spec. 3.182	1
Spec. 3.182	1
Spec. 3.190	4-neu/3
Spec. 4.23	1
Spec. 4.122	3
Spec. 4.123	3
Spec. 4.123	3
Spec. 4.150	1
Spec. 4.159	1
Spec. 4.187	4-neg
Spec. 4.207	5
Spec. 4.215	1
Spec. 4.235	4-pos
Spec. 4.237	4-neu
Virt. 85	4-pos
Virt. 162	3
Virt. 215	3
Praem. 54	1
Prob. 35	1
Contempl. 7	4-neu
Contempl. 13	1
Contempl. 14	1
Contempl. 16	1
Contempl. 18	1
Contempl. 61	1
Contempl. 61	1
Aet. 4	4-neu
Aet. 20	5
Aet. 21	4-neu
Aet. 29	5
Aet. 48	5
Aet. 49	5
Aet. 51	4-neu
Aet. 81	5
Aet. 85	5
Aet. 86	5
Aet. 90	5
Aet. 102	5
Aet. 103	5
Aet. 123	5
Aet. 135	5
Flacc. 94	1
Flacc. 130	1
Flacc. 132	1
Flacc. 148	1

Flacc. 150	1	*QG* 1.92	3/4-pos
Flacc. 151	1	*QG* 2.12	4-neu
Flacc. 171	1	*QG* 2.15	4-neu
Legat. 80	5	*QG* 2.59	3
Legat. 105	1	*QG* 2.59	3
Legat. 114	3/4-neu	*QG* 2.59	3
Legat. 343	1	*QG* 2.59	3
Legat. 344	1	*QG* 3.38	4-neu
Prov. 2.50	4-neu	*QG* 3.49	4-neu
Prov. 2.50	4-neu	*QG* 4.8	4-pos
Prov. 2.50	4-pos	*QG* 4.30	5
Prov. 2.51	3		

Appendix 2

Philo's Usage of Ὕλη

All occurrences of ὕλη were categorised on the basis of definitions modified from LSJ 1847b–48a. Each occurrence of 'matter' (#4) was assigned a value as positive (pos), neutral (neu), or negative (neg).

1. Forest
2. Wood that has been cut down (e.g., firewood); fuel
3. Stuff from which a thing is made
   a. Material
   b. Subject-matter (often for a poem or treatise)
   c. Medical-related
   d. Material resources (in the plural)
4. Philosophical: matter; often opposed to νοῦς

Opif. 40	1	*Leg.* 3.240	3a
Opif. 42	1	*Leg.* 3.243	4-neg
Opif. 62	4-neu	*Leg.* 3.252	4-neg
Opif. 136	4-pos	*Cher.* 80	3a
Opif. 137	4-pos	*Cher.* 100	3a
Opif. 142	3a	*Cher.* 125	3a
Opif. 146	4-neu	*Cher.* 126	3a
Opif. 153	1	*Cher.* 127	3a
Opif. 171	4-neu	*Det.* 20	3a
Leg. 1.3	4-neu	*Det.* 105	1
Leg. 1.29	3b	*Det.* 109	3a
Leg. 1.31	4-neg	*Det.* 111	1
Leg. 1.42	4-neg	*Det.* 117	3a
Leg. 1.49	1	*Post.* 61	4-neg
Leg. 1.83	4-neg	*Post.* 115	4-neg
Leg. 1.88	4-neg	*Post.* 116	3b
Leg. 2.19	4-neu	*Post.* 120	3b
Leg. 2.51	4-neg	*Post.* 128	3d
Leg. 2.80	4-neu	*Post.* 163	4-neg
Leg. 2.107	3b	*Post.* 165	4-neg
Leg. 3.114	3a	*Deus* 8	3a–4-neg
Leg. 3.152	4-neg	*Deus* 153	3d

Agr. 19	1	*Mut.* 215	3d
Agr. 25	3d	*Somn.* 1.126	3d
Agr. 40	3c	*Somn.* 2.93	2
Agr. 48	3d	*Somn.* 2.181	2
Agr. 95	3a	*Abr.* 220	3d
Agr. 97	3a	*Abr.* 223	3d
Plant. 5	4-neu	*Mos.* 1.60	3a
Plant. 8	4-neu	*Mos.* 1.65	2
Plant. 22	4-neg	*Mos.* 1.153	3d
Plant. 97	1	*Mos.* 1.192	1
Ebr. 61	4-neu	*Mos.* 1.317	3a
Ebr. 86	3a	*Mos.* 2.58	2
Ebr. 88	3b	*Mos.* 2.72	3a
Ebr. 89	3a	*Mos.* 2.76	4-neu
Ebr. 90	3a	*Mos.* 2.88	3a
Ebr. 109	3a	*Mos.* 2.90	3a
Ebr. 132	4-neg	*Mos.* 2.93	3a
Ebr. 217	3a	*Mos.* 2.136	3a
Sobr. 36	2	*Mos.* 2.139	3a
Sobr. 39	3d	*Mos.* 2.214	2
Sobr. 43	2	*Mos.* 2.220	3a
Conf. 83	3a	*Mos.* 2.220	3a
Conf. 107	3a	*Decal.* 12	3a
Migr. 97	3a	*Decal.* 66	3a
Migr. 120	3a	*Decal.* 72	3a
Migr. 204	3d	*Decal.* 133	3a
Her. 137	1	*Decal.* 173	1/2
Her. 157	3a–4-neu	*Spec.* 1.21	3a
Her. 158	3a	*Spec.* 1.22	3a
Her. 158	3a	*Spec.* 1.22	3a
Her. 159	3a–4-neg	*Spec.* 1.25	3a
Her. 160	4-neg–3a	*Spec.* 1.47	3a
Her. 216	3a	*Spec.* 1.71	3a
Her. 307	2	*Spec.* 1.74	1
Congr. 11	3b	*Spec.* 1.86	3a
Congr. 55	2	*Spec.* 1.104	3a
Congr. 112	3a	*Spec.* 1.248	3d
Congr. 144	3b	*Spec.* 1.254	2
Fug. 9	4-neg	*Spec.* 1.273	3a
Fug. 35	3d	*Spec.* 1.276	3a
Fug. 45	3d	*Spec.* 1.328	4-neg
Fug. 129	3d	*Spec.* 1.329	4-neg
Fug. 133	3a	*Spec.* 3.180	4-neg
Fug. 134	4-neu	*Spec.* 3.180	4-neg
Fug. 198	4-neg	*Spec.* 4.26	3a
Mut. 89	3d	*Spec.* 4.83	2
Mut. 152	3d	*Spec.* 4.118	2

Spec. 4.125	2
Spec. 4.209	1
Spec. 4.229	1
Virt. 149	3b
Virt. 162	2
Praem. 132	3a
Prob. 65	3d
Prob. 71	2
Contempl. 4	4-neg
Contempl. 49	3a
Contempl. 69	3a
Aet. 64	1
Aet. 96	1
Aet. 127	2
Aet. 132	1
Flacc. 68	2
Flacc. 148	3a
Legat. 9	3d
Legat. 129	2
Legat. 130	2
Legat. 132	2
Legat. 170	3b
Legat. 201	3a
Legat. 222	3a
Prov. 2.40	2
Prov. 2.50	4-neu
Prov. 2.50	3a
Prov. 2.50	3a
Prov. 2.50	3a
Prov. 2.50	3a
Prov. 2.59	3a
QG 1.58	4-neu
QG 2.12a	4-neg
QG 2.12a	4-neg
QG 4.172	2
QE 2.15a	2
QE 2.47	2
QE 2.50a	3d

Appendix 3

Philo's Usage of Γένεσις

All occurrences of γένεσις were categorised on the basis of definitions modified from LSJ 343b. Each occurrence of definitions #1–#4 was assigned a value as positive (pos), neutral (neu), or negative (neg). Moreover, negativity was sometimes judged to be relative (rel.); for example, that Israel thinks only God could nourish him, not any 'created thing' (*Deus* 157), is a *relatively* negative assessment, since such nourishment nonetheless remains necessary for embodied existence.

1. Origin, source
2. Manner of birth, birth, race, descent
3. Production, generation, coming into being, becoming
4. Creation, i.e., created things
5. Race, kind, sort
6. Generation, age
7. Generation of a figure (mathematical)

Opif. 12	3-neg	*Opif.* 64	3-neu
Opif. 12	4-neg	*Opif.* 67	3-neu
Opif. 12	1-pos	*Opif.* 67	3-neu
Opif. 14	4-neu	*Opif.* 68	3-pos
Opif. 25	3-neu	*Opif.* 72	3-neu
Opif. 27	3-neu	*Opif.* 75	3-neu
Opif. 31	3-neu	*Opif.* 77	3-pos
Opif. 34	3-neu	*Opif.* 79	3-neu
Opif. 37	3-neu	*Opif.* 100	3-neu
Opif. 40	3-neu	*Opif.* 129	3-neu/1-neu
Opif. 42	3-pos	*Opif.* 133	3-neu
Opif. 43	3-neu	*Opif.* 139	4-neu
Opif. 46	3-pos	*Opif.* 140	1-neu/3-neu
Opif. 52	3-pos	*Opif.* 151	4-neg
Opif. 52	3-neu	*Opif.* 152	3-neu
Opif. 54	3-neu	*Opif.* 161	3-neu
Opif. 58	3-neu	*Opif.* 168	3-pos
Opif. 59	2-neu	*Opif.* 171	3-pos

Leg. 1.1	3-pos	*Sacr.* 66	4-neg rel
Leg. 1.7	2-neu	*Sacr.* 66	4-neg rel
Leg. 1.18	3-neg	*Sacr.* 70	4-neg
Leg. 1.18	3-neu	*Sacr.* 70	4-neg
Leg. 1.19	3-neu/1-neu	*Sacr.* 72	4-neg rel
Leg. 1.19	3-neu/1-neu	*Sacr.* 72	4-neg
Leg. 1.21	3-neu	*Sacr.* 73	3-neu
Leg. 2.2	3-neu	*Sacr.* 98	2-neu
Leg. 2.6	3-neg	*Sacr.* 102	3-neu
Leg. 2.11	3-neu	*Sacr.* 102	3-neu
Leg. 2.15	1-neu/3-neu	*Sacr.* 120	4-neg
Leg. 2.24	3-neu	*Det.* 46	4-neg
Leg. 2.74	3-neu	*Det.* 80	3-neu
Leg. 2.83	4-neg	*Det.* 114	3-pos
Leg. 2.83	4-neg	*Det.* 121	2-neu
Leg. 3.7	4-neg	*Det.* 124	4-neg
Leg. 3.73	4-neg	*Det.* 138	2-neu
Leg. 3.77	2-neu	*Det.* 139	3-neu
Leg. 3.78	4-neg	*Det.* 146	4-neg
Leg. 3.78	3-pos	*Det.* 147	3-pos
Leg. 3.85	2-neu	*Det.* 148	4-neg
Leg. 3.86	2-neu	*Post.* 5	4-neu
Leg. 3.89	3-neg	*Post.* 23	4-neg
Leg. 3.101	4-pos	*Post.* 23	4-neg
Leg. 3.185	3-neu	*Post.* 29	4-neg
Cher. 16	4-neg	*Post.* 30	4-neg
Cher. 19	4-neg	*Post.* 33	3-neu
Cher. 43	3-neu	*Post.* 42	4-pos
Cher. 50	3-neg	*Post.* 65	3-neu
Cher. 51	3-neg	*Post.* 89	4-neu
Cher. 54	3-neu	*Post.* 125	3-neu
Cher. 62	4-neu	*Post.* 133	4-pos
Cher. 75	4-neg	*Post.* 168	4-neg
Cher. 97	4-neg	*Post.* 171	3-neu
Cher. 108	4-neu	*Post.* 172	4-neu
Cher. 109	4-neu	*Post.* 177	3-neu
Cher. 114	2-neu	*Post.* 182	4-neg
Cher. 114	2-neu	*Gig.* 1	2-neu
Cher. 120	2-neu	*Gig.* 3	2-neu
Cher. 125	3-neu	*Gig.* 42	4-neu
Sacr. 4	3-neu	*Gig.* 53	4-neg
Sacr. 10	2-neu	*Deus* 4	4-neg
Sacr. 14	2-neu	*Deus* 21	3-pos
Sacr. 17	2-neu	*Deus* 31	3-neu
Sacr. 42	2-neu	*Deus* 56	4-neu
Sacr. 58	4-neg	*Deus* 58	3-neu
Sacr. 64	4-neg rel	*Deus* 61	4-neg rel

Deus 75	2-neu
Deus 77	4-neg rel
Deus 87	2-neu
Deus 108	3-pos
Deus 117	6
Deus 119	3-neu
Deus 119	2-neg
Deus 123	2-neu
Deus 157	4-neg rel
Deus 179	4-neg
Agr. 6	2-neu
Agr. 25	2-neu
Agr. 103	2-neu
Plant. 12	3-neu
Plant. 53	4-neg
Plant. 61	4-neg rel
Plant. 61	4-neg rel
Plant. 64	4-neg
Plant. 66	4-neg rel
Plant. 86	4-pos
Plant. 93	4-neg rel
Plant. 117	3-pos
Plant. 130	4-pos
Ebr. 30	4-pos
Ebr. 31	2-neu
Ebr. 42	3-neu
Ebr. 69	4-neg
Ebr. 73	4-neg
Ebr. 77	4-neu
Ebr. 171	2-neu
Ebr. 208	2-neu
Ebr. 208	2-neu
Ebr. 211	3-neu
Sobr. 4	4-neg
Sobr. 8	2-neu
Sobr. 22	2-neu
Sobr. 22	2-neu
Sobr. 23	2-neu
Sobr. 26	2-neu
Sobr. 28	2-neu
Sobr. 60	5
Sobr. 62	4-pos
Conf. 42	3-neu
Conf. 57	4-neg
Conf. 98	4-neu
Conf. 106	2-neu
Conf. 114	3-neu/4-neu
Conf. 144	3-neu
Conf. 149	2-neu/3-neu
Conf. 175	3-neu
Conf. 186	3-neu
Conf. 187	5
Conf. 190	1-neu
Conf. 191	1-neu
Conf. 192	5
Conf. 196	3-neu
Migr. 6	4-neu
Migr. 22	4-neu
Migr. 95	2-neu
Migr. 115	4-neg rel
Migr. 136	3-pos
Migr. 183	4-pos
Migr. 207	5
Her. 30	4-neg
Her. 38	2-neu
Her. 45	4-neg
Her. 45	4-neg
Her. 50	2-neu
Her. 93	4-neg
Her. 97	2-neu
Her. 103	4-neg rel
Her. 115	3-neu
Her. 121	4-neu
Her. 122	3-pos
Her. 146	3-pos
Her. 163	3-pos
Her. 164	3-neu
Her. 170	4-neg
Her. 170	4-pos
Her. 171	3-pos
Her. 171	3-neu
Her. 172	3-pos
Her. 179	4-neg
Her. 206	4-neu
Her. 209	3-neu
Her. 246	3-neu
Her. 247	3-neu
Her. 257	3-neu
Her. 280	2-neu
Her. 314	2-neu
Congr. 13	3-neg
Congr. 14	2-neu
Congr. 59	3-neg
Congr. 81	3-neg

Congr. 84	3-neg
Congr. 91	7
Congr. 130	2-neg
Congr. 134	4-neg
Fug. 70	3-neg
Fug. 84	1-neg
Fug. 109	3-pos
Fug. 136	4-neg rel
Fug. 160	4-neg rel
Fug. 161	4-neu
Fug. 173	4-neu
Fug. 176	3-neu
Fug. 204	4-neg rel
Mut. 10	5
Mut. 13	4-neg rel
Mut. 18	4-neu
Mut. 27	3-pos
Mut. 27	3-pos
Mut. 28	4-pos
Mut. 36	3-neu
Mut. 46	3-pos
Mut. 46	3-pos
Mut. 48	4-neu
Mut. 74	3-neu
Mut. 127	4-neg
Mut. 130	2-neu
Mut. 156	4-neg
Mut. 157	3-neu
Mut. 166	4-neu
Mut. 177	2-neu
Mut. 188	3-neu
Mut. 195	4-neg rel
Mut. 218	2-neu
Mut. 223	2-pos
Mut. 228	4-neu
Mut. 255	2-neu
Mut. 264	4-neg rel
Mut. 268	3-neu
Somn. 1.37	2-neu
Somn. 1.37	2-neu
Somn. 1.38	2-neu
Somn. 1.66	4-neg
Somn. 1.77	4-neu
Somn. 1.184	4-neg
Somn. 1.189	2-neu
Somn. 1.197	3-neu
Somn. 1.211	4-neg
Somn. 1.244	4-neg rel
Somn. 1.249	4-neg rel
Somn. 2.28	4-neg
Somn. 2.59	3-neu
Somn. 2.67	4-neg
Somn. 2.68	4-neg
Somn. 2.100	4-neg
Somn. 2.107	4-neg
Somn. 2.131	3-neg
Somn. 2.221	3-neu
Somn. 2.221	2-pos
Somn. 2.231	4-neu
Somn. 2.253	4-neg
Somn. 2.273	4-neg
Somn. 2.290	4-neg
Abr. 1	3-pos
Abr. 1	3-pos
Abr. 9	3-neu
Abr. 11	3-neu
Abr. 31	6
Abr. 110	2-neu
Abr. 162	3-neu
Abr. 195	2-neu
Abr. 248	2-pos
Abr. 254	2-neu
Mos. 1.96	3-pos
Mos. 1.98	3-pos/1-pos
Mos. 1.116	3-neu
Mos. 1.212	3-pos
Mos. 1.279	3-neu
Mos. 2.1	2-neu
Mos. 2.37	3-pos
Mos. 2.47	3-pos
Mos. 2.48	3-pos
Mos. 2.51	3-pos
Mos. 2.60	6-neu
Mos. 2.64	3-neu
Mos. 2.80	3-pos/1-pos
Mos. 2.111	5
Mos. 2.119	3-neu
Mos. 2.147	4-neg
Mos. 2.260	3-neg
Mos. 2.263	3-neu
Mos. 2.266	3-pos
Decal. 58	3-neg
Decal. 117	3-neu
Decal. 163	3-neu

Spec. 1.6	3-neu
Spec. 1.10	3-pos
Spec. 1.16	3-neu
Spec. 1.27	3-neg
Spec. 1.43	4-neg
Spec. 1.80	2-neu
Spec. 1.102	3-neu
Spec. 1.112	3-neu
Spec. 1.112	3-neu
Spec. 1.114	2-neg
Spec. 1.140	2-neu
Spec. 1.210	3-pos
Spec. 1.277	4-neu
Spec. 1.295	2-neu
Spec. 1.326	2-neg
Spec. 2.5	3-neu
Spec. 2.6	4-neu
Spec. 2.42	2-neu
Spec. 2.58	3-pos
Spec. 2.58	3-neu
Spec. 2.133	2-neu
Spec. 2.152	3-pos
Spec. 2.154	3-pos
Spec. 2.160	3-pos
Spec. 2.166	4-neg
Spec. 2.233	2-neu
Spec. 2.248	3-neu
Spec. 3.23	2-neu
Spec. 3.36	5
Spec. 3.47	2-neg
Spec. 3.58	2-neu
Spec. 3.62	2-neu
Spec. 3.112	2-neu
Spec. 3.178	2-neg
Spec. 3.178	4-neg rel
Spec. 3.179	2-neg
Spec. 3.179	2-neu
Spec. 3.188	3-neu
Spec. 3.199	2-neu
Spec. 4.68	2-neu
Spec. 4.187	3-pos
Spec. 4.208	3-neu
Spec. 4.209	3-neu
Virt. 62	2-neu/3-neu
Virt. 72	2-neu
Virt. 93	3-neu
Virt. 112	2-neu
Virt. 130	2-pos
Virt. 132	3-neu
Virt. 134	3-neu
Virt. 203	4-neu
Virt. 218	4-neg rel
Praem. 1	3-pos
Praem. 1	4-neu
Praem. 9	3-pos
Praem. 13	3-pos
Praem. 22	3-neu
Praem. 63	2-neu
Praem. 68	3-neu
Praem. 132	1-neu
Praem. 145	3-neu
Praem. 149	3-neu
Praem. 160	2-neu
Praem. 160	2-neu
Prob. 80	3-pos
Prob. 105	2-neu
Contempl. 6	2-neu
Contempl. 65	3-pos/1-pos
Aet. 8	3-neu
Aet. 8	3-neu/1-neu
Aet. 8	3-neu
Aet. 14	3-neu
Aet. 14	3-neu
Aet. 27	3-neg
Aet. 53	3-neu
Aet. 57	2-neu
Aet. 62	3-neu
Aet. 65	3-neu
Aet. 66	3-neu
Aet. 73	3-neu/4-neu
Aet. 78	1-neu
Aet. 79	5
Aet. 89	3-neu
Aet. 94	3-neu
Aet. 95	3-neu
Aet. 99	3-pos
Aet. 100	1-neu
Aet. 100	2-neu
Aet. 111	3-neu
Aet. 111	3-neu
Aet. 117	3-neu
Aet. 118	3-neu
Aet. 134	3-neu
Aet. 137	3-neu

Flacc. 187	3-neu	*QG* 2.34a	3-pos
Legat. 56	2-neu	*QG* 2.66	3-pos
Prov. 2.50 (A)	3-pos	*QG* 3.12	3-neu
Prov. 2.10 (LCL)	3-neu	*QG* 3.21	3-neu
Prov. 2.59 (LCL)	3-neu	*QG* 4.8a	3-pos
Prov. 2.71 (LCL)	3-neu	*QG* 4.8b	3-neg
QG 1.1	3-neu	*QG* 4.8b	3-neg
QG 1.1	3-neu	*QG* 4.51b	3-neu
QG 1.64c	3-neu	*QE* 1.1	3-neu
QG 2.13	3-pos	*QE* 2.19	3-pos
QG 2.15a	3-neu	*QE* 2.46	3-pos
QG 2.17b	3-neu	*QE* 2.46	2-neu
QG 2.31	3-pos	*QE isf* 10	4-neg

Appendix 4

Philo's Usage of Κόσμος

All occurrences of κόσμος were categorised on the basis of definitions derived from LSJ 985a.

1. Order
2. Form, fashion
3. Government
4. Ornament, decoration
5. World-order, universe (no differentiation)
   a. Sensible
   b. Intelligible
   c. Some part of
6. World metaphorically: microcosm
7. Inhabited world

Opif. 3	5a
Opif. 3	5a
Opif. 3	5a
Opif. 7	5a
Opif. 9	5a
Opif. 11	5a
Opif. 12	5a
Opif. 13	5a
Opif. 14	5a
Opif. 15	5b
Opif. 16	5a
Opif. 17	5b
Opif. 19	5b
Opif. 20	5b
Opif. 24	5b
Opif. 25	5a
Opif. 25	5b
Opif. 26	5a
Opif. 26	5a
Opif. 26	5a
Opif. 33	5a
Opif. 35	5b
Opif. 36	5b
Opif. 52	5a
Opif. 53	4
Opif. 55	5b
Opif. 62	4
Opif. 69	5a
Opif. 77	5a
Opif. 77	5a
Opif. 78	5a
Opif. 89	5a
Opif. 89	5a
Opif. 111	5a
Opif. 131	5a
Opif. 139	4
Opif. 142	5a
Opif. 143	5a
Opif. 146	5a
Opif. 151	5a
Opif. 171	5a
Opif. 171	5a

Opif. 171	5a	*Sacr.* 40	5a
Opif. 171	5a	*Sacr.* 65	5a
Opif. 172	5a	*Sacr.* 97	5a
Leg. 1.1	5a & 5b	*Det.* 8	5a
Leg. 1.1	5a & 5b	*Det.* 54	5a
Leg. 1.2	5a	*Det.* 62	5a
Leg. 1.2	5a	*Det.* 75	5a
Leg. 1.2	5a	*Det.* 89	5a
Leg. 1.2	5a	*Det.* 90	5a
Leg. 1.44	5a	*Det.* 90	5a
Leg. 2.2	5a	*Det.* 116	5a
Leg. 2.3	5a	*Det.* 154	5a
Leg. 2.3	5a	*Det.* 154	5a
Leg. 3.5	5a	*Post.* 5	5a
Leg. 3.5	5a	*Post.* 6	5a
Leg. 3.6	5a	*Post.* 7	5a
Leg. 3.6	5a	*Post.* 14	5a
Leg. 3.7	5a	*Post.* 58	6
Leg. 3.7	5a	*Post.* 144	5c
Leg. 3.30	5a	*Post.* 166	4
Leg. 3.78	5a	*Post.* 167	5
Leg. 3.78	5a	*Gig.* 7	5a
Leg. 3.84	5a	*Gig.* 61	5a
Leg. 3.97	5a	*Gig.* 61	5b
Leg. 3.99	5a	*Gig.* 64	5a
Leg. 3.100	5a	*Deus* 19	5a
Leg. 3.175	5b	*Deus* 30	5a
Cher. 23	5a	*Deus* 31	5a
Cher. 26	5a	*Deus* 31	5a
Cher. 26	5a	*Deus* 57	5a
Cher. 86	5a	*Deus* 62	5a
Cher. 88	5a	*Deus* 79	5a
Cher. 99	4	*Deus* 97	5a
Cher. 104	4	*Deus* 106	5a
Cher. 110	5a	*Deus* 107	5a
Cher. 112	5a	*Deus* 107	5a
Cher. 119	5a	*Deus* 108	5a
Cher. 119	5a	*Agr.* 51	5a
Cher. 120	5a	*Agr.* 52	5a
Cher. 127	5a	*Agr.* 152	4
Sacr. 8	5a	*Plant.* 2	5a
Sacr. 8	5a	*Plant.* 4	5a
Sacr. 21	4	*Plant.* 6	5a
Sacr. 25	4	*Plant.* 7	5a
Sacr. 26	4	*Plant.* 8	5a
Sacr. 34	5a	*Plant.* 22	5a
Sacr. 40	5a	*Plant.* 28	5a

Plant. 28	6
Plant. 33	5a
Plant. 45	5a
Plant. 48	5a
Plant. 50	5a
Plant. 69	5a
Plant. 120	5c
Plant. 126	5a
Plant. 127	5a
Plant. 128	4
Plant. 131	5a
Plant. 139	5a
Plant. 162	1
Ebr. 30	5a
Ebr. 32	5a
Ebr. 62	5a
Ebr. 75	5a
Ebr. 108	5a
Ebr. 118	5a
Ebr. 187	5a
Ebr. 199	5a
Sobr. 53	5a
Sobr. 54	5a
Sobr. 55	5a
Conf. 56	5a
Conf. 96	5a
Conf. 97	5a
Conf. 98	5a
Conf. 98	5a
Conf. 99	5a
Conf. 106	5a
Conf. 114	5a
Conf. 136	5a
Conf. 170	5a
Conf. 172	5b
Conf. 173	5a & 5b
Conf. 185	1
Conf. 196	5a
Migr. 41	5a
Migr. 59	5a
Migr. 97	4
Migr. 97	4
Migr. 103	5b
Migr. 105	5c
Migr. 131	5
Migr. 136	5a
Migr. 138	5a

Migr. 179	5a
Migr. 180	5a
Migr. 181	5a
Migr. 181	5a
Migr. 186	5a
Migr. 194	5a
Migr. 203	4
Migr. 220	5a
Her. 37	5a
Her. 75	5a
Her. 97	5a
Her. 98	5a
Her. 99	5a
Her. 110	5a
Her. 111	5b
Her. 111	5a
Her. 120	5a
Her. 122	5a
Her. 126	5a
Her. 133	5a
Her. 134	5a
Her. 140	5a
Her. 152	5a
Her. 152	5a
Her. 155	5a
Her. 155	6
Her. 155	5a
Her. 169	5a
Her. 197	5a
Her. 199	5a
Her. 199	5a
Her. 200	5a
Her. 206	1
Her. 207	5a
Her. 226	5a
Her. 233	5a
Her. 236	5a
Her. 263	5a
Her. 281	5a
Her. 301	5a
Her. 311	5a
Congr. 21	5a
Congr. 48	5a
Congr. 49	5a
Congr. 49	5a
Congr. 104	5a
Congr. 105	5a

Congr. 113	4
Congr. 117	5a
Congr. 133	5a
Congr. 144	5a
Fug. 12	5a
Fug. 95	5a
Fug. 103	5a
Fug. 110	5a
Fug. 161	5a
Fug. 164	5a
Fug. 198	5a
Mut. 16	5a
Mut. 18	5a
Mut. 27	5a
Mut. 30	5a
Mut. 44	5a
Mut. 45	5a
Mut. 46	5a
Mut. 46	5a
Mut. 76	5a
Mut. 111	4
Mut. 135	5a
Mut. 140	5a
Mut. 246	4
Mut. 267	5b
Somn. 1.15	5a
Somn. 1.16	5a
Somn. 1.23	5a
Somn. 1.24	5a
Somn. 1.33	5a
Somn. 1.34	5a
Somn. 1.39	5a
Somn. 1.102	4
Somn. 1.104	4
Somn. 1.109	4
Somn. 1.116	5a
Somn. 1.134	5a
Somn. 1.135	5a
Somn. 1.146	5a
Somn. 1.149	5a
Somn. 1.157	5a
Somn. 1.159	5a
Somn. 1.175	5a
Somn. 1.184	5a
Somn. 1.185	5a
Somn. 1.186	5a
Somn. 1.186	5b
Somn. 1.188	5b
Somn. 1.188	5b
Somn. 1.188	5b
Somn. 1.203	5a
Somn. 1.207	5a
Somn. 1.215	5a
Somn. 1.215	5a
Somn. 1.241	1
Somn. 1.243	5a
Somn. 2.6	5a
Somn. 2.26	5a
Somn. 2.28	5a
Somn. 2.44	4
Somn. 2.45	5a
Somn. 2.51	1
Somn. 2.81	5a
Somn. 2.116	5a
Somn. 2.117	5a
Somn. 2.139	1
Somn. 2.173	5a
Somn. 2.220	5a
Somn. 2.220	5a
Somn. 2.248	5a
Somn. 2.289	5a
Somn. 2.291	5a
Somn. 2.294	5a
Abr. 1	5a
Abr. 2	5a
Abr. 2	5a
Abr. 28	5a
Abr. 44	5a
Abr. 46	5a
Abr. 57	5a
Abr. 61	5a
Abr. 69	5a
Abr. 69	5a
Abr. 70	5a
Abr. 71	5a
Abr. 74	5a
Abr. 75	5a
Abr. 77	5a
Abr. 78	5a
Abr. 84	5a
Abr. 88	5a
Abr. 159	5a
Abr. 159	5a
Abr. 159	5a

Abr. 162	5a
Abr. 163	5a
Abr. 164	5a
Abr. 166	5a
Abr. 207	5a
Abr. 267	4
Abr. 272	5a
Ios. 29	5a
Ios. 69	5a
Ios. 147	5a
Ios. 150	4
Ios. 150	4
Mos. 1.41	5a
Mos. 1.96	5a
Mos. 1.112	5a
Mos. 1.155	5a
Mos. 1.157	5a
Mos. 1.201	5a
Mos. 1.207	5a
Mos. 1.213	5a
Mos. 1.272	5a
Mos. 1.284	5a
Mos. 1.317	4
Mos. 2.14	5a
Mos. 2.47	5a
Mos. 2.48	5a
Mos. 2.51	5a
Mos. 2.53	5a
Mos. 2.64	5a
Mos. 2.88	5a
Mos. 2.101	5a
Mos. 2.108	5a
Mos. 2.117	5a
Mos. 2.120	5a
Mos. 2.127	5b
Mos. 2.133	5a
Mos. 2.134	5a
Mos. 2.135	5a
Mos. 2.135	5a
Mos. 2.135	6
Mos. 2.145	4
Mos. 2.191	5c
Mos. 2.194	5a
Mos. 2.209	5a
Mos. 2.210	5a
Mos. 2.238	5a
Mos. 2.243	4
Mos. 2.263	5a
Mos. 2.266	5a
Mos. 2.266	5a
Mos. 2.267	5a
Decal. 28	1
Decal. 31	5a
Decal. 37	5a
Decal. 38	5a
Decal. 44	5a
Decal. 51	5a
Decal. 53	5a
Decal. 58	5a
Decal. 60	5a
Decal. 66	5a
Decal. 81	5a
Decal. 90	5a
Decal. 97	5a
Decal. 99	5a
Decal. 100	5a
Decal. 101	5a
Decal. 120	5a
Decal. 133	4
Decal. 134	5a
Decal. 155	5a
Spec. 1.13	5a
Spec. 1.14	5a
Spec. 1.15	1
Spec. 1.31	5a
Spec. 1.34	5a
Spec. 1.35	5a
Spec. 1.41	5a
Spec. 1.44	5a
Spec. 1.49	5a
Spec. 1.66	5a
Spec. 1.76	5a
Spec. 1.81	5a
Spec. 1.84	5a
Spec. 1.93	5a
Spec. 1.96	5a
Spec. 1.96	5a
Spec. 1.97	5a
Spec. 1.134	4
Spec. 1.163	1
Spec. 1.170	5a
Spec. 1.210	5a
Spec. 1.269	5a
Spec. 1.294	5a

Spec. 1.296	5a	*Virt*. 220	5a
Spec. 1.300	5a	*Praem*. 1	5a
Spec. 1.302	5a–5b	*Praem*. 23	5a
Spec. 1.331	7	*Praem*. 34	5a
Spec. 1.336	5a	*Praem*. 34	5a
Spec. 2.5	5a	*Praem*. 37	5b
Spec. 2.45	5a	*Praem*. 41	5a
Spec. 2.52	5a	*Praem*. 41	5a
Spec. 2.58	5a	*Praem*. 41	5a
Spec. 2.59	5a	*Praem*. 76	1
Spec. 2.62	1	*Prob*. 81	4
Spec. 2.70	5a	*Contempl*. 5	5a
Spec. 2.130	5a	*Contempl*. 66	1
Spec. 2.150	5a	*Contempl*. 75	1
Spec. 2.151	5a	*Contempl*. 80	1
Spec. 2.152	5a	*Contempl*. 90	5a
Spec. 2.156	5a	*Aet*. 1	5a
Spec. 2.160	5a	*Aet*. 1	5a
Spec. 2.160	5a	*Aet*. 3	5a
Spec. 2.165	5a	*Aet*. 3	5a
Spec. 2.198	5a	*Aet*. 4	5a
Spec. 2.198	5a	*Aet*. 4	5c
Spec. 2.210	5a	*Aet*. 4	5a
Spec. 2.224	5a	*Aet*. 6	5a
Spec. 2.225	5a	*Aet*. 7	5a
Spec. 2.255	5a	*Aet*. 8	5a
Spec. 3.1	5a	*Aet*. 8	5a
Spec. 3.1	5a	*Aet*. 8	5a
Spec. 3.83	5a	*Aet*. 8	5a
Spec. 3.152	5a	*Aet*. 9	5a
Spec. 3.187	5a	*Aet*. 10	5a
Spec. 3.187	5a	*Aet*. 11	5a
Spec. 3.189	5a	*Aet*. 12	5a
Spec. 3.190	5a	*Aet*. 14	5a
Spec. 3.191	5a	*Aet*. 15	5a
Spec. 3.202	5a	*Aet*. 17	5a
Spec. 4.118	5a	*Aet*. 18	5a
Spec. 4.131	5a	*Aet*. 19	5a
Spec. 4.187	5a	*Aet*. 21	5a
Spec. 4.210	1–4	*Aet*. 21	5a
Spec. 4.237	5a	*Aet*. 22	5a
Virt. 21	4	*Aet*. 24	5a
Virt. 62	5	*Aet*. 25	5a
Virt. 73	5a	*Aet*. 25	5a
Virt. 74	5a	*Aet*. 27	5a
Virt. 212	5a	*Aet*. 32	5a
Virt. 216	5a	*Aet*. 32	5a

Aet. 34	5a
Aet. 34	5a
Aet. 37	5a
Aet. 37	5a
Aet. 39	5a
Aet. 41	5a
Aet. 47	5a
Aet. 47	5a
Aet. 49	5a
Aet. 50	5a
Aet. 50	5a
Aet. 50	5a
Aet. 51	5a
Aet. 51	5a
Aet. 51	5a
Aet. 51	5a
Aet. 52	5a
Aet. 52	5a
Aet. 52	5a
Aet. 53	5a
Aet. 53	5a
Aet. 54	5a
Aet. 54	5a
Aet. 54	5a
Aet. 55	5a
Aet. 55	5a
Aet. 55	5a
Aet. 56	4
Aet. 69	5a
Aet. 70	5a
Aet. 70	5a
Aet. 71	5a
Aet. 72	5a
Aet. 74	5a
Aet. 75	5a
Aet. 75	5a
Aet. 75	5a
Aet. 75	5a
Aet. 75	5a
Aet. 76	5a
Aet. 78	5a
Aet. 78	5a
Aet. 80	5a
Aet. 83	5a
Aet. 84	5a
Aet. 85	5a
Aet. 87	5a
Aet. 88	5a
Aet. 89	5a
Aet. 90	5a
Aet. 93	5a
Aet. 94	5a
Aet. 94	5a
Aet. 95	5a
Aet. 99	5a
Aet. 101	5a
Aet. 102	5a
Aet. 102	5a
Aet. 106	5a
Aet. 107	5a
Aet. 107	5a
Aet. 108	5a
Aet. 109	5a
Aet. 112	5a
Aet. 113	5a
Aet. 114	5a
Aet. 114	5a
Aet. 114	5a
Aet. 116	5a
Aet. 117	5a
Aet. 124	5a
Aet. 124	5a
Aet. 129	5a
Aet. 129	5a
Aet. 130	5a
Aet. 131	5a
Aet. 132	5a
Aet. 137	5a
Aet. 142	5a
Aet. 144	5a
Aet. 145	5a
Aet. 150	5a
Flacc. 92	1
Flacc. 123	5c
Flacc. 148	4
Flacc. 169	5a
Flacc. 169	5a
Legat. 115	5a
Legat. 118	5a
Legat. 151	4
Legat. 295	4
Legat. 309	7
Hypoth. 7.12	1
Prov. 1	5a

Prov. 1	5a	*QG* 2.13b	5a
Prov. 2.2	5a	*QG* 2.31	5a
Prov. 2.3	5a	*QG* 2.34a	5a
Prov. 2.6	5a	*QG* 2.54a	5a
Prov. 2.17	4	*QG* 2.66	5a
Prov. 2.39	5a	*QG* 3.38b	5a
Prov. 2.44	5a	*QG* 4.8b	5b
Prov. 2.45	5a	*QG* 4.33b	5a
Prov. 2.54	5a	*QG* 4.51a	5a
Prov. 2.58	1	*QG* isf 1	5a
Prov. 2.69	5a	*QG* isf 10	5a
QG 1.1	5a	*QG* par 2.4	5b
QG 1.64a	5a	*QE* 2.46	5a
QG 1.74	5a	*QE* 2.46	5a

Appendix 5

Philo's Usage of Φύσις

All occurrences of φύσις were categorised on the basis of definitions modified from Martens 2003: 67–81. Philo frequently utilises the polyvalence of φύσις, which is demonstrated in nearly 25% of its 1342 occurrences bearing multiple definitions for a single referent (signified by an en dash). That does not include when φύσις is part of the educational triad (#3) or metonymic for God (#6), since neither are actually distinct meanings.

1. Natura creatrix/power and growth inherent in life
2. Inherent character of a thing
    - c. Existence/things in general/universe
    - d. Divine (not God)
    - h. Human nature
        - s. Specific
        - u. Universal
    - g. God's nature
    - o. Other
3. Part of instruction-nature-practice triad
4. World or universe
    - r. Realm in general
5. Order of the cosmos
    - nl. Natural law
6. Metonymy for God
7. Kind/type/genus

Opif. 3	5
Opif. 8	4–5
Opif. 13	5nl
Opif. 15	2o
Opif. 21	2g
Opif. 23	2o
Opif. 29	2o
Opif. 33	2o–5
Opif. 35	2o
Opif. 36	2o
Opif. 38	2o
Opif. 44	1–4
Opif. 45	4
Opif. 49	2o
Opif. 49	2o
Opif. 49	2o
Opif. 53	4
Opif. 54	2o

Opif. 55	2o
Opif. 60	2o
Opif. 61	2o
Opif. 66	2c
Opif. 67	2o
Opif. 67	1
Opif. 67	1
Opif. 68	1
Opif. 69	2o
Opif. 73	2o
Opif. 73	2hu
Opif. 79	1
Opif. 82	2hu–1
Opif. 82	2o–5
Opif. 83	2hu/2o–5
Opif. 83	2o
Opif. 84	2hu–5
Opif. 85	1
Opif. 85	5
Opif. 89	2o
Opif. 90	2o
Opif. 95	2o
Opif. 97	2o
Opif. 97	2o
Opif. 102	2o
Opif. 105	2hu
Opif. 106	4
Opif. 111	2o
Opif. 113	1
Opif. 114	2hu
Opif. 124	1
Opif. 126	2o
Opif. 128	4
Opif. 129	2o–1–5
Opif. 130	1–6
Opif. 133	1
Opif. 133	1
Opif. 134	2hu
Opif. 134	2hu
Opif. 135	2g
Opif. 135	2hu
Opif. 139	4
Opif. 140	4
Opif. 143	5–5nl
Opif. 144	2d
Opif. 146	2d
Opif. 149	2hu
Opif. 150	2hu
Opif. 150	2o
Opif. 151	2g
Opif. 154	2o–5
Opif. 159	2o–5
Opif. 169	2g
Opif. 171	5nl
Leg. 1.1	2d
Leg. 1.2	2o
Leg. 1.8	5–4
Leg. 1.16	2o
Leg. 1.18	2o
Leg. 1.18	2hs
Leg. 1.28	1
Leg. 1.38	2g
Leg. 1.50	1
Leg. 1.52	2o
Leg. 1.77	2o
Leg. 1.92	2hs/2hu
Leg. 1.107	1
Leg. 1.107	1–5
Leg. 2.2	2g
Leg. 2.10	2d
Leg. 2.22	1
Leg. 2.22	1
Leg. 2.23	1
Leg. 2.23	2d
Leg. 2.37	1
Leg. 2.42	2o
Leg. 2.47	2o
Leg. 2.67	2o
Leg. 2.75	1
Leg. 2.89	2h/2o
Leg. 2.99	2o
Leg. 2.105	2o–2hs
Leg. 3.7	(2g & 2c)–5
Leg. 3.12	5–4
Leg. 3.24	2h
Leg. 3.61	2o
Leg. 3.64	1
Leg. 3.67	2o
Leg. 3.71	2o–5
Leg. 3.75	2o & 2o
Leg. 3.77	2hs
Leg. 3.78	2c
Leg. 3.84	2g
Leg. 3.89	2o–5

Leg. 3.91	2o & 2o
Leg. 3.104	2hs & 2hs
Leg. 3.108	2o–5
Leg. 3.110	5
Leg. 3.115	1
Leg. 3.130	2o
Leg. 3.145	1
Leg. 3.147	1
Leg. 3.157	2o
Leg. 3.161	2d
Leg. 3.162	4r
Leg. 3.206	2g
Leg. 3.206	2g
Leg. 3.207	2g
Leg. 3.210	2o
Leg. 3.213	2hs
Leg. 3.219	2hs
Leg. 3.226	1
Leg. 3.242	2hs
Leg. 3.252	2g
Cher. 9	2o
Cher. 19	2c
Cher. 36	2o
Cher. 38	2o
Cher. 39	1–5
Cher. 41	2d
Cher. 43	1
Cher. 50	2h/2d
Cher. 51	2o
Cher. 54	2hs
Cher. 61	2o
Cher. 67	2o
Cher. 76	5
Cher. 86	2g
Cher. 87	2g
Cher. 90	2g
Cher. 92	5
Cher. 97	2d
Cher. 111	2o
Cher. 115	2d
Sacr. 4	2hs & 2hs
Sacr. 21	5
Sacr. 28	2o–5
Sacr. 30	2o
Sacr. 33	2hs
Sacr. 36	1
Sacr. 40	1–5
Sacr. 44	1
Sacr. 66	2o
Sacr. 68	2g
Sacr. 69	2d
Sacr. 73	2hs
Sacr. 75	1
Sacr. 82	2o
Sacr. 86	2hs–1
Sacr. 98	1–6
Sacr. 99	1–6
Sacr. 100	1–6
Sacr. 101	1–6
Sacr. 101	2h
Sacr. 102	1
Sacr. 114	2hs
Sacr. 114	2h
Sacr. 116	2hs
Sacr. 117	2hs
Sacr. 125	1
Sacr. 125	1
Sacr. 127	2hu
Det. 7	2o
Det. 28	2o–5
Det. 29	2hs
Det. 33	1
Det. 52	5
Det. 62	1–5
Det. 68	1
Det. 75	2c
Det. 76	2o
Det. 77	2o
Det. 83	2h
Det. 84	2h
Det. 87	2h
Det. 88	2d
Det. 88	2o
Det. 89	2g
Det. 101	1
Det. 106	2o
Det. 108	2o & 2o
Det. 125	1
Det. 138	2h
Det. 151	1
Det. 152	2o
Det. 154	2o
Det. 177	2o
Post. 4	1

Post. 5	1–4
Post. 13	2g
Post. 16	2g
Post. 20	2g
Post. 26	1
Post. 28	2g
Post. 31	2h
Post. 32	2o–5
Post. 52	2h–5
Post. 62	1
Post. 66	2o
Post. 71	1–2hs
Post. 81	1–2hs
Post. 83	1–5
Post. 93	2o–5
Post. 99	2o
Post. 100	2o–5
Post. 103	1–6
Post. 104	1
Post. 106	1
Post. 109	2h–5
Post. 109	2h
Post. 115	2o
Post. 118	2o–5
Post. 127	1
Post. 130	1–4
Post. 133	2o
Post. 134	2d
Post. 150	2hs
Post. 150	2hs
Post. 154	2hs
Post. 160	2hu
Post. 162	1
Post. 173	2d
Post. 182	2c
Post. 185	5nl
Gig. 4	2o–5
Gig. 25	2o
Gig. 30	2h
Gig. 43	2o
Gig. 59	2o
Gig. 62	2o
Gig. 65	2h
Deus 13	2o–2hs
Deus 24	2o
Deus 25	1
Deus 32	2o
Deus 35	1
Deus 37	1
Deus 38	1
Deus 41	1
Deus 45	2c
Deus 45	2o
Deus 46	2d
Deus 55	2d
Deus 56	2hs
Deus 61	2hs
Deus 63	2hs
Deus 72	2g
Deus 77	2c/2hu
Deus 93	2hs–3
Deus 104	2o
Deus 108	2g
Deus 112	5–2hu–6
Deus 151	2d
Agr. 1	2c
Agr. 8	1
Agr. 24	4r
Agr. 30	1
Agr. 30	2o (7 referents)
Agr. 31	5nl
Agr. 37	2o–5
Agr. 38	1
Agr. 43	5nl
Agr. 46	2hs–5
Agr. 51	4r
Agr. 56	2o
Agr. 59	2hs
Agr. 62	2hs
Agr. 66	5nl
Agr. 133	1
Agr. 134	2c
Agr. 142	2c
Agr. 164	2o
Agr. 168	1–2hs–3 –6
Agr. 171	2o
Agr. 180	7
Plant. 3	2o
Plant. 9	4–1
Plant. 13	2o
Plant. 18	4r
Plant. 24	2g
Plant. 25	2d
Plant. 27	2c

Plant. 41	2o	*Ebr.* 172	1
Plant. 44	2o	*Ebr.* 180	2h–5
Plant. 49	2h	*Ebr.* 180	2h–5
Plant. 49	5–6	*Ebr.* 182	1
Plant. 68	4r	*Ebr.* 189	2o
Plant. 75	2o	*Ebr.* 190	2hu–5
Plant. 79	2c	*Ebr.* 190	2hu–5
Plant. 91	2g	*Ebr.* 190	2o
Plant. 110	2hs	*Ebr.* 201	2o
Plant. 110	1	*Ebr.* 211	1
Plant. 114	2o	*Ebr.* 212	5
Plant. 118	2o	*Sobr.* 14	2hu
Plant. 127	4r	*Sobr.* 25	5nl
Plant. 130	2o	*Sobr.* 36	1
Plant. 132	5nl	*Sobr.* 38	2hs–1
Plant. 135	2h	*Sobr.* 46	2o
Plant. 135	2h	*Sobr.* 53	2o
Plant. 157	2o–5	*Sobr.* 67	2o–5
Plant. 159	5	*Conf.* 32	5
Plant. 171	2h–1	*Conf.* 43	2hs
Ebr. 8	2o–5	*Conf.* 46	2d–5
Ebr. 13	(2hs & 2o)–5	*Conf.* 49	2hs–5
Ebr. 13	1–5	*Conf.* 52	2hs–5
Ebr. 14	2hs–5	*Conf.* 68	5
Ebr. 24	5	*Conf.* 73	2o
Ebr. 25	2hs	*Conf.* 75	2o
Ebr. 34	5	*Conf.* 77	2h
Ebr. 37	5nl	*Conf.* 87	2o
Ebr. 47	5nl	*Conf.* 90	2hs
Ebr. 48	2d	*Conf.* 102	2o
Ebr. 55	5	*Conf.* 106	2d
Ebr. 55	5	*Conf.* 110	2o
Ebr. 68	5nl	*Conf.* 121	5–6
Ebr. 70	2d	*Conf.* 126	5
Ebr. 90	1	*Conf.* 133	2d
Ebr. 90	4	*Conf.* 133	2o–5
Ebr. 105	2o–5	*Conf.* 141	2o
Ebr. 115	2o	*Conf.* 154	2c
Ebr. 121	1	*Conf.* 154	2d
Ebr. 131	1	*Conf.* 154	2d
Ebr. 133	2o	*Conf.* 157	2o
Ebr. 135	2hs	*Conf.* 159	2o–5
Ebr. 141	5nl–2c	*Conf.* 173	2c
Ebr. 164	2o	*Conf.* 176	4–2c–1
Ebr. 166	2hu	*Conf.* 180	2g
Ebr. 167	2c	*Conf.* 181	2g
Ebr. 169	1	*Migr.* 12	2o

Migr. 26	2hs–5
Migr. 31	1–2hs–3
Migr. 33	2o
Migr. 46	4
Migr. 68	2h
Migr. 75	2hs–1
Migr. 78	2hs
Migr. 83	2o
Migr. 85	1
Migr. 94	5nl
Migr. 95	2hs
Migr. 105	5
Migr. 108	5
Migr. 118	2h
Migr. 128	5
Migr. 132	2g
Migr. 138	2d
Migr. 139	2g
Migr. 145	2o–5
Migr. 150	2hs
Migr. 156	2hs–5
Migr. 167	2hs–3
Migr. 167	1–3
Migr. 167	1–2o–4
Migr. 185	2h
Migr. 189	2o
Migr. 192	4
Migr. 197	2hs
Migr. 198	2o & 2d
Migr. 202	2o
Migr. 206	2o
Migr. 207	2o
Migr. 210	2hu
Migr. 212	2hu
Migr. 216	2o
Migr. 224	2hs/2hu
Her. 33	2hu
Her. 36	2hs
Her. 49	2o–5
Her. 53	1
Her. 66	2d
Her. 71	4–5
Her. 75	4
Her. 76	1–4
Her. 88	2d
Her. 95	5
Her. 110	4
Her. 115	1–6
Her. 115	1–6
Her. 116	1–6
Her. 116	1–6
Her. 116	1–6
Her. 121	1–6
Her. 121	1–6
Her. 130	2o & 2o
Her. 135	2o
Her. 137	1
Her. 142	2hu
Her. 146	2o
Her. 152	4
Her. 154	2o
Her. 164	1–6
Her. 172	2d
Her. 176	2d
Her. 180	4
Her. 182	2o–5
Her. 184	1
Her. 204	2o
Her. 213	4
Her. 217	2d
Her. 232	2h–5
Her. 233	2hu & 2d
Her. 234	2hu & 2d
Her. 235	4
Her. 237	2o–5
Her. 238	2o–5
Her. 238	2o–5
Her. 246	4–5
Her. 246	2c–5
Her. 252	2hs–5
Her. 258	2o–5
Her. 274	2h
Her. 279	4–5
Her. 302	1–6
Her. 312	2o & 2d
Congr. 2	2o–5
Congr. 4	1
Congr. 17	1–6
Congr. 25	2hs
Congr. 25	2o
Congr. 36	2hs–3
Congr. 37	2hs–3
Congr. 52	4
Congr. 59	2hs

Congr. 61	2hs
Congr. 61	2g
Congr. 71	2o–5
Congr. 85	1
Congr. 88	2o
Congr. 108	5
Congr. 113	2o
Congr. 117	2o
Congr. 122	2hu
Congr. 129	2hs & 2hs
Congr. 133	4r
Congr. 143	2o
Congr. 144	4
Congr. 144	2c
Congr. 146	2o
Congr. 165	1
Congr. 169	2o–5
Fug. 11	2o–5
Fug. 14	2o–5
Fug. 22	2o–5
Fug. 34	2o
Fug. 50	2d
Fug. 51	2d
Fug. 63	2o
Fug. 66	2g
Fug. 72	2h & 2h
Fug. 74	2o
Fug. 99	2g
Fug. 112	2hu–5
Fug. 118	2d
Fug. 122	4–1
Fug. 141	2g
Fug. 141	2c
Fug. 146	2hs
Fug. 148	2o
Fug. 154	2hs
Fug. 155	2hs
Fug. 162	2d
Fug. 163	2d
Fug. 164	2g
Fug. 167	2hs
Fug. 168	1
Fug. 169	2h–1
Fug. 170	2o
Fug. 171	1–2o–5–6
Fug. 172	1–2o–5–6
Fug. 172	2hs
Fug. 172	2hs
Fug. 172	2g
Fug. 179	2o–4–5
Mut. 2	1–2hs
Mut. 7	2g
Mut. 12	4–3
Mut. 12	2c
Mut. 14	2d
Mut. 46	2h
Mut. 60	2o–4–5
Mut. 71	4r
Mut. 84	2hs–3
Mut. 86	4–5–3
Mut. 88	2hs–3
Mut. 89	1–4–5
Mut. 90	1–4–5
Mut. 101	2hs–3
Mut. 105	2g
Mut. 108	2hs–5
Mut. 112	2h–5
Mut. 117	2o
Mut. 133	2hs
Mut. 140	2g
Mut. 151	5–6
Mut. 158	1–4–5
Mut. 159	1
Mut. 162	1
Mut. 167	2o–5
Mut. 173	2o–5
Mut. 178	2o
Mut. 184	2g
Mut. 186	2hu–5
Mut. 197	2hu
Mut. 199	2d
Mut. 211	2hs–3
Mut. 211	2hs–3
Mut. 219	2d–3
Mut. 225	2hu
Mut. 231	4
Mut. 246	1
Mut. 247	2o
Mut. 257	1–2hs–3
Mut. 260	1–2o–3
Mut. 264	2o & 2o
Mut. 266	2o
Mut. 270	2o
Somn. 1.6	2o

Somn. 1.11	5
Somn. 1.18	2o
Somn. 1.19	2o
Somn. 1.20	2o
Somn. 1.21	2o
Somn. 1.27	1
Somn. 1.31	2hu
Somn. 1.33	2o
Somn. 1.34	2d
Somn. 1.49	2o
Somn. 1.53	4
Somn. 1.53	2o
Somn. 1.59	2hs
Somn. 1.94	2g
Somn. 1.97	1
Somn. 1.102	1
Somn. 1.103	1–6
Somn. 1.106	2h
Somn. 1.109	2h
Somn. 1.111	2hu–5
Somn. 1.114	2o–5
Somn. 1.123	1
Somn. 1.126	1–4
Somn. 1.129	2hs
Somn. 1.131	2d
Somn. 1.136	1
Somn. 1.137	1–5
Somn. 1.138	5
Somn. 1.145	2o
Somn. 1.150	2o–5
Somn. 1.157	2d
Somn. 1.157	4
Somn. 1.160	2hs–3
Somn. 1.162	2hs–3
Somn. 1.167	2hs–3
Somn. 1.168	2hs–3
Somn. 1.169	2hs–3
Somn. 1.171	2hs
Somn. 1.172	4–5
Somn. 1.176	2h
Somn. 1.206	2d/2o
Somn. 1.210	1
Somn. 1.232	2g
Somn. 1.236	2hs
Somn. 1.241	2c
Somn. 2.8	2o
Somn. 2.40	1
Somn. 2.44	1–4–5
Somn. 2.54	2hs
Somn. 2.60	1
Somn. 2.79	2d–5
Somn. 2.90	2o–5
Somn. 2.115	2c
Somn. 2.117	4
Somn. 2.118	2o
Somn. 2.122	4
Somn. 2.136	2o/2d–5
Somn. 2.147	1–2hs
Somn. 2.174	5nl
Somn. 2.186	4
Somn. 2.188	2d
Somn. 2.194	2c
Somn. 2.213	2o
Somn. 2.223	2hs
Somn. 2.228	2d
Somn. 2.234	2d & 2h
Somn. 2.240	2o
Somn. 2.243	5–6
Somn. 2.262	1
Somn. 2.271	2o
Somn. 2.283	4–5
Abr. 5	5
Abr. 6	5
Abr. 6	5nl
Abr. 11	5
Abr. 14	2o & 2o
Abr. 15	5
Abr. 16	5nl
Abr. 19	2hs–5
Abr. 21	2hs–5
Abr. 27	2hu–5
Abr. 35	4
Abr. 37	2hs
Abr. 38	5–4–6
Abr. 43	2o
Abr. 46	1–5
Abr. 52	2hs–3
Abr. 52	2hs–3
Abr. 53	2hs–3
Abr. 53	2hs–3
Abr. 53	2hs–3
Abr. 54	2hs–3
Abr. 55	2hu
Abr. 58	4

Abr. 60	1–4–5
Abr. 61	1–4–5
Abr. 75	2o
Abr. 77	4r
Abr. 79	2g
Abr. 83	2o–5
Abr. 84	2c
Abr. 87	2g
Abr. 88	4r
Abr. 102	2o–5
Abr. 105	2o & 2o
Abr. 105	2o
Abr. 107	2d
Abr. 115	2d
Abr. 135	5nl
Abr. 135	2h
Abr. 137	1–2hu–5
Abr. 144	2g
Abr. 153	2d
Abr. 157	2o
Abr. 159	2o
Abr. 162	2o
Abr. 165	2d
Abr. 185	5
Abr. 193	1–2h–5
Abr. 195	1
Abr. 199	2o
Abr. 200	2o
Abr. 202	2g
Abr. 207	2o
Abr. 208	2hs
Abr. 218	2o–5
Abr. 237	5
Abr. 248	1
Abr. 249	1–5nl
Abr. 256	2o–5
Abr. 257	1–5
Abr. 259	1–5
Abr. 275	5
Ios. 1	2hs–3
Ios. 4	2hs
Ios. 10	2o
Ios. 24	1–5
Ios. 25	2hu
Ios. 28	5
Ios. 29	5nl
Ios. 30	5nl
Ios. 31	5
Ios. 31	5
Ios. 31	5
Ios. 38	5
Ios. 40	2hs
Ios. 81	2hs
Ios. 82	2hs
Ios. 83	5
Ios. 118	2hs
Ios. 129	1–5
Ios. 142	2c
Ios. 167	2hs
Ios. 170	2o
Ios. 189	2hs
Ios. 192	1–5
Ios. 248	2hs
Ios. 254	2hs–5
Ios. 264	2d
Mos. 1.3	1–2hs
Mos. 1.5	2hu
Mos. 1.8	1–2hs
Mos. 1.21	2hs
Mos. 1.22	2hs
Mos. 1.26	2o
Mos. 1.28	1
Mos. 1.32	1
Mos. 1.39	1–5
Mos. 1.48	5
Mos. 1.59	2hs
Mos. 1.60	2hs
Mos. 1.68	2o
Mos. 1.70	2o
Mos. 1.72	2g
Mos. 1.76	2hs
Mos. 1.83	2hs
Mos. 1.93	2o
Mos. 1.101	2g
Mos. 1.103	1–5
Mos. 1.113	4
Mos. 1.117	1–5
Mos. 1.124	1
Mos. 1.130	4
Mos. 1.143	4
Mos. 1.149	2hs–5
Mos. 1.153	1–4
Mos. 1.158	2hu
Mos. 1.160	1–2hs

Mos. 1.165	1
Mos. 1.185	1
Mos. 1.190	2hs
Mos. 1.197	2o
Mos. 1.211	2o
Mos. 1.218	2o
Mos. 1.226	1
Mos. 1.241	2hu
Mos. 2.5	2g
Mos. 2.7	5nl
Mos. 2.9	2o–5
Mos. 2.14	5
Mos. 2.22	2o–5
Mos. 2.27	5
Mos. 2.37	4
Mos. 2.48	5
Mos. 2.52	5
Mos. 2.58	2hs
Mos. 2.61	2g
Mos. 2.63	4
Mos. 2.65	2g
Mos. 2.66	2hs–3
Mos. 2.68	2o
Mos. 2.81	5nl
Mos. 2.84	1
Mos. 2.88	2o
Mos. 2.100	2g–5
Mos. 2.118	2o
Mos. 2.127	2hu
Mos. 2.128	4
Mos. 2.128	4
Mos. 2.135	2c
Mos. 2.139	5
Mos. 2.154	1
Mos. 2.161	2hs
Mos. 2.180	4
Mos. 2.181	5
Mos. 2.191	2c
Mos. 2.207	2hs-1
Mos. 2.209	5–4
Mos. 2.211	5nl
Mos. 2.211	2o–5
Mos. 2.216	4–5
Mos. 2.222	1–4
Mos. 2.222	4
Mos. 2.236	1–5
Mos. 2.240	2hs
Mos. 2.245	5nl–1
Mos. 2.249	4
Mos. 2.251	4
Mos. 2.263	4
Mos. 2.281	1
Mos. 2.288	2hu
Decal. 3	2o
Decal. 6	2o–5
Decal. 8	1–2hs
Decal. 24	4
Decal. 25	4
Decal. 30	4
Decal. 41	1
Decal. 43	1–2h–4
Decal. 51	2g
Decal. 59	2hs
Decal. 64	2c–5
Decal. 75	2o
Decal. 76	1
Decal. 81	5
Decal. 84	2hu
Decal. 87	2o
Decal. 98	4–5
Decal. 99	2hu
Decal. 100	4–5
Decal. 101	2hu
Decal. 102	2o–5
Decal. 103	2c
Decal. 104	2d
Decal. 107	2hs
Decal. 110	2o
Decal. 111	5
Decal. 112	1–5
Decal. 115	2o
Decal. 117	2o–1–5
Decal. 132	1–5
Decal. 132	5nl
Decal. 136	2hs
Decal. 137	2h–5
Decal. 142	2d
Decal. 150	5
Decal. 163	1
Decal. 175	2g
Decal. 177	2g
Decal. 177	2o–5
Spec. 1.13	2o
Spec. 1.19	2o–5

Spec. 1.31	5
Spec. 1.39	2hu–5
Spec. 1.44	2hu
Spec. 1.47	2g
Spec. 1.61	2o–5
Spec. 1.62	2o
Spec. 1.66	2h
Spec. 1.81	2h
Spec. 1.85	2o
Spec. 1.89	2d
Spec. 1.91	2d
Spec. 1.96	2c
Spec. 1.97	4
Spec. 1.97	2g
Spec. 1.116	2d
Spec. 1.137	1–5
Spec. 1.146	1
Spec. 1.155	5nl
Spec. 1.162	2o
Spec. 1.162	2o
Spec. 1.172	1–4
Spec. 1.176	4–5
Spec. 1.180	2g
Spec. 1.191	5
Spec. 1.202	5nl
Spec. 1.216	1
Spec. 1.217	1
Spec. 1.219	2o
Spec. 1.220	2o
Spec. 1.246	2o
Spec. 1.266	1
Spec. 1.269	2d
Spec. 1.273	5
Spec. 1.294	1–2hu–5
Spec. 1.295	2hu–5
Spec. 1.300	2g
Spec. 1.305	1
Spec. 1.306	2o
Spec. 1.306	5nl
Spec. 1.310	2g
Spec. 1.311	2o
Spec. 1.313	2hs
Spec. 1.318	5–6
Spec. 1.322	1–4–5
Spec. 1.325	2hu–5
Spec. 1.335	2o
Spec. 2.3	1–5
Spec. 2.6	1–6
Spec. 2.13	5
Spec. 2.16	2hs
Spec. 2.21	2hs–3
Spec. 2.23	5
Spec. 2.23	2g
Spec. 2.29	5
Spec. 2.39	2hu–5
Spec. 2.40	2o
Spec. 2.42	5
Spec. 2.45	4
Spec. 2.45	2o
Spec. 2.48	1–5
Spec. 2.50	2hs
Spec. 2.51	2hu
Spec. 2.52	5
Spec. 2.55	2o
Spec. 2.58	5
Spec. 2.69	2hu–5
Spec. 2.69	2hu–5
Spec. 2.73	1–2hs
Spec. 2.84	2hu–5
Spec. 2.100	1–5
Spec. 2.103	1–5
Spec. 2.109	5
Spec. 2.122	2hu–5
Spec. 2.124	4–5
Spec. 2.129	1–5
Spec. 2.130	1–5
Spec. 2.137	2hs
Spec. 2.141	2d
Spec. 2.150	5
Spec. 2.158	1–4
Spec. 2.159	1
Spec. 2.159	1
Spec. 2.161	1
Spec. 2.165	2g
Spec. 2.166	2c–5
Spec. 2.170	5nl
Spec. 2.172	1–6
Spec. 2.173	1–6
Spec. 2.177	2o
Spec. 2.178	2o
Spec. 2.190	4–5
Spec. 2.191	1–4
Spec. 2.196	2g
Spec. 2.198	1–4

Spec. 2.205	1
Spec. 2.210	1–4
Spec. 2.212	4r
Spec. 2.225	2g & 2hu
Spec. 2.230	2d
Spec. 2.231	5–6
Spec. 2.232	1–5
Spec. 2.233	1–5nl
Spec. 2.235	1–5
Spec. 2.239	1–5
Spec. 2.241	2hu–5
Spec. 2.253	2g
Spec. 3.9	2o
Spec. 3.21	2hs
Spec. 3.23	1
Spec. 3.28	1–2o
Spec. 3.28	1
Spec. 3.32	5nl–1
Spec. 3.33	1
Spec. 3.33	1
Spec. 3.36	1–6
Spec. 3.37	2hs
Spec. 3.38	2hs–1–5
Spec. 3.39	2hs–1–5
Spec. 3.45	2o
Spec. 3.46	1–5nl
Spec. 3.47	1–5
Spec. 3.48	1–5
Spec. 3.51	1
Spec. 3.52	4–6
Spec. 3.97	2o
Spec. 3.99	2o
Spec. 3.100	1–4
Spec. 3.103	2hu
Spec. 3.108	1
Spec. 3.109	1
Spec. 3.111	1–4
Spec. 3.112	5nl
Spec. 3.118	2hu
Spec. 3.121	5–6
Spec. 3.125	2hs
Spec. 3.129	2g
Spec. 3.136	5–6
Spec. 3.137	5
Spec. 3.137	5
Spec. 3.151	2hs
Spec. 3.156	2hs
Spec. 3.158	2hs
Spec. 3.163	2hs
Spec. 3.173	1–2hs–5
Spec. 3.176	5nl–1
Spec. 3.176	5–1
Spec. 3.178	2g
Spec. 3.180	5
Spec. 3.184	1–5
Spec. 3.189	5nl
Spec. 3.198	1
Spec. 3.205	1–2hu–5
Spec. 4.14	2hu–5
Spec. 4.18	2hu–5
Spec. 4.24	5
Spec. 4.24	2o
Spec. 4.29	2o
Spec. 4.40	1–5
Spec. 4.46	5
Spec. 4.46	5
Spec. 4.48	2g
Spec. 4.51	1–5
Spec. 4.55	1–5
Spec. 4.64	1–5
Spec. 4.68	2h
Spec. 4.68	1
Spec. 4.71	2o
Spec. 4.77	2o
Spec. 4.79	2hu–5
Spec. 4.89	2hs
Spec. 4.92	2d
Spec. 4.104	2o
Spec. 4.109	2o
Spec. 4.114	2hs–5
Spec. 4.116	2o
Spec. 4.119	1
Spec. 4.123	2g
Spec. 4.131	5
Spec. 4.140	2o–5
Spec. 4.155	2o
Spec. 4.175	2hu
Spec. 4.178	2hu–5
Spec. 4.204	5nl
Spec. 4.208	1–5
Spec. 4.210	2o & 2o
Spec. 4.212	5nl
Spec. 4.215	5nl–1
Spec. 4.225	2hs–5

Spec. 4.227	2o
Spec. 4.231	4–5
Spec. 4.233	1
Spec. 4.236	2o
Virt. 2	2hs–3
Virt. 6	1–4
Virt. 7	1–4
Virt. 8	1–4
Virt. 9	2d & 2o
Virt. 12	2d
Virt. 18	5
Virt. 19	5
Virt. 19	5
Virt. 36	2o
Virt. 39	1
Virt. 59	1–2hs–5
Virt. 76	2d–5
Virt. 79	2hu
Virt. 80	2hs
Virt. 81	7
Virt. 87	7
Virt. 93	1–4
Virt. 94	1–4
Virt. 97	1
Virt. 105	2o–5
Virt. 117	4
Virt. 125	7
Virt. 127	5
Virt. 129	1
Virt. 132	5nl–1
Virt. 133	1–5–3
Virt. 133	1
Virt. 135	2o
Virt. 140	1–2hu
Virt. 143	1
Virt. 152	2hs
Virt. 154	1
Virt. 160	2o
Virt. 168	2h
Virt. 172	2hu
Virt. 173	2hs
Virt. 192	1
Virt. 203	2hu
Virt. 217	2hs
Virt. 225	1–2hs
Praem. 9	1–6
Praem. 11	2c
Praem. 13	2d & 2h
Praem. 15	2o
Praem. 23	2c
Praem. 26	4
Praem. 27	2hs–3
Praem. 31	2hs–3
Praem. 34	4–5
Praem. 36	2hs–3
Praem. 36	4r
Praem. 39	2hu
Praem. 42	5nl
Praem. 46	2g
Praem. 50	1–2hs
Praem. 50	1–2hs
Praem. 59	2hs–3
Praem. 62	2hu–5
Praem. 63	2hs–3
Praem. 64	2hs–3
Praem. 65	2hs–3
Praem. 77	2hs
Praem. 83	2hs
Praem. 85	2o
Praem. 89	2hu–5
Praem. 91	2o–5
Praem. 92	2hu
Praem. 99	1–4
Praem. 100	1–4
Praem. 108	5nl–1
Praem. 128	1–4
Praem. 130	1–4
Praem. 149	2o–4–5
Praem. 153	1
Praem. 155	1
Praem. 160	2o
Praem. 162	2g
Praem. 165	2g
Prob. 19	2hu–5
Prob. 30	5nl
Prob. 31	5
Prob. 37	5nl
Prob. 38	1–2hs
Prob. 40	2hu–5
Prob. 43	4
Prob. 46	5
Prob. 50	4
Prob. 62	5nl
Prob. 63	4–5

Prob. 70	2o	*Aet.* 37	1–2c
Prob. 74	4–5	*Aet.* 44	2hu
Prob. 79	5nl	*Aet.* 47	2d
Prob. 80	2hu	*Aet.* 53	2o
Prob. 89	2hs	*Aet.* 57	1
Prob. 91	2hs–5	*Aet.* 58	1
Prob. 102	2hs	*Aet.* 59	5nl–1
Prob. 105	2hu	*Aet.* 59	2c–5
Prob. 106	2hs	*Aet.* 63	2o
Prob. 108	4	*Aet.* 66	1
Prob. 114	2hs	*Aet.* 68	1
Prob. 117	2hs–5	*Aet.* 68	2hu
Prob. 123	2hs–5	*Aet.* 69	1
Prob. 125	2hs–5	*Aet.* 75	2o
Prob. 129	1–2hs	*Aet.* 75	2c
Prob. 130	2hs	*Aet.* 75	2c–1
Prob. 143	2o	*Aet.* 75	2c
Prob. 158	2d	*Aet.* 94	2c
Prob. 160	5	*Aet.* 103	2o
Contempl. 2	5	*Aet.* 105	2o–5
Contempl. 9	1–5	*Aet.* 112	5–1
Contempl. 9	2hs	*Aet.* 115	2o–5
Contempl. 17	1–4	*Aet.* 115	2o–5
Contempl. 28	2o–4–5	*Aet.* 119	2o
Contempl. 33	2hs	*Aet.* 130	4–1
Contempl. 37	1	*Aet.* 130	2hu–5
Contempl. 54	4	*Aet.* 132	2o & 2o
Contempl. 59	5nl–1	*Aet.* 133	1
Contempl. 64	4–5	*Aet.* 136	2o–5
Contempl. 70	1–5	*Aet.* 144	2o
Contempl. 90	4–5	*Aet.* 147	2o
Aet. 12	2c	*Aet.* 148	2o–5
Aet. 19	2o	*Flacc.* 1	2hs
Aet. 21	2o	*Flacc.* 4	2hs
Aet. 28	2o–5	*Flacc.* 25	2hs–3
Aet. 28	2o–5	*Flacc.* 29	2hs
Aet. 29	2o–5	*Flacc.* 29	2hs
Aet. 30	2o–5	*Flacc.* 59	2hs
Aet. 31	2o–5	*Flacc.* 66	2hs
Aet. 31	2o	*Flacc.* 79	2o
Aet. 32	2o–5	*Flacc.* 106	2o
Aet. 33	2o–5	*Flacc.* 154	2hs
Aet. 34	2o–5	*Flacc.* 176	2o–5
Aet. 34	2o–5	*Flacc.* 180	2hs
Aet. 35	1–2o–5	*Flacc.* 187	1
Aet. 35	1–2o–5	*Legat.* 1	5
Aet. 37	2c	*Legat.* 1	1

Legat. 1	1	*Prov.* 2.16	2hs–3
Legat. 23	1–2hs	*Prov.* 2.18	1–5
Legat. 30	2o	*Prov.* 2.18	2o–5
Legat. 34	2hs	*Prov.* 2.22	1–5
Legat. 50	5	*Prov.* 2.23	5nl–1
Legat. 56	1	*Prov.* 2.27	2d
Legat. 57	2hs	*Prov.* 2.38	2hs
Legat. 68	5nl	*Prov.* 2.47	1
Legat. 70	2o–5	*Prov.* 2.49	1
Legat. 75	2hu	*Prov.* 2.50	2d
Legat. 81	2o	*Prov.* 2.51	1
Legat. 91	2hu	*Prov.* 2.52	2d
Legat. 106	2hs–3	*Prov.* 2.53	1
Legat. 112	4r	*Prov.* 2.57	2hs
Legat. 114	2hs	*Prov.* 2.57	2o
Legat. 118	2hu	*Prov.* 2.58	1
Legat. 126	1	*Prov.* 2.59	1
Legat. 143	2hu	*Prov.* 2.61	5–6
Legat. 159	2hs	*Prov.* 2.69	1–5
Legat. 161	2hs	*Prov.* 2.70	2hu–5
Legat. 162	2hu	*QG* 1.28	2hs
Legat. 168	2hs	*QG* 1.55b	2hu
Legat. 190	1	*QG* 1.74	1–5
Legat. 190	1	*QG* 1.76b	2hu
Legat. 193	2hs	*QG* 2.34a	4
Legat. 213	2hs–5	*QG* 2.41	2o
Legat. 229	1	*QG* 2.41	1
Legat. 230	2hs	*QG* 2.54a	2o
Legat. 243	2hs	*QG* 2.62	2hu & 2d
Legat. 244	2hs	*QG* 3.7	2o
Legat. 245	2hs	*QG* 3.38b	2hs
Legat. 301	2hs	*QG* 4.51	2o–5
Legat. 310	2g	*QG* 4.184	5–1
Legat. 320	2hs–3	*QG* 4.184	5–1
Legat. 339	2hs	*QG* 4.193	2hs
Legat. 355	2hu	*QG* 4.9*	2hu
Legat. 359	2o	*QG isf* 2	2d
Legat. 367	2d	*QG isf* 10	2hu
Hypoth. 6.4	2hs	*QG par* 2.2	2hu
Hypoth. 7.20	2hu	*QG par* 2.3	2o
Hypoth. 11.13	2hu–5	*QG par* 2.4	2d
Hypoth. 11.17	2hs	*QG par* 2.7	1
Prov. 1	4–5	*QE* 2.1	1–4
Prov. 2.3	5nl	*QE* 2.1	1–4
Prov. 2.6	2g	*QE* 2.1	1–4
Prov. 2.12	1	*QE* 2.3b	5nl
Prov. 2.16	2hs–3	*QE* 2.19	5nl–1

QE 2.25a	2o–5	*QE isf* 3	2g
QE 2.26	5	*QE isf* 4	1–4–5
QE 2.46	2o/2d	*QE isf* 5	4–5
QE isf 3	2hu	*QE isf* 31	2o

Bibliography

I. Primary Sources

Aëtius. 1993. *Plutarch Œuvres Morales. Tome XII[2]. Opinions des Philosophes*. Translated by Guy Lachenaud. Collection des Universités de France 356. Paris: Belles Lettres.

Alcinous. 1990. *Alcinoos, Enseignement des doctrines de Platon / introduction, texte établi et commenté et traduit*. Edited by John Whittaker. Translated by Pierre Louis. Collection des Universités de France. Paris: Belles Lettres.

–. 1995. *The Handbook of Platonism / Alcinous; Translated with an Introduction and Commentary*. Translated by John Dillon. Clarendon Later Ancient Philosophers. Oxford: Clarendon.

Apuleius. 1973. *Opuscules philosophieques (Du dieu de Socrate, Platon et sa doctrine, Du monde) et fragments/Apulée: Texte établi, traduit et commenté*. Edited by Jean Beaujeu. Collection des Universités de France. Paris: Belles Lettres.

Aquinas, St. Thomas. 1964. *Summa Theologiæ*. Edited by Thomas Gilby, O.P. 60 vols. London: Eyre & Spottiswoode.

Aristotle. 1934. *Works*. Translated by H. P. Cooke, et al. 23 vols. Loeb Classical Library. Cambridge: Harvard University Press.

–. 1955. *Aristotelis Fragmenta Selecta*. Edited by W. D. Ross. Scriptorum Classicorum Bibliotheca Oxoniesis. Oxford: Clarendon.

Arnim, Ioannes Ab. 1968. *Stoicorum Veterum Fragments*. 4 vols. Sammlung Wissenschaftlicher Commentare. Stuttgart: Teubner.

Arrian. 1976–83. *Anabasis Alexandri*. Translated by P. A. Brunt and E. Iliff Robson. 2 vols. Loeb Classical Library. Cambridge: Harvard University Press.

Athenaeus. 1927–41. *The Deipnosophists*. Translated by Charles Burton Gulick. 7 vols. Loeb Classical Library. Cambridge: Harvard University Press.

Atticus. 1977. *Fragments*. Translated by Édouard des Places, S.J. Collection des Universités de France. Paris: Belles Lettres.

Babylonian Talmud. 1948–52. Edited by Isidore Epstein. 18 vols. London: Soncino.

Borgen, Peder, Kåre Fuglseth, and Roald Skarsten. 2005. *The Works of Philo: Greek Text with Morphology*. Bellingham, Wash.: Logos Research Systems, Inc.

Charlesworth, James H. 1983a. *The Old Testament Pseudepigrapha*. 2 vols. Anchor Bible Reference Library. New York: Doubleday.

–. 1983b. "Treatise of Shem. A New Translation and Introduction." Pp. 473–86 in *The Old Testament Pseudepigrapha*, edited by James H. Charlesworth. 2 vols. Anchor Bible Reference Library. New York: Doubleday.

Chrysostom, Dio. 1932–51. *Discourses*. Translated by J. W. Cohoon and H. Lamar Crosby. 5 vols. Loeb Classical Library. Cambridge: Harvard University Press.

Cicero, Marcus Tullius. 1913–33. *Philosophical Treatises*. Translated by Clinton W. Keyes, et al. 6 vols. Loeb Classical Library. Cambridge: Harvard University Press.

–. 1952–54. *The Letters to His Friends*. Rev. ed. Translated by W. Glynn Williams. 3 vols. Loeb Classical Library. Cambridge: Harvard University Press.

–. 1990. *Laelius, On Friendship (*Laelivs de Amicitia*) and the Dream of Scipio (*Somnivm Scipionis*)*. Translated by J. G. F. Powell. Classical Texts. Warminster: Aris & Phillips.

Demosthenes. 1926–88. *Orations*. Translated by A. T. Murray, C. A. Vince, J. H. Vince, Norman W. DeWitt, and Norman J. DeWitt. 7 vols. Loeb Classical Library. Cambridge: Harvard University Press.

Diels, Hermann, and Walther Kranz, eds. 1951. *Die Fragmente der Vorsokratiker*. 6th ed. 3 vols. Berlin: Weidmann.

Diodorus Siculus. 1933–67. *Bibliotheca Historica*. Translated by C. H. Oldfather and et al. 12 vols. Loeb Classical Library. Cambridge: Harvard University Press.

Diogenes Laertius. 1925. *Lives of Eminent Philosophers*. Translated by R. D. Hicks. 2 vols. Loeb Classical Library. Cambridge: Harvard University Press.

Epictetus. 1925–28. *Discourses*. Translated by W. A. Oldfather. 2 vols. Loeb Classical Library. Cambridge: Harvard University Press.

Hadas, Moses. 1951. *Aristeas to Philocrates (Letter of Aristeas)*. Jewish Apocryphal Literature. New York: Dropsie College.

Hanhart, Robert, ed. 1966. *Esther*. Septuaginta. Vetus Testamentum Graecum 8,3. Göttingen: Vandenhoeck & Ruprecht.

Harris, J. Rendel, ed. 1886. *Fragments of Philo Judœus*. Cambridge: Cambridge University Press.

Holladay, Carl R., ed. 1983. *Historians*. Vol. 1 of *Fragments from Hellenistic Jewish Authors*. Texts and Translations 20. Chico, Calif.: Scholars Press.

–, ed. 1995. *Aristobulus*. Vol. 3 of *Fragments from Hellenistic Jewish Authors*. Texts and Translations 39. Atlanta: Scholars Press.

Horst, Pieter W. van der. 1978. *The Sentences of Pseudo-Phocylides*. Studia in Veteris Testamenti pseudepigraphica 4. Leiden: Brill.

Iamblichus. 1975 [1937]. *Iamblichi De vita Pythagorica liber*. Edited by Ludwig Deubner and Ulrich Klein. Bibliotheca scriptorum Graecorum et Romanorum Teubneriana. Stuttgart: Teubner.

–. 2002. *De Anima: Text, Translation, and Commentary*. Translated by John F. Finamore and John M. Dillon. Philosophia Antiqua 92. Leiden: Brill.

Isocrates. 1928–45. *Works*. Translated by George Norlin and Larue Van Hook. 3 vols. Loeb Classical Library. Cambridge: Harvard University Press.

Josephus. 1930–65. *Works*. Translated by H. St. J. Thackeray, et al. 10 vols. Loeb Classical Library. Cambridge: Harvard University Press.

Long, A. A., and D. N. Sedley, eds. 1987. *The Hellenistic Philosophers*. 2 vols. Cambridge: Cambridge University Press.

Martínez, Florentino García, and Eibert J. C. Tigchelaar, eds. 1997–98. *The Dead Sea Scrolls Study Edition*. 2 vols. Leiden: Brill.

Midrash Rabbah. 1939. Edited by H. Freedman and Maurice Simon. 10 vols. London: Soncino.

Numenius. 1973. *Fragments*. Translated by Édouard des Places, S.J. Collection des Universités de France. Paris: Belles Lettres.

Petit, Françoise. 1978. *Quaestiones in Genesim et in Exodum. Fragmenta Graeca*. Les Œuvres de Philon d'Alexandrie 33. Paris: Cerf.

Philo. 1929–1953. *Works*. Translated by F. H. Colson, G. H. Whitaker, and Ralph Marcus. 12 vols. Loeb Classical Library. Cambridge: Harvard University Press.

Philonis Alexandrini opera quae supersunt. 1896–1915. Edited by Leopold Cohn, Paul Wendland, and Sigfreid Reiter. 6 vols. Berlin: George Reimer.

Plato. 1914–35. *Dialogues*. Translated by H. N. Fowler, et al. 12 vols. Loeb Classical Library. Cambridge: Harvard University Press.

Plotinus. 1966–88. *Works*. Translated by A. H. Armstrong. 7 vols. Loeb Classical Library. Cambridge: Harvard University Press.

Plutarch. 1927–2004. *Moralia*. Translated by Frank C. Babbit, et al. 16 vols. Loeb Classical Library. Cambridge: Harvard University Press.

Porphyry. 1979–95. *De l'Abstinence*. Translated by Jean Bouffartigue and Michel Patillon. 3 vols. Collection des Universités de France. Paris: Belles Lettres.

Posidonius. 1972–88. *Posidonius: The Fragments*. Translated by I. G. Kidd. 2 vols. in 3. Cambridge Classical Texts and Commentaries 13, 14, 36. Cambridge: Cambridge University Press.

Seneca. 1917–25. *Ad Lucilium Epistulae Morales*. Translated by Richard M. Gummere. 3 vols. Loeb Classical Library. Cambridge: Harvard University Press.

–. 1928–35. *Moral Essays*. Translated by John W. Basore. 3 vols. Loeb Classical Library. Cambridge: Harvard University Press.

Sextus Empiricus. 1933–49. *Works*. Translated by R. G. Bury. 4 vols. Loeb Classical Library. Cambridge: Harvard University Press.

Siegert, Folker. 1988. *Philon von Alexandrien: Über die Gottesbezeichnung „wohltätig verzehrendes Feuer"* (De Deo). *Rückübersetzung des Fragments aus dem Armenischen, deutsche Übersetzung und Kommentar*. Wissenschaftliche Untersuchungen zum Neuen Testament 46. Tübingen: Mohr Siebeck.

–. 1998. "The Philonian Fragment *De Deo*: First English Translation." *Studia Philonica Annual* 10:1–33.

Stern, Menahem. 1974–84. *Greek and Latin Authors on Jews and Judaism*. 3 vols. Publications of the Israel Academy of Sciences and Humanities, Section of Humanities. Jerusalem: Israel Academy of Sciences and Humanities.

Stobaeus. 1884–1912. *Ioannis Stobaeus Anthologii*. Edited by Curtius Wachsmuth and Otto Hense. 5 vols. Berlin: Weidmann.

Le Testament grec d'Abraham. Introduction, édition critique des deux recensions grecques, traduction. 1986. Translated by Francis Schmidt. Texte und Studien zum Antiken Judentum 11. Tübingen: Mohr Siebeck.

The Testaments of the Twelve Patriarchs. A Critical Edition of the Greek Text. 1978. Edited by M. de Jonge. Pseudepigrapha Veteris Testamenti Graece 1. Leiden: Brill.

Xenophon. 1914–35. *Works*. Translated by Carleton L. Brownson, et al. 7 vols. Loeb Classical Library. Cambridge: Harvard University Press.

II. Reference Works

Bauer, Walter, Frederick William Danker, W. F. Arndt, and F. W. Gingrch. 2000. *A Greek-English Lexicon of the New Testament and Other Early Christian Literature*. 3d ed. Chicago: University of Chicago Press.

Bertram, Georg, and Bo Reicke. 1967. "πᾶς, ἅπας." Pp. 5.886–96 in *TDNT*.

Blass, F., A. Debrunner, and Robert W. Funk. 1961. *A Greek Grammar of the New Testament and Other Early Christian Literature*. Chicago: University of Chicago.

Borgen, Peder, Kåre Fuglseth, and Roald Skarsten. 2000. *The Philo Index: A Complete Greek Word Index to the Writings of Philo of Alexandria.* Grand Rapids/Leiden: Eerdmans/Brill.

Cotterell, Peter. 1997. "Linguistics, Meaning, Semantics, and Discourse Analysis." Pp. 1:134–60 in *NIDOTTE.*

de Vries, Ad. 1974. *Dictionary of Symbols and Imagery.* Amsterdam: North-Holland.

Foerster, Werner. 1965. "κτίζω, etc." Pp. 3.1000–35 in *TDNT.*

Kittel, Gerhard, and Gerhard Friedrich, eds. 1964–76. *Theological Dictionary of the New Testament.* Translated by Geoffrey W. Bromiley. 10 vols. Grand Rapids: Eerdmans.

Kleinknecht, H., and W. Gutbrod. 1967. "νόμος, etc." Pp. 4.1022–91 in *TDNT.*

Koester, Helmut. 1974. "φύσις, etc." Pp. 9.251–77 in *TDNT.*

Leisegang, Hans. 1894–1972. "Physis." Pp. 20.1: col. 1129–64 in *Paulys Real-Encyclopädie der classischen Altertumswissenschaft.* New ed., edited by Georg Wissowa, Wilhelm Kroll, Karl Mittelhaus, Konrat Ziegler, and Walther John. 34 vols. in 56. Stuttgart: J. B. Metzler.

–. 1926. *Indices ad Philonis Alexandrini opera.* Vol. 7 of *Philonis Alexandrini opera quae supersunt.* Berlin: De Gruyter.

Liddell, H. G., R. Scott, and H. S. Jones. 1996. *A Greek-English Lexicon.* 9th Ed. with Revised Supplement. Oxford: Clarendon.

Louw, Johannes P., and Eugene A. Nida, eds. 1988–89. *Greek-English Lexicon of the New Testament Based on Semantic Domains.* 2 vols. New York: United Bible Societies.

Mayer, Günter. 1974. *Index Philoneus.* Berlin: De Gruyter.

Rengstorf, Karl Heinrich, ed. 1973–83. *A Complete Concordance to Flavius Josephus.* 4 vols. Leiden: Brill.

Sasse, Hermann. 1965. "κοσμέω, etc." Pp. 3.867–98 in *TDNT.*

VanGemeren, Willem A., ed. 1997. *New International Dictionary of Old Testament Theology and Exegesis.* 5 vols. Grand Rapids: Zondervan.

Wallace, Daniel B. 1996. *Greek Grammar Beyond the Basics: An Exegetical Syntax of the New Testament.* Grand Rapids: Zondervan.

Walton, John H. 1997. "Principles for Productive Word Study." Pp. 1:161–71 in *NIDOTTE.*

III. Secondary Literature

Adams, Edward. 2000. *Constructing the World: A Study in Paul's Cosmological Language.* Studies of the New Testament and Its World. Edinburgh: T&T Clark.

Adams, James Luther. 1945a. "The Law of Nature in Greco-Roman Thought." *Journal of Religion* 25:97–118.

–. 1945b. "The Law of Nature: Some General Considerations." *Journal of Religion* 25:88–96.

Alexandre, Monique. 1967. *De Congressu Eruditonis gratia. Introduction, traduction et notes.* Les Œuvres de Philon d'Alexandrie 16. Paris: Cerf.

Algra, Kempe. 2003. "Stoic Theology." Pp. 153–78 in *The Cambridge Companion to the Stoics*, edited by Brad Inwood. Cambridge: Cambridge University Press.

Allison, Dale C., Jr. 2003. *Testament of Abraham.* Commentaries on Early Jewish Literature. Berlin: De Gruyter.

Andersen, Francis I., and David Noel Freedman. 1989. *Amos.* Anchor Bible 24a. New York: Doubleday.

Anderson, William H. U. 1997. *Qoheleth and Its Pessimistic Theology: Hermeneutical Struggles in Wisdom Literature*. Mellen Biblical Press Series 54. Lewiston: Mellen Biblical.

Annas, Julia. 1993. *The Morality of Happiness*. New York: Oxford University Press.

Arnaldez, R. 1984. "La Bible de Philon d'Alexandrie." Pp. 37–54 in *Le monde grec ancien et la Bible 1*, edited by Claude Mondésert. Bible de tous les temps. Paris: Beauchesne.

Aune, David C. 1994. "Mastery of the Passions: Philo, 4 Maccabees and Early Christianity." Pp. 125–58 in *Hellenization Revisted: Shaping a Christian Response Within the Greco-Roman World*, edited by Wendy E. Helleman. Lanham: University Press of America.

Aune, David E. 1995. "Human Nature and Ethics in Hellenistic Philosophical Traditions and Paul: Some Issues and Problems." Pp. 291–312 in *Paul in His Hellenistic Context*, edited by Troels Engberg-Pedersen. Minneapolis: Fortress.

Badley, Karen Jo-Ann. 2005. "Paul's Use of Creation Narratives in 1 Corinthians: Indications for a Pauline Theology of Creation." Ph.D. diss. University of St. Michael's College (Canada).

Baer, Richard A., Jr. 1970. *Philo's Use of the Categories Male and Female*. Arbeiten zur Literatur und Geschichte des hellenistischen Judentums 3. Leiden: Brill.

Baltes, Matthias. 1976–78. *Die Weltentstehung des platonischen Timaios nach den antiken Interpreten*. 2 vols. Philosophia Antiqua 30, 35. Leiden: Brill.

Bamberger, Bernard J. 1977. "Philo and the Aggadah." *Hebrew Union College Annual* 48:153–85.

Bar Ilan, Meir. 2004. "Astrology in Ancient Judaism." Pp. 2031–37 in *The Encyclopaedia of Judaism*. Volume 5: Supplement 2, edited by Jacob Neusner, Alan J. Avery-Peck, and William Scott Green. Leiden: Brill.

Barclay, John M. G. 1996. *Jews in the Mediterranean Diaspora: From Alexander to Trajan (323 BCE – 117 CE)*. Edinburgh: T&T Clark.

–. 2002. "Apologetics in the Jewish Diaspora." Pp. 129–48 in *Jews in the Hellenistic and Roman Cities*, edited by John R. Bartlett. London: Routledge.

–. 2006. "'By the Grace of God I Am What I Am': Grace and Agency in Philo and Paul." Pp. 140–57 in *Divine and Human Agency in Paul and His Cultural Environment*, edited by John M. G. Barclay and Simon J. Gathercole. Library of New Testament Studies 335. London: T&T Clark.

Barr, James. 1961. *The Semantics of Biblical Language*. Oxford: Oxford University Press.

Barraclough, Ray. 1984. "Philo's Politics: Roman Rule and Hellenistic Judaism." Pp. 417–553 in *Aufstieg und Niedergang der römischen Welt.* Part 2, *Principat, 21.1*, edited by Wolfgang Haase. Berlin: De Gruyter.

Barton, John. 1979. "Natural Law and Poetic Justice in the Old Testament." *Journal of Theological Studies, NS* 30:1–14.

–. 1980. *Amos's Oracles Against the Nations*. Society for Old Testament Studies Monograph Series 6. Cambridge: Cambridge University Press.

–. 1990. "History and Rhetoric in the Prophets." Pp. 51–64 in *The Bible as Rhetoric: Studies in Biblical Persuasion and Credibility*, edited by Martin Warner. Warwick Studies in Philosophy and Literature. London/New York: Routledge.

–. 2002. *Ethics and the Old Testament*. 2d ed. London: SCM.

Barton, Stephen C. 1994. *Discipleship and Family Ties in Mark and Matthew*. Society for New Testament Studies Monograph Series 80. Cambridge: Cambridge University Press.

Barton, Tamsyn. 1994. *Ancient Astrology*. Sciences of Antiquity. London: Routledge.

Bauckham, Richard. 1999. "The Throne of God and the Worship of Jesus." Pp. 43–69 in *The Jewish Roots of Christological Monotheism: Papers from the St. Andrews Conference on the Historical Origins of the Worship of Jesus*, edited by Carey C. Newman, James R. Davlia, and Gladys S. Lewis. Supplements to the Journal for the Study of Judaism in the Persian, Hellenistic, and Roman Periods 63. Leiden: Brill.

Beale, G. K. 2004. *The Temple and the Church's Mission: A Biblical Theology of the Dwelling Place of God.* New Studies in Biblical Theology. Downers Grove, Ill.: InterVarsity.

Benn, Alfred. 1896. "The Idea of Nature in Plato." *Archiv für Geschichte der Philosophie* 9:24–49.

Berchman, Robert M. 1984. *From Philo to Origen: Middle Platonism in Transition.* Brown Judaic Studies 69. Chico: Scholars Press.

–. 2000. "Philo and Philosophy." Pp. 49–70 in *Where We Stand: Issues and Debates in Ancient Judaism*, edited by Alan J. Avery-Peck and Jacob Neusner. Part 3 vol. 3 of *Judaism in Late Antiquity*. Handbuch der Orientalistik 53. Leiden: Brill.

Betegh, Gábor. 2003. "Cosmological Ethics in the *Timaeus* and Early Stoicism." *Oxford Studies in Ancient Philosophy* 24:273–302.

Bianchi, Ugo, ed. 1967. *The Origins of Gnosticism. Colloquium of Messina 13–18 April 1966.* Studies in the History of Religions (Supplements to *Numen*) 12. Leiden: Brill.

Birnbaum, Ellen. 1995. "What Does Philo Mean by 'Seeing God'? Some Methodological Considerations." *Society of Biblical Literature Seminar Papers* 34:535–52.

–. 1996a. *The Place of Judaism in Philo's Thought: Israel, Jews, and Proselytes.* Brown Judaic Studies 290. Atlanta: Scholars Press.

–. 1996b. "Review of Naomi G. Cohen, *Philo Judaeus: His Universe of Discourse.*" *Studia Philonica Annual* 8:189–96.

–. 2001. "Philo on the Greeks: A Jewish Perspective on Culture and Society in First-Century Alexandria." *Studia Philonica Annual* 13:37–58.

–. 2003. "Allegorical Interpretation and Jewish Identity Among Alexandrian Jewish Writers." Pp. 307–29 in *Neotestamentica et Philonica: Studies in Honor of Peder Borgen*, edited by David E. Aune, Torrey Seland, and Jarl Henning Ulrichsen. Supplements to Novum Testamentum 106. Leiden: Brill.

–. 2004. "Portrayals of the Wise and Virtuous in Alexandrian Jewish Works: Jews' Perceptions of Themselves and Others." Pp. 125–60 in *Ancient Alexandria Between Egypt and Greece*, edited by W. V. Harris and Giovanni Ruffini. Columbia Studies in the Classical Tradition 26. Leiden: Brill.

–. 2006. "Two Millennia Later: General Resources and Particular Perspectives on Philo the Jew." *Currents in Biblical Research* 4:241–76.

Bix, Brian H. 2002. "Natural Law: The Modern Tradition." Pp. 61–103 in *The Oxford Handbook of Jurisprudence and Philosophy of Law*, edited by Jules Coleman and Scott Shapiro. Oxford: Oxford University Press.

Bockmuehl, Markus. 2003. *Jewish Law in Gentile Churches: Halakhah and the Beginning of Christian Public Ethics*. Grand Rapids: Baker Academic.

–. 2009. "The Dead Sea Scrolls and Ancient Commentary." Pp. 3–29 in *Text, Thought, and Practice in Qumran and Early Christianity.* Proceedings of the Ninth International Symposium of the Orion Center for the Study of the Dead Sea Scrolls and Associated Literature, edited by Daniel R. Schwartz and Ruth A. Clements. Studies on the Texts of the Desert of Judah 84. Leiden: Brill.

Borgen, Peder. 1965. *Bread from Heaven: An Exegetical Study of the Concept of Manna in the Gospel of John and the Writings of Philo*. Supplements to Novum Testamentum 10. Leiden: Brill.

–. 1987a. "Aristobulus and Philo." Pp. 7–16 in *Philo, John and Paul: New Perspectives on Judaism and Early Christianity*. Brown Judaic Studies 131. Atlanta: Scholars Press.

–. 1987b. "Philo's Writings." Pp. 17–59 in *Philo, John and Paul: New Perspectives on Judaism and Early Christianity*. Brown Judaic Studies 131. Atlanta: Scholars Press.

–. 1992a. "Philo and the Jews in Alexandria." Pp. 122–38 in *Ethnicity in Hellenistic Egypt*, edited by Per Bilde, Troels Engberg-Pedersen, Lise Hannestad, and Jan Zahle. Studies in Hellenistic Civilization 3. Aarhus: Aarhus University Press.

–. 1992b. "'There Shall Come Forth a Man': Reflections on Messianic Ideas in Philo." Pp. 341–61 in *The Messiah: Developments in Earliest Judaism and Christianity*, edited by James H. Charlesworth. Minneapolis: Fortress.

–. 1993. "Heavenly Ascent in Philo: An Examination of Selected Passages." Pp. 246–68 in *The Pseudepigrapha and Early Biblical Interpretation*, edited by James H Charlesworth and Craig A Evans. Journal for the Study of the Pseudepigrapha Supplement Series 14. Sheffield: JSOT Press.

–. 1995. "Philo of Alexandria – Systematic Philosopher or Eclectic Editor?" *Symbolae osloenses* 71:115–34.

–. 1997. *Philo of Alexandria: An Exegete for His Time*. Supplements to Novum Testamentum 86. Leiden: Brill.

Bos, Abraham P. 2003. "God as 'Father' and 'Maker' in Philo of Alexandria and Its Background in Aristotelian Thought." *Elenchos* 24:311–32.

–. 2009. "Philo on God as 'Arche Geneseos'." *Journal of Jewish Studies* 60:32–47.

Bousset, D. W. 1915. *Jüdisch-Christlicher Schulbetrieb in Alexandria und Rom: Literarische Untersuchungen zu Philo und Clemens von Alexandria, Justin und Irenäus*. Forschungen zur Religion und Literatur des Alten und Neuen Testaments 6. Göttingen: Vandenhoeck & Ruprecht.

Boyancé, P. 1954. "Le platonisme à Rome: Platon et Cicéron." *Association Guillaume Budé. Congrès de Tours et Poitiers. Actes du Congrès*:195–221.

Boyd-Taylor, Cameron, Peter C. Austin, and Andrey Feuerverger. 2001. "The Assessment of Manuscript Affiliation Within a Probabilistic Framework: A Study of Alfred Rahlfs's Core Manuscript Groupings for the Greek Psalter." Pp. 98–124 in *The Old Greek Psalter: Studies in Honour of Albert Pietersma*, edited by Robert J. V. Hiebert, Claude E. Cox, and Peter J. Gentry. Journal for the Study of the Old Testament Supplement Series 332. Sheffield: Sheffield Academic Press.

Böhm, Martina. 2005. *Rezeption und Funktion der Vätererzählungen bei Philo von Alexandria: Zum Zusammenhang von Kontext, Hermeneutik und Exegese im frühen Judentum*. Beihefte zur Zeitschrift für die neutestamentliche Wissenschaft und die Kunde der älteren Kirche 128. Berlin: De Gruyter.

Bradshaw, David. 1998. "The Vision of God in Philo of Alexandria." *Catholic Philosophical Quarterly* 72:483–500.

Bréhier, Émile. 1925. *Les idées philosophiques et religieuses de Philon d'Alexandrie*. 2d ed. Études de philosophie médiévale 8. Paris: Librairie philosophique J. Vrin.

Buchheim, Thomas. 2001. "The Functions of the Concept of *Physis* in Aristotle's Metaphysics." *Oxford Studies in Ancient Philosophy* 20:201–34.

Bultmann, Rudolf. ET 1952–55. *Theology of the New Testament*. Translated by Kendrick Grobel. 2 vols. London: SCM.

Burkhardt, Helmut. 1988. *Die Inspiration heiliger Schriften bei Philo von Alexandrien*. Giessen: Brunnen.

Calvert, Nancy L. 1994. "Philo's Use of Jewish Traditions About Abraham." *Society of Biblical Literature Seminar Papers* 33:463–76.

Cambronne, Patrice. 1984. "Loi et législateur chez Philon d'Alexandrie: remarques sur la formation d'un concept judéo-hellénistique." *Cahiers du Centre George-Radet, Talence, Université de Bordeaux III* 4:1–19.

Carone, Gabriela Roxana. 1997. "The Ethical Function of Astronomy in Plato's *Timaeus*." Pp. 341–50 in *Interpreting the* Timaeus – Critias. *Proceedings of the IV Symposium Platonicum Selected Papers*, edited by Tomás Calvo and Luc Brisson. International Plato Studies 9. Sankt Augustin: Academia.

Carson, D. A. 1996. *Exegetical Fallacies*. Rev. ed. Grand Rapids: Baker.

Cazeaux, Jacques, trans. 1965. *De Migratione Abrahami. Introduction, traduction et notes*. Les Œuvres de Philon d'Alexandrie 14. Paris: Cerf.

Chadwick, Henry. 1966. "St. Paul and Philo of Alexandria." *Bulletin of the John Rylands University Library of Manchester* 48:286–307.

–. 1967. "Philo." Pp. 137–57 in *The Cambridge History of Later Greek and Early Medieval Philosophy*, edited by A. H. Armstrong. Cambridge: Cambridge University Press.

Charlesworth, James H. 1987. "Jewish Interest in Astrology during the Hellenistic and Roman period." Pp. 926–50 in *Aufstieg und Niedergang der römischen Welt*. Part 2, *Principat, 20.2*, edited by Wolfgang Haase. Berlin: De Gruyter.

Clines, David J. A. 1984. *The Esther Scroll: The Story of the Story*. Journal for the Study of the Old Testament Supplement Series 30. Sheffield: JSOT.

–. 1989. *Word Biblical Commentary: Job 1–20*. Dallas: Word.

Cohen, Naomi G. 1987. "The Jewish Dimension of Philo's Judaism—An Elucidation of *de Spec. Leg. IV* 132–150." *Journal of Jewish Studies* 38:165–86.

–. 1995. *Philo Judaeus: His Universe of Discourse*. Beiträge zur Erfoschung des Alten Testaments und des antiken Judentum 24. Frankfurt: Peter Lang.

Cohen, Shaye D. 1990. "Religion, Ethnicity and 'Hellenism' in the Emergence of Jewish Identity in Maccabean Palestine." Pp. 204–23 in *Religion and Religious Practice in the Seleucid Kingdom*, edited by Per Bilde, Troels Engberg-Pedersen, Lise Hannestad, and Jan Zahle. Studies in Hellenistic Civilization 1. Aarhus: Aarhus University Press.

Collingwood, R. G. 1945. *The Idea of Nature*. Oxford: Clarendon.

Collins, John J. 1977. "Cosmos and Salvation: Jewish Wisdom and Apocalyptic in the Hellenistic Age." *History of Religions* 17:121–42.

–. 2000. *Between Athens and Jerusalem: Jewish Identity in the Hellenistic Diaspora*. 2d ed. The Biblical Resource Series. Grand Rapids: Eerdmans.

Cooper, John M. 1996. "Eudaimonism, the Appeal to Nature, and 'Moral Duty' in Stoicism." Pp. 261–84 in *Aristotle, Kant, and the Stoics: Rethinking Happiness and Duty*, edited by Stephen Engstrom and Jennifer Whiting. Cambridge: Cambridge University Press.

Courcelle, Pierre. 1965. "Tradition platonicienne et Traditions chrétiennes du Corps-Prison (*Phédon* 62 *b*; *Cratyle* 400 *c*.)." *Revue des études latines* 43:406–43.

–. 1966. "Le Corps-Tombeau (Platon, *Gorgias*, 493 *a*, *Cratyle* 400 *c*, *Phèdre*, 250 *c*)." *Revue des études anciennes* 63:101–22.

–. 1974–75. *Connais-toi toi-même de Socrate à saint Bernard*. 3 vols. Paris: Études augustiniennes.

Cox, Ronald. 2007. *By the Same Word. Creation and Salvation in Hellenistic Judaism and Early Christianity*. Beihefte zur Zeitschrift für die neutestamentliche Wissenschaft und die Kunde der älteren Kirche 145. Berlin: De Gruyter.

Crenshaw, James L. 1995a. "The Eternal Gospel (Ecclesiastes 3:11)." Pp. 548–72 in *Urgent Advice and Probing Questions: Collected Writings on Old Testament Wisdom*. Macon, Ga.: Mercer University Press.

–. 1995b. "Studies in Ancient Israelite Wisdom: Prolegomenon." Pp. 90–140 in *Urgent Advice and Probing Questions: Collected Writings on Old Testament Wisdom*. Macon, Ga.: Mercer University Press.

–. 1998. *Old Testament Wisdom: An Introduction*. Rev. ed. Louisville: Westminster.

Cumont, Franz. 1912. *Astrology and Religion Among the Greeks and Romans*. Translated by J. B. Baker. American Lectures on the History of Religions. New York: G. P. Putnam.

Dahl, N. A. 1956. "Christ, Creation and the Church." Pp. 422–43 in *The Background of the New Testament and Its Eschatology*, edited by W. D. Davies and D. Daube. Cambridge: Cambridge University Press.

Daubercies, P. 1995. "La vertu chez Philon d'Alexandrie." *Revue théologique de Louvain* 26:185–210.

Dawson, David. 1992. *Allegorical Readers and Cultural Revision in Ancient Alexandria*. Berkeley: University of California Press.

Decharneux, Baudouin. 1994. *L'ange, le devin et le prophète: chemins de la parole dans l'œuvre de Philon d'Alexandrie dit "le Juif"*. Spiritualités et pensées libres. Brussels: Editions de l'universite de Bruxelles.

Deines, Roland, and Karl-Wilhelm Niebuhr, eds. 2004. *Philo und das Neue Testament. Wechselseitige Wahrnehmungen. I. Internationales Symposium zum Corpus Judaeo-Hellenisticum 1.-4. Mai 2003, Eisenach/Jena*. Wissenschaftliche Untersuchungen zum Neuen Testament 172. Tübingen: Mohr Siebeck.

Dell, Katherine J. 1991. *The Book of Job as Sceptical Literature*. Beihefte zur Zeitschrift für die alttestamentliche Wissenschaft 197. Berlin: De Gruyter.

–. 2006. *The Book of Proverbs in Social and Theological Context*. Cambridge: Cambridge University Press.

Demandt, Alexander. 1996. "Hellenismus – die moderne Zeit des Altertums?" Pp. 17–27 in *Hellenismus: Beiträge zur Erforschung von Akkulturation und politischer Ordnung in den Staaten des hellenistischen Zeitalters*, edited by Bernd Funck. Tübingen: Mohr Siebeck.

deSilva, David A. 2006. "The Perfection of 'Love for Offspring': Greek Representations of Maternal Affection and the Achievement of the Heroine of 4 Maccabees." *New Testament Studies* 52:251–68.

Di Mattei, Steven. 2006. "Moses' *Physiologia* and the Meaning and Use of *Physikôs* in Philo of Alexandria's Exegetical Method." *Studia Philonica Annual* 18:3–32.

Dillon, John M. 1977. *The Middle Platonists: A Study of Platonism 80 B.C. to A.D. 220*. London: Duckworth.

–. 1990. "Review of Clara Klaus Reggiani, Roberto Radice, and Giovanni Reale. *Filone di Alessandria: La Fiosofia Mosaica*." *Studia Philonica Annual* 2:177–82.

–. 1993. "A Response to Runia and Sterling." *Studia Philonica Annual* 5:151–55.

–. 1995. "Reclaiming the Heritage of Moses: Philo's Confrontation with Greek Philosophy." *Studia Philonica Annual* 7:108–23.

–. 2005. "Cosmic Gods and Primordial Chaos in Hellenistic and Roman Philosophy: The Context of Philo's Interpretation of Plato's Timaeus and the Book of Genesis." Pp. 97–

107 in *The Creation of Heaven and Earth: Re-Interpretations of Genesis 1 in the Context of Judaism, Ancient Philosophy, Christianity, and Modern Physics*, edited by George H. van Kooten. Themes in Biblical Narrative 8. Leiden/Boston: Brill.

Driver, S. R. 1897. *The Books of Joel and Amos*. The Cambridge Bible for Schools and Colleges. Cambridge: Cambridge University Press.

Droge, Arthur J. 1989. *Homer or Moses? Early Christian Interpretations of the History of Culture*. Hermeneutische Untersuchungen zur Theologie 26. Tübingen: Mohr Siebeck.

Droysen, Johann Gustav. 1836–43. *Geschichte des Hellenismus*. Repr. 1952–53. Edited by Erich Bayer. 3 vols. Basel: Schwabe.

Dunn, James D. G. 1998. *The Theology of Paul the Apostle*. Grand Rapids: Eerdmans.

Dyck, Jonathan. 2002. "Philo, Alexandria and Empire: The Politics of Allegorical Interpretation." Pp. 149–74 in *Jews in the Hellenistic and Roman Cities*, edited by John R. Bartlett. London: Routledge.

Evernden, Neil. 1992. *The Social Creation of Nature*. Baltimore/London: Johns Hopkins University Press.

Feldman, Louis H. 1993. *Jew and Gentile in the Ancient World: Attitudes and Interactions from Alexander to Justinian*. Princeton, N.J.: Princeton University Press.

–. 2005. "Philo's Account of the Golden Calf Incident." *Journal for the Study of Judaism in the Persian, Hellenistic, and Roman Periods* 56:245–64.

Festugière, A. J. 1944–54. *La révélation d'Hermès Trismégiste*. 4 vols. Études bibliques. Paris: Lecoffre.

Field, David. 2008. Personal communication.

Finnis, John M. 1980. *Natural Law and Natural Rights*. Clarendon Law Series. Oxford: Clarendon.

–. 1981. "Natural Law and the 'Is'-'Ought' Question: An Invitation to Professor Veatch." *Catholic Lawyer* 26:266–77 [In *Natural Law: Volume 1*. The International Library of Essays in Law and Legal Theory. Edited by John Finnis. Dartmouth: Aldershot, 1991].

–. 2002. "Natural Law: The Classical Tradition." Pp. 1–60 in *The Oxford Handbook of Jurisprudence and Philosophy of Law*, edited by Jules L. Coleman and Scott Shapiro. Oxford: Oxford University Press.

Forstner, Dorothea, OSB. 1967. *Die Welt der Symbole*. 2d ed. Tyrolia: Innsbruck.

Fraser, P. M. 1972. *Ptolemaic Alexandria*. 3 vols. Oxford: Clarendon.

Frede, Michael. 1999. "Monotheism and Pagan Philosophy in Later Antiquity." Pp. 41–67 in *Pagan Monotheism in Late Antiquity*, edited by Polymnia Athanassiadi and Michael Frede. Oxford: Clarendon.

Früchtel, Ursula. 1968. *Die kosmologischen Vorstellungen bei Philo von Alexandrien*. Arbeiten zur Literatur und Geschichte des hellenistischen Judentums 2. Leiden: Brill.

Fyall, Robert S. 2002. *Now My Eyes Have Seen You: Images of Creation and Evil in the Book of Job*. New Studies in Biblical Theology 12. Downers Grove, Ill.: InterVarsity.

Gaca, Kathy L. 1996. "Philo's Principles of Sexual Conduct and Their Influence on Christian Platonist Sexual Principles." *Studia Philonica Annual* 8:21–39.

Garnsey, Peter. 1996. *Ideas of Slavery from Aristotle to Augustine*. The W. B. Stanford Memorial Lectures. Cambridge: Cambridge University Press.

Geiger, Franz. 1932. *Philon von Alexandreia als socialer Denker*. Tübinger Beiträge zur Altertumswissenschaft 14. Stuttgart: W. Kohlhammer.

Goldstein, Jonathan A. 1981. "Jewish Acceptance and Rejection of Hellenism." Pp. 64–87 in *Aspects of Judaism in the Graeco-Roman Period*, edited by E. P. Sanders, A. I. Baumgar-

ten, and Alan Mendelson. Vol.2 of *Jewish and Christian Self-Definition*. Philadelphia: Fortress.
–. 1983. *II Maccabees: A New Translation with Introduction and Commentary*. Anchor Bible 41a. New York: Doubleday.
Goodenough, Erwin R. 1933. "Philo's Exposition of the Law and His *De Vita Mosis*." *Harvard Theological Review* 26:109–25.
–. 1935. *By Light, Light: The Mystic Gospel of Hellenistic Judaism*. New Haven: Yale University Press.
Goody, Jack. 1993. *The Culture of Flowers*. Cambridge: Cambridge University Press.
Gordon, Lesley. 1977. *Green Magic: Flowers, Plants and Herbs in Lore and Legend*. London: Ebury.
Goudriaan, Koen. 1992. "Ethnical Strategies in Graeco-Roman Egypt." Pp. 74–99 in *Ethnicity in Hellenistic Egypt*, edited by Per Bilde, Troels Engberg-Pedersen, Lise Hannestad, and Jan Zahle. Studies in Hellenistic Civilization 3. Aarhus: Aarhus University Press.
Goulet, Richard. 1987. *La philosophie de Moïse: essai de reconstitution d'un commentaire philosophique préphilonien du Pentateuque*. Histoire des doctrines de l'antiquité classique 11. Paris: J. Vrin.
Grabbe, Lester L. 1992. *The Persian and Greek Periods*. Vol. 1 of *Judaism from Cyrus to Hadrian*. Minneapolis: Fortress.
–. 1993. "Philo and the Aggada: A Response to B. J. Bamberger." *Studia Philonica Annual* 2:153–66.
–. 2008. "Jewish Identity and Hellenism in the Fragmentary Jewish Writings in Greek." Pp. 21–32 in *Scripture and Traditions: Essays on Early Judaism and Christianity in Honor of Carl R. Holladay*, edited by Patrick Gray and Gail R. O'Day. Novum Testamentum Supplements 129. Leiden: Brill.
Grant, Robert M. 1952. *Miracle and Natural Law in Early Graeco-Roman and Early Christian Thought*. Amsterdam: North-Holland.
Gruen, Erich S. 2002. *Diaspora: Jews Amidst Greeks and Romans*. Cambridge: Harvard University Press.
Hadas, Moses. 1953. *The Third and Fourth Books of Maccabees*. New York: Harper.
Hadas-Lebel, Mireille, trans. 1973. *De Providentia I et II. Introduction, traduction et notes*. Les Œuvres de Philon d'Alexandrie 35. Paris: Cerf.
Hagner, Donald A. 1971. "The Vision of God in Philo and John: A Comparative Study." *Journal of the Evangelical Theological Society* 14:81–93.
Hahm, David E. 1977. *The Origins of Stoic Cosmology*. Columbus: Ohio State University Press.
Hall, Jonathan M. 1997. *Ethnic Identity in Greek Antiquity*. Cambridge: Cambridge University Press.
–. 2002. *Hellenicity: Between Ethnicity and Culture*. Chicago: University of Chicago Press.
Hamerton-Kelly, Robert G. 1972. "Sources and Traditions in Philo of Alexandria: Prologomena to an Analysis of His Writings." *Studia Philonica* 1:3–26.
Hankinson, R. J. 2003. "Philosophy and Science." Pp. 271–99 in *The Cambridge Companion to Greek and Roman Philosophy*, edited by David Sedley. Cambridge: Cambridge University Press.
Harder, Richard. 1929. *Über Ciceros Somnium Scipionis*. Schriften der Königsberger Gelehrten Gesellschaft 6.H3. Halle: Niemeyer.

Harl, Marguerite. 1967. "Cosmologie grecque et représentations juives chez Philon." Pp. 189–205 in *Philon d'Alexandrie: Lyon 11–15 Septembre 1966*, edited by R. Arnaldez, C. Mondésert, and J. Poullioux. Paris: Centre National de la Recherche Scientifique.

–. 1966. *Quis Rerum Divinarum Heres Sit. Introduction, traduction et notes*. Les Œuvres de Philon d'Alexandrie 15. Paris: Cerf.

Hartog, Paul. 2006. "'Not Even Among the Pagans' (1 Cor 5:1): Paul and Seneca on Incest.". In *The New Testament and Early Christian Literature in Greco-Roman Context: Studies in Honor of David E. Aune*, edited by John Fotopoulos. Supplements to Novum Testamentum 122. Leiden: Brill.

Hay, David M. 1979–80. "Philo's References to Other Allegorists." *Studia Philonica* 6:41–75.

–. 1987. "The Psychology of Faith in Hellenistic Judaism." Pp. 881–925 in *Aufstieg und Niedergang der Römischen Welt.* Part 2, *Principat, 20.2*, edited by Wolfgang Haase. Berlin: De Gruyter.

–. 1991a. "Philo's View of Himself as an Exegete: Inspired, but not Authoritative." *Studia Philonica Annual* 3:40–52.

–. 1991b. "References to Other Exegetes." Pp. 81–97 in *Both Literal and Allegorical: Studies in Philo of Alexandria'* Questions and Answers on Genesis and Exodus, edited by David M. Hay. Brown Judaic Studies 232. Atlanta: Scholars Press.

–. 1997. "Putting Extremism in Context: The Case of Philo, *De Migratione* 89–93." *Studia Philonica Annual* 9:126–42.

–. 2001–04. "Philo of Alexandria." Pp. 1.357–79 in *Justification and Variegated Nomism*, edited by D. A. Carson, Peter T. O'Brien, and Mark A. Seifrid. 2 vols. Wissenschaftliche Untersuchungen zum Neuen Testament 140, 181. Tübingen: Mohr Siebeck.

Heinemann, Isaak. 1927. "Die Lehre vom ungeschriebenen Gesetz im Jüdischen Schrifttum." *Hebrew Union College Annual* 4:149–71.

–. 1932. *Philons grieschische und jüdische Bildung: Kulturvergleichende Untersuchungen zu Philons Darstellung der jüdischen Gesetze*. Breslau: M. & H. Marcus.

Helleman, Wendy E. 1990. "Philo of Alexandria on Deification and Assimilation to God." *Studia Philonica Annual* 2:51–71.

Hengel, Martin. 2001. "Judaism and Hellenism Revisited." Pp. 6–37 in *Hellenism in the Land of Israel*, edited by John J. Collins and Gregory E. Sterling. Christianity and Judaism in Antiquity 13. Notre Dame: University of Notre Dame Press.

–. ET 1974. *Judaism and Hellenism: Studies in Their Encounter in Palestine During the Early Hellenistic Period.* Translated by John Bowden. 2 vols. London: SCM.

–. ET 1990. *The 'Hellenization' of Judea in the First Century After Christ.* Translated by John Bowden. London: SCM.

Hilgert, Earle. 1995. "Philo Judaeus et Alexandrinus: The State of the Problem." Pp. 1–15 in *The School of Moses: Studies in Philo and Hellenistic Religion in Memory of Horst R. Moehring*, edited by John Peter Kenney. Brown Judaic Studies 304. Studia Philonica Monographs 1. Atlanta: Scholars Press.

Hilhorst, Anton. 1992. "Was Philo Read by Pagans? The Statement on Heliodorus in Socrates *Hist. Eccl.* 5.22." *Studia Philonica Annual* 4:75–77.

Himmelfarb, Martha. 2005. "The Torah Between Athens and Jerusalem: Jewish Difference in Antiquity." Pp. 113–30 in *Ancient Judaism in Its Hellenistic Context*, edited by Carol Bakhos. Journal for the Study of the Pseudepigrapha: Supplement Series 95. Leiden: Brill.

Holladay, Carl R. 1992. "Jewish Responses to Hellenistic Culture in Early Ptolemaic Egypt." Pp. 139–63 in *Ethnicity in Hellenistic Egypt*, edited by Per Bilde, Troels Engberg-Pedersen, Lise Hannestad, and Jan Zahle. Studies in Hellenistic Civilization 3. Aarhus: Aarhus University Press.

Hollander, H. W., and M. de Jonge. 1985. *The Testaments of the Twelve Patriarchs: A Commentary*. Studia in Veteris Testamenti pseudepigraphica 8. Leiden: Brill.

Horbury, William. 2004. "Jewish and Christian Monotheism in the Herodian Age." Pp. 16–44 in *Early Jewish and Christian Monotheism*, edited by Loren T. Stuckenbruck and Wendy E. S. North. Journal for the Study of the New Testament: Supplement Series 263. London: T&T Clark.

Horsley, Richard A. 1978. "The Law of Nature in Philo and Cicero." *Harvard Theological Review* 71:35–60.

Horst, Friedrich. 1961. "Naturrecht und Altes Testament." Pp. 235–59 in *Gottes Recht: gessammelte Studien zum Recht im Alten Testament. Aus Anlaß der Vollendung seines 65. Lebensjahres*, edited by Hans Walter Wolff. Munich: Chr. Kaiser.

Hubbard, David Allan. 1989. *Joel and Amos*. Tyndale Old Testament Commentaries. Leicester: InterVarsity.

Inwood, Brad. 1985. *Ethics and Human Action in Early Stoicism*. New York: Oxford University Press.

Inwood, Brad, and Pierluigi Donini. 1999. "Stoic Ethics." Pp. 675–738 in *The Cambridge History of Hellenistic Philosophy*, edited by Keimpe Algra, Jonathan Barnes, Jaap Mansfeld, and Malcolm Schofield. Cambridge: Cambridge University Press.

Isaac, Benjamin. 2004. *The Invention of Racism in Classical Antiquity*. Princeton, N.J.: Princeton University Press.

Jackson-McCabe, Matt A. 2001. *Logos and Law in the Letter of James: The Law of Nature, the Law of Moses and the Law of Freedom*. Supplements to Novum Testamentum 100. Leiden: Brill.

Jacobson, Howard. 2004. "A Philonic Rejection of Plato." *Mnemosyne* 57:488.

Johnson, Luke Timothy. 1999. *The Writings of the New Testament: An Interpretation*. Rev. ed. Minneapolis: Fortress.

Jones, Alexander. 2003. "The Stoics and the Astronomical Sciences." Pp. 328–44 in *The Cambridge Companion to the Stoics*, edited by Brad Inwood. Cambridge: Cambridge University Press.

Kahn, Jean-George. 1973. "Connais-toi toi-même à la manière de Philon." *Revue d'Histoire et de Philosophie Religieuses* 53:293–307.

–. 1986. "The Concept of 'Physis' in the Philosophy of Philo." Pp. 139–44 in *Proceedings of the Ninth World Congress of Jewish Studies. Jerusalem, August 4–12, 1985. Division A: The Period of the Bible*. Jerusalem: World Union of Jewish Studies.

Kee, Howard Clark. 1978. "The Ethical Dimensions of the *Testaments of the XII* as a Clue to Provenance." *New Testament Studies* 24:259–70.

Kelsey, Sean. 2003. "Aristotle's Definition of Nature." *Oxford Studies in Ancient Philosophy* 25:59–87.

Knox, Wilfred Lawrence. 1935. "Abraham and the Quest for God." *Harvard Theological Review* 38:55–60.

Koester, Helmut. 1968. "ΝΟΜΟΣ ΦΥΣΕΩΣ: The Concept of Natural Law in Greek Thought." Pp. 521–41 in *Religions in Antiquity: Essays in Memory of Erwin Ramsdell Goodenough*, edited by Jacob Neusner. Leiden: Brill.

Kolarcik, Michael. 1992. "Creation and Salvation in the Book of Wisdom." Pp. 97–107 in *Creation in the Biblical Traditions*, edited by Richard J. Clifford and John J. Collins. Catholic Biblical Quarterly Monograph Series 24. Washington, D.C.: Catholic Biblical Association of America.

–. 1997. "The Book of Wisdom: Introduction, Commentary, and Reflections.". In *New Interpreter's Bible*, edited by Leander Keck. Vol. 5. Nashville: Abingdon.

Kraft, Robert A. 1991. "Philo and the Sabbath Crisis: Alexandrian Jewish Politics and the Dating of Philo's Works." Pp. 131–41 in *The Future of Early Christianity: Essays in Honor of Helmut Koester*, edited by Birger A. Pearson. Minneapolis: Fortress.

Kroll, Josef. 1914. *Die Lehren des Hermes Trismegistos*. Beiträge zur Geschichte der Philosophie des Mittelalters: Texte und Untersuchungen 12. Münster: Aschendorffsche.

Kuhrt, Amélie, and Susan Sherwin-White, eds. 1987. *Hellenism in the East: The Interaction of Greek and Non-Greek Civilizations from Syria to Central Asia After Alexander*. London: Duckworth.

Laks, André. 1989. "Commentary on Annas." Pp. 172–85 in *Proceedings of the Boston Area Colloquium in Ancient Philosophy. Volume IV*, John J. Cleary and Daniel C. Shartin. Lanham: University Press of America.

Lamberton, Robert. 1986. *Homer the Theologian: Neoplatonist Allegorical Reading and the Growth of the Epic Tradition*. Transformation of the Classical Heritage 9. Berkeley: University of California Press.

Laporte, Jean. 1972. *La doctrine eucharistique chez Philon d'Alexandrie*. Théologie historique 16. Paris: Beauchesne.

Leonhardt, Jutta. 2001. *Jewish Worship in Philo of Alexandria*. Texte und Studien zum antiken Judentum 84. Tübingen: Mohr Siebeck.

Levenson, Jon D. 1988. *Creation and the Persistence of Evil: The Jewish Drama of Divine Omnipotence*. Mythos. Princeton: Princeton University Press.

Lévy, Carlos. 2008. "Philo's Ethics." Pp. 146–71 in *The Cambridge Companion to Philo*, edited by Adam Kamesar. Cambridge: Cambridge University Press.

Lilla, Salvatore R. C. 1971. *Clement of Alexandria: A Study in Christian Platonism and Gnosticism*. Oxford Theological Monographs. Oxford: Oxford University Press.

Long, A. A. 1982. "Astrology: Arguments Pro and Contra." Pp. 165–92 in *Science and Speculation: Studies in Hellenistic Theory and Practice*, edited by Jonathan Barnes, Jacques Brunschwig, Myles Burnyeat, and Malcolm Schofield. Cambridge/Paris: Cambridge University Press/Editions de la Maison des Sciences de l'Homme.

–. 1989. "Stoic Eudaimonism." Pp. 77–101 in *Proccedings of the Boston Area Colloquium in Ancient Philosophy. Volume VII*, edited by John J. Cleary and Daniel C. Shartin. Lanham: University Press of America.

–. 1996. *Stoic Studies*. Cambridge: Cambridge University Press.

–. 2003. "Eudaimonism, Divinity, and Rationality in Greek Ethics." Pp. 123–43 in *Proceedings of the Boston Area Colloquium in Ancient Philosophy. Volume XIX*, edited by John J. Cleary and Gary M. Gurtler, S.J. Leiden: Brill.

–. 2005. "Law and Nature in Greek Thought." Pp. 412–30 in *The Cambridge Companion to Ancient Greek Law*, edited by Michael Gagarin and David Cohen. Cambridge: Cambridge University Press.

–. 2008. "Philo on Stoic Physics." Pp. 121–40 in *Philo of Alexandria and Post-Aristotelian Philosophy*, edited by Francesca Alesse. Studies in Philo of Alexandria 5. Leiden: Brill.

Longman, Tremper, III. 1998. *The Book of Ecclesiastes*. New International Commentary on the Old Testament. Grand Rapids: Eerdmans.

Lucas, Alec J. 2009. Personal communication.

Mach, Michael F. 1999. "Concepts of Jewish Monotheism in the Hellenistic Period." Pp. 21–42 in *The Jewish Roots of Christological Monotheism: Papers from the St. Andrews Conference on the Historical Origins of the Worship of Jesus*, edited by Carey C. Newman, James R. Davlia, and Gladys S. Lewis. Supplements to the Journal for the Study of Judaism in the Persian, Hellenistic, and Roman Periods 63. Leiden: Brill.

–. 2005. "Lernentraditionen im hellenistischen Judentum unter besonderer Berücksichtigung Philons von Alexandrien." Pp. 117–39 in *Religiöses Lernen in der biblischen, frühjüdischen und frühchristlichen Überlieferung*, edited by Beate Ego and Helmut Merkel. Wissenschaftliche Untersuchungen zum Neuen Testament 180. Tübingen: Mohr Siebeck.

Mack, Burton L. 1984. "Philo Judaeus and Exegetical Traditions in Alexandria." Pp. 227–71 in *Aufstieg und Niedergang der römischen Welt.* Part 2, *Principat, 21.1*, edited by Wolfgang Haase. Berlin: De Gruyter.

–. 1991. "Wisdom and Apocalyptic in Philo." *Studia Philonica Annual* 3:21–39.

Mackie, Scott D. 2009. "Seeing God in Philo of Alexandria: The Logos, the Powers, or the Existent One?" *Studia Philonica Annual* 21:25–47.

Malingrey, Anne-Marie. 1961. *'Philosophia': Étude d'un groupe de mots dans la littérature grecque, des Présocratiques au IVe siècle après J.-C.* Études et commentaires 40. Paris: C. Klincksieck.

Mansfeld, Jaap. 1981. "Bad World and Demiurge: A 'Gnostic' Motif from Parmenides and Empedocles to Lucretius and Philo." Pp. 261–314 in *Studies in Gnosticism and Hellenistic Religions: Presented to Gilles Quispel on the Occasion of His 65th Birthday*, edited by R. Van den Broek and M. J. Vermaseren. Études préliminaires aux religions orientales dans l'empire romain 91. Leiden: Brill.

–. 1988. "Philosophy in the Service of Scripture: Philo's Exegetical Strategies." Pp. 70–102 in *The Question of "Eclecticism"*, edited by John M. Dillon and A. A. Long. Berkley: University of California Press.

Martens, John W. 2003. *One God, One Law: Philo of Alexandria on the Mosaic and Greco-Roman Law.* Studies in Philo of Alexandria 2. Leiden: Brill.

Mason, Steve. 1996. "*Philosophiai*: Graeco-Roman, Judean and Christian." Pp. 31–58 in *Voluntary Associations in the Graeco-Roman World*, edited by J. S. Kloppenborg and S. G. Wilson. London: Routledge.

Mattila, Sharon Lea. 1996. "Wisdom, Sense Perception, Nature, and Philo's Gender Gradient." *Harvard Theological Review* 89:103–29.

McGrath, Alister. 2001. *Nature.* Vol. 1 of *A Scientific Theology.* London/Grand Rapids: T&T Clark/Eerdmans.

McKirahan, Richard D., Jr. 1994. *Philosophy Before Socrates: An Introduction with Texts and Commentary.* Indianapolis: Hackett.

Mendels, D. 1988. "'Creative History' in the Hellenistic Near East in the Third and Second Centuries BCE: The Jewish Case." *Journal for the Study of the Pseudepigrapha* 2:13–20.

Mendelson, Alan. 1982. *Secular Education in Philo of Alexandria.* Monographs of the Hebrew Union College 7. Cincinnati: Hebrew Union College Press.

–. 1988. *Philo's Jewish Identity.* Brown Judaic Studies 161. Atlanta: Scholars Press.

Merki, Hubert, OSB 1952. *Ὁμοίωσις Θεῷ: Von der platonischen Angleichung an Gott zur Gottähnlichkeit bei Gregor von Nyssa.* Pardosis 7. Freiburg: Paulusverlag.

Mitsis, Phillip. 1994. "Natural law and natural right in Post-Aristotelian philosophy." Pp. 4812–50 in *Aufstieg und Niedergang der römischen Welt.* Part 2. *Principat, 36.7.* Berlin: De Gruyter.

–. 2003. "The Stoics and Aquinas on Virtue and Natural Law." *Studia Philonica Annual* 15:35–53.

Modrzejewski, J. M. 1991. "How to be a Greek and Yet a Jew in Hellenistic Alexandria." Pp. 65–92 in *Diasporas in Antiquity*, edited by Shaye J. D. Cohen and Ernest S. Frerichs. Atlanta: Scholars Press.

Momigliano, Arnaldo. 1975. *Alien Wisdom: The Limits of Hellenization*. Cambridge: Cambridge University Press.

Mondésert, Claude. 1999. "Philo of Alexandria." Pp. 877–900 in *The Early Roman Period*, edited by William Horbury, W. D. Davies, and John Sturdy. Vol. 3 of *The Cambridge History of Judaism*. Cambridge: Cambridge University Press.

Montefiore, C. G. 1895. "Florilegium Philonis." *Jewish Quarterly Review* 7:481–545.

Moo, Douglas J. 2008. *The Letters to the Colossians and to Philemon*. Pillar New Testament Commentary. Grand Rapids: Eerdmans.

Moo, Jonathan. 2008. "Creation, Nature and Hope in Fourth Ezra." Ph.D. dissertation. University of Cambridge.

Morris, Jenny. 1987. "The Jewish Philosopher Philo." Pp. 809–89 in *The History of the Jewish People in the Age of Jesus Christ (175 B.C.–A.D. 135)* III.2, Emil Schürer, Geza Vermes, Fergus Millar, and Martin Goodman. Edinburgh: T&T Clark.

Murphy-O'Connor, Jerome. 1978. "I Cor VIII, 6: Cosmology or Soteriology?" *Revue Biblique* 85:253–67.

Myre, André, S.J. 1972. "La loi dans l'ordre cosmique et politique selon Philon d'Alexandrie." *Science et Esprit* 24:217–47.

–. 1976. "La loi de la nature et la loi mosaïque selon Philon d'Alexandrie." *Science et Esprit* 28:163–81.

Naddaf, Gerard. 2005. *The Greek Concept of Nature*. Albany: State University of New York Press.

Najman, Hindy. 1999. "The Law of Nature and the Authority of Mosaic Law." *Studia Philonica Annual* 11:55–73.

–. 2003a. *Seconding Sinai: The Development of Mosaic Discourse in Second Temple Judaism*. Supplements to the Journal for the Study of Judaism in the Persian, Hellenistic, and Roman Periods 77. Leiden: Brill.

–. 2003b. "A Written Copy of the Law of Nature: An Unthinkable Paradox?" *Studia Philonica Annual* 15:54–63.

Neudorfer, Heinz-Werner. 1990. "Das Diasporajudentum und der Kanon." Pp. 83–101 in *Der Kanon der Bibel*, edited by Gerhard Maier. Giessen/Basel: Brunnen/R. Brockhaus.

Niebuhr, K.-W. 1987. *Gesetz und Paränese: Katechismusartige Weisungsreihen in der frühjüdischen Literatur*. Wissenschaftliche Untersuchungen zum Neuen Testament 28. Tübingen: Mohr Siebeck.

Niehoff, Maren R. 1998. "Philo's Views on Paganism." Pp. 135–58 in *Tolerance and Intolerance in Early Judaism and Christianity*, edited by Graham N. Stanton and Guy G. Stroumsa. Cambridge: Cambridge University Press.

–. 2001. *Philo on Jewish Identity and Culture*. Texte und Studien zum antiken Judentum 86. Tübingen: Mohr Siebeck.

Nikiprowetzky, Valentin. 1965. *De Decalogo. Introduction, traduction et notes*. Les Œuvres de Philon d'Alexandrie 23. Paris: Cerf.

–. 1977. *Le commentaire de l'Écriture chez Philon d'Alexandrie*. Arbeiten zur Literatur und Geschichte des hellenistischen Judentums 11. Leiden: Brill.

Novak, David. 1998. *Natural Law in Judaism*. Cambridge: Cambridge University Press.

Novick, Tzvi. 2009. "Perspective, Paideia, and Accommodation in Philo." *Studia Philonica Annual* 21:49–62.

O'Neill, J. C. 2002. "How Early is the Doctrine of Creatio Ex Nihilo?" *Journal of Theological Studies, NS* 53:449–65.

Paul, Shalom M. 1991. *Amos*. Hermeneia. Minneapolis: Fortress.

Pearce, Sarah. 2007. *The Land of the Body: Studies in Philo's Representation of Egypt*. Wissenschaftliche Untersuchungen zum Neuen Testament 208. Tübingen: Mohr Siebeck.

Pearson, Birger A. 1984. "Philo and Gnosticism." Pp. 295–342 in *Aufstieg und Niedergang der römischen Welt*. Part 2, *Principat, 21.1*, edited by Wolfgang Haase. Berlin: De Gruyter.

Pease, Arthur Stanley. 1941. "Caeli Enarrant." *Harvard Theological Review* 34:163–200.

Pelikan, Jaroslav. 1971–89. *The Christian Tradition: A History of the Development of Doctrine*. 5 vols. Chicago: University of Chicago Press.

Pembroke, S. G. 1971. "Oikeiosis." Pp. 114–49 in *Problems in Stoicism*, edited by A. A. Long. London: Athlone.

Perdue, Leo G. 1994. *Wisdom and Creation: The Theology of Wisdom Literature*. Nashville: Abingdon.

Pépin, Jean. 1967. "Remarques sur la théorie de l'exégèse allégorique chez Philon." Pp. 131–67 in *Philon d'Alexandrie: Lyon 11–15 Septembre 1966*, edited by R. Arnaldez, C. Mondésert, and J. Poullioux. Paris: Centre National de la Recherche Scientifique.

–. 1976. *Mythe et allégorie. Les origines grecques et les contestations judéo-chrêtiennes*. 2d ed. Philosophie de l'esprit. Paris: Études Augustiniennes.

–. 1986. "Cosmic Piety." Pp. 408–35 in *Classical Mediterranean Spirituality: Egyptian, Greek, Roman*, edited by A. H. Armstrong, translated by Jane Curran. World Spirituality: An Encyclopedic History of the Religious Quest. London: SCM.

Piccione, Rosa Maria. 2004. "De Vita Mosis I 60–62. Philon und die griechische Paideia." Pp. 345–57 in *Philo und das Neue Testament. Wechselseitige Wahrnehmungen. I. Internationales Symposium zum Corpus Judaeo-Hellenisticum 1.-4. Mai 2003, Eisenach/Jena*, edited by Roland Deines and Karl-Wilhelm Niebuhr. Wissenschaftliche Untersuchungen zum Neuen Testament 172. Tübingen: Mohr Siebeck.

Pilhofer, Peter. 1990. *Presbyteron Kreitton: der Altersbeweis der jüdischen und christlichen Apologeten und seine Vorgeschichte*. Wissenschaftliche Untersuchungen zum Neuen Testament 39. Tübingen: Mohr Siebeck.

Popović, Mladen. 2007. *Reading the Human Body: Physiognomics and Astrology in the Dead Sea Scrolls and Hellenistic-Early Roman Period Judaism. Studies on the Texts of the Desert of Judah* 67. Leiden: Brill.

Radice, Roberto. 2008. "Philo's Theology and Theory of Creation." Pp. 124–45 in *The Cambridge Companion to Philo*, edited by Adam Kamesar. Cambridge: Cambridge University Press.

Redditt, Paul L. 1983. "The Concept of *Nomos* in Fourth Maccabees." *Catholic Biblical Quarterly* 45:249–70.

Reed, Annette Yoshiko. 2004. "Abraham as Chaldean Scientist and Father of the Jews: Josephus, *Ant*. 1.154–168, and the Greco-Roman Discourse About Astronomy/Astrology." *Journal for the Study of Judaism in the Persian, Hellenistic, and Roman Periods* 35:119–58.

Reinhartz, Adele. 1986. "The Meaning of *Nomos* in Philo's *Exposition of the Law*." *Studies in Religion* 15:337–45.

–. 1993. "Parents and Children: A Philonic Perspective." Pp. 61–88 in *The Jewish Family in Antiquity*, edited by Shaye J.D. Cohen. Brown Judaic Studies 289. Atlanta: Scholars Press.

Renehan, R. 1972. "The Greek philosophical background of Fourth Maccabees."

Reydams-Schils, Gretchen J., ed. 2003. *Plato's Timaeus as Cultural Icon*. Notre Dame, Ind.: University of Notre Dame Press.

–. 1995. "Stoicized Readings of Plato's *Timaeus* in Philo of Alexandria." *Studia Philonica Annual* 7:85–102.

–. 1999. *Demiurge and Providence: Stoic and Platonist Readings of Plato's "Timaeus"*. Monothéismes et Philosophie. Turnhout: Brepols.

Riedweg, Christoph. 1993. *Jüdisch-hellenistische Imitation eines orphischen Hieros Logos: Beobachtungen zu OF 245 und 247 (sog. Testament des Orpheus)*. Classica Monacensia 7. Tübingen: Gunter Narr.

Rist, John M. 1962. *Eros and Psyche: Studies in Plato, Plotinus, and Origen*. Journal of the Classical Association of Canada Supplementary Volume 6. Toronto: University of Toronto Press.

Rodd, C. S. 2001. *Glimpses of a Strange Land: Studies in Old Testament Ethics*. Old Testament Studies. Edinburgh: T&T Clark.

Rosner, Brian S. 1994. *Paul, Scripture and Ethics: A Study of 1 Corinthians 5–7*. Arbeiten zur Geschichte des antiken Judentums und des Urchristentums 22. Leiden: Brill.

Roth, Norman. 1978. "The 'Theft of Philosophy' by the Greeks from the Jews." *Classical Folia* 32:53–67.

Royse, James R. 1976–77. "The Original Structure of Philo's *Quaestiones*." *Studia Philonica* 4:41–78.

–. 2008. "The Works of Philo." Pp. 32–64 in *The Cambridge Companion to Philo*, edited by Adam Kamesar. Cambridge: Cambridge University Press.

Rudolph, David J. 2006. "A Jew to the Jews: Jewish Contours of Pauline Flexibility in 1 Cor 9:19–23." Ph.D. diss. University of Cambridge.

Runia, David T. 1986. *Philo of Alexandria and the* Timaeus *of Plato*. Philosophia Antiqua 44. Leiden: Brill.

–. 1988a. "God and Man in Philo of Alexandria." *Journal of Theological Studies, NS* 39:48–75.

–. 1988b. "Naming and Knowing: Themes in Philonic Theology with Special Reference to the *De Mutatione Nominum*." Pp. 69–91 in *Knowledge of God in the Graeco-Roman World*, edited by R. van der Broek, T. Baarda, and J. Mansfeld. Études préliminaires aux religions orientales dans l'empire romain 112. Leiden: Brill.

–. 1989. "Review of Robert Goulet, *La Philosophie de Moïse*." *Journal of Theological Studies, NS* 40:590–602.

–. 1990. "How to Search Philo." *Studia Philonica Annual* 2:106–39.

–. 1993a. *Philo in Early Christian Literature: A Survey*. Compendia rerum iudaicarum ad Novum Testamentum 3/3. Assen/Minneapolis: Van Gorcum/Fortress.

–. 1993b. "Was Philo a Middle Platonist? A Difficult Question Revisited." *Studia Philonica Annual* 5:112–40.

–. 1997. "The Reward for Goodness: Philo, *De Vita Contemplativa* 90." *Studia Philonica Annual* 9:3–18.

–. 1999. "A Brief History of the Term *Kosmos Noétos* from Plato to Plotinus." Pp. 151–72 in *Traditions of Platonism: Essays in Honour of John Dillon*, edited by John J. Cleary. Aldershot: Ashgate.

–. 2001. *On the Creation of the Cosmos According to Moses*. Philo of Alexandria Commentary Series 1. Leiden: Brill.

–. 2002a. "The Beginnings of the End: Philo of Alexandria and Hellenistic Theology." Pp. 281–316 in *Traditions of Theology: Studies in Hellenistic Theology, Its Background, and Aftermath*, Dorothea Frede and André Laks. Philosophia Antiqua 89. Leiden: Brill.

–. 2002b. "Eudaimonism in Hellenistic-Jewish Literature." Pp. 131–57 in *Shem in the Tents of Japheth: Essays on the Encounter of Judaism and Hellenism*, edited by James L. Kugel. Supplements to the Journal for the Study of Judaism in the Persian, Hellenistic, and Roman Periods 74. Leiden: Brill.

–. 2004. "Clement of Alexandria and the Philonic Doctrine of the Divine Power(s)." *Vigiliae Christianae* 58:256–76.

Sandbach, F. H. 1985. *Aristotle and the Stoics*. Cambridge Philological Society Supplementary Volume 10. Cambridge: Cambridge Philological Society.

Sandmel, Samuel. 1951. "Abraham's Knowledge of the Existence of God." *Harvard Theological Review* 44:137–39.

–. 1955. "Philo's Place in Judaism: A Study of Conceptions of Abraham in Jewish Literature, II." *Hebrew Union College Annual* 26:151–332.

–. 1978. "Philo's Knowledge of Hebrew." *Studia Philonica* 5:107–12.

–. 1979. *Philo of Alexandria: An Introduction*. New York: Oxford University Press.

Satlow, Michael L. 2008. "Philo on Human Perfection." *Journal of Theological Studies* 59:500–19.

Schmidt, Francis. 1974. "Le monde à l'image du bouclier d'Achille: sur la naissance et l'incorruptibilité du monde dans le 'Testament d'Abraham'." *Revue de l'histoire des religions* 185:122–26.

Schrage, Wolfgang. 2005. "Schöpfung und Neuschöpfung in Kontinuität und Diskontinuität bei Paulus." *Evangelische Theologie* 65:245–59.

Schwarzschild, Steven S. 1962. "Do Noachites Have to Believe in Revelation? (Part 1 and 2)." *Jewish Quarterly Review* 52–53:297–308; 30–65.

Scott, Alan. 1991. *Origen and the Life of the Stars*. Oxford Early Christian Studies. Oxford: Clarendon.

Sedley, David. 1997. "'Becoming Like God' in the *Timaeus* and Aristotle." Pp. 327–39 in *Interpreting the* Timaeus – Critias. *Proceedings of the IV Symposium Platonicum Selected Papers*, edited by Tomás Calvo and Luc Brisson. International Plato Studies 9. Sankt Augustin: Academia.

–. 1999. "Hellenistic Physics and Metaphysics." Pp. 355–411 in *The Cambridge History of Hellenistic Philosophy*, edited by Keimpe Algra, Jonathan Barnes, Jaap Mansfeld, and Malcolm Schofield. Cambridge: Cambridge University Press.

Seifrid, Mark A. 2001–04. "Righteousness Language in the Hebrew Scriptures and Early Judaism." Pp. 1.415–42 in *Justification and Variegated Nomism*, edited by D. A. Carson, Peter T. O'Brien, and Mark A. Seifrid. 2 vols. Wissenschaftliche Untersuchungen zum Neuen Testament 140, 181. Tübingen: Mohr Siebeck.

Seland, Torrey. 1996. "Philo and the Clubs and Associations of Alexandria." Pp. 110–27 in *Voluntary Associations in the Graeco-Roman World*, edited by J. S. Kloppenborg and S. G. Wilson. London: Routledge.

Sharples, Robert W., and Anne Sheppard, eds. 2003. *Ancient Approaches to Plato's* Timaeus. Bulletin of the Institute of Classical Studies Supplement 78. London: Institute of Classical Studies/University of London.

Shroyer, Montgomery J. 1936. "Alexandrian Jewish Literalists." *Journal of Biblical Literature* 55:261–84.

Siegert, Folker. 1996. "Early Jewish Interpretation in a Hellenistic Style." Pp. 130–98 in *From the Beginnings to the Middle Ages (Until 1300).* Part 1 *Antiquity*, edited by Magne Sæbø. Vol. 1 of *Hebrew Bible/Old Testament The History of its Interpretation.* Göttingen: Vandenhoeck & Ruprecht.

–. 2008. "Philo and the New Testament." Pp. 175–209 in *The Cambridge Companion to Philo*, edited by Adam Kamesar. Cambridge: Cambridge University Press.

Silva, Moisés. 1994. *Biblical Words and Their Meaning: An Introduction to Lexical Semantics.* Rev. ed. Grand Rapids: Zondervan.

Simon, Heinrich, and Marie Simon. 1956. *Die alte Stoa und ihr Naturbegriff; ein Beitrag zur Philosophiegeschichte des Hellenismus.* Berlin: Aufbau.

Simon, Marcel. 1967. "Eléments gnostiques chez Philon." Pp. 359–76 in *The Origins of Gnosticism. Colloquium of Messina 13–18 April 1966*, edited by Ugo Bianchi. Studies in the History of Religions (Supplements to *Numen*) 12. Leiden: Brill.

Slingerland, Dixon. 1986. "The Nature of *Nomos* (Law) Within the *Testaments of the Twelve Patriarchs.*" *Journal of Biblical Literature* 105:39–48.

Sly, Dorothy. 1990. *Philo's Perception of Women.* Brown Judaic Studies 209. Atlanta: Scholars.

Smith, Morton. 1987. *Palestinian Parties and Politics That Shaped the Old Testament.* 2d ed. London: SCM.

Sorabji, Richard. 2000. *Emotion and Peace of Mind: From Stoic Agitation to Christian Temptation.* Oxford: Oxford University Press.

Sterling, Gregory E. 1991. "Philo's *Quaestiones*: Prolegomena or Afterthought?" Pp. 99–123 in *Both Literal and Allegorical: Studies in Philo of Alexandria's* Questions and Answers on Genesis and Exodus, edited by David M. Hay. Brown Judaic Studies 232. Atlanta: Scholars Press.

–. 1992. "*Creatio Temporalis, Aeterna, Vel Continua*? An Analysis of the Thought of Philo of Alexandria." *Studia Philonica Annual* 4:15–41.

–. 1993. "Platonizing Moses: Philo and Middle Platonism." *Studia Philonica Annual* 5:96–111.

–. 1995a. "'Thus Are Israel': Jewish Self-Definition in Alexandria." *Studia Philonica Annual* 7:1–18.

–. 1995b. "Wisdom Among the Perfect: Creation Traditions in Alexandrian Judaism and Corinthian Christianity." *Novum Testamentum* 37:355–84.

–. 1997. "Prepositional Metaphysics in Jewish Wisdom Speculation and Early Christian Liturgical Texts." *Studia Philonica Annual* 9:219–38.

–. 1999a. "Recherché or Representative? What is the Relationship Between Philo's Treatises and Greek-Speaking Judaism?" *Studia Philonica Annual* 11:1–30.

–. 1999b. "'The School of Sacred Laws': The Social Setting of Philo's Treatises." *Vigiliae Christianae* 53:148–64.

–. 2001. "Judaism Between Jerusalem and Alexandria." Pp. 263–301 in *Hellenism in the Land of Israel*, edited by John J. Collins and Gregory E. Sterling. Christianity and Judaism in Antiquity 13. Notre Dame: University of Notre Dame Press.

–. 2003a. "'Philo Has Not Been Used Half Enough': The Significance of Philo of Alexandria for the Study of the New Testament." *Perspectives in Religious Studies* 30:251–70.

–. 2003b. "Universalizing the Particular: Natural Law in Second Temple Jewish Ethics." *Studia Philonica Annual* 15:64–80.

–. 2005. "'The Jewish Philosophy': The Presence of Hellenistic Philosophy in Jewish Exegesis in the Second Temple Period." Pp. 131–53 in *Ancient Judaism in Its Hellenistic Context*, edited by Carol Bakhos. Supplements to the Journal for the Study of Judaism in the Persian, Hellenistic, and Roman Periods 95. Leiden: Brill.
–. 2006. "'The Queen of the Virtues': Εὐσέβεια In Philo of Alexandria." *Studia Philonica Annual* 18:103–23.
–. 2007. "The First Theologian: The Originality of Philo of Alexandria." Pp. 145–62 in *Renewing Tradition: Studies in Texts and Contexts in Honor of James W. Thompson*, edited by Mark W. Hamilton, Thomas H. Olbricht, and Jeffrey Peterson. Princeton Theological Monograph Series 65. Eugene, Oreg.: Pickwick.
Striker, Gisela. 1986. "Antipater, or the Art of Living." Pp. 185–204 in *The Norms of Nature: Studies in Hellenistic Ethics*, edited by Malcom Schofield and Gisela Striker. Cambridge/Paris: Cambridge University Press/Editions de la Maison des Sciences de l'Homme.
–. 1996. *Essays on Hellenistic Epistemology and Ethics*. Cambridge: Cambridge University Press.
Stuckrad, Kocku von. 2000. "Jewish and Christian Astrology in Late Antiquity – a New Approach." *Numen* 47:1–40.
Tcherikover, Viktor. 1956. "Jewish Apologetic Literature Reconsidered." *Eos* 48:169–93.
–. 1958. "The Ideology of the Letter of Aristeas." *Harvard Theological Review* 51:59–85.
Terian, Abraham. 1997. "Back to Creation: The Beginning of Philo's Third Grand Commentary." *Studia Philonica Annual* 9:19–36.
Termini, Cristina. 2000. *Le Potenze di Dio. Studio su δύναμις in Filone di Alessandria*. Studia Ephemeridis Augustinianum 71. Rome: Institutum Patristicum Augustinianum.
Theiler, Willy. 1930. *Die Vorbereitung des Neuplatonismus*. Problemata: Forschungen zur klassischen Philologie 1. Berlin: Weidmannsche.
–. 1965. "Philo von Alexandria und der Beginn des kaiserzeitlichen Platonismus." Pp. 199–218 in *Parusia: Studien zur Philosophie Platons und zur Problemgeschichte des Platonismus; Festgabe für J. Hirschberger*, edited by K. Flasch. Frankfurt: Minerva.
Thiselton, Anthony C. 2000. *The First Epistle to the Corinthians: A Commentary on the Greek Text*. New International Greek Testament Commentary. Grand Rapids: Eerdmans.
Thorne, Gary W. A. 1989. "The Structure of Philo's Commentary on the Pentateuch." *Dionysius* 13:17–50.
Tigay, Jeffrey H. 1996. *Deuteronomy: The Traditional Hebrew Text with the New JPS Translation Commentary*. JPS Torah Commentary. Philadelphia: Jewish Publication Society.
Tobin, Thomas H., S.J. 1983. *The Creation of Man: Philo and the History of Interpretation*. Catholic Biblical Quarterly Monograph Series 14. Washington, D. C.: Catholic Biblical Assocation.
–. 1993. "Was Philo a Middle Platonist? Some Suggestions." *Studia Philonica Annual* 5:147–50.
Urbach, Ephraim E. 1987. *The Sages: Their Concepts and Beliefs*. Translated by Israel Abrahams. Cambridge: Harvard University Press.
Van Kooten, George H. 1999. "Enoch, the 'Watchers', Seth's Descendants and Abraham as Astronomers: Jewish Applications of the Greek Motif of the First Inventor (300 BCE–CE 100)." Pp. 292–316 in *Recycling Biblical Figures. Papers Read at a NOSTER Colloquium in Amsterdam 12–13 May 1997*, edited by Athalya Brenner and Jan Willem van Henten. Studies in Theology and Religion 1. Leiden: Deo.
Van Zyl, D. H. 1986. "Cicero and the Law of Nature." *South African Law Journal* 103:55–68.

Vander Waerdt, Paul A. 1994. "Philosophical Influence on Roman Jurisprudence? The Case of Stoicism and Natural Law." Pp. 4851–900 in *Aufstieg und Niedergang der römischen Welt.* Part 2. *Principat, 36.7.* Berlin: De Gruyter.

–. 2003. "The Original Theory of Natural Law." *Studia Philonica Annual* 15:17–34.

Veatch, Henry. 1981. "Natural Law and the 'Is'-'Ought' Question: Queries to Finnis and Griesz." Pp. 293–311 in *Swimming Against the Current in Contemporary Philosophy.* Washington, D. C.: Catholic University of America Press [In *Natural Law: Volume 1.* The International Library of Essays in Law and Legal Theory. Edited by John Finnis. Dartmouth: Aldershot, 1991].

Völker, Walther. 1938. *Fortschritt und Vollendung bei Philo von Alexandrien: eine Studie zur Geschichte der Frömmigkeit.* Texte und Untersuchungen zur Geschichte der altchristlichen Literatur 49. Leipzig: J. C. Hinrich.

Walbank, F. W. 1992. *The Hellenistic World.* Rev. ed. Fontana History of the Ancient World. London: Fontana.

Walter, Nikolaus. 1964. *Der Thoraausleger Aristobulos: Untersuchungen zu seinen Fragmenten und zu pseudepigraphischen Resten der jüdisch-hellenistischen Literatur.* Texte und Untersuchungen zur Geschichte der altchristlichen Literatur 86. Berlin: Akademie-Verlag.

–. 1983. "Pseudepigraphische jüdische-hellenistische Dichtung: Pseudo-Phokylides, Pseudo-Orpheus, gefälschte Verse auf Namen griechischer Dichter." Pp. 173–278 in *Jüdische Schriften aus hellenistisch-römischer Zeit.* 4.3 "Poetische Schriften", edited by Werner Georg Kümmel. Gütersloh: Gerd Mohn.

Wanamaker, Charles A. 2005. "Metaphor and Morality: Examples of Paul's Moral Thinking in 1 Corinthians 1–5." *Neotestamentica* 39:409–33.

Watson, Gerard. 1966. "The Early History of Natural Law." *Irish Theological Quarterly* 33:65–74.

–. 1971. "The Natural Law and Stoicism." Pp. 216–38 in *Problems in Stoicism*, edited by A. A. Long. London: Athlone.

Weinandy, Thomas G., OFM Cap. 1985. *Does God Change? The Word's Becoming in the Incarnation.* Studies in Historical Theology 4. Still River, Mass.: St. Bede's.

Werman, Cana. 2004. "God's House: Temple or Universe." Pp. 309–20 in *Philo und das Neue Testament. Wechselseitige Wahrnehmungen. I. Internationales Symposium Zum Corpus Judaeo-Hellenisticum 1.-4. Mai 2003, Eisenach/Jena*, edited by Roland Deines and Karl-Wilhelm Niebuhr. Wissenschaftliche Untersuchungen zum Neuen Testament 172. Tübingen: Mohr Siebeck.

White, Michael J. 2003. "Stoic Natural Philosophy (Physics and Cosmology)." Pp. 124–52 in *The Cambridge Companion to the Stoics*, edited by Brad Inwood. Cambridge: Cambridge University Press.

White, Nicholas P. 1979. "The Basis of Stoic Ethics." *Harvard Studies in Classical Philology* 83:143–78.

–. 1985. "The Role of Physics in Stoic Ethics." *Southern Journal of Philosophy* 23 Supplement:57–74.

Wilson, R. McL. 1993. "Philo and Gnosticism." *Studia Philonica Annual* 5:84–92.

Winston, David. 1979. *The Wisdom of Solomon: A New Translation with Introduction and Commentary.* Anchor Bible 43. Garden City, NY: Doubleday.

–. 1981. *Philo of Alexandria: The Contemplative Life, the Giants, and Selections.* The Classics of Western Spirituality. London: SPCK.

–. 1984. "Philo's Ethical Theory." Pp. 372–416 in *Aufstieg und Niedergang der römischen Welt*. Part 2, *Principat, 21.1*, edited by Wolfgang Haase. Berlin: De Gruyter.
–. 1985. *Logos and Mystical Theology in Philo of Alexandria*. Cincinnati: Hebrew Union College Press.
–. 1986. "Theodicy and Creation of Man in Philo of Alexandria." Pp. 105–11 in *Hellenica et Judaica. Hommage á Valentin Nikiprowetzky*, edited by A. Caquot, M. Hadas-Lebel, and J. Riaud. Leuven: Peeters.
–. 1988. "Two Types of Mosaic Prophecy According to Philo." *Society of Biblical Literature Seminar Papers* 27:442–55.
–. 1990. "Judaism and Hellenism: Hidden Tensions in Philo's Thought." *Studia Philonica Annual* 2:1–19.
–. 1996a. "Philo's Mysticism." *Studia Philonica Annual* 8:74–82.
–. 1996b. "Review of Naomi G. Cohen, *Philo Judaeus: His Universe of Discourse*." *Jewish Quarterly Review* 86:510–15.
–. 2001. "Philo and the Rabbis on Sex and the Body." Pp. 199–219 in *The Ancestral Philosophy: Hellenistic Philosophy in Second Temple Judaism; Essays of David Winston*, edited by Gregory E. Sterling. Brown Judaic Studies 331. Providence.
–. 2002. "Philo and the Wisdom of Solomon on Creation, Revelation, and Providence: The High-Water of Jewish Hellenistic Fusion." Pp. 109–30 in *Shem in the Tents of Japheth: Essays on the Encounter of Judaism and Hellenism*, edited by James L. Kugel. Supplements to the Journal for the Study of Judaism in the Persian, Hellenistic, and Roman Periods 74. Leiden: Brill.
Winter, Bruce W. 2002. *Philo and Paul Among the Sophists: Alexandrian and Corinthian Responses to a Julio-Claudian Movement*. 2d ed. Grand Rapids: Eerdmans.
Witmer, Stephen E. 2008. *Divine Instruction in Early Christianity*. Wissenschaftliche Untersuchungen zum Neuen Testament 246. Tübingen: Mohr Siebeck.
Wolff, Hans Walter. 1969. *Dodekapropheton 2. Joel und Amos*. Biblischer Kommentar, Altes Testament 14/2. Neukirchen-Vlyun: Neukirchener Verlag.
Wolfson, Harry Austryn. 1947. *Philo: Foundations of Religious Philosophy in Judaism, Christianity, and Islam*. 2 vols. Cambridge: Harvard University Press.
Wolters, Albert M. 1994. "*Creatio Ex Nihilo* in Philo." Pp. 107–24 in *Hellenization Revisited: Shaping a Christian Response Within the Greco-Roman World*, edited by Wendy E. Helleman. Lanham: University Press of America.
Wong, Chan-Kok. 1992. "Philo's Use of *Chaldaioi*." *Studia Philonica Annual* 4:1–14.
Zeller, Dieter. 1990. *Charis bei Philon und Paulus*. Stuttgarter Bibelstudien 142. Stuttgart: Katholisches Bibelwerk.
Ziesler, J. A. 1972. *The Meaning of Righteousness in Paul: A Linguistic and Theological Enquiry*. Society for New Testament Studies Monograph Series 20. Cambridge: Cambridge University Press.

Index of Ancient Sources

I. Philo

II. Tanakh

III. Apocrypha and Septuagint

IV. New Testament

V. Pseudepigrapha

VI. Other Jewish Writings

VII. Greco-Roman Writings

Index of Modern Authors

Index of Subjects

Wissenschaftliche Untersuchungen zum Neuen Testament

Alphabetical Index of the First and Second Series

ing the Earliest Gospels in their First Century Settings. 2011. *Vol. 271.*

Becker, Michael: Wunder und Wundertäter im frührabbinischen Judentum. 2002. *Vol. II/144.*

Becker, Michael and *Markus Öhler* (Ed.): Apokalyptik als Herausforderung neutestamentlicher Theologie. 2006. *Vol. II/214.*

Bell, Richard H.: Deliver Us from Evil. 2007. *Vol. 216.*

– The Irrevocable Call of God. 2005. *Vol. 184.*

– No One Seeks for God. 1998. *Vol. 106.*

– Provoked to Jealousy. 1994. *Vol. II/63.*

Bennema, Cornelis: The Power of Saving Wisdom. 2002. *Vol. II/148.*

Bergman, Jan: see *Kieffer, René*

Bergmeier, Roland: Das Gesetz im Römerbrief und andere Studien zum Neuen Testament. 2000. *Vol. 121.*

Bernett, Monika: Der Kaiserkult in Judäa unter den Herodiern und Römern. 2007. *Vol. 203.*

Betz, Otto: Jesus, der Messias Israels. 1987. *Vol. 42.*

– Jesus, der Herr der Kirche. 1990. *Vol. 52.*

Beyschlag, Karlmann: Simon Magus und die christliche Gnosis. 1974. *Vol. 16.*

Bieringer, Reimund: see *Koester, Craig.*

Bittner, Wolfgang J.: Jesu Zeichen im Johannesevangelium. 1987. *Vol. II/26.*

Bjerkelund, Carl J.: Tauta Egeneto. 1987. *Vol. 40.*

Blackburn, Barry Lee: Theios Aner and the Markan Miracle Traditions. 1991. *Vol. II/40.*

Blanton IV, Thomas R.: Constructing a New Covenant. 2007. *Vol. II/233.*

Bock, Darrell L.: Blasphemy and Exaltation in Judaism and the Final Examination of Jesus. 1998. *Vol. II/106.*

– and *Robert L. Webb* (Ed.): Key Events in the Life of the Historical Jesus. 2009. *Vol. 247.*

Bockmuehl, Markus: The Remembered Peter. 2010. *Vol. 262.*

– Revelation and Mystery in Ancient Judaism and Pauline Christianity. 1990. *Vol. II/36.*

Bøe, Sverre: Cross-Bearing in Luke. 2010. *Vol. II/278.*

– Gog and Magog. 2001. *Vol. II/135.*

Böhlig, Alexander: Gnosis und Synkretismus. Vol. 1 1989. *Vol. 47* – Vol. 2 1989. *Vol. 48.*

Böhm, Martina: Samarien und die Samaritai bei Lukas. 1999. *Vol. II/111.*

Börstinghaus, Jens: Sturmfahrt und Schiffbruch. 2010. *Vol. II/274.*

Böttrich, Christfried: Weltweisheit – Menschheitsethik – Urkult. 1992. *Vol. II/50.*

– and *Herzer, Jens* (Ed.): Josephus und das Neue Testament. 2007. *Vol. 209.*

Bolyki, János: Jesu Tischgemeinschaften. 1997. *Vol. II/96.*

Bosman, Philip: Conscience in Philo and Paul. 2003. *Vol. II/166.*

Bovon, François: New Testament and Christian Apocrypha. 2009. *Vol. 237.*

– Studies in Early Christianity. 2003. *Vol. 161.*

Brändl, Martin: Der Agon bei Paulus. 2006. *Vol. II/222.*

Braun, Heike: Geschichte des Gottesvolkes und christliche Identität. 2010. *Vol. II/279.*

Breytenbach, Cilliers: see *Frey, Jörg.*

Broadhead, Edwin K.: Jewish Ways of Following Jesus Redrawing the Religious Map of Antiquity. 2010. *Vol. 266.*

Brocke, Christoph vom: Thessaloniki – Stadt des Kassander und Gemeinde des Paulus. 2001. *Vol. II/125.*

Brunson, Andrew: Psalm 118 in the Gospel of John. 2003. *Vol. II/158.*

Büchli, Jörg: Der Poimandres – ein paganisiertes Evangelium. 1987. *Vol. II/27.*

Bühner, Jan A.: Der Gesandte und sein Weg im 4. Evangelium. 1977. *Vol. II/2.*

Burchard, Christoph: Untersuchungen zu Joseph und Aseneth. 1965. *Vol. 8.*

– Studien zur Theologie, Sprache und Umwelt des Neuen Testaments. Ed. by D. Sänger. 1998. *Vol. 107.*

Burnett, Richard: Karl Barth's Theological Exegesis. 2001. *Vol. II/145.*

Byron, John: Slavery Metaphors in Early Judaism and Pauline Christianity. 2003. *Vol. II/162.*

Byrskog, Samuel: Story as History – History as Story. 2000. *Vol. 123.*

Cancik, Hubert (Ed.): Markus-Philologie. 1984. *Vol. 33.*

Capes, David B.: Old Testament Yaweh Texts in Paul's Christology. 1992. *Vol. II/47.*

Caragounis, Chrys C.: The Development of Greek and the New Testament. 2004. *Vol. 167.*

– The Son of Man. 1986. *Vol. 38.*

– see *Fridrichsen, Anton.*

Carleton Paget, James: The Epistle of Barnabas. 1994. *Vol. II/64.*

– Jews, Christians and Jewish Christians in Antiquity. 2010. *Vol. 251.*

Carson, D.A., O'Brien, Peter T. and *Mark Seifrid* (Ed.): Justification and Variegated Nomism.
Vol. 1: The Complexities of Second Temple Judaism. 2001. *Vol. II/140.*
Vol. 2: The Paradoxes of Paul. 2004. *Vol. II/181.*

Chae, Young Sam: Jesus as the Eschatological Davidic Shepherd. 2006. *Vol. II/216.*
Chapman, David W.: Ancient Jewish and Christian Perceptions of Crucifixion. 2008. *Vol. II/244.*
Chester, Andrew: Messiah and Exaltation. 2007. *Vol. 207.*
Chibici-Revneanu, Nicole: Die Herrlichkeit des Verherrlichten. 2007. *Vol. II/231.*
Ciampa, Roy E.: The Presence and Function of Scripture in Galatians 1 and 2. 1998. *Vol. II/102.*
Classen, Carl Joachim: Rhetorical Criticsm of the New Testament. 2000. *Vol. 128.*
Colpe, Carsten: Griechen – Byzantiner – Semiten – Muslime. 2008. *Vol. 221.*
– Iranier – Aramäer – Hebräer – Hellenen. 2003. *Vol. 154.*
Cook, John G.: Roman Attitudes Towards the Christians. 2010. *Vol. 261.*
Coote, Robert B. (Ed.): see *Weissenrieder, Annette.*
Coppins, Wayne: The Interpretation of Freedom in the Letters of Paul. 2009. *Vol. II/261.*
Crump, David: Jesus the Intercessor. 1992. *Vol. II/49.*
Dahl, Nils Alstrup: Studies in Ephesians. 2000. *Vol. 131.*
Daise, Michael A.: Feasts in John. 2007. *Vol. II/229.*
Deines, Roland: Die Gerechtigkeit der Tora im Reich des Messias. 2004. *Vol. 177.*
– Jüdische Steingefäße und pharisäische Frömmigkeit. 1993. *Vol. II/52.*
– Die Pharisäer. 1997. *Vol. 101.*
Deines, Roland, Jens Herzer and *Karl-Wilhelm Niebuhr* (Ed.): Neues Testament und hellenistisch-jüdische Alltagskultur. III. Internationales Symposium zum Corpus Judaeo-Hellenisticum Novi Testamenti. 21.–24. Mai 2009 in Leipzig. 2011. *Vol. 274.*
– and *Karl-Wilhelm Niebuhr* (Ed.): Philo und das Neue Testament. 2004. *Vol. 172.*
Dennis, John A.: Jesus' Death and the Gathering of True Israel. 2006. *Vol. 217.*
Dettwiler, Andreas and *Jean Zumstein* (Ed.): Kreuzestheologie im Neuen Testament. 2002. *Vol. 151.*
Dickson, John P.: Mission-Commitment in Ancient Judaism and in the Pauline Communities. 2003. *Vol. II/159.*
Dietzfelbinger, Christian: Der Abschied des Kommenden. 1997. *Vol. 95.*
Dimitrov, Ivan Z., James D.G. Dunn, Ulrich Luz and *Karl-Wilhelm Niebuhr* (Ed.): Das Alte Testament als christliche Bibel in orthodoxer und westlicher Sicht. 2004. *Vol. 174.*
Dobbeler, Axel von: Glaube als Teilhabe. 1987. *Vol. II/22.*
Docherty, Susan E.: The Use of the Old Testament in Hebrews. 2009. *Vol. II/260.*
Dochhorn, Jan: Schriftgelehrte Prophetie. 2010. *Vol. 268.*
Downs, David J.: The Offering of the Gentiles. 2008. *Vol. II/248.*
Dryden, J. de Waal: Theology and Ethics in 1 Peter. 2006. *Vol. II/209.*
Dübbers, Michael: Christologie und Existenz im Kolosserbrief. 2005. *Vol. II/191.*
Dunn, James D.G.: The New Perspective on Paul. 2005. *Vol. 185.*
Dunn , James D.G. (Ed.): Jews and Christians. 1992. *Vol. 66.*
– Paul and the Mosaic Law. 1996. *Vol. 89.*
– see *Dimitrov, Ivan Z.*
–, *Hans Klein, Ulrich Luz,* and *Vasile Mihoc* (Ed.): Auslegung der Bibel in orthodoxer und westlicher Perspektive. 2000. *Vol. 130.*
Ebel, Eva: Die Attraktivität früher christlicher Gemeinden. 2004. *Vol. II/178.*
Ebertz, Michael N.: Das Charisma des Gekreuzigten. 1987. *Vol. 45.*
Eckstein, Hans-Joachim: Der Begriff Syneidesis bei Paulus. 1983. *Vol. II/10.*
– Verheißung und Gesetz. 1996. *Vol. 86.*
–, *Christoph Landmesser* and *Hermann Lichtenberger* (Ed.): Eschatologie – Eschatology. The Sixth Durham-Tübingen Research Symposium. 2011. *Vol. 272.*
Ego, Beate: Im Himmel wie auf Erden. 1989. *Vol. II/34.*
Ego, Beate, Armin Lange and *Peter Pilhofer* (Ed.): Gemeinde ohne Tempel – Community without Temple. 1999. *Vol. 118.*
– and *Helmut Merkel* (Ed.): Religiöses Lernen in der biblischen, frühjüdischen und frühchristlichen Überlieferung. 2005. *Vol. 180.*
Eisele, Wilfried: Welcher Thomas? 2010. *Vol. 259.*
Eisen, Ute E.: see *Paulsen, Henning.*
Elledge, C.D.: Life after Death in Early Judaism. 2006. *Vol. II/208.*
Ellis, E. Earle: Prophecy and Hermeneutic in Early Christianity. 1978. *Vol. 18.*
– The Old Testament in Early Christianity. 1991. *Vol. 54.*
Elmer, Ian J.: Paul, Jerusalem and the Judaisers. 2009. *Vol. II/258.*
Endo, Masanobu: Creation and Christology. 2002. *Vol. 149.*
Ennulat, Andreas: Die 'Minor Agreements'. 1994. *Vol. II/62.*
Ensor, Peter W.: Jesus and His 'Works'. 1996. *Vol. II/85.*

Eskola, Timo: Messiah and the Throne. 2001. *Vol. II/142.*
– Theodicy and Predestination in Pauline Soteriology. 1998. *Vol. II/100.*
Farelly, Nicolas: The Disciples in the Fourth Gospel. 2010. *Vol. II/290.*
Fatehi, Mehrdad: The Spirit's Relation to the Risen Lord in Paul. 2000. *Vol. II/128.*
Feldmeier, Reinhard: Die Krisis des Gottessohnes. 1987. *Vol. II/21.*
– Die Christen als Fremde. 1992. *Vol. 64.*
Feldmeier, Reinhard and *Ulrich Heckel* (Ed.): Die Heiden. 1994. *Vol. 70.*
Felsch, Dorit: Die Feste im Johannesevangelium. 2011. *Vol. II/308.*
Finnern, Sönke: Narratologie und biblische Exegese. 2010. *Vol. II/285.*
Fletcher-Louis, Crispin H.T.: Luke-Acts: Angels, Christology and Soteriology. 1997. *Vol. II/94.*
Förster, Niclas: Marcus Magus. 1999. *Vol. 114.*
Forbes, Christopher Brian: Prophecy and Inspired Speech in Early Christianity and its Hellenistic Environment. 1995. *Vol. II/75.*
Fornberg, Tord: see *Fridrichsen, Anton.*
Fossum, Jarl E.: The Name of God and the Angel of the Lord. 1985. *Vol. 36.*
Foster, Paul: Community, Law and Mission in Matthew's Gospel. *Vol. II/177.*
Fotopoulos, John: Food Offered to Idols in Roman Corinth. 2003. *Vol. II/151.*
Frank, Nicole: Der Kolosserbrief im Kontext des paulinischen Erbes. 2009. *Vol. II/271.*
Frenschkowski, Marco: Offenbarung und Epiphanie. Vol. 1 1995. *Vol. II/79* – Vol. 2 1997. *Vol. II/80.*
Frey, Jörg: Eugen Drewermann und die biblische Exegese. 1995. *Vol. II/71.*
– Die johanneische Eschatologie. Vol. I. 1997. *Vol. 96.* – Vol. II. 1998. *Vol. 110.* – Vol. III. 2000. *Vol. 117.*
Frey, Jörg and *Cilliers Breytenbach* (Ed.): Aufgabe und Durchführung einer Theologie des Neuen Testaments. 2007. *Vol. 205.*
– *Jens Herzer, Martina Janßen* and *Clare K. Rothschild* (Ed.): Pseudepigraphie und Verfasserfiktion in frühchristlichen Briefen. 2009. *Vol. 246.*
– *Stefan Krauter* and *Hermann Lichtenberger* (Ed.): Heil und Geschichte. 2009. *Vol. 248.*
– and *Udo Schnelle (Ed.):* Kontexte des Johannesevangeliums. 2004. *Vol. 175.*
– and *Jens Schröter* (Ed.): Deutungen des Todes Jesu im Neuen Testament. 2005. *Vol. 181.*
– Jesus in apokryphen Evangelienüberlieferungen. 2010. *Vol. 254.*
–, *Jan G. van der Watt,* and *Ruben Zimmermann* (Ed.): Imagery in the Gospel of John. 2006. *Vol. 200.*
Freyne, Sean: Galilee and Gospel. 2000. *Vol. 125.*
Fridrichsen, Anton: Exegetical Writings. Edited by C.C. Caragounis and T. Fornberg. 1994. *Vol. 76.*
Gadenz, Pablo T.: Called from the Jews and from the Gentiles. 2009. *Vol. II/267.*
Gäbel, Georg: Die Kulttheologie des Hebräerbriefes. 2006. *Vol. II/212.*
Gäckle, Volker: Die Starken und die Schwachen in Korinth und in Rom. 2005. *Vol. 200.*
Garlington, Don B.: 'The Obedience of Faith'. 1991. *Vol. II/38.*
– Faith, Obedience, and Perseverance. 1994. *Vol. 79.*
Garnet, Paul: Salvation and Atonement in the Qumran Scrolls. 1977. *Vol. II/3.*
Gemünden, Petra von (Ed.): see *Weissenrieder, Annette.*
Gese, Michael: Das Vermächtnis des Apostels. 1997. *Vol. II/99.*
Gheorghita, Radu: The Role of the Septuagint in Hebrews. 2003. *Vol. II/160.*
Gordley, Matthew E.: The Colossian Hymn in Context. 2007. *Vol. II/228.*
– Teaching through Song in Antiquity. 2011. *Vol. II/302.*
Gräbe, Petrus J.: The Power of God in Paul's Letters. 2000, [2]2008. *Vol. II/123.*
Gräßer, Erich: Der Alte Bund im Neuen. 1985. *Vol. 35.*
– Forschungen zur Apostelgeschichte. 2001. *Vol. 137.*
Grappe, Christian (Ed.): Le Repas de Dieu / Das Mahl Gottes. 2004. *Vol. 169.*
Gray, Timothy C.: The Temple in the Gospel of Mark. 2008. *Vol. II/242.*
Green, Joel B.: The Death of Jesus. 1988. *Vol. II/33.*
Gregg, Brian Han: The Historical Jesus and the Final Judgment Sayings in Q. 2005. *Vol. II/207.*
Gregory, Andrew: The Reception of Luke and Acts in the Period before Irenaeus. 2003. *Vol. II/169.*
Grindheim, Sigurd: The Crux of Election. 2005. *Vol. II/202.*
Gundry, Robert H.: The Old is Better. 2005. *Vol. 178.*
Gundry Volf, Judith M.: Paul and Perseverance. 1990. *Vol. II/37.*
Häußer, Detlef: Christusbekenntnis und Jesusüberlieferung bei Paulus. 2006. *Vol. 210.*

Hafemann, Scott J.: Suffering and the Spirit. 1986. *Vol. II/19.*
– Paul, Moses, and the History of Israel. 1995. *Vol. 81.*
Hahn, Ferdinand: Studien zum Neuen Testament.
Vol. I: Grundsatzfragen, Jesusforschung, Evangelien. 2006. *Vol. 191.*
Vol. II: Bekenntnisbildung und Theologie in urchristlicher Zeit. 2006. *Vol. 192.*
Hahn, Johannes (Ed.): Zerstörungen des Jerusalemer Tempels. 2002. *Vol. 147.*
Hamid-Khani, Saeed: Relevation and Concealment of Christ. 2000. *Vol. II/120.*
Hannah, Darrel D.: Michael and Christ. 1999. *Vol. II/109.*
Hardin, Justin K.: Galatians and the Imperial Cult? 2007. *Vol. II /237.*
Harrison, James R.: Paul and the Imperial Authorities at Thessolanica and Rome. 2011. *Vol. 273.*
– Paul's Language of Grace in Its Graeco-Roman Context. 2003. *Vol. II/172.*
Hartman, Lars: Text-Centered New Testament Studies. Ed. von D. Hellholm. 1997. *Vol. 102.*
Hartog, Paul: Polycarp and the New Testament. 2001. *Vol. II/134.*
Hasselbrook, David S.: Studies in New Testament Lexicography. 2011. *Vol. II/303.*
Hays, Christopher M.: Luke's Wealth Ethics. 2010. *Vol. 275.*
Heckel, Theo K.: Der Innere Mensch. 1993. *Vol. II/53.*
– Vom Evangelium des Markus zum viergestaltigen Evangelium. 1999. *Vol. 120.*
Heckel, Ulrich: Kraft in Schwachheit. 1993. *Vol. II/56.*
– Der Segen im Neuen Testament. 2002. *Vol. 150.*
– see *Feldmeier, Reinhard.*
– see *Hengel, Martin.*
Heemstra, Marius: The Fiscus Judaicus and the Parting of the Ways. 2010. *Vol. II/277.*
Heiligenthal, Roman: Werke als Zeichen. 1983. *Vol. II/9.*
Heininger, Bernhard: Die Inkulturation des Christentums. 2010. *Vol. 255.*
Heliso, Desta: Pistis and the Righteous One. 2007. *Vol. II/235.*
Hellholm, D.: see *Hartman, Lars.*
Hemer, Colin J.: The Book of Acts in the Setting of Hellenistic History. 1989. *Vol. 49.*
Henderson, Timothy P.: The Gospel of Peter and Early Christian Apologetics. 2011. *Vol. II/301.*
Hengel, Martin: Jesus und die Evangelien. Kleine Schriften V. 2007. *Vol. 211.*
– Die johanneische Frage. 1993. *Vol. 67.*
– Judaica et Hellenistica. Kleine Schriften I. 1996. *Vol. 90.*
– Judaica, Hellenistica et Christiana. Kleine Schriften II. 1999. *Vol. 109.*
– Judentum und Hellenismus. 1969, [3]1988. *Vol. 10.*
– Paulus und Jakobus. Kleine Schriften III. 2002. *Vol. 141.*
– Studien zur Christologie. Kleine Schriften IV. 2006. *Vol. 201.*
– Studien zum Urchristentum. Kleine Schriften VI. 2008. *Vol. 234.*
– Theologische, historische und biographische Skizzen. Kleine Schriften VII. 2010. *Vol. 253.*
– and *Anna Maria Schwemer:* Paulus zwischen Damaskus und Antiochien. 1998. *Vol. 108.*
– Der messianische Anspruch Jesu und die Anfänge der Christologie. 2001. *Vol. 138.*
– Die vier Evangelien und das eine Evangelium von Jesus Christus. 2008. *Vol. 224.*
Hengel, Martin and *Ulrich Heckel* (Ed.): Paulus und das antike Judentum. 1991. *Vol. 58.*
– and *Hermut Löhr* (Ed.): Schriftauslegung im antiken Judentum und im Urchristentum. 1994. *Vol. 73.*
– and *Anna Maria Schwemer* (Ed.): Königsherrschaft Gottes und himmlischer Kult. 1991. *Vol. 55.*
– Die Septuaginta. 1994. *Vol. 72.*
–, *Siegfried Mittmann* and *Anna Maria Schwemer* (Ed.): La Cité de Dieu / Die Stadt Gottes. 2000. *Vol. 129.*
Hentschel, Anni: Diakonia im Neuen Testament. 2007. *Vol. 226.*
Hernández Jr., Juan: Scribal Habits and Theological Influence in the Apocalypse. 2006. *Vol. II/218.*
Herrenbrück, Fritz: Jesus und die Zöllner. 1990. *Vol. II/41.*
Herzer, Jens: Paulus oder Petrus? 1998. *Vol. 103.*
– see *Böttrich, Christfried.*
– see *Deines, Roland.*
– see *Frey, Jörg.*
Hill, Charles E.: From the Lost Teaching of Polycarp. 2005. *Vol. 186.*
Hoegen-Rohls, Christina: Der nachösterliche Johannes. 1996. *Vol. II/84.*
Hoffmann, Matthias Reinhard: The Destroyer and the Lamb. 2005. *Vol. II/203.*
Hofius, Otfried: Katapausis. 1970. *Vol. 11.*

– Der Vorhang vor dem Thron Gottes. 1972. *Vol. 14.*
– Der Christushymnus Philipper 2,6–11. 1976, 21991. *Vol. 17.*
– Paulusstudien. 1989, 21994. *Vol. 51.*
– Neutestamentliche Studien. 2000. *Vol. 132.*
– Paulusstudien II. 2002. *Vol. 143.*
– Exegetische Studien. 2008. *Vol. 223.*
– and *Hans-Christian Kammler:* Johannesstudien. 1996. *Vol. 88.*
Holloway, Paul A.: Coping with Prejudice. 2009. *Vol. 244.*
– see *Ahearne-Kroll, Stephen P.*
Holmberg, Bengt (Ed.): Exploring Early Christian Identity. 2008. *Vol. 226.*
– and *Mikael Winninge* (Ed.): Identity Formation in the New Testament. 2008. *Vol. 227.*
Holtz, Traugott: Geschichte und Theologie des Urchristentums. 1991. *Vol. 57.*
Hommel, Hildebrecht: Sebasmata.
Vol. 1 1983. *Vol. 31.*
Vol. 2 1984. *Vol. 32.*
Horbury, William: Herodian Judaism and New Testament Study. 2006. *Vol. 193.*
Horn, Friedrich Wilhelm and *Ruben Zimmermann* (Ed.): Jenseits von Indikativ und Imperativ. Vol. 1. 2009. *Vol. 238.*
Horst, Pieter W. van der: Jews and Christians in Their Graeco-Roman Context. 2006. *Vol. 196.*
Hultgård, Anders and *Stig Norin* (Ed): Le Jour de Dieu / Der Tag Gottes. 2009. *Vol. 245.*
Hume, Douglas A.: The Early Christian Community. 2011. *Vol. II/298.*
Hvalvik, Reidar: The Struggle for Scripture and Covenant. 1996. *Vol. II/82.*
Jackson, Ryan: New Creation in Paul's Letters. 2010. *Vol. II/272.*
Janßen, Martina: see *Frey, Jörg.*
Jauhiainen, Marko: The Use of Zechariah in Revelation. 2005. *Vol. II/199.*
Jensen, Morten H.: Herod Antipas in Galilee. 2006; 22010. *Vol. II/215.*
Johns, Loren L.: The Lamb Christology of the Apocalypse of John. 2003. *Vol. II/167.*
Jossa, Giorgio: Jews or Christians? 2006. *Vol. 202.*
Joubert, Stephan: Paul as Benefactor. 2000. *Vol. II/124.*
Judge, E. A.: The First Christians in the Roman World. 2008. *Vol. 229.*
– Jerusalem and Athens. 2010. *Vol. 265.*
Jungbauer, Harry: „Ehre Vater und Mutter". 2002. *Vol. II/146.*
Kähler, Christoph: Jesu Gleichnisse als Poesie und Therapie. 1995. *Vol. 78.*
Kamlah, Ehrhard: Die Form der katalogischen Paränese im Neuen Testament. 1964. *Vol. 7.*
Kammler, Hans-Christian: Christologie und Eschatologie. 2000. *Vol. 126.*
– Kreuz und Weisheit. 2003. *Vol. 159.*
– see *Hofius, Otfried.*
Karakolis, Christos: see *Alexeev, Anatoly A.*
Karrer, Martin und *Wolfgang Kraus* (Ed.): Die Septuaginta – Texte, Kontexte, Lebenswelten. 2008. *Vol. 219.*
– see *Kraus, Wolfgang.*
Kelhoffer, James A.: The Diet of John the Baptist. 2005. *Vol. 176.*
– Miracle and Mission. 1999. *Vol. II/112.*
– Persecution, Persuasion and Power. 2010. *Vol. 270.*
– see *Ahearne-Kroll, Stephen P.*
Kelley, Nicole: Knowledge and Religious Authority in the Pseudo-Clementines. 2006. *Vol. II/213.*
Kennedy, Joel: The Recapitulation of Israel. 2008. *Vol. II/257.*
Kensky, Meira Z.: Trying Man, Trying God. 2010. *Vol. II/289.*
Kieffer, René and *Jan Bergman* (Ed.): La Main de Dieu / Die Hand Gottes. 1997. *Vol. 94.*
Kierspel, Lars: The Jews and the World in the Fourth Gospel. 2006. *Vol. 220.*
Kim, Seyoon: The Origin of Paul's Gospel. 1981, 21984. *Vol. II/4.*
– Paul and the New Perspective. 2002. *Vol. 140.*
– "The 'Son of Man'" as the Son of God. 1983. *Vol. 30.*
Klauck, Hans-Josef: Religion und Gesellschaft im frühen Christentum. 2003. *Vol. 152.*
Klein, Hans, Vasile Mihoc und *Karl-Wilhelm Niebuhr* (Ed.): Das Gebet im Neuen Testament. Vierte, europäische orthodox-westliche Exegetenkonferenz in Sambata de Sus, 4. – 8. August 2007. 2009. Vol. 249.
– see Dunn, James D.G.
Kleinknecht, Karl Th.: Der leidende Gerechtfertigte. 1984, 21988. *Vol. II/13.*
Klinghardt, Matthias: Gesetz und Volk Gottes. 1988. *Vol. II/32.*
Kloppenborg, John S.: The Tenants in the Vineyard. 2006, student edition 2010. *Vol. 195.*
Koch, Michael: Drachenkampf und Sonnenfrau. 2004. *Vol. II/184.*
Koch, Stefan: Rechtliche Regelung von Konflikten im frühen Christentum. 2004. *Vol. II/174.*
Köhler, Wolf-Dietrich: Rezeption des Matthäusevangeliums in der Zeit vor Irenäus. 1987. *Vol. II/24.*

Köhn, Andreas: Der Neutestamentler Ernst Lohmeyer. 2004. *Vol. II/180.*
Koester, Craig and *Reimund Bieringer* (Ed.): The Resurrection of Jesus in the Gospel of John. 2008. *Vol. 222.*
Konradt, Matthias: Israel, Kirche und die Völker im Matthäusevangelium. 2007. *Vol. 215.*
Kooten, George H. van: Cosmic Christology in Paul and the Pauline School. 2003. *Vol. II/171.*
– Paul's Anthropology in Context. 2008. *Vol. 232.*
Korn, Manfred: Die Geschichte Jesu in veränderter Zeit. 1993. *Vol. II/51.*
Koskenniemi, Erkki: Apollonios von Tyana in der neutestamentlichen Exegese. 1994. *Vol. II/61.*
– The Old Testament Miracle-Workers in Early Judaism. 2005. *Vol. II/206.*
Kraus, Thomas J.: Sprache, Stil und historischer Ort des zweiten Petrusbriefes. 2001. *Vol. II/136.*
Kraus, Wolfgang: Das Volk Gottes. 1996. *Vol. 85.*
– see *Karrer, Martin.*
– see *Walter, Nikolaus.*
– and *Martin Karrer* (Hrsg.): Die Septuaginta – Texte, Theologien, Einflüsse. 2010. *Bd. 252.*
– and *Karl-Wilhelm Niebuhr* (Ed.): Frühjudentum und Neues Testament im Horizont Biblischer Theologie. 2003. *Vol. 162.*
Krauter, Stefan: Studien zu Röm 13,1-7. 2009. *Vol. 243.*
– see *Frey, Jörg.*
Kreplin, Matthias: Das Selbstverständnis Jesu. 2001. *Vol. II/141.*
Kuhn, Karl G.: Achtzehngebet und Vaterunser und der Reim. 1950. *Vol. 1.*
Kvalbein, Hans: see *Ådna, Jostein.*
Kwon, Yon-Gyong: Eschatology in Galatians. 2004. *Vol. II/183.*
Laansma, Jon: I Will Give You Rest. 1997. *Vol. II/98.*
Labahn, Michael: Offenbarung in Zeichen und Wort. 2000. *Vol. II/117.*
Lambers-Petry, Doris: see *Tomson, Peter J.*
Lampe, Peter: Die stadtrömischen Christen in den ersten beiden Jahrhunderten. 1987, [2]1989. *Vol. II/18.*
Landmesser, Christof: Wahrheit als Grundbegriff neutestamentlicher Wissenschaft. 1999. *Vol. 113.*
– Jüngerberufung und Zuwendung zu Gott. 2000. *Vol. 133.*
– see *Eckstein, Hans-Joachim.*
Lange, Armin: see *Ego, Beate.*
Lau, Andrew: Manifest in Flesh. 1996. *Vol. II/86.*
Lawrence, Louise: An Ethnography of the Gospel of Matthew. 2003. *Vol. II/165.*
Lee, Aquila H.I.: From Messiah to Preexistent Son. 2005. *Vol. II/192.*
Lee, Pilchan: The New Jerusalem in the Book of Relevation. 2000. *Vol. II/129.*
Lee, Sang M.: The Cosmic Drama of Salvation. 2010. *Vol. II/276.*
Lee, Simon S.: Jesus' Transfiguration and the Believers' Transformation. 2009. *Vol. II/265.*
Lichtenberger, Hermann: Das Ich Adams und das Ich der Menschheit. 2004. *Vol. 164.*
– see *Avemarie, Friedrich.*
– see *Eckstein, Hans-Joachim.*
– see *Frey, Jörg.*
Lierman, John: The New Testament Moses. 2004. *Vol. II/173.*
– (Ed.): Challenging Perspectives on the Gospel of John. 2006. *Vol. II/219.*
Lieu, Samuel N.C.: Manichaeism in the Later Roman Empire and Medieval China. [2]1992. *Vol. 63.*
Lindemann, Andreas: Die Evangelien und die Apostelgeschichte. 2009. *Vol. 241.*
Lincicum, David: Paul and the Early Jewish Encounter with Deuteronomy. 2010. *Vol. II/284.*
Lindgård, Fredrik: Paul's Line of Thought in 2 Corinthians 4:16–5:10. 2004. *Vol. II/189.*
Livesey, Nina E.: Circumcision as a Malleable Symbol. 2010. *Vol. II/295.*
Loader, William R.G.: Jesus' Attitude Towards the Law. 1997. *Vol. II/97.*
Löhr, Gebhard: Verherrlichung Gottes durch Philosophie. 1997. *Vol. 97.*
Löhr, Hermut: Studien zum frühchristlichen und frühjüdischen Gebet. 2003. *Vol. 160.*
– see *Hengel, Martin.*
Löhr, Winrich Alfried: Basilides und seine Schule. 1995. *Vol. 83.*
Lorenzen, Stefanie: Das paulinische Eikon-Konzept. 2008. *Vol. II/250.*
Luomanen, Petri: Entering the Kingdom of Heaven. 1998. *Vol. II/101.*
Luz, Ulrich: see *Alexeev, Anatoly A.*
– see *Dunn, James D.G.*
Mackay, Ian D.: John's Raltionship with Mark. 2004. *Vol. II/182.*
Mackie, Scott D.: Eschatology and Exhortation in the Epistle to the Hebrews. 2006. *Vol. II/223.*
Magda, Ksenija: Paul's Territoriality and Mission Strategy. 2009. *Vol. II/266.*
Maier, Gerhard: Mensch und freier Wille. 1971. *Vol. 12.*

– Die Johannesoffenbarung und die Kirche. 1981. *Vol. 25.*
Markschies, Christoph: Valentinus Gnosticus? 1992. *Vol. 65.*
Marshall, Jonathan: Jesus, Patrons, and Benefactors. 2009. *Vol. II/259.*
Marshall, Peter: Enmity in Corinth: Social Conventions in Paul's Relations with the Corinthians. 1987. *Vol. II/23.*
Martin, Dale B.: see *Zangenberg, Jürgen.*
Maston, Jason: Divine and Human Agency in Second Temple Judaism and Paul. 2010. *Vol. II/297.*
Mayer, Annemarie: Sprache der Einheit im Epheserbrief und in der Ökumene. 2002. *Vol. II/150.*
Mayordomo, Moisés: Argumentiert Paulus logisch? 2005. *Vol. 188.*
McDonough, Sean M.: YHWH at Patmos: Rev. 1:4 in its Hellenistic and Early Jewish Setting. 1999. *Vol. II/107.*
McDowell, Markus: Prayers of Jewish Women. 2006. *Vol. II/211.*
McGlynn, Moyna: Divine Judgement and Divine Benevolence in the Book of Wisdom. 2001. *Vol. II/139.*
Meade, David G.: Pseudonymity and Canon. 1986. *Vol. 39.*
Meadors, Edward P.: Jesus the Messianic Herald of Salvation. 1995. *Vol. II/72.*
Meißner, Stefan: Die Heimholung des Ketzers. 1996. *Vol. II/87.*
Mell, Ulrich: Die „anderen" Winzer. 1994. *Vol. 77.*
– see *Sänger, Dieter.*
Mengel, Berthold: Studien zum Philipperbrief. 1982. *Vol. II/8.*
Merkel, Helmut: Die Widersprüche zwischen den Evangelien. 1971. *Vol. 13.*
– see *Ego, Beate.*
Merklein, Helmut: Studien zu Jesus und Paulus. Vol. 1 1987. *Vol. 43.* – Vol. 2 1998. *Vol. 105.*
Merkt, Andreas: see *Nicklas, Tobias*
Metzdorf, Christina: Die Tempelaktion Jesu. 2003. *Vol. II/168.*
Metzler, Karin: Der griechische Begriff des Verzeihens. 1991. *Vol. II/44.*
Metzner, Rainer: Die Rezeption des Matthäusevangeliums im 1. Petrusbrief. 1995. *Vol. II/74.*
– Das Verständnis der Sünde im Johannesevangelium. 2000. *Vol. 122.*
Mihoc, Vasile: see *Dunn, James D.G.*
– see *Klein, Hans.*
Mineshige, Kiyoshi: Besitzverzicht und Almosen bei Lukas. 2003. *Vol. II/163.*
Mittmann, Siegfried: see *Hengel, Martin.*
Mittmann-Richert, Ulrike: Magnifikat und Benediktus. *1996. Vol. II/90.*
– Der Sühnetod des Gottesknechts. 2008. *Vol. 220.*
Miura, Yuzuru: David in Luke-Acts. 2007. *Vol. II/232.*
Moll, Sebastian: The Arch-Heretic Marcion. 2010. *Vol. 250.*
Morales, Rodrigo J.: The Spirit and the Restorat. 2010. *Vol. 282.*
Mournet, Terence C.: Oral Tradition and Literary Dependency. 2005. *Vol. II/195.*
Mußner, Franz: Jesus von Nazareth im Umfeld Israels und der Urkirche. Ed. von M. Theobald. 1998. *Vol. 111.*
Mutschler, Bernhard: Das Corpus Johanneum bei Irenäus von Lyon. 2005. *Vol. 189.*
– Glaube in den Pastoralbriefen. 2010. *Vol. 256.*
Myers, Susan E.: Spirit Epicleses in the Acts of Thomas. 2010. *Vol. 281.*
Nguyen, V. Henry T.: Christian Identity in Corinth. 2008. *Vol. II/243.*
Nicklas, Tobias, Andreas Merkt und *Joseph Verheyden* (Ed.): Gelitten – Gestorben – Auferstanden. 2010. *Vol. II/273.*
– see *Verheyden, Joseph*
Niebuhr, Karl-Wilhelm: Gesetz and Paränese. 1987. *Vol. II/28.*
– Heidenapostel aus Israel. 1992. *Vol. 62.*
– see *Deines, Roland.*
– see *Dimitrov, Ivan Z.*
– see *Klein, Hans.*
– see *Kraus, Wolfgang.*
Nielsen, Anders E.: "Until it is Fullfilled". 2000. *Vol. II/126.*
Nielsen, Jesper Tang: Die kognitive Dimension des Kreuzes. 2009. *Vol. II/263.*
Nissen, Andreas: Gott und der Nächste im antiken Judentum. 1974. *Vol. 15.*
Noack, Christian: Gottesbewußtsein. 2000. *Vol. II/116.*
Noormann, Rolf: Irenäus als Paulusinterpret. 1994. *Vol. II/66.*
Norin, Stig: see *Hultgård, Anders.*
Novakovic, Lidija: Messiah, the Healer of the Sick. 2003. *Vol. II/170.*
Obermann, Andreas: Die christologische Erfüllung der Schrift im Johannesevangelium. 1996. *Vol. II/83.*
Öhler, Markus: Barnabas. 2003. *Vol. 156.*
– see *Becker, Michael.*
Okure, Teresa: The Johannine Approach to Mission. 1988. *Vol. II/31.*
Onuki, Takashi: Heil und Erlösung. 2004. *Vol. 165.*

Oropeza, B. J.: Paul and Apostasy. 2000. *Vol. II/115.*
Ostmeyer, Karl-Heinrich: Kommunikation mit Gott und Christus. 2006. *Vol. 197.*
– Taufe und Typos. 2000. *Vol. II/118.*
Pao, David W.: Acts and the Isaianic New Exodus. 2000. *Vol. II/130.*
Park, Eung Chun: The Mission Discourse in Matthew's Interpretation. 1995. *Vol. II/81.*
Park, Joseph S.: Conceptions of Afterlife in Jewish Insriptions. 2000. *Vol. II/121.*
Parsenios, George L.: Rhetoric and Drama in the Johannine Lawsuit Motif. 2010. *Vol. 258.*
Pate, C. Marvin: The Reverse of the Curse. 2000. *Vol. II/114.*
Paulsen, Henning: Studien zur Literatur und Geschichte des frühen Christentums. Ed. von Ute E. Eisen. 1997. *Vol. 99.*
Pearce, Sarah J.K.: The Land of the Body. 2007. *Vol. 208.*
Peres, Imre: Griechische Grabinschriften und neutestamentliche Eschatologie. 2003. *Vol. 157.*
Perry, Peter S.: The Rhetoric of Digressions. 2009. *Vol. II/268.*
Pierce, Chad T.: Spirits and the Proclamation of Christ. 2011. *Vol. II/305.*
Philip, Finny: The Origins of Pauline Pneumatology. 2005. *Vol. II/194.*
Philonenko, Marc (Ed.): Le Trône de Dieu. 1993. *Vol. 69.*
Pilhofer, Peter: Presbyteron Kreitton. 1990. *Vol. II/39.*
– Philippi. Vol. 1 1995. *Vol. 87.* – Vol. 2 ^{2}2009. *Vol. 119.*
– Die frühen Christen und ihre Welt. 2002. *Vol. 145.*
– see *Becker, Eve-Marie.*
– see *Ego, Beate.*
Pitre, Brant: Jesus, the Tribulation, and the End of the Exile. 2005. *Vol. II/204.*
Plümacher, Eckhard: Geschichte und Geschichten. 2004. *Vol. 170.*
Pöhlmann, Wolfgang: Der Verlorene Sohn und das Haus. 1993. *Vol. 68.*
Poirier, John C.: The Tongues of Angels. 2010. *Vol. II/287.*
Pokorný, Petr and *Josef B. Souček:* Bibelauslegung als Theologie. 1997. *Vol. 100.*
– and *Jan Roskovec* (Ed.): Philosophical Hermeneutics and Biblical Exegesis. 2002. *Vol. 153.*
Popkes, Enno Edzard: Das Menschenbild des Thomasevangeliums. 2007. *Vol. 206.*
– Die Theologie der Liebe Gottes in den johanneischen Schriften. 2005. *Vol. II/197.*
Porter, Stanley E.: The Paul of Acts. 1999. *Vol. 115.*
Prieur, Alexander: Die Verkündigung der Gottesherrschaft. 1996. *Vol. II/89.*
Probst, Hermann: Paulus und der Brief. 1991. *Vol. II/45.*
Puig i Tàrrech, Armand: Jesus: An Uncommon Journey. 2010. *Vol. II/288.*
Rabens, Volker: The Holy Spirit and Ethics in Paul. 2010. *Vol. II/283.*
Räisänen, Heikki: Paul and the Law. 1983, ^{2}1987. *Vol. 29.*
Rehkopf, Friedrich: Die lukanische Sonderquelle. 1959. *Vol. 5.*
Rein, Matthias: Die Heilung des Blindgeborenen (Joh 9). 1995. *Vol. II/73.*
Reinmuth, Eckart: Pseudo-Philo und Lukas. 1994. *Vol. 74.*
Reiser, Marius: Bibelkritik und Auslegung der Heiligen Schrift. 2007. *Vol. 217.*
– Syntax und Stil des Markusevangeliums. 1984. *Vol. II/11.*
Reynolds, Benjamin E.: The Apocalyptic Son of Man in the Gospel of John. 2008. *Vol. II/249.*
Rhodes, James N.: The Epistle of Barnabas and the Deuteronomic Tradition. 2004. *Vol. II/188.*
Richards, E. Randolph: The Secretary in the Letters of Paul. 1991. *Vol. II/42.*
Riesner, Rainer: Jesus als Lehrer. 1981, ^{3}1988. *Vol. II/7.*
– Die Frühzeit des Apostels Paulus. 1994. *Vol. 71.*
Rissi, Mathias: Die Theologie des Hebräerbriefs. 1987. *Vol. 41.*
Röcker, Fritz W.: Belial und Katechon. 2009. *Vol. II/262.*
Röhser, Günter: Metaphorik und Personifikation der Sünde. 1987. *Vol. II/25.*
Rose, Christian: Theologie als Erzählung im Markusevangelium. 2007. *Vol. II/236.*
– Die Wolke der Zeugen. 1994. *Vol. II/60.*
Roskovec, Jan: see *Pokorný, Petr.*
Rothschild, Clare K.: Baptist Traditions and Q. 2005. *Vol. 190.*
– Hebrews as Pseudepigraphon. 2009. *Vol. 235.*
– Luke Acts and the Rhetoric of History. 2004. *Vol. II/175.*
– see *Frey, Jörg.*
Rudolph, David J.: A Jew to the Jews. 2011. *Vol. II/304.*
Rüegger, Hans-Ulrich: Verstehen, was Markus erzählt. 2002. *Vol. II/155.*
Rüger, Hans Peter: Die Weisheitsschrift aus der Kairoer Geniza. 1991. *Vol. 53.*

Ruf, Martin G.: Die heiligen Propheten, eure Apostel und ich. 2011. *Vol. II/300.*
Runesson, Anders: see *Becker, Eve-Marie.*
Sänger, Dieter: Antikes Judentum und die Mysterien. 1980. *Vol. II/5.*
– Die Verkündigung des Gekreuzigten und Israel. 1994. *Vol. 75.*
– see *Burchard, Christoph*
– and *Ulrich Mell* (Ed.): Paulus und Johannes. 2006. *Vol. 198.*
Salier, Willis Hedley: The Rhetorical Impact of the Semeia in the Gospel of John. 2004. *Vol. II/186.*
Salzmann, Jörg Christian: Lehren und Ermahnen. 1994. *Vol. II/59.*
Samuelsson, Gunnar: Crucifixion in Antiquity. 2011. *Vol. II/310.*
Sandnes, Karl Olav: Paul – One of the Prophets? 1991. *Vol. II/43.*
Sato, Migaku: Q und Prophetie. 1988. *Vol. II/29.*
Schäfer, Ruth: Paulus bis zum Apostelkonzil. 2004. *Vol. II/179.*
Schaper, Joachim: Eschatology in the Greek Psalter. 1995. *Vol. II/76.*
Schimanowski, Gottfried: Die himmlische Liturgie in der Apokalypse des Johannes. 2002. *Vol. II/154.*
– Weisheit und Messias. 1985. *Vol. II/17.*
Schlichting, Günter: Ein jüdisches Leben Jesu. 1982. *Vol. 24.*
Schließer, Benjamin: Abraham's Faith in Romans 4. 2007. *Vol. II/224.*
Schnabel, Eckhard J.: Law and Wisdom from Ben Sira to Paul. 1985. *Vol. II/16.*
Schnelle, Udo: see *Frey, Jörg.*
Schröter, Jens: Von Jesus zum Neuen Testament. 2007. *Vol. 204.*
– see *Frey, Jörg.*
Schutter, William L.: Hermeneutic and Composition in I Peter. 1989. *Vol. II/30.*
Schwartz, Daniel R.: Studies in the Jewish Background of Christianity. 1992. *Vol. 60.*
Schwemer, Anna Maria: see *Hengel, Martin*
Scott, Ian W.: Implicit Epistemology in the Letters of Paul. 2005. *Vol. II/*205.
Scott, James M.: Adoption as Sons of God. 1992. *Vol. II/48.*
– Paul and the Nations. 1995. *Vol. 84.*
Shi, Wenhua: Paul's Message of the Cross as Body Language. 2008. *Vol. II/254.*
Shum, Shiu-Lun: Paul's Use of Isaiah in Romans. 2002. *Vol. II/156.*
Siegert, Folker: Drei hellenistisch-jüdische Predigten. Teil I 1980. *Vol. 20* – Teil II 1992. *Vol. 61.*
– Nag-Hammadi-Register. 1982. *Vol. 26.*
– Argumentation bei Paulus. 1985. *Vol. 34.*
– Philon von Alexandrien. 1988. *Vol. 46.*
Siggelkow-Berner, Birke: Die jüdischen Feste im Bellum Judaicum des Flavius Josephus. 2011. *Vol. II/306.*
Simon, Marcel: Le christianisme antique et son contexte religieux I/II. 1981. *Vol. 23.*
Smit, Peter-Ben: Fellowship and Food in the Kingdom. 2008. *Vol. II/234.*
Snodgrass, Klyne: The Parable of the Wicked Tenants. 1983. *Vol. 27.*
Söding, Thomas: Das Wort vom Kreuz. 1997. *Vol. 93.*
– see *Thüsing, Wilhelm.*
Sommer, Urs: Die Passionsgeschichte des Markusevangeliums. 1993. *Vol. II/58.*
Sorensen, Eric: Possession and Exorcism in the New Testament and Early Christianity. 2002. *Vol. II/157.*
Souček, Josef B.: see *Pokorný, Petr.*
Southall, David J.: Rediscovering Righteousness in Romans. 2008. *Vol. 240.*
Spangenberg, Volker: Herrlichkeit des Neuen Bundes. 1993. *Vol. II/55.*
Spanje, T.E. van: Inconsistency in Paul? 1999. *Vol. II/110.*
Speyer, Wolfgang: Frühes Christentum im antiken Strahlungsfeld. Vol. I: 1989. *Vol. 50.*
– Vol. II: 1999. *Vol. 116.*
– Vol. III: 2007. *Vol. 213.*
Spittler, Janet E.: Animals in the Apocryphal Acts of the Apostles. 2008. *Vol. II/247.*
Sprinkle, Preston: Law and Life. 2008. *Vol. II/241.*
Stadelmann, Helge: Ben Sira als Schriftgelehrter. 1980. *Vol. II/6.*
Stein, Hans Joachim: Frühchristliche Mahlfeiern. 2008. *Vol. II/255.*
Stenschke, Christoph W.: Luke's Portrait of Gentiles Prior to Their Coming to Faith. *Vol. II/108.*
Stephens, Mark B.: Annihilation or Renewal? 2011. *Vol. II/307.*
Sterck-Degueldre, Jean-Pierre: Eine Frau namens Lydia. 2004. *Vol. II/176.*
Stettler, Christian: Der Kolosserhymnus. 2000. *Vol. II/131.*
– Das letzte Gericht. 2011. *Vol. II/299.*
Stettler, Hanna: Die Christologie der Pastoralbriefe. 1998. *Vol. II/105.*
Stökl Ben Ezra, Daniel: The Impact of Yom Kippur on Early Christianity. 2003. *Vol. 163.*
Strobel, August: Die Stunde der Wahrheit. 1980. *Vol. 21.*
Stroumsa, Guy G.: Barbarian Philosophy. 1999. *Vol. 112.*
Stuckenbruck, Loren T.: Angel Veneration and Christology. 1995. *Vol. II/70.*

–, *Stephen C. Barton* and *Benjamin G. Wold* (Ed.): Memory in the Bible and Antiquity. 2007. *Vol. 212.*

Stuhlmacher, Peter (Ed.): Das Evangelium und die Evangelien. 1983. *Vol. 28.*

– Biblische Theologie und Evangelium. 2002. *Vol. 146.*

Sung, Chong-Hyon: Vergebung der Sünden. 1993. *Vol. II/57.*

Svendsen, Stefan N.: Allegory Transformed. 2009. *Vol. II/269.*

Tajra, Harry W.: The Trial of St. Paul. 1989. *Vol. II/35.*

– The Martyrdom of St.Paul. 1994. *Vol. II/67.*

Tellbe, Mikael: Christ-Believers in Ephesus. 2009. *Vol. 242.*

Theißen, Gerd: Studien zur Soziologie des Urchristentums. 1979, [3]1989. *Vol. 19.*

Theobald, Michael: Studien zum Corpus Iohanneum. 2010. *Vol. 267.*

– Studien zum Römerbrief. 2001. *Vol. 136.*

– see *Mußner, Franz.*

Thornton, Claus-Jürgen: Der Zeuge des Zeugen. 1991. *Vol. 56.*

Thüsing, Wilhelm: Studien zur neutestamentlichen Theologie. Ed. von Thomas Söding. 1995. *Vol. 82.*

Thurén, Lauri: Derhethorizing Paul. 2000. *Vol. 124.*

Thyen, Hartwig: Studien zum Corpus Iohanneum. 2007. *Vol. 214.*

Tibbs, Clint: Religious Experience of the Pneuma. 2007. *Vol. II/230.*

Toit, David S. du: Theios Anthropos. 1997. *Vol. II/91.*

Tolmie, D. Francois: Persuading the Galatians. 2005. *Vol. II/190.*

Tomson, Peter J. and *Doris Lambers-Petry* (Ed.): The Image of the Judaeo-Christians in Ancient Jewish and Christian Literature. 2003. *Vol. 158.*

Toney, Carl N.: Paul's Inclusive Ethic. 2008. *Vol. II/252.*

Trebilco, Paul: The Early Christians in Ephesus from Paul to Ignatius. 2004. *Vol. 166.*

Treloar, Geoffrey R.: Lightfoot the Historian. 1998. *Vol. II/103.*

Troftgruben, Troy M.: A Conclusion Unhindered. 2010. Vol. II/280.

Tso, Marcus K.M.: Ethics in the Qumran Community. 2010. *Vol. II/292.*

Tsuji, Manabu: Glaube zwischen Vollkommenheit und Verweltlichung. 1997. *Vol. II/93.*

Twelftree, Graham H.: Jesus the Exorcist. 1993. *Vol. II/54.*

Ulrichs, Karl Friedrich: Christusglaube. 2007. *Vol. II/227.*

Urban, Christina: Das Menschenbild nach dem Johannesevangelium. 2001. *Vol. II/137.*

Vahrenhorst, Martin: Kultische Sprache in den Paulusbriefen. 2008. *Vol. 230.*

Vegge, Ivar: 2 Corinthians – a Letter about Reconciliation. 2008. *Vol. II/239.*

Verheyden, Joseph, Korinna Zamfir and *Tobias Nicklas* (Ed.): Prophets and Prophecy in Jewish and Early Christian Literature. 2010. *Vol. II/286.*

– see *Nicklas, Tobias*

Visotzky, Burton L.: Fathers of the World. 1995. *Vol. 80.*

Vollenweider, Samuel: Horizonte neutestamentlicher Christologie. 2002. *Vol. 144.*

Vos, Johan S.: Die Kunst der Argumentation bei Paulus. 2002. *Vol. 149.*

Waaler, Erik: The *Shema* and The First Commandment in First Corinthians. 2008. *Vol. II/253.*

Wagener, Ulrike: Die Ordnung des „Hauses Gottes". 1994. *Vol. II/65.*

Wagner, J. Ross: see *Wilk, Florian.*

Wahlen, Clinton: Jesus and the Impurity of Spirits in the Synoptic Gospels. 2004. *Vol. II/185.*

Walker, Donald D.: Paul's Offer of Leniency (2 Cor 10:1). 2002. *Vol. II/152.*

Walter, Nikolaus: Praeparatio Evangelica. Ed. von Wolfgang Kraus und Florian Wilk. 1997. *Vol. 98.*

Wander, Bernd: Gottesfürchtige und Sympathisanten. 1998. *Vol. 104.*

Wardle, Timothy: The Jerusalem Temple and Early Christian Identity. 2010. *Vol. II/291.*

Wasserman, Emma: The Death of the Soul in Romans 7. 2008. *Vol. 256.*

Waters, Guy: The End of Deuteronomy in the Epistles of Paul. 2006. *Vol. 221.*

Watt, Jan G. van der: see *Frey, Jörg*

– see *Zimmermann, Ruben*

Watts, Rikki: Isaiah's New Exodus and Mark. 1997. *Vol. II/88.*

Webb, Robert L.: see *Bock, Darrell L.*

Wedderburn, Alexander J.M.: Baptism and Resurrection. 1987. *Vol. 44.*

– Jesus and the Historians. 2010. *Vol. 269.*

Wegner, Uwe: Der Hauptmann von Kafarnaum. 1985. *Vol. II/14.*

Weiß, Hans-Friedrich: Frühes Christentum und Gnosis. 2008. *Vol. 225.*

Weissenrieder, Annette: Images of Illness in the Gospel of Luke. 2003. Vol. II/164.

–, and *Robert B. Coote* (Ed.): The Interface of Orality and Writing. 2010. *Vol. 260.*

–, *Friederike Wendt* and *Petra von Gemünden* (Ed.): Picturing the New Testament. 2005. *Vol. II/193.*
Welck, Christian: Erzählte ‚Zeichen'. 1994. *Vol. II/69.*
Wendt, Friederike (Ed.): see *Weissenrieder, Annette.*
Wiarda, Timothy: Peter in the Gospels. 2000. *Vol. II/127.*
Wifstrand, Albert: Epochs and Styles. 2005. *Vol. 179.*
Wilk, Florian and *J. Ross Wagner* (Ed.): Between Gospel and Election. 2010. *Vol. 257.*
– see *Walter, Nikolaus.*
Williams, Catrin H.: I am He. 2000. *Vol. II/113.*
Wilson, Todd A.: The Curse of the Law and the Crisis in Galatia. 2007. *Vol. II/225.*
Wilson, Walter T.: Love without Pretense. 1991. *Vol. II/46.*
Winn, Adam: The Purpose of Mark's Gospel. 2008. *Vol. II/245.*
Winninge, Mikael: see *Holmberg, Bengt.*
Wischmeyer, Oda: Von Ben Sira zu Paulus. 2004. *Vol. 173.*
Wisdom, Jeffrey: Blessing for the Nations and the Curse of the Law. 2001. *Vol. II/133.*
Witmer, Stephen E.: Divine Instruction in Early Christianity. 2008. *Vol. II/246.*
Wold, Benjamin G.: Women, Men, and Angels. 2005. *Vol. II/2001.*
Wolter, Michael: Theologie und Ethos im frühen Christentum. 2009. *Vol. 236.*
– see *Stuckenbruck, Loren T.*
Wright, Archie T.: The Origin of Evil Spirits. 2005. *Vol. II/198.*
Wucherpfennig, Ansgar: Heracleon Philologus. 2002. *Vol. 142.*
Yates, John W.: The Spirit and Creation in Paul. 2008. *Vol. II/251.*
Yeung, Maureen: Faith in Jesus and Paul. 2002. *Vol. II/147.*
Zamfir, Corinna: see *Verheyden, Joseph*
Zangenberg, Jürgen, Harold W. Attridge and *Dale B. Martin* (Ed.): Religion, Ethnicity and Identity in Ancient Galilee. 2007. *Vol. 210.*
Zimmermann, Alfred E.: Die urchristlichen Lehrer. 1984, [2]1988. *Vol. II/12.*
Zimmermann, Johannes: Messianische Texte aus Qumran. 1998. *Vol. II/104.*
Zimmermann, Ruben: Christologie der Bilder im Johannesevangelium. 2004. *Vol. 171.*
– Geschlechtermetaphorik und Gottesverhältnis. 2001. *Vol. II/122.*
– (Ed.): Hermeneutik der Gleichnisse Jesu. 2008. *Vol. 231.*
– and *Jan G. van der Watt* (Ed.): Moral Language in the New Testament. Vol. II. 2010. *Vol. II/296.*
– see *Frey, Jörg.*
– see *Horn, Friedrich Wilhelm.*
Zugmann, Michael: „Hellenisten" in der Apostelgeschichte. 2009. *Vol. II/264.*
Zumstein, Jean: see *Dettwiler, Andreas*
Zwiep, Arie W.: Christ, the Spirit and the Community of God. 2010. *Vol. II/293.*
– Judas and the Choice of Matthias. 2004. *Vol. II/187.*

For a complete catalogue please write to the publisher
Mohr Siebeck • P.O. Box 2030 • D–72010 Tübingen/Germany
Up-to-date information on the internet at www.mohr.de